The Motion Picture Mega-Industry

Barry R. Litman
Michigan State University

Allyn and Bacon
Boston • London • Toronto • Sydney • Tokyo • Singapore

Vice President, Editor in Chief: Paul Smith
Series Editor: Karon Bowers
Editorial Assistant: Leila Scott
Marketing Manager: Kris Farnsworth
Editorial Production Service: Chestnut Hill Enterprises, Inc.
Manufacturing Buyer: Megan Cochran
Cover Administrator: Jennifer Hart

Library of Congress Cataloging-in-Publication Data
Litman, Barry Russell
    The motion picture mega-industry / Barry R. Litman.
        p.   cm.
    Includes bibliographical references.
    ISBN 0-205-20026-5
    1. Motion picture industry--United States.   I. Title.
PN1993.5.U6L53   1997
384.8'0973--dc21   97-22703
                                                              CIP

Printed in the United States of Amerca

10   9   8   7   6   5   4   3   2   1   02   01   00   99   98

To my beloved mother, Roselyn, who instilled in me the value of education and insisted on high achievement;

To my loving wife, Lesli, who continues to support and believe in me and my goals and who always reminds me of the truly important values in life;

To my mother-in-law and father-in-law, Josephine and Clarence, whose strong work ethic has inspired me to work at my maximum potential;

To my dedicated graduate students who believed in my ideas, corrected my faulty logic, carried forward the message to others, and gave it more meaning and importance than it deserved.

Contributing Authors

Hoekyun Ahn is a doctoral student in the Mass Media Ph.D. program at Michigan State University.

Larry Collette is Assistant Professor of Department of Mass Communication at University of Denver.

Indra De Silva is Assistant Professor of Communications at Mount Union College.

Anne Hoag is Assistant Professor of Telecommunication at Pennsylvania State University.

Gary Hoppenstand is Associate Professor and Assistant Chairperson of American Thought and Language at Michigan State University.

Barry Litman is Professor of Telecommunication at Michigan State University.

Erik S. Lunde is Professor of American Thought and Language at Michigan State University.

Contents

Preface

The entertainment world of the year 2000 will be quite different from that of over a hundred years ago when the great master inventor Thomas Edison first introduced his moving pictures to a disbelieving public. No longer are people naïvely interested in the novelty of moving figures viewed through a peephole on a kinetoscope or projected on a silver screen. However, the creation of visual imagery to manipulate time and space still captures the imagination of over one billion movie theater patrons a year in the United States alone.

Far from being a cultural artifact of a bygone era, the motion picture is strong, solid, and constantly evolving and adapting to its environment. With the exception of major league championship sporting events such as the Super Bowl or the World Series, there is no media event that can match the excitement that comes with an opening night or opening weekend for a widely heralded, major motion picture. It is truly remarkable that, at its venerable age, the motion picture is the centerpiece attraction driving a whole new array of exhibition windows that already allows consumers the luxury of seeing movies at different times in different settings and at affordable prices.

In the new millennium, with the arrival of the information superhighway to the home, consumers will achieve the ultimate sovereignty—the freedom to order "on demand" whatever recent or classic movie they want to see at whatever time. Nonetheless, even the most advanced technology yet unveiled may not have the power to destroy the motion picture theater and the "moviegoing experience" that has been ingrained as part of American culture for many generations, and still creates a wonderful, shared family experience.

The major companies that provide this special cultural form are remarkable in their own right and are survivors in a creative rivalry that is the fiercest in all media and perhaps in all American business. It is hard to imagine that small creative production houses that began in the 1920s, such as Warner Bros. and Fox, would last through the century. Or, that they would evolve into giant media conglomerates in the 1990s and still be versatile enough to tell stories that entertain and please so many viewers and create the special level of excitement surrounding the opening of a new film. They certainly are the "dream merchants" of this century. What makes the "major" studios "major" is not their corporate wealth or luxurious surroundings but their talent in recognizing creative new ideas and consistently turning them into hit movies. What makes this creative success so difficult is that, with the exception of sequels, they must start from the ground up and develop each picture as a separate handcrafted entity.

To understand the rich corporate histories of these studios is to recreate the storied history of the industry itself, and it is a proud history of cherished cultural memories and fantasies that are preserved for all new generations to enjoy. As Robert Frost once wrote: "something to look backward to with pride"—and a promise of a rewarding future, filled with new promises and new dreams—"something to look forward to with hope."

ACKNOWLEDGMENTS

Thanks to all the contributing authors whose material has helped complete the scope of this text. Thanks also to the following reviewers who provided many insightful comments: Joseph Dominick, University of Georgia; Gorham Kindem, University of North Carolina; Bruce A. Austin, Rochester Institute of Technology; and Michael Wirth, University of Denver.

1

Introduction

This chapter will serve as a basic introduction to the special characteristics of the motion picture product that distinguish it from the other mass media and the vast group of products in the private enterprise system. A brief description of the surrounding motion picture industry will then be presented to act as an introduction for the organizational structure of this book.

The motion picture product is one of the most unique products in the marketplace since it changes from a kind of service to a tangible product and then back to a service as it travels through its product life cycle. When a movie first debuts at the theaters, there are several thousand positive prints for simultaneous national release, yet consumers may only access/view it at the theater and then have no tangible product on its completion. However, this is only the first stage in the useful life of the film. After its theatrical run, both here and abroad, it generally becomes available in the videocassette market where millions of copies of the film have been transferred to VHS videocassettes for sale or rental to the home consumer market. As the movie then advances through the sequence of exhibition windows from pay-per-view, pay cable, network television, and broadcast and cable syndication, the product once again is available in these markets as an entertainment service. In short, while the content of the film is fixed, the changing nature of transmission technologies changes the physical nature of the film experience over its product life cycle. Whereas in former times people had to watch movies at the theaters themselves, this is no longer true; the theaters now act as "launching pads" to provide a kind of lift that carries a film through all its subsequent windows.

The optimal sequencing of motion pictures through these exhibition outlets is known as the process of "windowing." Windowing stripped to its bare essentials is a clear example of price discrimination, with the age of the film (time since theatrical release) affecting the value and price that consumers will pay at each successive exhibition outlet. It is interesting to note that the film would not have such value in so many exhibition windows if it did not have the special property of a "public good." Public goods are products that do not behave very well in a private market economy and are generally relegated to the political realm where taxes are levied and governments provide the services themselves. The private market fails because consumers are hesitant to reveal their true consumption preference since they believe that the products will somehow be produced by someone else and there will be no way to exclude them, and thus they can have a "free ride." The key factor that distinguishes public from private goods is the infinite amount of utility in the former and the finite amount in the latter. Hence, there is an infinite amount of national defense, police protection, city streets, and so on for all to consume and no one person's consumption of these services forecloses another. This is contrasted with private goods, in which the utility is gradually exhausted with usage, so that it is not equally available for all to enjoy. Mass media are said to have properties of public goods because once the content is produced, it is equally available for all to consume in infinite supply. In this context, if I watch a movie or television program or read a book, that does not diminish the utility available for others to consume—it is reusable.

This parsimonious property of sharing content across many markets and people is the foundation of "networking," which relies on the sharing and spreading of high "first copy" programming costs across as many households as possible to achieve economies of scale. While the other mass media network by distributing content through high speed telecommunication transmission links, the motion picture industry still relies on personal distribution networks from theater to theater, orchestrated by the central district office of the movie distributor. But it would be wrong to think of this process as a relic of the past, because these same distributors have negotiated the rights for all the subsequent windows and international distribution. It is this package of software distribution rights that has made these distributors, and especially the major studios, the acquisition targets of the international media conglomerates that are in desperate search of software to bundle with their media hardware technologies.

It should also be recalled that motion pictures are also among that vast array of communication mass media that are covered by the First Amendment protection against government infringement of free speech. While motion pictures are often thought by many to be exclusively entertainment oriented, and this is generally considered one of the prime motives for individuals to go to the theaters, there is no easy separation between information, news, and entertainment—they are simply different sides of the same coin—and should receive the same Constitutional protections. Nonetheless, there is not complete freedom of speech in any mass media, especially if the content approaches the limits of taste associated with obscenity or depicts extreme acts of violence. Government must naturally tread softly when it seeks to place limits on motion picture content. Yet, it cannot stand idly by and permit extremely distasteful and potentially harmful actions in such an influential, persuasive, and imitative medium as motion pictures. Under the threat of rigid government rules, the industry has established its own set of self-censorship standards and a corresponding "rating system" to guide parents with respect to the level of sex and violence in any particular movie. This information warning label is not entirely unique in the mass media. It has been copied by the recording industry and, beginning in 1997, by the broadcasting and cable industries, and it is prevalent in other industries in which consumption of the product (e.g., smoking, drinking) may lead to several unhealthy results or in which the nutritional value of foods is considered important in maintaining a balanced diet.

The protection of the marketplace of discourse has led to a different response by other agencies of government whose responsibility is to protect the economic system against the entrenchment of monopoly power and to restore competition wherever possible as the long-term substitute for day-to-day government interference with the functioning of the marketplace. The antitrust authorities have paid special attention to motion pictures and other mass media because the concentration of market power, especially in the hands of the major studios, could tamper with the free play of forces in the marketplace of ideas and thus threaten the vitality of the First Amendment. With censorship, the role of government was to remove itself or else play an advisory role; however, with antitrust, government must play an active role in restructuring the industry by breaking down barriers to entry, preventing harmful mergers, or exposing and then undoing illegal conspiracies that undermine the automatic functioning of the marketplace and substitute private gain for social good.

In the antitrust context, two major cases against motion picture companies, the *Motion Picture Patents Co.* and *Paramount* cases, have led to major restructuring of the industry. The former broke up the original trust and, in conjunction with other forces at hand, created a whole new industry prepared to distribute feature films of major stars; the latter dissolved the ownership ties between the theaters and the producer–distributors, and, in conjunction with the arrival of television, forced motion picture distributors to enter into new business arrangements based on film quality rather than the historic system of vertical control and assured access. These two monumental antitrust victories for the government helped set the stage and became precedents for further major cases in the communications industry, including the historic vertical dissolution of AT&T. With such a rich antitrust legacy, the motion picture industry must continue to act cautiously and seek governmental approval when new mega-merger plans emerge, such as Disney–ABC, Viacom–Paramount, Seagrams–MCA, and Time Warner–TBS.

In another light, the motion picture product differs from the other mass media in its approach to supplying consumer satisfaction and value and the associated impact on diversity of program content. To explain this idea in simpler terms, we can return to the basic functioning of a marketplace, which is really the interaction between suppliers of product (producers) and demanders of product (consumers). The consumers achieve their greatest degree of collective power when their expression of

effective demand causes differential profits for certain types of product and corresponding movement of scarce economic resources toward the more favored product
and away from others not as popular. In short, effective consumer demand directs
supply and strong "consumer sovereignty" prevails. This is clearly the case in the
motion picture marketplace where movie patrons register their dollar votes directly
for the kinds of movies they prefer, and the differential box office rewards create the
financial incentive for the next round of motion picture investment. This direct link
between consumers and producers is further solidified in the other early exhibition
windows of VCRs and pay-per-view where each movie is made available on an
individual basis for a specified price. As we move farther down the chain of exhibition windows, eventually the individual movie is grouped with others, as in pay
cable, and sold for a packaged price, or is made available at a zero direct price for
network television, basic cable, or local syndication. With the advent of video
dialtone or video-on-demand, made possible through maturation of the information
infrastructure, this rich tradition of direct consumer sovereignty will continue uninterrupted for the motion picture industry well into the twenty-first century.

Related to consumer sovereignty is the concept of product diversity. Product
diversity is a performance goal that permeates the entire landscape of mass media. In
simple terms, consumers are expected to have greater utility when they have more
product choices from which to purchase. These additional choices can come from:
(1) more options within a certain category or genre or (2) more genres. Hence, consumers who like certain kinds of movies, say science fiction, will have increased
satisfaction when there are multiple movies of this sort simultaneously available,
while others, who have more eclectic choices, prefer to choose from among a
broader array of different genres, say dramas, musicals, comedies, action–adventure, *and* science fiction. With the rise of the multiplex theaters and the ability of
distributors to use many different exhibition windows to make back their investment, there has been a record number of new feature films released each year over
the last several years, and these movies have represented a wide range of genres,
rather than being concentrated in a particular category. Thus, the moviegoing audience has the best of both worlds—more choices within each genre and more genres
and this industry continues to set the example for the other media of a diverse product line that satisfies the expectations of the customer.

Finally, it should be noted that the motion picture is a worldwide phenomenon
and has been one throughout its long history. There are few industries that have
consistently contributed to a net foreign trade balance of payments as motion pictures have. The strength and domination of the majors in distributing their product
abroad is unmatched throughout the rest of American private industry, yet has led to
strong criticisms of attempts to export only specific U.S. values and lifestyles to less
advantaged countries. The indigenous culture and traditions of these developing societies is threatened by the omnipresent imagery of U.S. culture and this exploitation
is sometimes criticized as being pernicious to these societies as former days when
their economies were raped under the yoke of economic imperialism.

It seems quite evident that the motion picture is a complex, unique, and interesting product that merits a fuller analysis in many different dimensions. The tool for conducting this industry analysis is the *industrial organizational approach,* a process derived from applied microeconomic theory that provides a convenient method for organizing elements of an industry into a comprehensive whole, yet is still flexible enough to permit examination of special industry circumstances or characteristics.

The industrial organization approach begins by examining the nature of the product and the structure of an industry in its basic components—demand, market concentration, barriers to entry, vertical integration, conglomerateness, and so on, in order to gain an overall picture of the distribution of current market power and the chances for deconcentration of power in the future. Often, an historical investigation provides a supplementary context for how the industry became so organized and the direction it is heading in.

The structure of an industry helps determine and direct the conduct of the firms in that industry. *Conduct* refers to how the industry members act and react to each other in such dimensions as pricing, product differentiation, and research and development. Under different conditions, the conduct of firms may evolve toward one of extreme competition or, alternatively, toward mutual cooperation and collusion. The final result of the interplay of structure and conduct is the performance of the industry according to well-defined economic categories of efficiency, productivity, technological progressivity, and profitability. Hence, the structure–conduct–performance paradigm provides a useful approach to examining the motion picture industry and sets the stage for public policy debate about such issues as antitrust or censorship or even cultural imperialism. Because the industrial organization approach often uses special economic terms that may be unfamiliar to the average reader of this book, a special appendix has been prepared to serve as a primer on this approach. Similarly, for those who are unfamiliar with the basic microeconomic building blocks, this material has been included in Appendix B. Appendix C provides a basic foundation in the principles of antitrust policy and enforcement.

The book is organized according to a very systematic and logical design. The first chapter after the introduction provides an historical context for the development of the industry and highlights some of the major events that have changed the organization of the industry. Chapters 3 and 4 then follow the structure–conduct–performance model and describe in great detail all the different elements that constitute the motion picture industry today. Chapters 5 and 6 then pick up on the importance and impact of antitrust rulings during the development of the industry and the blossoming of the "windowing" distribution strategy and the exploitation of new markets, including foreign ones. The final chapters deal with current research topics of major importance to industry development. For example, Chapters 7 and 8 explore the concept of company investment and diversification into the theater business and into network broadcast television, respectively. Chapter 9 investigates the reasons why consumers continue to attend movies at theaters and the forces of change that are shifting their consumption toward the other exhibition windows. Chapter 10 attempts to pull together most of the industry behavioral research to ask the critical question of whether it is possible to predict the financial success of motion pictures and to identify those ingredients that are associated with the financial success of movies released in the last several years. Chapters 11 and 12 look at the relationship between the economic structure of the industry and the resulting content—the intersection of art and commerce—and industry attempts to self-regulate content through applying voluntary rating standards. The appendices provide a basic background in the fundamentals of microeconomics, industrial organization, and antitrust.

2

Business History of the Industry

EARLIEST ORIGINS

Shortly after receiving his patent for the motion picture camera (kinetograph) and its viewing machine (the kinetoscope), Edison introduced motion pictures to an unbelieving public in 1894. These early "peep" hole viewing machines with their continually rotating fifty-foot (forty seconds) strips of celluloid film proved to be an instantaneous success and were easily added novelties to a penny arcade, curio hall, or storefront amusement center. Yet, the novelty stage of motion picture development could not sustain a growing industry.[1]

By failing to protect his patents abroad, Edison "invited" in a series of foreign inventors who soon foresaw the wisdom of a more sophisticated projector system using the same stop action technique of the kinetoscope. By 1896, when Edison belatedly caught up with the European and new U.S. inventors by teaming up with Thomas Armat to introduce a new projector called the "vitascope," the long-range potential of the industry started to take shape.[2] The projector meant that a crowd of people could simultaneously view a single strip of film, thus reducing the capital investment of the amusement parlor operator. Edison was suddenly faced with domestic competition from Biograph, Vitagraph, and the Latham Brothers, and foreign competition from Lumiere, Pathe Freres, and others. Each of the rival projector manufacturers produced their own films. There was no standardization in the industry and cameras were not freely licensed. Thus, machines and films were tied to each other, requiring parlor operators to choose one incompatible projector system over another or purchase all the different systems.

Once again, the public grew weary of this novelty act and attendance faltered until more sophisticated movies could be developed. By the early 1900s, the "story" (with plot, characterization, etc.) had developed to replace the "home movie" era of actualities.[3] Stories of approximately fifteen-minutes duration (a so-called one-reeler) soon became the industry standard and shortly thereafter incorporated more complex production techniques such as the manipulation of time through crosscut editing techniques. Essentially, the movie industry had passed across the imaginary line from being merely a novelty to an art form, and this would be its beginning as the creator of cultural artifacts that, alongside popular music, would clearly identify the U.S. experience.

The arrival of the nickelodeon theater in 1905 provided the movie industry with its first true opportunity to stand on its own as an entertainment industry rather than being used as filler for vaudeville shows. The nickelodeon was not really a theater in its modern sense (although today's shopping center mini-auditoria are only about twice its original size), but a converted storefront with one-hundred chairs and a projector and screen. Nevertheless, the motion picture program consisting of four or five consecutive one-reelers (shorts), often emphasizing different genres (e.g., newsreels, comedy, drama), was soon to overshadow its vaudevillian counterparts.[4]

These fundamental changes in the industry brought forth corresponding new business practices. The emergence of the film exchange and the conversion of the industry from purchase to *leasing* of motion pictures was a critical factor in maintaining the rapid turnover of film product—a factor thought critical to luring the customer back to the nickelodeon continually and establishing a loyal clientele. With production costs rising more than proportionately with the development of the story, the only way that nickelodeons could hold the line on admission prices *and* maintain turnover of product would be to share the burden amongst themselves by sharing the pool of available films. Hence, the exchange was an intermediary for facilitating the operation of a rental system at approximately one-fourth the purchase price of a one-reeler. While problems of incompatibility of film product still remained, the exchange system of distribution was clearly a force working to standardize the product to facilitate its leasing practices. Later on, as one-reelers gave way to two-reelers and eventually feature films, and the nickelodeon was replaced by first-class and then deluxe movie theaters, rising production costs would have to be met by lengthened runs (less turnover) and higher admission prices.[5]

In short, the story and nickelodeon were only the first steps in the development of motion pictures as a full-fledged mass medium. The arrival a decade later of feature films (four reels or more) and then deluxe theaters meant that the motion picture industry had indeed displaced the legitimate and illegitimate theaters as the primary entertainment medium for the American people.[6] The development of motion pictures as a mass medium involved a series of cycles, each with some driving force that could help cultivate a mass audience that would develop the moviegoing habit. Each new invention, improvement in content, and in the luxuriousness of the exhibition hall would propel the industry through a ratchet-type effect to a new, higher equilibrium level (see Figure 2-1).

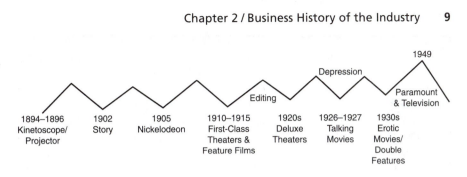

FIGURE 2-1   Time Line Development of Motion Picture (1894–1949)

THE SEARCH FOR MARKET POWER

Concomitant with the development of motion pictures as a cultural habit was the attempt by a small group of companies to acquire monopoly power in the fledgling industry. As is typical with most new industries, the original power brokers were enthroned through manipulation of the patent process. As alluded to above, Edison and a small group of inventors tried to dominate the market by exploiting their patents on cameras, projectors, film, and other integrated components. At first, they refused to license others in the use of their cameras, which meant that exhibitors were tied to the manufacturers for the provision of film unless they were willing to import films made with bootleg equipment from abroad. Because of the simplicity of the film content, the manufacturers were initially able to supply the burgeoning industry with all its film product needs. However, with the development of the story and the one-reeler, filmmaking (the production stage) now became a more skilled and specialized venture and was beyond the scope of many of the original independent bootleggers.[7] Eventually, a small specialized group of skilled artisans were able to enter and compete successfully with the equipment manufacturers in the production of films and help fill the demand from the nickelodeons for enough product to maintain a daily turnover of their program fare. Essentially, partial vertical disintegration of the industry was taking place into four, largely separate, strata: manufacture of equipment, production of film product, distribution of product via local exchanges, and, finally, exhibition of product at nickelodeons. The industry was on the threshold of competition, especially at the exhibition level, where the capital cost of setting up a single nickelodeon was minimal.

There was tremendous patent litigation during this early era, with the biggest conflict over the basic camera and projector patents of Edison and Biograph, especially following a Supreme Court decision sanctioning both patents (i.e., Biograph's had no sprockets). Filmmakers lined up behind one or the other patent and this created an atmosphere of uncertainty and instability that inhibited the further development of the motion picture industry. Eventually, a truce was called in 1909 between the major patent holders and a new cartel arrangement, in the form of a trust, was established to solve the conflicting claims and collectively monopolize the industry. This trust form of business organization was perfectly in keeping with the times. It should be recalled that this was the "muckraker" era, when such captains of industry as the Rockefellers, Carnegie, Mellon, Gould, and even Marconi had taken control of strategic U.S. industries through trust combinations.

The Motion Picture Patents Company was a patent pooling arrangement between the holders of the sixteen key motion picture patents, including Edison, Biograph, Armat, and Eastman–Kodak (with the former two receiving the overwhelming majority of patent royalties).[8] (See Chapter 5 for more detail on the era of the trust.) The major domestic and foreign producers of that era were also members but they didn't explicitly share in the royalties accruing from the patents. Each of the producers, exchanges, and nickelodeons were exclusively aligned to the Trust and could not contract with independents for film product or theaters or anything without risking loss of their Trust franchise. Therefore, by cornering the market on cameras, projectors, and film stock and offering top quality producers, the Trust believed that their product was indispensable and they could monopolize all of the vertical stages of the motion picture industry and exclude independents at all access points, since no other source could supply the vast input needs of the industry at this time.

Troubles arose for the Trust when they were unable to prevent maverick exchanges and nickelodeons from dealing with independents for additional needed supply of product. To control this uncertainty over distribution, the General Film distribution subsidiary was established to acquire or drive out of business all of the previously licensed exchanges with the exception of a few in the major cities.[9] Only the exhibition stage remained in private hands following the acquisition practices of General Film; all the other stages were under the corporate umbrella of the Trust. For the next several years, the Trust was able to completely dominate the nascent motion picture industry. However, a growing list of problems threatened the smooth functioning of monopoly control.

First, the Trust was unable to enforce its court-ordered injunctions against patent infringers using bootlegged equipment. These independents, often aided and abetted by Trust members, quickly escaped from the grasp of the U.S. marshalls and private company security guards to the sunny Los Angeles area—just a few miles from the Mexican border where they could conveniently flee if their illegal operations were discovered by the Pinkerton guards. Second, William Fox, one of the few remaining independent exchange operators in New York City, filed an antitrust suit against the Trust, alleging a series of antitrust violations whose effect was to drive independents out of business.[10] This private antitrust suit was soon joined by the Department of Justice and was tried in District Court in 1915 and appealed to the Supreme Court in 1918.[11] The courts found against the Trust and disbanded it (see Chapter 5). Many commentators feel that the adverse court decision merely formalized an internal decaying process already in the terminal stage.

Not only was there internal bickering among the Trust members over the failure of Edison and Biograph to share royalties more equitably, but many of the producers and directors moved from one company to another and to independents, thereby weakening industry stability.[12] There also was evidence that some of the Trust members secretly aided the independents, further harming the overall resolve and morale. More crucially, because of the Trust's inflexible standard of using single reels coupled with daily turnover, they were slow to adapt to changing consumer tastes for motion pictures. When the defiant independents introduced the feature film (at higher rentals and slower turnover rates) and simultaneously began publicizing their stars and paying them higher salaries to attract repeat patronage, the Trust refused to meet this competitive challenge since these practices would destroy their carefully crafted production standards and system of royalties. With unattractive and uncompetitive product, the Trust soon began to lose their customers.[13]

With the rise of feature films, a new distribution organization was needed to handle such a different species of film. In the period 1914–1925, the tight oligopolistic market structure in the film industry was formed.[14] Adolph Zukor, head of Famous Players, a film production company, was trying to introduce feature films to the American audience. In 1914, he signed a twenty-five-year exclusive contract with Wadsworth Hodkinson who had just formed an association of states' rights distributors known as Paramount. In 1916, Hodkinson was forced out as President of Paramount and Zukor assumed control and soon merged his Famous Players company with Paramount. Zukor's feature films were superior to the competition and, with his acquisition of famous stars such as Mary Pickford, Douglas Fairbanks, and Gloria Swanson, he was able to charge high fees and license his films in blocks by tying the star films to lesser films on an all-or-nothing basis. Thus, at this time, the production–distribution stage had the upper hand with quality product, and the exhibitors had to accept the terms or suffer the loss of this popular fare.

When the terms became too dear, the one-hundred largest first-run exhibitors formed their own organization called First National Exhibitors Circuit.[15] They integrated backwards into production by long-term contract and merger in an attempt to supply their own needs and thereby circumvent the power of the Zukor organization. Zukor realized that even quality films had to have first-run exhibition to earn high box office dollars, and he sought an agreement with First National to jointly control the industry. When First National refused, he had no other choice but to acquire a string of theaters in order to guarantee access for his films. This triggered a vast merger race as all the large companies in each stage of production sought merger partners to guarantee either an assured supply of films or access at reasonable terms. This raised the capital requirements for entry and for successfully competing in the industry. By 1925, there were only a handful of giant vertically integrated firms left in the industry and, from this point on, the industry would forever fall under the control of strong oligopoly firms.

The arrival of sound occurred in the mid-twenties at precisely that point in time when something new and exciting was once again needed to stimulate movie attendance (see Figure 2-1). While silents had reached their zenith of artistic achievement, the industry seemed listless, without momentum, and its product was relatively expensive now that it had to compete with the burgeoning mass medium of radio. As a series of competing and incompatible technologies sought market-place approval,[16] Western Electric finally joined up with Warner Brothers, a small production house seeking to expand into distribution and exhibition, to introduce the first "talkies" in late 1926. Within a year, buoyed by the phenomenal success of *The Jazz Singer,* Western Electric severed its exclusive ties to Warner Brothers and sought industry-wide approval and exclusive use of its sound-on-film technology. The remaining major distributors/exhibitors (the Big 5) soon signed exclusive arrangements with Western Electric to use its equipment in both the filming and exhibition of motion pictures.[17] Furthermore, as distributors, they would not permit their films to be shown in independent theaters unless they used Western Electric equipment.

Thus, once again, the tendency of the industry toward oligopolistic consensus was manifest, this time with the invention of sound as the catalytic agent and the indispensable technology needed to maintain a competitive posture in the industry. Yet, even with the propulsion that sound gave to companies like Warner Brothers and RCA, they still could not be viable without a chain of theaters providing an assured point of access for their films. To coexist with such industry giants as Fox, Loew's, and Paramount, these companies were forced to integrate into the exhibition stage, and the trend toward vertical integration continued unabated.[18]

While the Depression of the early thirties did dampen the box office revival induced by sound, the motion picture industry was not as severely impacted as many large smokestack industries. This is not to minimize the corporate reorganizations (and receiverships) that several of the companies with substantial theater holdings experienced when they couldn't make their debt (interest) payments. Nevertheless, the industry did attempt to improve its popularity by resorting to more salacious themes as well as introducing the double feature and contests to hold their loyal customers. Most importantly, the industry participated in the New Deal's suspension of the antitrust laws (the National Industrial Recovery Act)—an antidote to the ravages of unbridled competition. "The Code of Fair Competition" was drawn up in 1933 and regulated trade practices among producers, distributors, and exhibitors. It was administered by the Motion Picture Producers and Distributors of America, the industry trade association. Participating distributors and exhibitors could now display the "blue eagle" logo on their films and in their theaters to show compliance with government economic stabilization policies. Such trade practices as block booking, blind selling, time clearances, zoning, and admission price discrimination[19] were now legally sanctioned and enforceable in a court of law. The net result of such practices was to disadvantage independents, especially at the exhibition level, by unreasonable theater classifications, zoning and clearance patterns, and minimum admission prices. Within two years, the National Industrial Recovery Act was declared illegal, but the lesson of the advantage of mutual cooperation had clearly been learned. The industry would now follow a tacit (indirect) form of shared monopoly[20] rather than the explicit form permitted by the Code; in the long run, the results would be indistinguishable.

THE PARAMOUNT CASE

During the late 1930s, the five fully integrated firms ("the majors")[21] set out on a deliberate course of action to eliminate the remaining independents within the industry (see Chapter 5 for more detail). Since none of the majors, individually, possessed enough first-run theaters (the cream of the business) nor produced enough "A" quality feature films to be self-sufficient, *they needed to depend on each other.* Acting in concert, they possessed enough first-run theaters to provide a solid nationwide exhibition showcase for their own films, and their combined production efforts (in association with three minor distributors)[22] were sufficient to fill an entire year's schedule of films. This near 100 percent self-sufficiency and self-preference severely restricted the freedom of independent producers, distributors, and exhibitors from access at any point along the vertical path.[23] It became an impenetrable barrier to entry and permitted the majors to monopolize the industry, fix prices, and earn excess profits.

It is important to understand the vertical nature of this industry and how vertical integration can be utilized as an anticompetitive tool to coalesce monopoly power. The Big 5 were fully integrated across the three critical strata and were the primary producer–distributors of "A" quality films. They were aligned with the Little 3 and some other minor independents who acceded to the stiff distribution fees demanded by the majors for access to the system. These companies collectively provided the lower quality, lower budgeted "B" films that would fill the lower half of the double bill. Collectively, the Big 5, Little 3, and aligned independents could supply virtually 100 percent of the program fare for an entire year's playbill at the exhibition stage. During this period, they released three-fourths of the total number of non-Western films and earned a comparable percentage of industry rentals.

At the exhibition level, the Big 5 either wholly owned or had significant financial interests in only 3,137 out of 18,076 U.S. theaters or 17.35 percent; yet, in the more significant first-run market, they collectively operated 70 percent of all first-run theaters in the 92 cities with 100,000 or more population and 60 percent in cities between 25,000 and 100,000 in size.[24]

The price-fixing conspiracy had both horizontal and vertical aspects, spanning the distribution and exhibition levels. Theaters were categorized according to their status in the temporal distribution scheme and assigned territorial (zoning) and time clearance to protect their status and earning power. Distributors, furthermore, fixed minimum admission prices for films according to their "run," and when they *uniformly* and unchangeably determined these designations and *arbitrarily* gave favorable terms to the vertically owned majors, this system of distribution became rigged. Hence, with high admission prices, excessive temporal and geographic clearances, the bulk of film revenues would be guaranteed for the first-run theaters controlled by the majors, thereby injuring the independents, who had, in many cases, been unfairly relegated to second-run or lower status.[25] When these practices were buttressed by a film licensing process that also favored the large theater owners, the exclusionary aspects of the conspiracy were vividly demonstrated.[26] While this vertical market structure with accompanying degree of self-sufficiency was not as stable as that of AT&T's interlocking subsidiary system nor as encompassing as the Motion Picture Patents Company, it still regimented the industry to an extraordinary degree and prevented nonaligned independents from access at any point.

This pattern of vertical organization was attacked by the Antitrust Division of the Justice Department beginning in 1938. The first resolution of action involved a consent decree in 1940 in which some of the most obnoxious trade practices would be ameliorated and an Arbitration Board established, but no structural reform would be instituted. Such a conduct solution did not prove very satisfying, and the original case was reinstated in 1944, asking for a divorcement of the vertical ownership bonds. While the Justice Department won at the district court level, this court found only anticompetitive conduct violations rather than the actual existence (or any dangerous probability) of monopolization. The district court outlawed these specific trade practices[27] and ordered a system of "competitive bidding" whereby films would be licensed picture by picture and theater by theater. The court believed that such a decentralized licensing procedure would automatically restore independent distributors and theaters to equal access to the best theaters/films.

On appeal, the Supreme Court basically agreed with the lower court's finding of facts but differed on interpretation. For example, the higher court believed that a separate submarket of "first-run" theaters rather than all theaters taken as a group was the proper relevant product market and the Big 5 clearly dominated these key theaters. Furthermore, the Court did not believe that "competitive bidding" would end the conduct abuses since the components of a bid encompassed many dimensions and required subjective judgment by distributors, the very parties that had engaged in the collusive conspiracy in the first place. Finally, the bureaucracy inherent in adjudicating a competitive bidding regime was beyond the scope (and expertise) of the judiciary branch of government.[28]

On remand from the higher court, the district court in 1949 ordered vertical divestiture of the exhibition level from the production–distribution level and furthermore required that theaters illegally obtained or used as part of the conspiracy had to be sold off by the newly reconfigured exhibition circuits. The divestiture process was fashioned through a series of consent decrees negotiated with each company on an individual basis. For the most part, the divested chains of theaters could not acquire new theaters without specific approval of the courts and none of the affected parties could reintegrate (either forward or backward). Furthermore, competitive bidding was suggested (but not mandated) as a way of further insuring that decentralization of power and open access would prevail in the exhibition level.

THE AFTERMATH OF PARAMOUNT

The dismantling of the vertical monopoly in the motion picture industry should have provided a laboratory setting to assess the impacts of antitrust structural remedies, but alas, the arrival of television at precisely the same point in time confounds the analysis. Nevertheless, some industry changes can be directly attributable to the breakup.[29]

With vertical disintegration and the end of block booking and franchising, assured access to theaters was no longer guaranteed; *films would have to compete according to their intrinsic quality.* This naturally opened up the market for independent producers and distributors whose products would now be judged according to merit rather than parentage. Many new independent producers entered the scene and, paradoxically, they were now welcomed with open arms by the major and minor distributors. The majors had decided to reduce their risks by cutting back on their in-house productions, which correspondingly meant the end of the studio system of star exploitation. Given their excess studio capacity and their need to obtain economies of scale in distribution, they courted the favor of the independent production sector—the same group of people they had sought to eliminate only a few years before.[30] Frequently, the majors had access internally or externally to the critical source of film financing, which they leveraged as a means of obtaining distribution rights for independently produced films.

For the Little 3 distributors, the opening up of the exhibition market meant that they could upgrade their product line and thus compete head-to-head with the majors; no longer were they relegated to the subservient role of producing B films. Within a few short years, their status as distributors became comparable to that of the Big 5 and continues to this day. Allied Artists (formerly Monogram) and Republic, two independent producer–distributors who had weathered the cartel years, also became more prominent after divestiture. Surprisingly, the distribution level that would soon become the new center of power and profits for the industry invited only sporadic entry. This is generally explainable by the fact that the arrival of television cut box office demand by an estimated one-third to one-half and eliminated the low-budget B film (which was similar to the "free" television program) from the marketplace. Given such adverse market conditions and the need to achieve economies of scale of two to three films distributed per month, entry was not feasible.[31]

The most striking changes occurred at the exhibition level. As noted, the divested circuits were further required to sell off those theaters that had been obtained illegally or were part of the conspiracy. They went even further than this by getting rid of marginal theaters, especially in small towns. Since such a large percentage of their remaining holdings were first-run theaters, they remained in a relatively advantageous position. Some 20 percent of the second-run theaters of independents had their classifications improved after divestiture, but the most significant change was the elimination of the third-run (and lower-run) theaters due primarily to the loss of B pictures induced by competition from television and the emergence of drive-ins.[32] While pictures were now supposed to be available on an equal basis to all local theaters, the deep pockets and superior efficiency and negotiating prowess of the chain organizations still "dominated the scene" in the exhibition sector.

Thus, divestiture meant the removal of the umbrella that artificially had been propping up many inefficient, small theaters. As the total number of features released gradually diminished (especially those by the majors), and production budgets also increased (in part as a way of conquering the uncertainty of theater access), there was inevitable pressure on admission prices to rise. Theater reclassification and upgrading further exacerbated the trend toward rising average admission prices for the moviegoing public, yet this was counterbalanced by a general improvement in the quality and diversity of films distributed.[33] Crandall explains the paradox of rising admission prices simultaneous with declining demand by claiming that the major distributors had consolidated their oligopolistic consensus during this time and distribution had become the focal point for industry power.[34] In a sense, it was a restoration to the era when Zukor was the kingpin of the industry and control over product was the key to success rather than control over access. This shifting of strategic control within a vertical industry structure is not unusual, yet Crandall blames the ineffective Paramount decrees for overlooking this eventuality and never coming to grips with the true source of market power in the industry.

THE IMPACT OF TELEVISION

The initial reaction of the motion picture industry to the fledgling television industry was one of ridicule, especially regarding the nature of the product. Because of the insatiable demand for product, the quality of TV programs often suffered. Indeed, in these early years, the live programs on network television were rather clumsily handled with very little production value, and for every high quality drama, there were many at the opposite extreme. It truly was *not* a golden age of television if one looks at the entire panorama of programs rather than focusing on the live dramas. Overall, these early television programs can best be compared to the B films of the 1940s era. Nevertheless, as TV penetration increased and people stayed at home to watch what was billed as "free television" rather than attend movies, the motion picture industry soon understood the enormity of their situation and plight.

Their initial response was to boycott the television industry.[35] This meant refusing to permit their creative personnel under contract (primarily actors) from appearing in television programs; "television" actors were stigmatized in the Hollywood community and informally blacklisted from motion pictures. Furthermore, none of the large producer–distributors would produce television series nor license current or past films from their library for television exhibition. They also tried to counter the television technology by introducing a number of product innovations to win back their lost patronage. They hoped to establish a clearer product identity and market niche, independent of television. These innovations included Cinerama, 3-dimensional, and finally big budgeted films, incorporating lavish production values.[36] Later on, such innovations as stereophonic sound and 70-millimeter screens and multiplex theater complexes were also added to the theater experience. However, none of these changes could slow down the advance of television. Its time had come.

After a number of years of absorbing the declining fortunes of theatrical distribution and recognizing the revenue-generating capability of television production, Warner Brothers became the first major distributor to break the boycott in 1955 by agreeing to produce a weekly series.[37] Shortly thereafter, the remainder of the large distributors decided to hitch their wagons to the rising star of television rather than retain their purity in producing films. They also realized that television networks (and later television stations) could become subsidiary markets for licensing recent and classic theatrical films, once those films had reached the saturation level of theatrical exhibition. In other words, the new television markets could now replace the third- and lower-run theatrical markets that had been lost. The temporal price discrimination pattern that had worked so well when only theaters were involved could now accommodate the new television technology. Therefore, what had begun in the late 1940s as a major confrontation between two entertainment media took on a pattern of stability, mutual interdependence, and economic symbiosis within a short span of ten to fifteen years.[38] This stable business relationship continues to exist, and in fact, has been extended to the newest technologies of cable, videocassette recorders, pay-per-view, and the emerging video-on-demand fiber-optic systems—all of which have been folded into the distribution price discrimination process now known as "windowing" that will be explained in greater detail in Chapter 6.

ADDITIONAL CHANGES IN THE MOTION PICTURE INDUSTRY

In addition to adjustments to the vertical restructuring and the emergence of new exhibition windows, the motion picture industry has been immersed in other social changes as well. The most prominent of these changes involves the migration of population out of the cities to the suburbs. Starting around 1960, this trend toward suburbanization changed the fundamental locus of movie theaters from the downtown area to the shopping malls in nearby suburbs. As malls grew to accommodate the influx of population, there was a transformation from the single deluxe theater of the downtown era to the multiscreen auditoriums of the theater complex. This transformation also affected the economics of operating motion picture theaters.

The process of downsizing average theaters and building multiple screen auditoriums illustrates a different approach to profit maximization by the theater owners. This permits a more cost-efficient utilization of seat capacity than was possible in the old single auditorium deluxe theaters. A good analogy is found in the airline industry since deregulation. To maintain a high "load factor," the airlines have downsized their planes (or formed alliances with commuter airlines) and adjusted the number of scheduled flights between smaller cities (with few passengers going to a common location) and hub cities. At the hub, passengers going to major destinations are collected from all the feeder lines and placed on larger planes.

For the theater owners, multiple auditoriums permit a theater complex to book movies for a portfolio of different screens, some of which may be larger than others. With, say, six to eight or more screens per site, a theater owner is fairly certain that at least one or two of its screens will have a hit, while the others will do moderate business until their run is over. In this way, average load factors can be increased compared to the "hit and miss" strategy associated with having a single screen.

The multiple screen concept is tied in with the shopping mall phenomenon.[39] For shopping malls, the greater the amount of foot traffic, the greater the total sales for all store owners. This explains why similar shoe stores, department stores, clothing stores, and the like will locate near each other even though they are natural competitors. The movie theater complex is an integral part of the modern shopping mall since it generates a lot of foot traffic for other store owners (sometimes vice versa). For this reason, Guback concluded that the recent construction boom in movie theaters was more a shopping mall phenomenon than related to fundamental industry economics. If one only looked at theaters as an isolated business, given the stagnant demand for admissions due to the VCR and pay cable alternatives, one could not explain the addition of nearly 1,000 new screens per year. In short, theater construction was only justified as part of the profit-maximizing calculus of building a successful shopping mall.[40] It shouldn't be surprising to thus find mall entrepreneurs cross-subsidizing such theaters through favorable leasing provisions or low-interest loans.

The theater concession stand also fits into this traffic flow analysis and multiple theater concept. Since the theater retains 100 percent of all concession revenues (which have an extremely high markup), yet only makes about 10 percent excess profits from box office gross, any strategy that maintains a high load factor can be very profitable. By having multiple screens in operation at staggered starting times and centrally locating the concession stand in the lobby, the theater can operate this aspect of its business at near capacity, although the peak traffic times—about ten minutes before each new showing, cannot be totally avoided. Thus, the modern theater multiplex is as much dedicated to selling high profit margin concessions as it is to showcasing recent released movies. Of course, a highly popular movie will naturally cause spillover benefits for the entire theater complex so movies plus popcorn are properly considered as a kind of joint economic product with interrelated demand. Given the stagnant demand for movie admissions over the last thirty years, the theaters have been forced to abandon their once exalted position as the exhibitor of cultural artifacts in favor of and in association with their new skills in selling fast-food concessions. Instead of modernizing theaters to make the moviegoing experience more special for patrons, the remodeling funds have gone toward improvements in the concession stands.

A few other trends have emerged in the production–distribution sphere that should now be highlighted. First, as the distributors jettisoned the star system and cut back on their investment in in-house productions, the independent producer took on a totally different role. Far from being shunned in the industry, the independents were now welcomed with open arms, since the majors could now lay off some of the high risk of flimmaking on the backs of these independents. What arose is what is commonly referred to as the "condominium" era of motion picture-making in which the studios rent out space on their lots to independent producers aligned with the majors; they become landlords over a kind of condominium with many independents simultaneously taking occupancy.

Not surprisingly, the terms of rent are quite high, and when a major agrees to distribute an independent's picture or loan money to cover the budget, the financial considerations are very substantial. The independent is virtually forced to mortgage all its rights and split the profits as a quid pro quo for landing a distribution contract with a major. In fact, the terms are not dissimilar from those of the television networks when they accept a new entertainment series for prime-time broadcast. Evidently, the major movie companies learned their lessons quite well from the TV networks when bargaining advantages were more favorable to them.

Finally, within the new competitive milieu, it is not surprising to see a realignment of power between the major studios, just as we have seen for the newly reconstituted theater circuits (see Chapter 3 for greater detail). The RKO organization failed under the misguided leadership of Howard Hughes in the 1950s and MGM, the once top production house, suffered several corporate reorganizations, eventually becoming a partner with United Artists with respect to distribution and selling its film library to Ted Turner for his TNT Network launch. TriStar was born as a combination of three strange bedfellows—CBS, Columbia, and HBO—and later was sold along with Columbia Pictures to Sony after first being owned by Coca-Cola. Perhaps most important has been the tremendous resurgence of Disney. While not really part of the *Paramount* conspiracy of the 1940s, Disney was always considered a specialty player in the industry, focusing on animated films and G-rated family pictures. With the arrival of Michael Eisner over a dozen years ago, Disney established a totally new identity. It retained its traditional trademark in animated and G-rated films but added new films of all genres through its new Touchstone and Hollywood Picture subsidiaries. A few years ago it also acquired a successful independent, Miramax, to round out its subsidiaries to four. Its films over the last half dozen years have been so popular that it has become the top producer–distributor. Its financial picture became so bright that it decided to expand its holdings into the TV network sphere with the acquisition of ABC–Capital Cities in 1995. Notwithstanding the tremendous success story of Disney, the major movie studios of the 1990s greatly resemble their earlier counterparts of the 1920s and 1930s, and it is their resilience to change that is a truly remarkable feat of endurance in the history of U.S. industry.

NOTES

[1] A. R. Fulton, *Motion Pictures: The Development of an Art from Silent Films to the Age of Television,* Norman, OK: University of Oklahoma Press, 1960, p. 7.
[2] Ibid, Chapter 1.

[3]Tino Balio (ed.), *The American Film Industry,* revised edition, Madison, WI: University of Wisconsin Press, 1985, part I introduction.

[4]Russell Merritt, "Nickelodeon Theaters, 1905–1914: Building an Audience for the Movies," in Tino Balio, op. cit., Chapter 4.

[5]Balio, op. cit., part I.

[6]Ibid, part II introduction.

[7]Ibid.

[8]Jeanne Thomas Allen, "The Decay of the Motion Picture Patents Company," in Tino Balio (ed.), *The American Film Industry,* Madison: University of Wisconsin Press, 1976, Chapter 6.

[9]Ibid.

[10]Ibid.

[11]*U.S. v. Motion Picture Patents Co.,* 225 Federal Reporter 800 (1915). The salient issue was whether legally granted patents could be cross licensed in such a fashion to regiment an entire industry. The Court ruled that the patent system did not supercede the antitrust laws; what might be legal for a single patent holder could not be done collectively "by combining in a vertical pattern and excluding non-members from access to trade."

[12]Robert Anderson, "The Motion Picture Patents Company: A Reevaluation," in Balio, op. cit., Chapter 5.

[13]Allen, op. cit.

[14]Balio, op. cit. (1985), part II.

[15]Ibid.

[16]The competing technologies can be grouped into the categories of synchronization of sound and picture (Western Electric) and sound-on-film (DeForest, Case, RCA). By 1927, Western Electric had signed patent pooling agreements with Case/Fox and the sound-on-film technology became the industry standard. For more detail on this section, see Douglas Gomery, "The Coming of Sound: Technological Change in the American Film Industry," in Balio, op. cit. (1985), Chapter 10.

[17]Ibid.

[18]Ibid. It should be mentioned that when RCA brought suit against Western Electric, charging them with antitrust violations in connection with their exclusive agreements on sound equipment, the case was settled out of court with Western Electric removing its exclusivity clause from such contracts.

[19]Block booking is the forced licensing of a package of feature films, tying high and low quality films together and offering them on an all-or-nothing basis.

Blind selling is the licensing of a film prior to its being available for commercial preview to the theaters.

Zoning is the geographical area of exclusivity afforded a local theater.

Time clearance is the temporal period of exclusivity granted a certain run of a feature film.

Price discrimination means charging different prices for a film depending on the the number of seats, location, and interior splendor.

[20]For the export market, the Webb–Pomerene Act permitted the industry to establish an export cartel known as the Motion Picture Export Association (MPEA) that could establish common policies and negotiate on behalf of its members. The MPEA continues to dominate the world markets, even though the Webb–Pomerene Act was finally repealed about a decade ago.

[21]The five majors were: Twentieth-Century Fox, Loew's, Paramount, RKO, and Warner Brothers.

[22]The three minor distributors were United Artists, Columbia, and Universal. None of these companies officially owned theaters, although United Artists had interlocking directorships with a major chain.

[23]The manufacturing stage had long since been separated as an integral stage of production.

[24]*U.S. v. Paramount Pictures,* 334 U.S. 131 (1948).

[25]Ibid.

[26]Ibid.

[27]Besides those practices already mentioned, master and formula deals involving chainwide licensing as well as franchise (full-line) forcing agreements exceeding a year's duration were also prohibited. Ibid.

[28]Ibid.

[29]The best accounts of these impacts are those of Michael Conant, "The Impact of the *Paramount* Decrees," in Balio, op. cit. (1976), Chapter 16 and "The *Paramount* Decrees Reconsidered," in Balio, op. cit. (1985), Chapter 20. This section draws heavily on these articles.

[30]Conant, "Impact of Decrees," op. cit. (1985).

[31]Ibid.

[32]Ibid.

[33]Ibid.

[34]Robert Crandall, "The Post-War Performance of the Motion Picture Industry," *The Antitrust Bulletin,* 20, Spring 1975: 49–87.

[35]Balio, op. cit. (1985), part IV introduction.

[36]Ibid.

[37]Ibid.

[38]Barry R. Litman, "Decision Making in the Film Industry: The Influence of the TV Market," *Journal of Commuinication*, 32, Summer, 1982: 33–52.

[39]Thomas Guback, "The Evolution of the Motion Picture Theater Business in the 1980s," *Journal of Communication,* 37, Spring, 1987: 60–77.

[40]Ibid.

3

The Current Structure of the Industry

DISTRIBUTION STAGE

The distribution stage still remains under the control of a handful of major companies, although a few names have changed since the *Paramount* divestiture.[1] In terms of the majors, RKO left the scene in the 1950s. In 1983, United Artists took over distribution from MGM and eight years later acquired the company completely; finally, its movie inventory was sold to Ted Turner to help launch his TNT cable network and then the production studio was spun off again and is currently for sale to the highest bidder. Monogram became Allied Artists and very recently was purchased by Lorimar, which in turn was acquired by Warner Brothers.[2] Another independent, Embassy, was sold in 1985 to Columbia and then resold that same year to Dino DeLaurentis and then underwent bankruptcy proceedings. American International was sold to Filmways in 1979 and its name changed to Orion in 1980. While still in business, its role has been relegated to that of a minor player. Another key player in the distribution realm is TriStar. Formed in 1983 as a joint venture of Columbia, HBO, and CBS, it was purchased late in 1987 (including its theater circuit) by Columbia and folded into the new Columbia Entertainment division that was first sold to Coca-Cola and then to Sony in the late 1980s.[3]

Finally, the latent Disney studio was reorganized in the mid-1980s, shed its exclusive family entertainment label ("G" rating) and established itself as the leading production–distribution company in the industry after its recent acquisition of Miramax.

In looking at the market shares in Table 3-1, it is quite evident that the distribution side of the motion picture industry is still highly concentrated. Only a handful of large major distributors control the industry. With remarkably few changes, the same group that dominated the industry during the Paramount era continues to lead the charge into the twenty-first century. With a CR_4 of about 65 and a Herfindahl–Hirschman Index of about 1400, the distribution side is clearly a moderately/highly concentrated industry. The two moderating influences that still keep the industry somewhat rivalrous are the relative parity that the top few distributors have with each other and the fact that industry leadership can change quickly if one or another studio hits big with a major blockbuster in any one year. This is shown by examining the instability index between any two years to see if market shares have significantly altered. Notwithstanding these facts and given the tremendous uncertainty that surrounds creating popular media programming, there must be continuing barriers to entry that make the life of the independent quite precarious, especially if it seeks to become a mini-major like New Line or Miramax.

The concentration in the distribution sector entered a period of flux in the late 1980s. With the successful entry of TriStar, the newly emerging strength of Disney, and the sustained presence of some mini-majors like Canon, DeLaurentis, New Line, and Orion, it appeared briefly that a new competitive element had finally caught hold in this sector of the industry. Unfortunately, this period of euphoria was short-lived. The disappointing results from the merger between TriStar and Columbia and the financial difficulties of the new mini-majors caused their market pres-

TABLE 3-1   Market Shares for North American Film Distribution (1990–95)

Company	1995	1994	1993	1992	1991	1990
Disney[a]	22.5%	23.1%	16.3%	19.4%	13.9%	15.5%
Warner Brothers	16.3	16.1	18.5	19.8	13.7	13.1
Universal	12.5	12.5	13.9	11.7	11.0	13.1
Sony (Columbia + TriStar)	12.8	9.2	17.5	19.1	20.0	13.9
Paramount	10.0	13.9	9.3	9.9	12.0	14.9
20th Fox	7.6	9.4	10.7	14.2	11.6	13.1
MGM-UA	6.2	2.8	1.8	1.2	2.3	2.8
New Line	6.6	6.2	3.4	2.1	4.0	4.4
Savoy	1.3	1.4	——			
Gramercy	1.1	1.8	.6			
Goldwyn			.7			
Miramax			2.9	1.1	1.4	1.2
Others	3.1	3.6	4.4	1.5	10.1	8.0
Total	100.0%	100.0%	100.0%	100.0%	100.0%	100.0%
CR_4	64.1	65.6	66.2	72.5	59.6	57.4
CR_8	94.5	93.2	92.5	97.4	88.5	90.8
H-H	1335	1367	1333	1577	1204	1200
Instability		15.2	35.6	20.2	29.7	18

[a]Includes Miramax for years 1994 and 1995 after merger.

ence to be quite dimmed, and when Miramax caught on as a new darling of the industry, it was shortly absorbed by Disney, seeking to expand its newfound market power. The same fate awaited New Line, which, along with Castle Rock, was absorbed by Turner Broadcasting Systems and later merged with Time Warner when it acquired Turner in 1996. Finally, in 1996, Kirk Kerkorian absorbed MGM-UA again under the auspices of his Tracinda Corporation with hopes of returning it to major studio status.

With Disney and Warner Brothers apparently firmly entrenched in the top two positions for the last few years and with promising production schedules already planned, it appears that the current market structure will continue indefinitely. There is one bright ray of hope still shining on the horizon, however. The formation of the new "Dreamworks" studio by Steven Spielberg, Jeffrey Katzenberg, and David Geffen promises to install a well-financed and highly respected creative team that can solve the age-old plight of the independent. And this new studio, with its hand in many multimedia applications, appears to have the best chance for success since the demise of the Zoetrope empire of Francis Ford Coppola some fifteen years ago.

BARRIERS TO ENTRY

It is not surprising that the distribution level is highly concentrated. This is a characteristic common to all the mass media and is largely explained by the economies of scale that accompany national distribution of entertainment product. To service the nearly 26,000 North American movie screens and take advantage of the foreign market potential, a distributor must have a vast worldwide network of offices. Furthermore, if other subsidiary markets like pay cable, pay-per-view, commercial television, and home video are to be tapped, additional bureaucratic layers must be established. Focusing on domestic distribution of motion pictures, for the moment, a major company needs somewhere between twenty to thirty-two regional offices and a full complement of salespeople and marketers to cover the territory. This is the first quantity dimension, Q1, that encompasses economies of scale. Furthermore, it is necessary to have a full lineup of features released throughout the year so that these offices can work at full capacity. This is the second quantity dimension, Q2, that encompasses economies of scale. If one uses 1995 as a typical year, (see Table 3-2) each of the large companies released at least fourteen features and most of them between twenty to thirty-five. There is a caveat here, however. The number of releases does not always correspond to the relative success of the distributor. Sony, with thirty-five, had nearly as many releases as Disney, with thirty-seven, yet a significantly lower market share; similarly, Warner Brothers and New Line had the same number of releases at twenty-nine, yet Warner Brothers was much more successful with its films. The "quality" of films (as reflected in box office popularity) is thus as important as the quantity of films released. At any one time, it is much better to employ one's workforce on a relatively small number of good prospects (those currently in release and those on the horizon) than to waste their efforts on films that

TABLE 3-2   Number of Films Released and Box Office Success, 1993–95

Firm	1995 B.O. Share	1995 # Films	1994 B.O. Share	1994 # Films	1993 B.O. Share	1993 # Films
Buena Vista	19.0%	37	19.3%	36	16.3	36
Warner Bros.	16.3	29	16.1	42	18.5	37
Paramount	10.0	22	13.9	19	9.3	15
Universal	12.5	21	12.5	22	13.9	22
Fox	7.6	14	9.4	18	10.7	21
Sony	12.8	35	9.2	35	17.5	39
New Line	6.6	29	6.2	14	3.4	13
Miramax	3.5	39	3.8	28	2.9	24
MGM UA	6.2	18	2.8	12	1.8	12
Gramercy	1.1	15	1.8	13	.6	6
Savoy	1.3	10	1.4	5	—	—
Others	3.1	137	3.6	138	5.1	119

may only last a few weeks. So the quantity of films adjusted by a quality index is a more proper designation of the second dimension of scale economies.

Figure 3-1 demonstrates the dual nature of cost efficiencies for the distribution sector. For the most part, only the majors and mini-majors have the requisite size across both quantity dimensions—thus creating a declining *long-run average cost surface.* Furthermore, while some critics would argue that vertical integration ownership of studios and back lots is an albatross hanging over the heads of the major distributors and merely drives up their overhead costs, there may still be some strategic nonpecuniary advantage and efficiency (in scheduling time and having creative experts on hand) that accrues to those so situated. This is especially important if there is a boom period in production during which access to sound stages is limited.

While cost efficiencies dictate large size, there must be a corresponding level of demand to justify such a large enterprise and to use the capacity most efficiently. Here is where product ideas, differentiation, and managerial skill play such an important role. The studio chief and his/her top creative lieutenants must consistently make the correct decisions (or educated guesses) concerning their product composition. This is not like a modern industrial enterprise in which assembling lines turn out large quantities over long manufacturing runs; rather, each film is hand crafted with a very short product life and only occasional opportunities for reuse of the creative inputs. In fact, the motion picture differs significantly from episodic television series in this key creative dimension. The successful studio needs to have a continual stream of new ideas since product and consumers' tastes change so often; this process of matching tastes and product is made more complicated by the nearly two-year lead time required to produce and release a new film. Therefore, it should not be surprising that one witnesses a high turnover and revolving door policy for studio production chiefs who often are personally blamed for box-office flops.

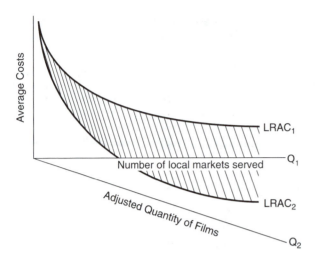

FIGURE 3-1 Dual Efficiencies of Distribution Networks

Given the escalating production and advertising costs of recent years, the average release by a major distributor runs nearly $35 million in "negative" costs plus at least half that amount to give it a national "day and date" launch. Understanding these economic risks and the fact that the major distributors have a **portfolio** of such projects at different stages in the two-year cycle, the distributors and their corporate parents tend to act rather conservatively. They seek to minimize their financial risks in whatever way is available; hence, like their television counterparts, they often seek some formulaic answer. This answer may take the form of employing "bankable" movie stars, top directors, and writers who at some point have touched the magic of a box office smash, or else "laying off" the risk through coproduction with foreign investors or financially backed independents.[4] Similarly, they may repeat ideas, themes, or characters that worked well in the past, thus leading to the ever-present sequel.[5] (For more detail on the factors that predict financial success, see Chapter 10) This risk-averse philosophy is not new; it simply has replaced the assured theatrical access in operation during the heyday of the Trust and the cartel. Yet, with all the new exhibition windows available, the real risk probably lies with only the most expensive budgeted films that absolutely must make a big splash in the theatrical market to capture high returns in the secondary windows. Moderately budgeted films are thus much better overall investments since there is less risk of complete failure in all the windows, taken together.

SURVIVABILITY

To get a better understanding of the average cost relationship, a survivor technique was conducted comparing the average number of annual films released with the average rate of profitability as measured by operating income and cash flow margins. The results are contained in Table 3-3 and in Figure 3-2. While this information is not complete and bearing in mind the caveat that quantity does not always equate with quality, it clearly demonstrates the strong relationship between the number of films released and the average rate of profitability, especially for industry leader Disney. By survivorship standards, this implies nearly a continuously declining long-run average cost relationship and, alongside the fact that very small distributors with a few market share points have enormous difficulty in remaining in business for five or more years, it suggests a clear tendency toward oligopoly in the distribution sector. Refinements of this technique would separate out the quality dimension associated with the number of released films so that the quantitative amount reflects a qualitative dimension as well.

It would also be useful to have similar information about the exhibition sector. Given the proclivity toward chain ownership, it would be nice to be able to answer the question about how many screens were necessary to achieve the economies of scale in booking, marketing, and related areas of interest. Regrettably, the profit information is sparse for the theater circuits because many of them are not publicly traded nor is information systematically gathered about them in the trade press. So this piece of the puzzle must for the time being remain unsolved.

TABLE 3-3 Number of Films Released and Long-Term Profitability, 1990–94

Distributor Companies	Annual Average Number of Films Released	Average Operating Income Margin %	Average Cash Flow Margin %
Majors			
Buena Vista	29.67	15.46%	16.38
Warner Brothers	31.67	5.92	12.44
Sony (Columbia + TriStar)	33.33	N/A	N/A
Universal	21.80	3.63	3.30
Paramount	19.00	4.34	6.58
Fox	19.50	6.00	7.48
MGM/UA	13.67	N/A	N/A
Independents			
New Line	17.17		
Miramax	24.50		
Savoy	7.50		
Gramercy	11.33		
Goldwyn	12.00		

Source: *Variety*, various annual issues; Veronis-Suhler, various annual industry reports.

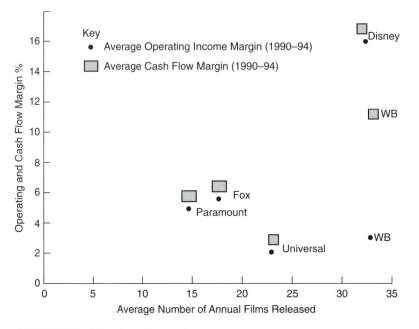

FIGURE 3-2   Survivor Technique

VERTICAL INTEGRATION AND CONGLOMERATENESS

Part of the risk can also be reduced if the distributors have vertical integration or deep corporate pockets. While the *Paramount* decrees forbade reintegration between the distribution and exhibition levels, as time has passed the original companies have been resold or absorbed into larger conglomerate corporations.[6] Furthermore, new entry has occurred at both levels, thus introducing new companies that were not covered by the original decrees. Most importantly, given the degree of competition from other subsidiary exhibition markets, the antitrust-tolerant Department of Justice has not even opposed reintegration by the original *Paramount* defendants during the 1980s.[7]

There currently exists a significant degree of vertical integration by the leading distributors into the exhibition realm. The advantages of vertical integration are numerous. They clearly give the distributor greater control over admission prices, release patterns, and the avoidance of antiblind-bidding statutes. Most importantly, they permit all of the box office dollars to flow to the distributor without worrying about too many remaining in the exhibition sector.[8]

While Disney has concentrated on theme parks and Twentieth-Century Fox has eschewed theater ownership in favor of TV stations and the new Fox Broadcasting

Network, and MGM–United Artists has been too busy with corporate takeovers (e.g., by Ted Turner and Kirk Kerkorian) and reorganizations to concentrate on this activity, most of the other major companies have obtained a foothold in domestic and international theaters. Most of the key acquisitions have occurred in the last decade.[9] For example, in 1986 MCA acquired a 50 percent interest in Cineplex–Odeon, then the second largest theater circuit in North America, which had grown by over a thousand theaters through acquiring Plitt and other medium-sized circuits. In recent years, the Bronfman family has retained working control of the company and continues to exert a major presence in both the U.S. and Canadian markets, with 1056 screens in the former and 575 in the latter. Viacom, the parent organization of Paramount, has approximately 368 domestic and 462 Canadian theaters, making it one of the top ten circuits in North America. The domestic theaters were acquired with long-time partner, Time Warner, in 1986 from Mann Theaters, Festival Enterprises, and Trans Lux and now operate under the corporate name Cinamerica. Viacom is also the owner of the Famous Players Circuit in Canada, one of the biggest chains of theaters in that country with 462 screens. Furthermore, it is a partner with MCA in the 76-screen circuit in Europe known as "Cinema International Corporation."[10] Warner Brothers has also made significant foreign theater investments, but they are too scattered and hidden to document for our purposes.

As mentioned above, in late 1987, Columbia Entertainment obtained full ownership control of TriStar, including its circuit of 310 theaters (the former Loew's circuit). In early 1988, the Loew's subsidiary acquired the USA circuit, thereby adding another 317 theaters to Columbia's holdings and making it the sixth largest circuit in North America. Since then, its holdings have grown and it has been acquired by Sony and its theater operations (some 946 screens) bear the Sony name.

In another light, Cannon, a mini-major distributor for a number of years in the 1980s, owned a 525-screen circuit in Europe (with a particularly strong position in the United Kingdom) and then bought the Commonwealth circuit (#9) in 1986 with its 432 screens to solidify its domestic holdings. Since then, it has undergone several reorganizations. As Table 3-4 shows, Sony, MCA, Viacom, and Warner Brothers collectively own 2370 screens in the United States and 1037 in Canada, giving them a strong position domestically and a commanding one in Canada. Their international holdings are also strategically placed to facilitate their export operations in many foreign countries.

Most interesting was the position of industry leader, United Artists Theater Circuit—not affiliated with MGM–United Artists. Not only did it aggressively seek merger partners and embrace new construction programs within the theater exhibition level, but for a while it was controlled by Tele-Communications, Inc. (TCI), by far the leading domestic multiple-system cable operator. At one point, TCI bought significant stock in Blockbuster video stores, an industry leader in videocassette sales with some 600 stores in its chain by the end of 1988.[11] Given this dominant position across so many exhibition windows and with partial ownership of such cable networks as Turner Broadcasting Systems (CNN, WTBS, TNT), Black Enter-

TABLE 3-4   Vertical Integration by Major Distributors

Parent Company (Major Distributor)	Theater	# U.S. Screens	# Canadian Screens
Sony (Columbia & TriStar)	Sony (#8)	946	——
MCA (Universal)	Cineplex-Odeon (#7)	1056	575
Viacom (Paramount) with			
Time Warner (Warner Brothers)	Cinameria (#16)	368	——
Viacom (Paramount)	Famous Players	——	462
Totals		U.S. Screens 2370	Canadian Screens 1037

Source: NATO, *Encyclopedia of Exhibition,* various years.

tainment Network, Cable Value Network, Tempo, and American Movie Classic (100 percent control), many people believed that we were witnessing a vertical chain of control, never even dreamed of by the *Paramount* conspirators. However, this coalescence of power never fully materialized when significant Congressional pressure forced TCI to reevaluate its total holdings. It decided to divest its interests in both the theater and video store sectors to focus more attention on its core cable programming and operating system subsidiaries.

CONGLOMERATENESS

In addition to examining market concentration and vertical integration, there is a special need in the motion picture industry to analyze the degree of conglomerateness or diversification among the leading firms. This diversification seems more prevalent in the distribution rather than the exhibition sector, so that will be the main focus here.

It seems fair to say that the distribution sector is an arena where only well-financed, deep pocket firms can play on a competitive level. The days of the independent are long past. Because of its strategic bottleneck position in the "windowing" process and the critical importance of the export market for entertainment and information product, the major studios have now become the targets of large global media conglomerates of one form or another. With corporate parents like Time Warner (Warner Brothers), Disney, Seagrams (Universal), Sony (Columbia and TriStar) and News Corporation (Fox), there is no lack of venture capital for these risk-bearing companies. Yet, surprisingly, most of them are cautious in tapping into the vast financial wealth of their parents, preferring instead to balance the long shots with conservative undertakings. This is not to say they are unwilling to gamble on big budgeted films; rather such large pictures must have bankable stars, be adaptations from other popular media, or be sequels to what has proven successful in the past before the "go" signal is given.

The high degree of conglomerateness can act as a barrier to entry to small independent distributors, with little industry experience or contacts and without the financial security and wherewithal that accrues to having a giant corporate parent. It must have been a daunting prospect for companies like New Line or Miramax (prior to their takeovers) to try to compete in an industry where one's size is so dwarfed by the large industry leaders and their giant parents.

The other advantage that comes from a high degree of conglomerateness is the possibility for creating significant synergies across many different planes of operation. If a parent corporation has holdings in other media, both domestically and internationally, this may pave an easier path for entry into the various exhibition windows. Similarly, ideas that develop in one subsidiary of the corporation can cross-fertilize and be exploited in another. A successful novel, TV program, or recording in one part of the business may be more easily transplanted into another or exploited better. This is the hope and dream of media conglomeration that only recently has found some positive evidence of fulfillment.

In summary, to the extent that these major distributors can rely on the resources of their parent corporations for production loans or capital expansion, this further enhances the barriers to entry in the industry and widens the gap between the majors and independents, perpetuating the negative connotation that still accompanies a truly independent release.

Table 3-5 gives a brief synopsis of each parent company, its total corporate sales, and the percentage of its 1994 revenues that came from its filmed entertainment division—a category broad enough to include film-related revenues earned in the broadcasting and home video markets. Columbia–TriStar and Universal are subsidiaries of very large consumer electronics corporate giants (like the NBC–General Electric connection). Consequently, they account for a rather small percentage of the parent company's operations. Twentieth-Century Fox, Warner Brothers, and Paramount are divisions of large media conglomerates, albeit somewhat smaller than the pure conglomerates associated with the first grouping of distributors. Nevertheless, these are still enormously large corporations with annual sales in the $2.3 to 5.0 billion range. The motion picture distributors in this grouping account for a higher percentage of total corporation sales, ranging from 26 to 31 percent. Disney is a somewhat diversified corporation with major holdings in amusement parks; yet, nearly half of its business is devoted to filmed entertainment. The final grouping consists of independents: Carolco, Goldwyn, Savoy, and Orion. These corporations are considerably smaller than the first two groupings with annual sales of slightly less than half a billion dollars. Correspondingly, their film entertainment divisions

TABLE 3-5   1994 Diversification Ratios and Profitability for Selected Film Distributors

Company	(A) Parent $ Sales (Millions)	(B) Film Distributor $ Sales (Millions)	(C) = B/A Distributors Diversification %	(D) Operating Income $Millions	(E) = D/B Operating Income Margin %
Sony (Columbia + TriStar)	$36,249.7	$3,182.0	8.78%	N/A	N/A
Walt Disney (Disney–Buena Vista)	10,055.1	4,793.3	47.67	856.1	17.9%
Viacom (Paramount)	7,363.2	2,285.2	31.04	−88.4	−3.86
News Corporation (20th-Fox)	7,985.0	2,126.0	26.62	97.0	4.6
Time Warner (Warner Brothers)	16,188.0	5,014.0	30.97	276.0	5.5
Matsushita (Universal)	64,306.7	5,696.7	8.86	225.7	4.0
MGM–UA (Tracinda)					
Independents					
Carolco	59.3	59.3	100.0%	−39.9	−67.3%
Goldwyn	108.8	68.5	62.96	6.7	9.8
Savoy	85.8	85.8	100.0%	−39.3	−45.8
Orion	175.7	175.7	100.0%	−89.0	−50.7

usually account for a very high percentage of the parent's sales. Of course, the remainder of distributors would rank farther down the list and would neither be very large in absolute terms nor very diversified.

PRODUCT DIFFERENTIATION

Product differentiation is quite important in the motion picture industry, especially on the distribution side. One of the greatest difficulties of newcomers in establishing a beachhead in this industry is battling the name recognition and trademarks of the major distributors, many of whom have been in the business for seventy or more years. In an age of information overload and with a plethora of motion pictures released each year, the consumer must navigate a steady course through this bewildering jungle. Knowing that a film was distributed by a trusted company provides a certain comfort to the consumer and helps direct his/her choice of movies. The factor of "being there first" provides an enormous "trademark" advantage to incumbent firms in the motion picture distribution sector. Of course, the type of movie, notoriety of the director, actors, and actresses also help with the decision process.

However, there is more involved here than just showing one's name and colors. Each film will have its own custom tailored publicity and advertising campaign that might include television appearances for the stars, trailers for prerelease promotional use, print and electronic advertising, billboards and theater displays, product tie-ins with fast-food restaurants, and many other "tools of the trade." To grab the attention of consumers, newcomers must be willing to match these expenditures dollar-for-dollar or even spend additional funds to lure away potential customers from their rivals; and it is a sustained level of expenditure, picture after picture, that is required. Without such a prolonged financial commitment, the newcomer distributor can scarcely hope to establish its name in the market. This is, of course, the essence of how product differentiation can represent a structural barrier to entry that ties in alongside economies of scale and vertical integration to dissuade new firms from entering as full-fledged competitive rivals and limits them to being fringe players.

EXHIBITION

To understand the degree of concentration in the exhibition stage, one should first differentiate between national and local markets. One commonality across both geographical delineations is the overwhelming prevalence of chain ownership, in the movie industry known as "theater circuits." Just as chain ownership has permeated the grocery, drug, and department store industries, so it has throughout the mass media. The days of the stand-alone theater owner, cable system, newspaper, or television station are fast diminishing. Chain ownership yields some significant efficiencies in spreading managerial (i.e., motion picture booking and scheduling) and legal expertise, advertising, and marketing costs across a large number of outlets. These economies are especially important within cities and regions where coordinated advertising and marketing campaigns can yield significant benefits to the exhibitor and distributor alike.

The national concentration indices given in Table 3-6 indicates a moderate degree of concentration of theater ownership, with a CR_4 about 26 percent and a CR_8 just over 40 percent of the total U.S. screens. The companion Herfindahl–Hirschman Index is well below the 1,000 threshold level, though it was highest in 1990 and 1993. The trend is somewhat upward since 1988 at the eight firm concentration level while quite stable at the four firm level. There was a large increase in concentration in the 1980s when the CR_4 increased by over eight points and CR_8 by

TABLE 3-6   Market Concentration of Top Dozen U.S. Theater Circuits, 1990–95

Circuit	1995 # Screens (%)	1994 # Screens (%)	1993 # Screens (%)	1990 # Screens (%)
United Art.	2295(8%)	2237(8%)	2312(9%)	2699(11%)
Carmike	2037(7%)	1735(7%)	1570(6%)	813(3%)
AMC	1632(6%)	1603(6%)	1628(6%)	1649(7%)
Cinemark	1224(4%)	1149(4%)	1059(4%)	645(3%)
Gen.Cinema	1202(4%)	1268(5%)	1355(5%)	1444(6%)
Cinpl.Odeon	1056(4%)	1055(4%)	1039(4%)	1365(6%)
Loews–Sony	946(3%)	904(3%)	885(3%)	837(4%)
Ntl.Amusement	870(3%)	840(3%)	780(3%)	625(3%)
Regal	861(3%)	454(2%)	——	——
Hoyt's	561(2%)	521(2%)	440(2%)	610(2%)
Act III	575(2%)	568(2%)	544(2%)	486(2%)
Cobb	575(2%)	507(2%)	410(2%)	261(1%)
Total Screens (Indoor & Drive-in)	27,843	26,689	25,626	23,814
CR_4	25.8%	25.6%	26.8%	30.1%
CR_8	40.4%	40.4%	41.5%	42.3%
HH	<500	<500	<1000	<1000

fifteen but that merger craze and building flurry by the industry leaders has clearly ameliorated in the last few years (see Chapter 7). United Artists has decreased its holdings by some 400 theater screens since 1990 while AMC has stayed perfectly the same. The real movement has come from industry newcomers Carmike and Cinemark, which have both entered significant acquisition programs to jump into the top four hierarchy of industry leadership. The other fast rising circuits are National Amusements, Sony, and Regal, while previous industry leader, General Cinema, and Cineplex Odeon–USA have all downsized in the 1990s. It should be noted that such expansion of circuit size is not limited to only the acquisition route; a net of some 4,000 new screens have also been built in the 1990s, mostly in new suburban shopping malls.

There is a point that needs to be made about this method of measuring market concentration. Implicit in merely counting screens as market shares is the idea that each screen is equivalent in terms of auditorium size and drawing power. Hence, having 500 screens is better than having 250 screens. As was demonstrated in the *Paramount* case, this logic is faulty and subject to great error because first-run screens are clearly bigger moneymakers than second-run ones and in more lucrative, attractive, and in less congested geographical territories that may produce a higher per screen dollar volume—the true source of market power.

While the switch of units from theaters to screens has in one sense made the measurement more uniform with smaller deviations in the standard auditorium size, it has not totally eliminated differentials between screens. At minimum, the differential between first- and second-run screens and (drive-ins) should be more effectively handled through data collection and publication. This separation of first- and second-run theaters is done below in the examination of several typical local markets. Finally, it should be noted that this method of measuring market concentration by examining the potential *reach* rather than actual revenues is common among the electronic mass media industries such as radio, broadcast TV, and cable.

Obviously, it would be wrong to only examine national concentration since movie theaters are really local retail outlets. Is the local degree of concentration better or worse than at the national level? The Detroit market is fairly typical of what is happening in metropolitan areas through the country. Looking at Table 3-7, it is seen that four chains collectively control 85.1 percent of the 261 first-run screens in the greater metropolitan area. This is an impressive increase of CR_4 measure of concentration since 1988. AMC is still the largest circuit in Detroit with 85 screens while National Amusement is second with 65. Hence, the top two circuits account for 150 screens themselves—more than half of all screens. It is also seen that the average number of screens per site in Detroit is 7.05, up from 4.32 just eight years ago. As Table 3-7 clearly indicates, the pattern of circuit ownership in Detroit has only slightly altered from the earlier period. General Cinema has reduced its first-run presence while Star cinemas, a regional circuit, has expanded its holdings to become the third largest theater owner, bypassing the national circuits of United Artists and General Cinema.

The Detroit market translates national trends quite closely. National circuits tend to have multiple screens located in the suburbs, generally in the major shopping centers while local circuits are smaller, spread throughout the central city or concentrated in the drive-in market. Most of the independent stand-alone theaters tend to be located in the old line suburbs or have been split into multiple parts. The national trend has been to downsize theaters into multiscreen auditoriums. This is a significant change from the deluxe theaters built in the 1920s and the willingness of owners to bank their entire business on a single feature. Another phenomenon is the gradual emergence of second-run theaters, with sixty-three screens in the greater Detroit area. Cinemark, the fourth largest national chain and one of the fastest growing, is the key player in the second-run arena with twenty-eight screens at four sites.

The same pattern of circuit ownership and domination is seen in Boston, a city comparable in size to Detroit, with roughly the same number of total screens. National Amusements is the top circuit in Boston with seventy-one first-run screens, followed by General Cinema with fifty-seven and Sony Theaters with forty-eight. Collectively, these three account for 176 screens. No other national circuit has any sort of presence in the Boston first-run market.

To contrast these large metropolitan markets, two smaller city areas were examined. In the Lansing, Michigan area, there are twenty-eight first-run screens, twelve

TABLE 3-7   Market Concentration in Exhibition in Detroit, 1988 and 1996

			1988			
Company	Local Rank	National Rank	# Screens	%	# Sites	Average No. Screens/Site
AMC	1	2	86	33.7%	17	5.06
Ntl. Amusement	2	9	44	17.3	6	7.33
United Artist	3	1	26	10.2	5	5.20
General Cinema	4	3	25	9.8	5	5.00
Total Screens			181	100.0%	33	4.32
CR$_4$ 71.0%						

			1996			
Company	Local Rank	National Rank	# Screens	%	# Sites	Average No. Screens/Site
AMC	1	3	85	32.6%	13	6.54
Ntl. Amusement	2	8	65	24.9	7	9.29
Star	3	42	43	16.5	6	7.17
United Artist	4	1	29	11.1	5	5.80
General Cinema	5	5	14	5.4	2	7.00
Others			25	9.6	4	6.25
Total Screens 261			261	100.0%	37	7.05
CR$_4$ 85.1%						

Source: *National Association of Theater Owners Encyclopedia,* various years.

second-run screens, and one art theater. AMC is the local monopolist with twenty-two of the twenty-eight screens (78.6 percent) at three sites. Only General Cinema with a six-screen complex (21.4 percent) competes against AMC in the important first-run arena. National Amusements maintains the only other theaters with a twelve-screen second-run complex. On the other hand, in the Grand Rapids, Michigan area, there are thirty-six first-run screens and thirty second-run screens. Here, the regional Jack Loek's and Jack Loek's–STAR circuits control twenty-seven of the thirty-six screens (75 percent). National Amusements is the only other national chain competing in Grand Rapids with a nine-screen complex accounting for the remaining 25 percent. The second-run market is split between local and regional theater circuits.

Therefore, in assessing the distribution of screens across these disparate markets, it seems clear that the pattern of domination prevalent during the *Paramount* era still remains, even though the industry has undergone some remarkable changes. The large theater circuits still prefer to locate and cluster themselves in favorite cities or regions, and then seek to dominate those areas. It is still true today that no theater circuit has enough screens to give a truly national release to a picture. While the names of the circuit owners have changed since *Paramount,* and the deluxe theaters have been replaced by multiplexes, the pattern of local and regional domination still holds after fifty years.

PRODUCTION SECTOR

It is very difficult to analyze the structure of the production sector because of the overall scarcity of data and the fact that it is so closely aligned to distribution that in many instances the two are inseparable. In general, all available evidence suggests that this sector is monopolistically competitive in nature with a large number of similar type firms and no substantial barriers to entry.

As explained in the history section above, the production sector now consists of hundreds of very small production companies of a few key employees each. They were founded around a major star or director and include a handful of writers, directors, and budgetary personnel. Oftentimes, the production company is created or recreated around a specific film project. Once the funding is secured to launch a new film, the production company will swell with new employees, hired specifically for that project. Since writers, actors, assistant directors, makeup personnel, and sound stage crew belong to the highly complex union system in Hollywood, it is possible to "rent" these people for whatever length of time is needed to complete the project. This obviates the need for retaining a large permanent staff of these people and having them underemployed or laid off during the down times between pictures. Similarly, office space and access time can be rented on studio lots to actually produce the picture, without the necessity of owning a studio. This reinforces the conclusion that production companies can be lean operations and that entry can be relatively easy and exit relatively painless. *This is not to suggest that producing a feature film is easy;* nothing could be further from the truth. The creative ideas and professional cinematography necessary today to capture the attention of filmgoers are quite impressive and beyond the reach of most curious or uninitiated people. Furthermore, in many instances, the deal needed to secure the funding to produce the film can be almost as creative as the film itself and requires significant business acumen. And the production company's reputation will largely rest on the financial (or sometimes artistic) success of its most recent picture. No one will be willing to back a production company that has continually been associated with box office failures.

While a film project must obviously bring together this complex assortment of creative and business personnel and mold them into a unified whole, the most important item in this mix must always be the creative idea itself. Without a strong concept to focus on, film projects can languish unfunded or never become completed once filming has commenced. This is often the reason why the most successful independent producers began as writers themselves. They have the inner wherewithal to initiate or seize on a vision and turn it into reality. Most importantly, they have the ability to convince others to join with them and take enormous risks.

Risk-taking and filmmaking are synonymous terms. To launch an average picture for national release today costs almost $35 million in negative costs and an advertising and marketing budget of an additional $10 to 15 million. Most production companies do not have these amounts of funds themselves and thus must figure out a deal to achieve financial backing. This involves either taking out a bank loan or locating investors. In both instances, the participation of a major distributor is indispensable to achieving these levels of financial commitment.

In the first instance, taking out a bank loan requires the establishment of either a line of credit or a specific amount of collateral. The *bank loan must be repaid* as revenues accrue from the film. It is a financial debt for the company much like an auto loan or home loan is for the individual. Because of the enormous risk and difficulty in predicting hit movies in advance, banks and other financial institutions require demonstrable proof of the wherewithal of borrowers to repay the loan, no matter what happens at the turnstiles. Furthermore, there usually will be an additional few interest points added on to cover this special risk. Their first requirement generally is that a major distributor (Fox, Paramount, Warner Brothers, etc.) actually handle distribution of the film throughout the thousands of theaters in the country. To achieve a major "pick up" contract, the producer must obviously have a sound vision but also must be willing to pay a 30 to 35 percent distribution fee and surrender rights in all subsidiary exhibition windows. These distribution fees are deducted *first* along with the bank loan debt, before the splitting up of any profits.

If the distributor is asked to guarantee the loan to the bank (i.e., pledge the full faith and assets of the distributor to cover any debt) or if the distributor decides to finance the loan itself, then it generally requires significant profit participation as its reward for this additional risk. An equal split of net profits is often demanded by the distributor as a quid pro quo for assuming the added risks of financing the film, in addition to distributing it.

An alternative means of financing is to solicit a group of investors to become equity participants in exchange for providing some or all of the funding. This funding may come from a stock offering or well-heeled relatives, if the film is a small project, or more likely from private solicitation of financial "angels"—people interested in sharing in the excitement and glamour of Hollywood filmmaking. An investment is different from a loan. It represents a stake in the project, a share of the profits or losses. If the project fails, the investors are all responsible. If the film is successful, they share in the net profits according to their equity ownership in the project. Often the film itself is incorporated to limit liability to corporate assets, rather than the personal assets of the investors. In such instances, the producer often is guaranteed a disproportionate share of the net profits because of his/her direct participation in making the film itself. Occasionally, there are additional government sources for filmmaking that originate with the Small Business Administration to provide funding or to guarantee a low interest rate. However, these are generally limited to very small film projects that hardly can be expected to be major entertainment motion pictures. Finally, presales of distribution rights to foreign markets or "coproduction" deals with foreign investors are alternative sources of film financing that are available if the producer wishes to handle distribution on an independent basis—without the involvement of a major distributor.

Market share data for the production sector is practically nonexistent. To gain some insight into what companies participate in this sector, the distribution of production companies was extracted from the list of top 100 films for the years 1993, 1994, and 1995. While the data is not presented, it clearly demonstrates the wide dispersal of film projects and the competitiveness of this sector. By correlating the overall box office receipts, one can gain further understanding of which companies have been associated with the biggest hits, although the distributor is usually given credit for box office smashes—not the producers.

Since the dawn of motion pictures, the major motion picture distributors have always maintained a fairly strong position in the production sphere through in-house production. The so-called studio system of star development was intricately intertwined with the distribution and exhibition plan in the *Paramount* era. Each studio had a nexus of sound stages, back lots, and other property that were used intensively to drive the engine of the *Paramount* conspiracy. The same observation could naturally be made with the even earlier period of the Trust during which production was vertically tied to all the other stages of the industry.

With the dismantling of the vertical stages of production following the *Paramount* decision, there was a rethinking on the parts of the major distributors concerning the role that production should play in the redesigned corporation. While some studios did sell part of their properties or combine with others to jointly operate the units, there remained the impression in the corporate boardrooms that studio production was somehow efficient and necessary to remain a major player in this industry. Nevertheless, a new concept of how this role should be played soon emerged with the simultaneous developments of vertical divestiture of motion picture theaters and the arrival of television. With the loss of assured access to theater outlets, the majors became more cautious and conservative about their in-house production operations. They clearly wished to keep a strong and steady hand in this sector but they also wished to lay off some of the risk and enormous costs on the rest of the production sector. Hence, they first dismantled the studio system of star development and switched to a system of hiring creative personnel on a need basis only, rather than keeping them under long-term contract. Secondly, they switched to the aforementioned "condominium" theory of studio management whereby the studio facilities would be made available to independents on a leased contractual basis at the point when the major distributor became involved in the financing or production of a film. In short, there no longer was a need for a company to do everything; outsourcing of a significant number of films each year would diversify the risk and increase the flexibility of the operation. Incidentally, this is the same approach toward production that the Big 3 television networks followed even before the enactment of the Financial Interest and Syndication Rules. Since the majors controlled access through their bottleneck position, they could maintain effective control over the production sector, even though they did not produce all the films themselves from internal sources. As with the commercial television industry, this partial integration approach by the major distributors probably benefited moviegoers the most by introducing new creative ideas from outside sources rather than becoming totally reliant on the studios for all new concepts.

NATURE OF DEMAND

One can be fairly confident in saying that the nature of consumer demand in the theatrical film business has been quite stagnant for the last twenty years. The number of theatrical admissions has been remarkably stable at slightly more than one billion, regardless of the quality of the product, nature of competing technologies or services (e.g., cable television, VCRs, pay-per-view), or even economic conditions (see Table 3-8). In this sense, it appears to be an industry that is truly recession proof.

Yet this focus on the stable admissions masks several important economic factors that often are overlooked but cast a different light on the state of the industry's health. First, while admissions have indeed remained steady, this must be considered within the context of a rising underlying population that has slowly but steadily increased over the last twenty or more years. If measured on a per household or per person basis, motion picture admissions would show a steady decline—contrary to the expectation and performance of most other industries during the same span of time. To say it slightly differently, the norm is to expect industry growth at least as fast as the rate of population increase. To fall behind this pace is a sign of weakness and not something to boast about.

On the other hand, when viewed in the broader context of the overall demand for motion pictures across all exhibition windows, the picture could not be any brighter. With the unbelievable increase in VCR penetration and sales/rental activity, the steady markets for premium and pay-per-view movies and syndication, all indications point to the conclusion that movies are more popular than ever before; people just view them in different settings than they used to (see Chapter 9 for more detail). This is great news for the motion picture producer–distributors but not for the theater owners unless they have diversified into other exhibition windows. To their credit, they have continued to maintain their absolute demand in the face of an

**TABLE 3.8   Motion Picture Theaters Box Office Attendance and
Admission Prices, 1970–1994**

Year	Admissions (in millions)	Admission Average Prices	Year	Admissions (in millions)	Admission Average Prices
1970	920.6	N/A	1982	1,175.4	2.94
1971	820.3	1.65	1983	1,196.9	3.15
1972	934.1	N/A	1984	1,199.1	3.36
1973	864.6	N/A	1985	1,056.0	3.55
1974	1,010.7	1.89	1986	1,017.2	3.71
1975	1,032.8	2.03	1987	1,088.5	3.91
1976	957.1	2.13	1988	1,084.8	4.11
1977	1,063.2	2.23	1989	1,262.8	3.99
1978	1,128.2	2.34	1990	1,188.6	4.22
1979	1,120.9	2.47	1991	1,140.6	4.21
1980	1,021.5	2.69	1992	1,173.2	4.15
1981	1,067.0	2.78	1993	1,244.0	4.14
			1994	1,291.0	4.18

Source: NATO, *Encyclopedia of Exhibition,* 1994, various years.

ever-increasing competitive challenge as tough as any in American private industry. Furthermore, there has been a corresponding change in the demographics of the moviegoing audience. While once thought to be predominantly the province of the young, the under-thirty generation, the demographics have skewed toward the older in the last decade so that over half of the audience is thirty or older. The reshuffling of attendance has favored patrons over fifty at the expense of those in their early twenties. *Movie attendance now has a demographic age profile not too dissimilar from that of the television audience.* There have been no major demographic shifts over the last decade in the categories of marital status, family status, or education— all of which are strongly linked to the moviegoing attribute. However, there has been a noticeable shift in gender, with more women self-reporting as frequent or occasional movie patrons in recent years.

It is important to make a judgment about the price elasticity of demand as well. To examine price elasticity (movements along a demand curve), we hypothesize a series of different price and output combinations, with all other substitute good prices and economic factors held constant. Looking at admission prices in Table 3-8 since 1990, we see a decline of about three cents in actual prices and a somewhat larger decline in real terms since we know that the prices of other entertainment goods and services have been rising at about 4 to 5 percent per year. So, we can calculate a gross estimate of elasticity by using admission data from 1990 and 1994 and assuming about a 20 percent decline in real admission prices over the four-year period.[12] The result of such a calculation shows approximately an 8.3 percent increase in admissions in response to a 20 percent decline in real admission prices for an elasticity coefficient of .415, which is less than one and therefore solidly in the *inelastic* range for price elasticity of demand.

BUYER CONCENTRATION

Oftentimes, when there is strong countervailing power on the buying side of the market, it can neutralize the selling power of a close-knit group of oligopolists. To determine just how strong the buyers are, we would need to examine every exhibition window for which the theatrical movies are important inputs. Clearly in a home market, the producer–distributors can dominate the more widely spread out theater circuits so buyer concentration overall is quite weak nationally, but there may be key cities or regions where large chains predominate and can negotiate on more favorable terms. In the VCR market the distributors have integrated themselves and therefore handle distribution in-house rather than deal with outsiders. In the pay cable market, the studios must face the very strong buying power of the HBO–Cinemax and Showtime–The Movie Channel organizations. Similarly, in the broadcast network market for theatrical films and first-run entertainment series, there is a collective strength in the hands of the historic Big 3 networks. For pay-per-view, the movie distributors must face strong buyers in Viewer's Choice and Request TV, but this market is so underdeveloped that a parity in bargaining power seems to have emerged. In the international markets, the majors clearly reign supreme as they generally do in the syndication market for classic and recent theatrical films where there are only pockets of power held by major multiple owners such as the television networks' owned and operated station groups.

In sum, the appearance of countervailing power may diminish the bargaining strength and freedom of the major distributors to set whatever terms they want. This will be most evident in broadcast network television and pay cable where well-established network distributors have the advantage of being there first and strong barriers to entry to solidify their power. This, of course, does not mean that any transaction savings arising from buying power will be passed along to consumers.

NOTES

[1]For a good overall accounting of the various mergers, see Conant, "The Decrees Reconsidered," op. cit. (1985); Thomas Guback, "The Theatrical Film," in Benjamin Compaine, *Who Owns the Media: Concentration of Ownership in the Mass Communications Industry,* second edition, White Plains, NY: Knowledge Industries, 1982, Chapter 5; and end of the year roundups in *Variety,* annual editions, January, various years.
[2]*Multichannel News,* May 16, 1988, p. 1 and June 20, 1988, p. 40.
[3]*Variety*, January 15, 1988, p. 1.

[4]Gorham Kindem, "Hollywood's Movie Star System: An Historical Overview," in Gorham Kindem, *The American Movie Industry: The Business of Motion Pictures,* Carbondale, IL: Southern Illinois University Press, 1982, Chapter 4.

[5]Thomas Simonet, "Conglomerate and Content Remakes, Sequels and Series in the New Hollywood," in Bruce A. Austin, *Current Research in Film: Audiences, Economics and Law,* Volume 3, Norwood, NJ: Ablex, 1987, Chapter 10.

[6]Conant, op. cit.

[7]"Merger Mania Facing Congress," *Variety,* January 14 1987, p. 1.

[8]Thomas Guback, "The Evolution of the Motion Picture Theater Business in the 1980s," *Journal of Communications,* 37 (Spring 1987): 60–77.

[9]Ibid.

[10]Ibid.

[11]*Satellite Times,* July 27, 1988, p. 10.

[12]Figuring the real decline in movie admission prices is an attempt to hold constant the prices of substitute entertainment products. In a fuller treatment, it would be necessary to run a linear regression equation for movie admissions and account for variation in admission prices and all the other factors that affect demand.

4

The Conduct and Performance of the Industry

DISTRIBUTOR CONDUCT

It is interesting to examine the actions of the major studios as they interact among themselves in the important dimensions of product prices and quality. While industrial organization theorists generally look for evidence of a "spirit of cooperation" achieved through standardized behavior, that type of collusive behavior is only partially realized in the distribution side of the industry, mainly in terms of price, while the tendency for heated rivalry in the other areas of contact seems to be an inevitable result of the peculiar nature of the motion picture product.

With respect to pricing, the distributors naturally would like to achieve a relatively uniform, high fixed price for their special product. Owing to the individualized, handcrafted nature of every motion picture, it would be completely impossible to find a single distribution rental price that would be acceptable for all pictures. Since the distributors instead prefer to allow the marketplace to determine returns for their invested efforts, they have established a revenue sharing approach with the exhibitors, allowing each picture to find its own financial harbor. Yet, even with all this individual economic freedom, there still remain other financial terms that can achieve similar ends. By the distributors all religiously following the standard sharing formula of a 90–10 split, they clearly reduce the range of rivalry in the price–revenue dimension. This simple revenue-sharing split is further modified by setting it against fixed minimum percentages of box office gross, as is often true in a bidding situation. As long as the fixed minimum percentages are virtually the same across all distributors, this guarantees a spirit of cooperation in its truest sense. This can never mean that films will be forced toward some common financial return—the box office potential is too variable to achieve this. Rather, it means that as films achieve certain box office plateaus, say $50, $100, or $200 million, the absolute share of this money returned to the distributors can be expected to reach an equilibrium parity. So the share of the wealth, rather than the wealth itself, can be standardized and fit the pattern of mutual cooperation. The exhibitors are seemingly willing allies in this venture by maintaining fixed admission prices (e.g., $6 for a nighttime performance) *regardless of film quality or popularity.* Whereas each film should find its own equilibrium admission price, based on the laws of supply and demand, the fixed admission price system employed by exhibitors guarantees a disequilibrium distribution of moviegoers across the pictures in play. In other words, some films will have widespread excess capacity because the value of the film doesn't merit $6, while other films will be sold out hours in advance because there is excessive demand relative to theater capacity. Under true equilibrium conditions, the theater owner should lower admission prices for the unattractive films and raise prices for the popular ones, thereby eliminating both surpluses and shortages of seats. But such is not the reality in admission pricing, and is too complex an undertaking that could cause confusion in the minds of consumers. It should be realized that some other event organizers do follow a differential pricing with live concerts or plays, while professional sports franchises do not adjust their fixed prices based on the level of quality of the opposing teams. In any case, the fixed standardization of prices by theater owners facilitates the standardization of revenue-sharing by the distributors.

Another dimension of interaction that can upset a spirit of cooperation among distributors is in the quantity of films released and in their quality. If the distributors were truly interested in achieving a cartel-like agreement among themselves, there would develop a mechanism for regulating the quantity of films that each distributor released each year and a corresponding release schedule that permitted a more even sharing and spreading of the customer base across the films released. This type of output allocation approach would therefore smooth out the flow of product into the market and prevent periods during which there were either too few films released or too many. A product equilibrium could thereby be achieved coincident with the price equilibrium mentioned above.

However, this type of output allocation scheme does not seem likely in the motion picture industry because of some sort of natural, innate tendency of movie distributors to mistrust each other concerning production schedules and budgets and to always envision more and more films released each year, especially if certain kinds of films were successful over the last several years. In simpler terms, it might be likened to a "get rich quick" strategy of continuing to up the ante, in hopes of striking the jackpot. As the major distributors each invest in a full production lineup, they globally produce too many films for the market to handle equitably, especially during the peak periods of summer and Christmas time release. This creates an extreme form of product competition, with many films failing to live up to their projected potential, as they might had there been more order to the schedule of films released. The exhibitors and consumers naturally love this heated competition since it generally means more choices and diversity of offerings for the consumer and a likelihood for the theater owner that several of its auditoriums will be filled to higher capacity than normal. Yet, it is contrary to the smooth functioning of a spirit of cooperation.

Another related program area is that of film budget (technically, "negative cost"). If the distributors cannot control their natural instinct to compete in the quantity dimension, maybe they can hold the line on average production costs and, thereby, achieve some degree of product control in this dimension. Unfortunately, this product area is even harder to control, owing to the individualized, handcrafted nature of each film and the desire to spend enough money on production values to make a big box office splash. The further tendency to bid for the rights of popular stars has led to a tremendous inflation in negative costs over the last several years. The average film now costs some $35 million, and many top stars like John Travolta, Arnold Swarzenegger, Kevin Costner, Tom Cruise, and Tom Hanks receive $10 to 20 million per film. While comparable stars may be partially substitutable for each other, this apparently does not diminish their market value nor cause them to openly fight over choice acting roles. Their agents generally maintain a strong bargaining hand once a studio decides to "get involved" with a major actor. This creates a kind of temporary monopoly power for the actor since his/her happiness and well-being can make or break a movie project. Furthermore, the inability of distributors to control "above the line costs" of top creative people will naturally spill over to the "below the line" union costs and continue the cost inflation that is so affecting distributor profits.

Finally, it should be remembered that there are significant additional costs involved with releasing a major motion picture that transcend the production budget. These are generally referred to as "marketing costs" and it may cost $15 to $20 million above production costs to launch an average $35 million film today. The marketing costs include such areas as advertising, publicity, promotion, research, and merchandising[1] and form a comprehensive strategy toward giving the newly released film the greatest opportunity for achieving success. By whetting the public's appetite about the content or the stars or any other aspect of the film, the distributor hopes to create a temporary excitement about the film that will stimulate the avid moviegoer whose opinions are influential toward creating the all important "word-of-mouth" informal communication network among friends, family, and workers that will make or break a new film. All the advertising and publicity about a film will be for nothing if the informal communication network does not favorably respond during the first two weeks after release.

Since the master marketing effort, including merchandising tie-ins to posters, dolls, T-shirts, or whatever, must be tailor-made for each film, there is little chance for standardization or coordination of this expense across distributors. It is too individualistic, too abstract, and too unpredictable to even think of cooperation or forming an industry standard. Given such conditions, this area of distributor conduct must necessarily remain competitive and forms a healthy outlet for distributors to maintain their aura of individuality.

In summary, with the exception of standard contract terms specifying the split of box office gross between distributors and exhibitors, there seems little hope for industry standardization or coordination of pricing, product distribution, or product marketing behavior. The tailor-made special nature of each film, in conjunction with the box office uncertainty, brings out the competitive instinct among the distributors as each tries to strike it rich and uncover the box office "mother lode." The fact that such outlandish success is only achieved by relatively few films per year does not apparently diminish its magical lure.

EXHIBITOR CONDUCT

The process of product pricing and revenue-sharing has altered very little since the *Paramount* restructuring. At the exhibition level, theaters either bid for upcoming features or individually negotiate the contract with the major or independent distributors. The *Paramount* decrees required that motion pictures should be contracted picture by picture at the *local* rather than chain level such that all theaters have an equal opportunity for obtaining product; yet this practice is hardly ever followed since nearly all theaters are now parts of theater circuits and contract negotiations have all been centralized at circuit headquarters for many years.

As mentioned above, this centralized negotiating process permits a kind of negotiating efficiency by reducing the number of individual transactions between theaters and distributors. It also provides for a cleaner and clearer plan for how the annual movie season will be structured, even with all the uncertainties inherent in predicting public taste—uncertainties at all levels of interaction.

For example, one must plan the annual schedule not only for each screen in the theater complex but across all complexes in the city or regional area. The circuit will naturally want to avoid direct competition between its own screens for the same pictures since this would just fractionalize the natural audience for the film. This is usually handled by insuring for reasonable geographic clearance if the theaters are not sufficiently far apart. Similarly, there must always be some flexibility built into the contract starting and ending dates to allow for unexpected failures (cancellations) or successes (extended runs, moveovers, etc.). The circuit will also benefit by having the same movies playing at its different complexes throughout the region so that it can make its print and electronic advertising more cost-efficient.

The process of film negotiations is obviously not done in a vacuum. The chain must be completely cognizant of its oligopolistic interdependence with rival chains, with special significance attached to their scheduling practices during the peak summer months and Christmas holiday season. The effect of competition can be both beneficial as well as harmful. It can be positive if it helps create a strong moviegoing climate when many hit movies are simultaneously playing; negative if one has only average quality movies to counter the blockbusters of one's rivals.

The basic contract generally has the following standard provisions: admission prices, beginning date, length of run, minimum guarantee, dollar advance, terms for extended runs and early cancellation, and most critically, the rental terms. By rental terms, one usually is referring to the percentage split of box office dollars between the exhibitor and distributor. The traditional industry standard has long been a 90–10 split in favor of the distributor *after the house expenses are deducted.* This represents a small excess profit margin for theater owners since some entrepreneurial costs are generally included in the "house nut." Nonetheless, this clearly demonstrates the relative bargaining advantage power of the distributors vis à vis the exhibitors.

Figure 4-1 illustrates the flow of money in the theatrical motion picture industry. Starting with box office gross and subtracting house overhead expenses and the theater's share yields gross rentals to the distributor. From these rentals, the distribution fee (usually standardized at 35 percent for domestic distribution) and all of the distribution expenses (advertising, print duplication) are deducted. This leaves gross profits for the producer. From profits are subtracted the production loan and interest payments, yielding net producer profits. Net profits are then split among all the profit participants, which may include financial investors ("angels"), deferred payments to actors, directors, and chief writers and major motion picture distributors if they have financed the production loan themselves or have guaranteed a bank loan. Often the major distributors obtain net profit shares of 50 percent because of their central importance and expertise in both financing and distribution. Any residual profits remain with the producer. Thus, the major distributors have achieved some industry consensus and standardization in terms of their splitting of the box office dollars, distribution fees, and profit-sharing. This cooperation also spills over into their subsidiary markets through a sophisticated price discrimination plan.

As mentioned above, the process of booking motion picture theaters has taken on a new complexity with the switchover from the single screen deluxe theater to the multiplex concept. With multiple screens available, the theater becomes the supplier of a new form of content diversity. With six to eight or more screens under control,

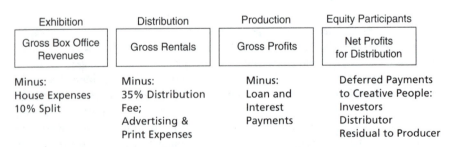

Exhibition	Distribution	Production	Equity Participants
Gross Box Office Revenues	Gross Rentals	Gross Profits	Net Profits for Distribution
Minus: House Expenses 10% Split	Minus: 35% Distribution Fee; Advertising & Print Expenses	Minus: Loan and Interest Payments	Deferred Payments to Creative People: Investors Distributor Residual to Producer

FIGURE 4-1   Revenue Flow for Motion Picture Industry

the theater owners are faced with quite a difficult problem of arranging a schedule for a constantly changing portfolio of movies. While the cable system operator faces a similar problem in choosing the twenty-five or more "basic" cable networks to fill its channel capacity, their dilemma is minuscule compared to the multiplex theater owners, since the latter's product must prove itself each and every day in the marketplace by pleasing the moviegoing public. On the other hand, the cable operator bundles the chosen networks together, sells them for a single subscription price, and only months later evaluates them based on local ratings data, local advertising revenues, and customer comments.

The multiplex theater owner must not only subject himself/herself to the vagaries of public taste for each and every movie, but it must guesstimate the length of run in signing contracts with distributors. This guesstimate is hard enough for a single screen for an entire season but is exponentially more difficult for six to eight screens taken as a group. Without some flexibility in starting dates and moveovers, the system of movie bookings would take on a very rigid pattern and could never respond to the spontaneous tastes of the public.

The obvious goal of the theater complex owner is to maximize admission profits by maximizing audience size. This leads to the added bonus of maximizing concession revenues as well. In practical terms, this means booking movies that have the greatest likelihood of attracting a mass audience—the least common denominator (LCD) type of movie. Thus, the movie theater offerings follow the same profit-maximizing principles as the broadcast networks and the same economic analysis for the latter can now be applied to the former.[1] While these mass taste offerings may not appeal to the most sophisticated movie-goer, there will be an opportunity with some of the smaller auditoriums in the complex to devote time to less heralded but fine quality dramas and comedies. Just as the cable system can appeal to the specialized minority taste audience for potential subscribers, so can a movie theater complex at the margin.

The Steiner and Owen and Wildman models[2] of mass media supply clearly apply to the situation of the theater complex owner. Those movies with the greatest potential draw will be booked first and even assigned to multiple screens, thereby splitting the audience, before the next highest-rated potential film is assigned. This iterative process continues sequentially until all the screens in the complex are booked. Only after the LCD movies have been fully served and have reached their equilibrium point of access will other more diverse films be offered. Hence, the appearance of movie diversity critically depends on the number of screens in the complex, the overall competition between films for access, and the season of the year.

During the peak summer months and holiday seasons surrounding Christmas and Easter, one can scarcely expect much access for the smaller films of independent distributors as the screens are dominated by big-budgeted films of the major studio distributors. Looking at the summer of 1996 as a prime example, by the July 4 midpoint and strong holiday weekend, the die was already cast with such high profile action–adventure films as *Twister, Eraser, Mission Impossible, The Rock,* and *Independence Day,* leaving little operating room for less attractive comedies or dramas.

SEARCHING FOR EFFICIENCY

The process of downsizing average theater size and building multiple-screen auditoriums illustrates a different approach to profit maximization by the theater owners. This permits a more cost-efficient utilization of seat capacity than was possible in the old single auditorium deluxe theaters. A good analogy is found in the airline industry since deregulation. To maintain a high "load factor," the airlines have downsized their planes (or formed alliances with commuter airlines) and adjusted the number of scheduled flights between smaller cities (with few passengers going to a common location) and central hub cities. At the hub, passengers going to major destinations are collected from all the feeder lines and placed on larger planes.

For the theater owners, the multiple theater concept permits a theater complex to book a portfolio of different pictures for its different screens, some of which may be larger than others. With, say, six to eight screens per site, a theater owner is fairly certain that at least one or two of its screens will have a hit while the others will do moderate business until their run is over. In this way, average load factors can be increased compared to the "hit and miss" strategy associated with having a single screen.

As mentioned earlier, the multiple screen concept is also tied in with the shopping mall phenomenon.[3] For shopping malls, the greater the amount of foot traffic, the greater the total sales for all store owners. This explains why similar shoe stores, department stores, clothing stores, and the like will locate near each other even though they are natural competitors.

The theater concession stand also fits into this traffic flow analysis and multiple theater concept. Since the theater retains 100 percent of all concession revenues (which have an extremely high markup), yet only makes about 10 percent excess profits from box office gross, any strategy that maintains a high load factor can be very profitable.

The theaters can further minimize their excess seat capacity by negotiating escape clauses in their booking contracts that permit shortened runs for unpopular films and, correspondingly, lengthened runs, additional screens, and moveovers (to a larger auditorium) for films that prove unexpectedly popular. Another pricing strategy would be to price according to film popularity, that is, charge higher admission prices for successful films and lower ones for limited appeal films. Yet, this is almost never done unless a special "roadshow" release pattern is followed by the distributor. Rather, the theater owners choose to abide by a fixed price regardless of "quality." The prices that local theaters charge for performances at comparable times tend to be similar, and most theaters follow a price discrimination pattern of discounting for off-peak time periods (e.g., matinees, twilight, midnight, and, occasionally, certain weekdays like Tuesdays) and for customers with elastic demands (e.g., children and senior citizens). Once again, this brings more customers into the theaters, sells more popcorn, and, since the theaters usually have unlimited number of showings per day and split the box office dollars with the distributor, it is still profitable to show a movie with only a couple of dozen patrons in the theater.

In terms of product differentiation among theaters these days, there is really very little difference in their interior designs. Granted, a few may have stereophonic sound or 70-millimeter screens, but the auditoriums in the shopping malls tend to have the same utilitarian look. Theaters can basically differentiate themselves in two dimensions: their location and the overall quality of their offerings. Since shopping malls tend to be located in either densely populated areas or places that are easy to reach, these theaters may have a built-in advantage over the "neighborhood" duplex. With their vast number of screens and the newest trend of multiple screens within or across the street from a shopping mall, they can have the full array of all possible movies, protected with sufficient geographical clearance to insure their exclusivity to their customer base. Hence, the competition that does exist is generally over which of the several chains successfully obtains the cream of the crop of promising movies. However, once films are booked, such competition does not break out over admission prices.

The local exhibitors have sought to countervail the power of the distributors who either explicitly, through open bidding, or implicitly, through the "grapevine," continually desire exhibitors to bid against each other for exclusive rights. The local theater owners formerly would band together and "split" the forthcoming product among themselves according to a preconceived plan.[5] In this way, the distributor could only negotiate with a single theater, and such a bilateral monopoly would even up the negotiation process for the theater owners. The courts originally permitted such an obvious price-fixing/territorial allocation plan provided distributors were not involved and nonaligned independents were still free to enter negotiations for any film. In April 1977, the Department of Justice reversed its position and announced that all splits were per se illegal and would be prosecuted.[6] This triggered a renewed series of legal proceedings, but the overall pattern of decisions forced a discontinuance of this attempt at price coordination.

Therefore, both distributors and exhibitors alike have practiced cooperative conduct strategies aimed at countervailing the oligopoly strength of the other side. At this juncture, the distributors seem to have the upper hand because of their control over the product and the proliferation of subsidiary markets to reach their U.S. and worldwide customers.

PERFORMANCE

If an industry has a concentrated market structure, attempts to coordinate pricing behavior, has significant barriers to entry, and an inelastic demand, the end result should be high prices for the consumer and excess profits for the industry. We now analyze these issues in turn. To assess the excess profits issue, it is necessary to choose a time period of sufficient duration to insure that the industry in question is clearly in for the long run, disaggregate key product lines from other corporate subsidiaries using annual reports, and compare the rate of return for this period to industries with comparable products, risks, and capital–labor ratios.

The data in Table 4-1 were obtained from Veronis and Suhler, a media analyst firm that has analyzed the communication industry for a number of years and has been able to separate out the different product lines for the conglomerate corporations involved in these industries.[7] Their measure of profits are the pretax operating income and pretax cash flow. (Cash flow is current operating income with depreciation and amortization of intangibles added back in.) For the film entertainment segment, they have analyzed annual reports and 10 K filings for forty-one publicly traded corporations. This should give us a better feel for the entire motion picture production–distribution industry than just the financial picture for the industry leaders contained in Table 4-1. The period under examination is 1990–1994.

For the five-year period, the average operating income margin (on sales) is 9.16 percent, while the cash flow margin is 12.18 percent. For the 420 companies occupying the ten communication industry segments, the corresponding margins are 13.44 percent and 20.44 percent, respectively. Similarly, the compound annual growth in operating income for the movie segment is 6.7 percent compared to 8.9 percent for the aggregate "communications" industry. On the other hand, comparing the pretax profit data for the top film distributors with other broadly defined industry aggregations leads to somewhat different conclusions. The average profit margin for 1994 for the distributors as a group is 9.0 percent while the average sales margin for 1995 for all Fortune 500 firms is 5.2 percent. The Fortune 500 data is unfortunately calculated after deduction of taxes, while the communications segment is before tax information, thereby clouding the direct comparison.

Nevertheless, it seems that the motion picture distributors have not been able to exert as significant a market control in their own industry segment as have some other mass communication distribution companies (ranking in the bottom quartile within the overall communications segment); yet, compared to a broader grouping of leisure and service companies throughout the economy, they do above average. This failure is undoubtedly due to the vast degree of product differentiation accompanying motion picture product, the unpredictability of consumer tastes, and the instability of market shares from one year to the next. This is compounded by the fact that industry leadership rotates among the top firms, and market shares are more evenly dispersed than in other industries with comparable concentration ratios. It may also reflect the fact that there are now a plethora of different media available for consumers to obtain their entertainment product, and that the theatrical film experience may be losing its luster.

What about the impact of this market structure on the public? One way to answer this is to examine inflationary trends in motion picture admission prices com-

TABLE 4-1 Comparisons of Profitability across Mass Media, 1990–1994

Industry Segments	Compound Annual Growth (%)	Operating					90 vs. 94 Margin (+ or – % Points)	Operating Income				91 vs. 94 ROA (+ or – % Points)
		1990	1991	1992	1993	1994		1991	1992	1993	1994	
1 Television & Radio Broadcasting	12.7%	14.3%	10.7%	12.6%	16.1%	19.2%	4.9	6.5%	8.4%	11.2%	14.3%	7.8
Television Network Companies	10.4	13.7	9.6	10.1	14.5	17.2	3.5	7.0	8.5	12.2	16.0	9.0
TV & Radio Station Broadcasters	15.8	15.3	12.5	16.6	18.6	22.4	7.1	5.9	8.4	10.1	12.6	6.7
2 Subscription Video Services	13.8	13.9	17.1	19.5	19.4	16.4	2.5	6.2	7.4	7.7	6.6	0.4
Subscription Video Services Operators	13.2	14.8	17.7	20.4	20.2	18.3	3.5	5.1	6.3	6.6	5.9	0.8
Cable and Pay-Per-View Networks	15.5	11.8	15.7	17.3	17.4	12.6	0.8	13.8	14.9	14.1	9.8	-4.0
3 Filmed Entertainment	6.7	10.8	7.7	9.7	8.6	9.0	-1.8	5.8	7.6	6.6	6.6	0.8
4 Recorded Music	13.1	10.0	10.2	10.8	10.8	11.8	1.8	6.7	7.4	7.4	8.8	2.1
5 Newspaper Publishing	1.4	15.8	12.0	14.1	14.2	15.9	0.1	12.6	15.0	15.0	17.0	4.4
6 Book Publishing	8.2	13.7	12.7	13.3	12.7	12.2	-1.5	14.5	14.2	12.7	10.7	-3.8
7 Magazine Publishing	4.3	10.7	8.2	9.8	10.5	11.1	0.4	8.6	10.4	11.4	12.3	3.7
Consumer Magazine Publishers	6.6	10.1	8.1	9.7	10.6	10.8	0.7	8.0	9.8	11.0	11.5	3.5
Business and Professional Publishers	-2.9	13.1	8.8	10.3	10.1	12.3	-0.8	12.1	13.7	13.5	17.0	4.9
8 Business Information Services	9.9	14.8	14.3	15.1	15.3	16.0	1.2	13.3	14.4	14.4	15.8	2.5
9 Advertising Agencies	6.9	9.3	8.2	9.1	9.3	10.0	0.7	6.1	7.1	6.9	7.0	0.9
10 Interactive Digital Media	26.2	10.6	10.9	13.9	10.1	8.5	-2.1	19.9	26.3	16.5	12.1	-7.8
11 Miscellaneous Communications	9.2	13.1	12.1	13.4	15.2	14.4	1.3	16.7	17.8	19.9	18.1	1.4
Communications Industry Total	8.9	13.4	11.9	13.5	14.0	14.4	1.0	8.4	9.9	10.4	10.8	2.4

Source: Veronis, Suhler & Associates, *Communications Industry Report/Executive Summary*, 1990–1994.

pared to other products and services in the economy at large. Using 1982–1984 as a common base year, indoor admission prices have risen by 32.7 percent over the ten year period ending in 1994 while the CPI category of "entertainment services and products" has increased by 50.1 percent and "all goods and services" has risen by 48.2 percent for the same period. Hence, admission price inflation has risen at about two-thirds the rate of these other categories. This evidence is consistent with the profitability data and implies that the full force of the concentrated market structure has not inflicted unusual pain on consumers' pocketbooks.

TECHNOLOGICAL PROGRESS

Given the creative nature of the motion picture product, it is not surprising to see technological progress surfacing only in the exhibition sphere. The rapid development of such subsidiary markets as pay cable, pay-per-view, and especially home video attests to the speed of diffusion of these new technologies and the added programming flexibility they provide for consumers. The willingness of the distributors to embrace these new markets and fold them into their sequential distribution plan clearly demonstrates the lesson they have learned from the boycott days of the early television industry.

The multiplicity of exhibition markets has also spurred the production side of the industry, especially small independents, to release record numbers of theatrical films. These shoestring films, of dubious quality, critically depend on presales to the subsidiary markets to finance their undertakings. The theaters themselves have lost a small amount of their total market demand to the new technologies but have not yet made a price or quantity competitive response. If the erosion of patronage becomes more pronounced or unfavorable demographics (e.g., the aging of the population) plague the industry, theaters may need to rethink their Spartan furnishings in favor of a more unique viewing experience. While more competition means even greater financial risk in the future, the fundamental truth is that this motion picture industry and especially the production and distribution sectors seem impervious to whatever technical marvels the twenty-first century brings forth.

DIVERSITY

Because the motion picture industry produces cultural products, one can add an unusual category of performance to the standard ones, namely, the diversity of product offerings. The critical question here is whether concentration of control over the production–distribution business affects product diversity to the American people. A variety of studies of the other mass media have all concluded that such control adversely impacts on product diversity—the amount and kinds of program choices available to consumers. Absent the spur of competition, oligopoly firms tend to lead a quiet imitative life rather than engage in costly product experimentation and new ideas. The end result is homogenization of content.

Given the strong oligopoly control of the leading distributors and recalling their conglomerate ties, the incentive may be to stress the bottom line rather than worry about the impact on motion pictures as an art or cultural form. This would mean the constant search for formulaic content, such as sequels, which reduces risks for a motion picture as it winds through all the subsidiary markets. It has been proposed that recognizing the historic importance of the international market, the leading distributors attempt to homogenize content by creating extravagant "spectacles" with universal themes and "international" stars that transcend the different cultures rather than focusing on a content area that is culture-bound.[8] Since the U.S. majors are the only companies that can afford to risk such sums of money, this big budget content strategy reinforces their collective financial clout. Similarly, because of the growing importance of the cable and home video markets, these motion pictures typically feature actors and actresses who are familiar to the television audience or have achieved fame in some other medium, such as records.

In recent studies, both Dominick[9] and Litman and Kohl[10] have documented the strong correlation between concentration of control and homogenization of content diversity. Dominick studied nearly 1,900 films that were released over the twenty-year period spanning 1964–1983. He correlated a Herfindahl–Hirschman index of market share concentration with a similar index measuring concentration of content into fewer film categories and discovered the significant relationship. Litman and Kohl studied some 700 films released during the 1980s and concluded that "almost every variable which represents some known factor or conveys information that reduces uncertainty seems to be correlated with financial success."[11] Thus, not only are the filmmakers seeking some secret formula for reducing risks, but the audience has also become conditioned to seek *familiarity* in their choice of movie entertainment.

The results of Chapter 10 reinforce these conclusions concerning the lack of diversity in the U.S. film industry. The examination of the top 100 box office champions for the last three years, in Table 4-2, shows a content concentration in only a few categories (comedy, drama, children's/family and action/adventure). However, it should be understood that this represents the demand side of the market! Consumers are clearly demanding certain genre and storylines, so the production–distribution sector may not be responsible for the homogenization process—they are merely serving the public taste.

X-INEFFICIENCY

One means of assessing the degree of X-inefficiency in an industry is to compare the wage structure with a comparable base to see if there are excessive payments to the workforce, significantly higher than for workers with comparable skills in similar

TABLE 4-2   Frequency Distribution of Genres, 1993–1995

Category	Frequency	Percent
Action/Adventure	38	15.77
Children/Family	38	15.77
Comedy	62	25.73
Drama	52	21.58
Foreign	2	0.83
Horror	5	2.07
Musical	1	0.41
Mystery/Suspense	17	7.05
Sci-Fi/Fantasy	18	7.47
Western	8	3.30
Total	241	100.00

Source: Calculated from *Variety*.

industries. This might also be a measure for the strength and effectiveness of the unionized sector of the motion picture industry compared to other industries in which unionization is less prevalent.

According to the Bureau of Labor Statistics, the 1995 annual average hourly earnings for workers in the motion picture industry overall were $14.84 and $19.48 for a subsegment of workers in "motion picture production and services"—the latter more closely aligned to the production sector—while the overall category includes both video, production and theater employment, which have always been a lower skilled occupation than production—just barely above the minimum wage. These average hourly earnings were then compared to a broader base of comparable industries. The annual average hourly earnings for 1995 for "all service" workers were $11.41; for all business services, $10.68; and for all amusement and recreational services, $8.82. Just using the "all service" category for a base of comparison, it clearly indicates that hourly earnings in motion pictures are $3.43 to $8.07 higher than for workers in similar occupations throughout the economy. This represents a 30–71 percent higher wage structure for the motion picture industry. Checking this wage differential over time shows that indeed this pattern has existed for many years. For example, in 1990, the differential between average hourly earnings for the overall motion picture and production service categories was $11.19 and $17.16, respectively, compared to $9.86 for "all service" workers. The percentage difference was 13.49 percent and 74.0 percent for these two categories.

Thus, one feels quite confident in concluding that the motion picture industry workforce is significantly better paid than workers with comparable skills in other service industries, especially for those in the production sector of this industry. This either means that excess profits are being more equally shared here than in other industries or that the industry executives simply tolerate excessive wages for such specialized work product. Unfortunately, comparable data on fringe benefits and other forms of add-on compensation are not available from the Bureau of Labor Statistics, and hence no conclusions can be drawn about this other dimension of X-inefficiency.

PRODUCTIVITY

To further understand the degree of efficiency in the various sectors of the motion picture industry, it is important to assess the dynamic conditions of worker productivity. Productivity is generally measured by dividing the industry output by the size of the workforce or comparable proxy variables. Unfortunately, the Bureau of Labor Statistics does not collect productivity information about this industry directly so it is necessary to construct some rough indices by combining data from various sources. A further problem in measuring productivity is determining the nature of the product produced, which is more of a service than a tangible good in the traditional sense.

Thus, when we deal with the production sector, it is proper to think of the number of movies produced as the relevant product, while for the exhibition sector the number of patrons (admissions) seems more appropriate to the service rendered. Similarly, while the number of employees seems like a reasonable measure for the size of the workforce, multiplying by the actual hours worked further refines this measure to more accurately reflect the total workforce commitment.

According to Table 4-3, spanning the years 1990–1995, for the production sector, there appears to be a very slight increase in the number of new films released per thousand employees (PR_1) and per weekly hour (PR_2). For the theater exhibition sector for the same timespan, there appears to be a small increase in the number of total films per 1,000 employees (PR_3) and the number of admissions per 1,000 employees (PR_4). In the most liberal reading of this measure for PR_3, the increase appears to be on the order of about 11 percent for the four-year period or slightly less than 3 percent per year. This is certainly consistent with the rates of increase in worker productivity of about 5 to 6 percent found throughout private industry during this same time frame.

Therefore, there appear to be only small increases in worker productivity in the production and exhibition sectors in this industry, which is not surprising given the overall impression of a very loose workforce and an indulgent management. With the continuing escalation in average production budgets reported each year, it seems predictable *not* to find countervailing worker productivity of any magnitude. The same conclusion undoubtedly applies to the rate of technological progress that, through improvements in process technology, directly affects worker productivity.

TABLE 4-3   Measures of Productivity in the Motion Picture Industry

	1990	1991	1992	1993	1994	1995
Number of Employees (A) (000)						
Production Services (1)	152.5	151.4	149.8	171.6	208.6	305.2
Theater Services (2)	111.1	109.6	104.3	107.1	114.7	118.1
Weekly Hours Worked (B) Production Services (1)	35.8	36.9	37.4	38.3	38.6	38.7
Number of Films Released (C)						
New (1)	379	415	431	450	420	N/A
New & Reissues (2)	404	448	484	469	462	N/A
Number of Admissions (D) (Millions)	1,188.6	1,140.6	1,173.2	1,244,0	1,291.0	N/A
PR_1	2.48	2.74	2.88	2.62	2.01	N/A
PR_2	.069	.074	.077	.068	.052	N/A
PR_3	3.64	4.09	4.64	4.38	4.03	N/A
PR_4	10.70	10.41	11.25	11.62	11.26	N/A

Productivity = Output/workforce
Production service sector

$$PR_1 = \frac{\text{Number of New Flims Released (C1)}}{\text{Number of Employees (A1)}}$$

$$PR_2 = \frac{\text{Number of New Films Released (C1)}}{\text{Number of Weekly Employee Hours (A1 × B)}}$$

Theater Service Sector

$$PR_3 = \frac{\text{Number of Total Films (C2)}}{\text{Number of Employees (A2)}}$$

$$PR_4 = \frac{\text{Number of Admissions (D)}}{\text{Number of Employees (A2)}}$$

Sources: Bureau of Labor Statistics, *Employment and Earnings,* various years; NATO, *Encyclopedia of Exhibition,* various years.

EXCESSIVE ADVERTISING

One area of conduct that often features excessive spending, waste, and inefficiency is that of product differentiation, particularly advertising. While all firms and industries rely on product differentiation to one degree or another, these expenditures can get carried to the extreme, become a substitute for price competition, and a drain on profits.

To determine whether an industry has excessive advertising expenditures, one usually compares the advertising to sales revenue ratio (the A/S ratio) for the industry under examination to a broader sector of similar product categories with comparable risks and capital-to-labor investment intensity. For the most recent year, 1996, motion picture production had a ratio of 6.1 percent, motion picture distribution was 5.8 percent, and motion picture theaters was 3.1 percent. This compares to a ratio of 2.1 percent for "all communication products and services" and "all services except health care" of 3.1 percent. The A/S ratio across all industries is 3.5, which includes the heavily advertised consumer product category. Hence, except for the category of motion picture theaters, whose advertising generally involves informative newspaper ads, listing times and locations, there does appear to be quite an excessive amount of advertising (nearly twice as high) in the production and distribution sectors of this industry compared to other areas of the economy. This is further evidence of the failure of the studios and other players to maintain a strong vigilance on cost. It could also be envisioned as an investment by the incumbent industry members in building a product differentiation barrier to entry.

CONCLUSIONS

The American people's love affair with the motion picture has lasted for over a century since that eventful day when Edison first introduced the kinetoscope, and thereby launched the early motion picture industry. While production budgets have skyrocketed since the days of the one-reelers and the space-age and computer technologies have opened up many new points of competitive access, the motion picture industry remains a cherished institution on the U.S. landscape, as venerable as the automobile. The basic structure of this industry was forged in the 1920s and continues largely intact except for the growth of subsidiary markets to replace the traditional system of theatrical runs. The concentration of market power that had its roots in economies of scale and a vertically interlocking, self-sufficient system of arrangements was decimated by the *Paramount* consent decrees, but has regrouped and refocused at the distribution stage. Throughout all of the technological innovations, truly remarkable has been the resilience and adaptive capability of the industry.

NOTES

[1]Bruce M. Owen and Stephen S. Wildman, *Video Economics,* Cambridge, MA: Harvard University Press, 1992, Chapter 3; Peter O. Steiner, "Program Patterns and Preferences and the Workability of Competition in Radio Broadcasting," *Quarterly Journal of Economics,* 66, 1952: 194–223.

[2]Ibid.

[3]Thomas Guback, "The Evolution of Theater Business in the 1980s," *Journal of Communication,* Spring 1987: 60–77.

[4]Ibid.

[5]Ibid.

[6]Ibid.

[7]Veronis, Suhler and Associates, *Thirteenth Annual Communications Industry Report* (New York: VS&A, 1996). Another good source for financial information is Harold L. Vogel, *Entertainment Industry Economics: A Guide for Financial Analysis* (Cambridge: Cambridge University Press, 1987, especially Chapters 2–4.

[8]Joseph D. Phillips, "Film Conglomerate Blockbusters: International Appeal and Product Homogenization," in Gorham Kindem, ed., *American Film History: A Case Studies Approach,* Carbondale, IL: Southern Illinois University Press, 1982, Chapter 15.

[9]Joseph Dominick, "Film Economics and Film Content: 1964–83," in Bruce H. Austin, ed., op. cit., Chapter 9.

[10]Barry R. Litman and Linda Kohl, "Predicting Financial Success of Motion Pictures: The 80s Experience," *Journal of Media Economics,* Fall 1989.

[11]Ibid.

5

Famous Antitrust Cases

The history of the motion picture industry in the United States is rich with many important examples of antitrust proceedings involving the key players in this industry. Each of these cases clearly shows how attempts were made to monopolize one or more phases of the industry and thereby prevent competition from destroying positions of market power and control. While each case comes from different eras of this long-standing industry, there are clear parallels in terms of motives and intentions and desired results.

THE MOTION PICTURE
PATENT COMPANY CASE—THE TRUST

When the Supreme Court sanctioned both the Edison and Biograph camera patents (Biograph's had no sprockets), a cycle of costly patent infringement suits cropped up that threatened the stability of the industry in its early years. Eventually, in 1908 a truce was called between the major patent holders and a collusive agreement, in the form of a trust, was forged to collectively monopolize the industry.[1] That such an arrangement should emerge as the "solution" for industrial warfare is not surprising if one recalls that this was the era of trust formation in the U.S. in many key areas of modern industry.

The Motion Picture Patents Company was a trustlike patent pooling arrangement between the holders of the sixteen key motion picture patents, including Edison, Biograph, Armat and Eastman–Kodak (with the former two receiving the overwhelming majority of patent royalties). The major domestic and foreign producers of that era (e.g., Selig, Essanay, Gaumont, Lumiere, Pathe, and Melies) were also members but they didn't explicitly share in the royalties accruing from the patents. Each of the producers was exclusive to the Trust and had to pay a royalty of one-half cent per foot of completed film. This royalty was collected on behalf of the Trust by Eastman–Kodak, the exclusive supplier of film stock to the producer members. The leading exchanges were also exclusively licensed and could not obtain film product for distribution from any other sources. They purchased film product at prices ranging from nine to thirteen cents per foot per copy and had to buy a minimum of $2,500 worth of product per month. The exchanges leased films at market prices to nickelodeon operators who also were signed to exclusive contracts with the Trust. Their contracts included provisions mandating their purchase of Trust sanctioned projectors at $150 each plus a two dollar weekly royalty payment for the use of the Trust-produced films. The exchanges collected the weekly royalty as part of their routine business with the theaters. Therefore, by cornering the market on cameras, projectors, and film stock and offering top quality producers, the Trust believed that their product was indispensable and they could monopolize the industry and exclude independents at all access points (see Figure 5-1).

At this point, control of equipment through patents appeared to be the key strategic source of monopoly power and the cornerstone of the tight interlocking vertical system of arrangements. Like any monopolist, the Trust tried to stabilize industry fluctuations by standardizing many of its practices such as the one-reeler (later the two-reeler), daily turnover, and fixed rental and minimum admission prices.

Troubles arose for the Trust when they were unable to prevent maverick exchanges and nickelodeons from dealing with independents for additional needed supply of product.[2] This instability could only be eliminated by exerting greater control over the distribution stage; hence, the General Film subsidiary was estab-

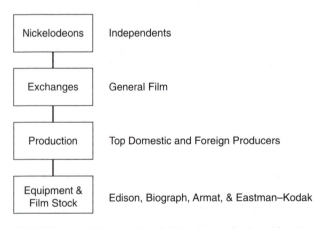

FIGURE 5-1   The Vertical Structure during the Era of the Trust

lished to acquire or drive out of business all licensed exchanges. On completion of this goal and now with control over every stage of production except exhibition, General Films was further able to standardize business practices by paying a straight ten cents per completed foot of film to each producer and establishing fixed "rentals" for exhibitors based on the size of their house, the nature of local competition, and general desirability of their location. While the Trust was able to dominate the industry during its first few years of existence, eventually a series of mutually reinforcing events caused its demise.[3]

Because of the Trust's inflexible standard of using single reels, coupled with daily turnover, they were slow to adapt to changing consumer tastes for motion pictures. When the independents introduced the feature film (at higher rentals and slower turnover rates) and simultaneously capitalized on the drawing power of box office stars by publicizing their names and paying them higher salaries, the Trust could not meet this competitive challenge and slowly fell by the wayside. Second, William Fox, one of the few remaining independent exchange operators, filed an antitrust suit against the Trust, alleging conduct violations seeking to drive independents out of business. This private antitrust suit was soon joined by the Department of Justice and the case was tried in district court in 1915.[4]

The salient legal issue was whether legally granted patents could be cross-licensed in such a fashion to regiment an entire industry and exclude competition. The Trust claimed that they had legal patents that were government sanctioned rights of monopoly protection for a period of seventeen years. As with any patented product, they had the right to exploit or license it in any way they chose during the term it was in force. This right included cross-licensing it with other patent holders to form a patent pool. They further argued that what was applicable to the single patent holder held true for the group of patent holders.

The district court in 1915 struck down this vertically integrated monopoly by saying that there was a fallacy of composition in the defendants' thinking. What was true for the single patent holder was not true for the group. While the single patent holder could exploit it as he/she chose, a group of such patent holders cannot combine in a vertical pattern to monopolize an industry and exclude nonmembers from access to trade. Hence, the Patent Acts and Sherman Acts are not contradictory; rather they work together. In the former, the patent holder is supreme: "he is the keeper of the gate of entrance." Yet, there is another field (the latter) that is in the "common occupancy of all."[5]

The court likened the open field to a race "in which all may enter, but in which there must be no unfair jostling or hampering of others. Each one is free to exert all his powers . . . and win all prizes; but he must run fairly and accord to others like freedom." In this race, if one has a patent, he can use it for all its advantages, but must not use it "as a weapon to disable a rival contestant or drive him from the field."[6]

In 1918, the Supreme Court dismissed the appeal and ordered the district court decision requiring dissolution of the Trust to be implemented. By this time, the issue was largely moot since the Trust had pretty much already collapsed from its own mistakes, inconsistencies, and instabilities. This famous antitrust decision was one of the earliest victories for the Justice Department in applying the Sherman Act to trusts and seeking major industrial restructuring. The motion picture trust, the tobacco trust, the Standard Oil trust, and others were reconfigured during this early era and forced to seek solace in oligopoly rather than monopoly power.

THE PARAMOUNT CASE

In the late 1930s and early 1940s, the motion picture industry sought a new level of stability and control. Already a strong oligopoly, the major studios sought to consolidate their power and insulate their market position against competitive threats arising from outside their inner circle. Cognizant of their high degree of mutual interdependence and no longer concerned with driving their rivals out of business, they sought a mechanism that would take advantage of their widespread vertical integration and their corresponding strength in first-run theaters and high quality "A" pictures. It is instructive to elaborate on this vertical integration to further understand the structural foundations of their market power and their conspiratorial plan to establish a shared monopoly.[7]

First, the "Big 5," as they came to be known, were fully integrated across all three vertical stages—production, distribution, and exhibition. This group consisted of MGM, Warner Brothers, RKO, Paramount, and Fox. Their subsidiaries are shown in Table 5-1. While each of these major companies was indeed fully integrated, *none of them was self-sufficient.* At the exhibition level, while they may have run a large circuit of 1,000 or more theaters, the theaters tended to be heavily clustered in different regions of the country and often in cities and contiguous suburban

TABLE 5-1   Vertical Structure of the Motion Picture Industry (Pre-Paramount Era)

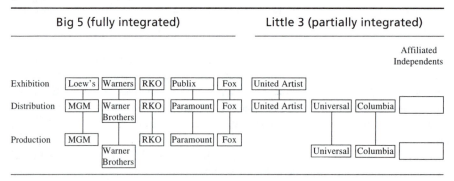

areas. Hence, none of these circuits could be said to be national in scope and no feature film could achieve a true national release by solely concentrating on the captive theaters of the major studio. In sum, they had to rely on other theater circuits to obtain national coverage.

Similarly, the production–distribution subsidiaries of the major companies were not self-sufficient in their supply of high quality feature films. While a single studio could possibly produce a few feature films each month, this was not a sufficient supply to satisfy the exhibition needs of the theater circuit that, during this period, showed double features with turnover every week or two. Hence, the exhibition arms of each major were forced to contract with their distributor competitors to obtain sufficient product to fill their annual needs, given their tendency for rapid turnover.

Therefore, the mutual interdependence that normally accompanies an oligopoly market structure was enhanced by the clearly evident need of each company for the feature film product and screens of the others in order for this group to be collectively self-sufficient in these key dimensions of product space. Strangely, the success of each studio in producing hit movies would reverberate throughout the whole industry. A hit movie would benefit the exhibition sector of all theater circuits, not just the one originating the film.

Even with a pooling of all the "A" product of the Big 5, there still was an insufficiency in the production of "B" quality films to fill out the double bill of the theaters. The Big 5, therefore, outsourced this need to the "Little 3" and some other independent affiliated firms. The "Little 3" included United Artists, Universal, and Columbia, none of which had specific theater holdings but were largely involved in the production and exhibition spheres. Independents like Monogram and Republic fulfilled similar roles in supplying filler product. Collectively, the Big 5, Little 3, and other affiliates were completely self-sufficient.

In a similar fashion, the clustered theater holdings of each major necessitated agreements among the majors and with affiliated independent circuits to cover all the markets needed in a national release pattern. In many towns and cities, the theater circuits were co-owned or cooperated with each other through pooling arrangements to "split" the films among themselves and, in this manner, to avoid unproductive bidding wars and to facilitate orderly scheduling of release patterns.

The distribution sector spearheaded the vertical conspiracy. Movies were to be distributed in a sequential fashion to first-run theaters, second-run theaters, and finally to lower-run theaters. The first-run theaters would be protected in their exhibition by having very generous time and spatial clearances. What this means is that there would be an abundant amount of elapsed time between the first and second run in order to enhance the revenue-generating power of these theaters. Without adequate clearance, filmgoers could easily wait for the film to complete its initial run and then attend at significantly reduced rates during the second and subsequent runs. To forestall such a diversion or leakage of patrons to the subsequent runs, the time in between first and second runs had to be protracted.

Similarly, each theater that had preferential first-run access must be guaranteed a certain geographical area of exclusivity, which is often known as *geographical clearance.* No other theater within this geographical clearance area could simultaneously exhibit the same film; only theaters outside the protected area could have simultaneous showings. By extending the geographical clearance areas far beyond their normal confines, the revenue-generating power of the first-run theaters could be enhanced to the detriment of nearby non-aligned theaters, similarly situated.

The conspirator defendants in league with their exhibition affiliates established uniform systems of runs and clearances that far exceeded the zone of reasonableness. Furthermore, by giving preferential first-run designations to their own theaters, they guaranteed a superior financial return to these theaters at the expense of independents, unaffiliated with the major distributors. While the majors only owned 17 percent of all theaters in the country during this era, they had 60 to 70 percent of all first-run theaters in the major cities, thereby giving them significant market power in the exhibition arena.

The conspirator distributors also set out on a deliberate course of action to fix admission prices by setting uniform minimum admission price floors below which no theater could charge. In this way, price competition between theaters would be eliminated and theaters could not lower prices for inferior product. With respect to the supply of movie product, the distributors negotiated for access at the circuit level rather than the local level. Hence "formula deals," "master agreements," and long term "franchise" agreements covering more than a year's worth of product were quite common and established effective access squeezes on independent, unaffiliated, local theaters seeking adequate product.

Other privileges were afforded to the integrated theaters and their affiliates to the detriment of the independents. Favorable terms regarding move-overs (from one theater to another) and extended runs, early cancellations, and other contract terms clearly aided in the smooth operation of the distribution conspiracy. Where independent theaters did participate, they often were discriminated against with *block booking* of films that tied superior and inferior pictures together in a single all-or-nothing package and *blind bidding* for these features with little or no advance trade showings prior to licensure.

At the district court level,[8] there was a clear condemnation of the *price-fixing* agreements. Also there was an understanding that the majors, minors, and affiliated companies produced over three-quarters of all distributor rental income and collected a majority of film box office receipts. Yet, with theater holdings of only 17 percent in this key area (and no written, express agreements), the district court was reluctant to rule that a shared monopoly truly existed at the exhibition level that somehow transmitted power back through the distribution and production stages. Instead they believed that conduct remedies would be sufficient to break up the price fixing-conspiracy, forestall attempts to monopolize, and restore competition to the industry.

The district court decree thus sought to prohibit the fixed admission prices, uniform theater designations, excessive time and geographical clearances, franchise, formula, master agreements, and unconditional block booking and blind bidding. It broke up all theater pooling arrangements and, most importantly, instituted a system of *competitive bidding* for films. Each film would be bid "picture by picture," "theater by theater" and thus all theaters would compete on an equal playing field in the bidding process with the highest responsible bidder "winning according to merit rather than lineage."[9]

The case was appealed to the Supreme Court and the same findings of fact were uncovered by this court but their interpretation was radically different.[10] The Supreme Court substituted first-run theaters in place of all theaters as the relevant product market at the exhibition level and then recalculated the defendants' market share to be 60 to 70 percent, clearly within the region of a shared monopoly and requiring a *structural* rather than a *conduct solution*. They distrusted the concept of competitive bidding as involving the courts too deeply in the day-to-day operation of the motion picture industry since the successful bid was a subjective decision composed of many different components, and the judiciary was not suited to administer this kind of business scrutiny.

Furthermore, the Court distrusted the concept of the level playing field and believed that competitive bidding would favor the major companies. They recommended therefore that the lower court reconsider a structural solution that vertically divested the theater circuits from the production–distribution holdings (with reintegration prohibited). Only in this way would truly independent, arms-length behavior emerge in negotiations between the exhibition and distribution levels. Further, the local theaters that were acquired or controlled as a result of the illegal restraint of trade must be given up and undone before competition could be restored.[11] On remand to the district court, these findings were put into place through the signing of consent decrees between the Court and the defendants.

In addition to its precedent-setting reaffirmation of the illegality of tying arrangements inherent in block booking, the case is also famous for its examination of vertical integration as a method of achieving monopolization. The famous dictum in *Paramount* that was used as a pattern in later cases involving vertical arrangements is:

> The legality of vertical integration under the Sherman Act turns on: (1) the purpose or intent with which it was conceived or (2) the power it creates and the attendant purpose and intent. First, it runs afoul of the Sherman Act if it was a calculated scheme to gain control over an appreciable segment of the market and to restrain or suppress competition, rather than an expansion to meet legitimate business needs. Second, a vertically integrated enterprise . . . will constitute monopoly provided a power to exclude competition is coupled with a purpose or intent to do so.[12]

APPLICATION OF THE PARAMOUNT DOCTRINE

In a rather ironic twist of fate, after having fought bitterly against the vertical disintegration of their industry, some twenty years later, the major motion picture studios initiated private antitrust litigation against the "Big 3" television networks, now using the same arguments and accusations that were employed against them. The case was soon joined by the Department of Justice and ended in consent decrees by the end of the seventies.[13]

The motion picture studios complained that the historic "Big 3" networks had established a fully integrated monopoly across the production, distribution, and exhibition stages and were using their protected status as television licensees to deny access to independent television series and motion pictures produced by the studios. The specific charge was that the network vertical affiliation contract process created a protected position of power that was transmitted backwards through the vertical chain and disadvantaged independent suppliers of television product. In specific terms, when the networks individually or through equity ownership with others, produced their own television fare, this acted to foreclose the open market to access for non-aligned independent producers such as the motion picture studios.

These charges of self-preference and discrimination for product produced "in-house" as compared to that licensed from outsiders were not really new. The broadcast networks had been investigated in the 1970s and the FCC had instituted the Prime-Time Access Rules and Financial Interest and Syndication Rules in 1971 to restore the balance of power in the industry. The former limited the number of hours that the networks could operate during the lucrative nighttime daypart while the latter rules removed the networks from active participation in the syndication industry and no longer permitted them to obtain equity consideration (profit shares) in the programming they obtained from independent suppliers. These rules did permit the networks to produce programming in-house (by themselves).

The motion picture industry had never complained in the past about the networks' production of their own television programs because the networks did so little of this, limiting themselves to news, sports, daytime, late night and only a few prime-time series. In fact, the major movie companies supplied the majority of prime-time entertainment programming, although they complained they had to suffer production deficits for the initial network run. What triggered the complaint was the entrance of CBS and ABC into feature film production as a means of reducing the license prices paid for network broadcast of feature films, and also the increasing use of made-for-television movies as a substitute product for theatrical films. These made-for-television movies were often coproduced by the networks themselves. The major studios saw these actions as a means of shrinking the market for television exhibition of feature films and foreclosing access if the networks favored their own theatrical product over that of the studios. A final concern was making sure that the Financial Interest and Syndication Rules were sanctified by the Courts rather than simply remaining administrative rules subject to change.

While there were different interpretations defining the relevant product market, the district court seemed to favor the Department of Justice in the early findings of fact, but the case never fully went to trial. Between 1976 and 1979 the networks entered into consent decrees stipulating certain conduct conditions that would be followed to settle the action. In basic terms, the settlements incorporate the Financial Interest and Syndication Rules (now deregulated by the FCC) and place strict limits on the amount of television programming that each network can produce for itself. For example, NBC's decree limited in-house production to 2.5 hours of prime-time programming, 8 hours of daytime, and 11 hours of fringe time. Of course, the ratification of the Financial Interest and Syndication Rules prevented networks from co-venturing programming with independents through equity interests and continued their ban from engaging in domestic syndication. Strangely, there were no provisions restricting networks from producing their own theatrical movies.[14]

Therefore, while the television networks were not disintegrated as with the *Paramount* decrees, their ability to tie together the production and distribution sectors was severely curtailed for the ten-year duration of the consent decrees (expiring in 1990). This proceeding clearly demonstrates the general applicability of the *Paramount* decrees to other industries. As a historical footnote, the Financial Interest and Syndication Rules were repealed by the FCC in 1995 and, in conjunction with the expiration of the consent decrees, the broadcast networks have begun to produce significantly more of their product themselves rather than rely on outsiders. On the other hand, their need for theatrical movie product has significantly diminished as new exhibition windows like VCR, pay-per-view, and pay cable became the primary outlets by which viewers watched movies on television. Furthermore, when the networks reentered filmmaking in the 1980s to compensate for their production limitations, their performance was lackluster, at best. Hence, the tremendous fear of the major motion picture distributors that they would be displaced by network produced theatrical films turned out to be overplayed in the first instance and reduced to nothing with the arrival of new technology and services that displaced networks in the "windowing" process. Note, for all these cases, that there was an attempt to use vertical integration and vertical tying arrangements to obtain and perpetuate market power and monopoly control throughout the motion picture industry. This is the connective tissue running through these cases and that is often quite prevalent in other sectors of the mass media.

THE LOEW'S CASE AGAINST BLOCK BOOKING

One of the clearest violations in the *Paramount* case involved the widespread practice of "block booking" feature films to theaters. Block booking is a form of a tying arrangement whereby one product is sold on condition of buying another one. This practice traces back to the earliest years of the motion picture industry when films of such illustrious superstars as Mary Pickford or Charles Chaplin were sold in conjunction and on condition with films of a lesser quality and value. The selling of products in combination or in packages or bundles is not inherently anticompetitive and may reflect the transaction savings of brokering multiple products. Nonetheless, where one of the products has significant market power, it may possess enough leverage in the market for inducing or conditioning the sale of this highly desirable product with that of a lesser or more competitive product. The product possessing market power is known as the *tying* good and the more competitive product is the *tied* good. This type of tying arrangement may force buyers into accepting less desirable or inferior product and thereby reduce the free play of market forces in the product for the tied good.[15] The necessity for showing significant market power for the tying good can be inferred from the product's desirability to consumers or its unique attributes. Also, if the tying product was patented, this would constitute evidence of sufficient economic power.

In the *Paramount* case, the principle of recognizing patents as constituting sufficient power was extended to copyrighted feature films. And in a similar fashion to the prohibition against extending patents, through tying arrangements, to unpatented product, the same was held to be true for feature films. According to the *Paramount* precedent:

> *Where a high quality film greatly desired is licensed only if an inferior one is taken, the latter borrows quality from the former and strengthens the monopoly by drawing on the other. This practice tends to equalize rather than differentiate the rewards for individual copyrights. Each film stands not on its own footing but in whole or in part on the appeal which another film may have.*[16]

The particular issue that arose in the Loew's case was whether this overall prohibition against block booking of films was applicable only to the theatrical exhibition area or should be extended into new media such as television. It has been mentioned in the history section that the motion picture industry had a difficult period of adjustment with the arrival of television. At first, they tried to boycott television by ridiculing it and forbidding their stars from appearing on television shows of any kind. They refused to produce television programs or to sell their film library to television networks or stations for broadcast. By 1955, the boycott started to fade and a new accommodation of mutual respect and business interaction occurred across many different product levels as the majors began producing prime-time series and negotiating for the broadcast rights of classic movies and recently released movies as well.

With respect to the classic movies, these were separately classified as *pre* or *post* 1948, recognizing this date as the beginning of the television era. The pre-1948 movies, in some instances representing hundreds of talking films in the library, were generally sold in syndication packages to television stations that wished to use them to fill in for times when network programs were unavailable. The sale of these feature films in packages was thought necessary to save transaction costs and, undoubtedly, to clear the unsold inventory in one fell swoop rather than on a piecemeal basis. Naturally, the libraries contained many first-class feature films but also other lower quality films with little television value.

When the television stations attempted to split up the packages of the distributors into smaller amounts or inquired what the license prices were for the first-class films, they were told by distributors that this was an all-or-nothing purchase and that individual prices were unavailable. The television stations appealed to the Justice Department, charging that such forms of packaged deals were illegal tying arrangements that were condemned under the *Paramount* decrees. The Justice Department instituted an antitrust case alleging violations of Section 1 of the Sherman Act,[17] even though no combination or conspiracy was alleged among the distributors nor was there any attempt to monopolize or monopolization under Section 2 of the Act. The sole complaint rested on the manner in which the films were licensed—pressuring television stations to accept inferior films along with desirable ones.

The Supreme Court affirmed the decision of the lower court and found in favor of the Justice Department, thereby reaffirming the *Paramount* decision in declaring such block booking arrangements as illegal antitrust practices.[18] The Court said that it was irrelevant that the film was being licensed to television stations rather than movie theaters. "A copyrighted feature film does not lose its legal or economic uniqueness because it is shown on a television rather than a movie screen."[19]

As a result of this case, there no longer was any doubt that block booking in any form was condemned as illegal and distributors were required to indicate individual film prices on request in their business practice. This does not, however, mean that it has totally disappeared from the entertainment industry. One frequently hears stories of how syndicated programming such as *Wheel of Fortune, Jeopardy,* and *Oprah Winfrey* was sold in combination on an all-or-nothing basis. Further, there continues to be the sale of classic movie packages to television stations and basic cable networks. The difference today is the requisite appearance of a clause indicating that the negotiation of a package deal is *voluntary* by both parties and not forced. Whether this natural tendency of film distributors to tie high quality and low quality product together in one fashion or another can ever be eliminated is questionable because the real source of uneven market and bargaining power traces back to the holder of the rights to the superior film product. The manner in which these negotiations occur cannot restore equality of bargaining power and hence cannot eliminate the source of the problem.

Theater Enterprise v. Paramount (1954)

Another key antitrust precedent in the history of the motion picture industry involved a very small theater in the suburbs of Baltimore that tried to upgrade its status but continually was rejected as a first-run theater. The time period was in the late 1940s and early 1950s when the movement of population to the suburbs was just starting. New suburban shopping centers were being built along the perimeter of major cities; each shopping center had a state-of-the-art motion picture theater as a main attraction. Yet, the vast majority of the population still resided in the central city and the luxurious downtown theaters had the largest attendance draw. These downtown theaters had been owned by the Big 5 individually, collectively, or in combination with independent owners. In the early 1950s, the divestiture process had just begun. Each major signed its own consent decree and started to sell off its theater circuit.

The Crest theater belonged to Theater Enterprises, Inc., and was located some six miles from the downtown shopping center in Baltimore, Maryland.[20] It began operations in February 1949 and continually requested exclusive first-run status for the major pictures of the day. Each time, the Crest was rejected by the major distributors in favor of the downtown theaters. Because of its proximity to the downtown theaters, the Crest was within the clearance zone of these theaters and none of them would grant clearance for simultaneous showing of first-run movies. This meant that the Crest had to obtain an exclusive, area-wide license in order to be a first-run exhibitor. The problem that plagued the Crest was that its suburban location had a drawing area less than one-tenth that of the downtown theaters and, even though the Crest claimed to have comparable or superior bids for first-run exclusive licenses, its overall earning capability simply could not equal that of the downtown theaters. No matter what the Crest said or did, this inferior economic position was cited as the reason for denial by each distributor.

The Crest felt that it was being discriminated against by the major distributors, each of which had already been found guilty in the *Paramount* case and forced to divest its theater holdings. While there was no charge or proof of conspiracy by the distributors to deny product or access to the Crest, nonetheless, each followed a uniform and unchanging policy of classifying the Crest as a second-run theater. Theater Enterprises further claimed that, under the "conscious parallelism" doctrine enunciated in the *American Tobacco* case, this uniform rejection of the Crest theater constituted a conspiracy to exclude competition and should be remedied under the Sherman Act. The lower courts found no conspiracy nor any other antitrust violations, and the Supreme Court concurred with these decisions. For the higher court, the key issue was whether the uniform rejection of the bids of the Crest Theater stemmed from independent decisions or from agreement among the distributors. The famous dictum emerging from this case reads:

> *To be sure, business behavior is admissible circumstantial evidence from which the fact finder may infer agreement. . . . But this Court has never held that proof of parallel behavior itself constitutes a Sherman Act offense. Circumstantial evidence of consciously parallel behavior may have made heavy inroads into the traditional judicial attitude toward conspiracy; but "conscious parallelism" has not yet read conspiracy out of the Sherman Act entirely.[21]*

Because each of the distributors arrived at this same business conclusion independently, this was merely good business judgment rather than a conspiracy to exclude others. This standard of "independent business judgment" has since become the standard defense in all cases involving shared monopolies or conspiracy to monopolize.

NOTES

[1]This section borrows from Jeanne Thomas Allen, "The Decay of the Motion Picture Patents Company," in Tino Balio, ed., *The American Film Industry,* Madison, WI: University of Wisconsin Press, 1976, Chapter 6.

[2]Ibid.

[3]Ibid.

[4]*United States v. Motion Picture Patents Co., et al.,* 225 F 2d., 800 (1915).

[5]Ibid., at 805.

[6]Ibid., at 805.

[7]This Chapter borrows from Barry Litman, "The Motion Picture Industry," in Walter Adams, ed., *The Structure of American Industry,* New York: McMillan, 1990, Chapter 7; *also,* Barry Litman, *The Vertical Structure of the Television Broadcast Industry: The Coalescence of Power,* East Lansing, MI: Michigan State University, 1979. There is also a good background in the lower and upper court decisions.

[8]*United States v. Paramount Pictures,* 66 F. Supp 323 (1946).

[9]Ibid.

[10]*United States v. Paramount Pictures, Inc.,* 334 U.S. 131 (1948).

[11]Ibid., at 178.

[12]Ibid., at 174.

[13]*United States v. National Broadcasting Company,* 449 F. Supp. 1127 (1978).

[14]Ibid.

[15]*International Salt Co. v. United States,* 332 U.S. 392 (1947), *Times-Picayune Publishing Co. v. United States,* 545 U.S. 594 (1953); also *U.S. v. Paramount,* op. cit.

[16]*U.S. v. Paramount,* 334 U.S. 131 (1948) at 334.

[17]There is also a general condemnation against such tying arrangments in the Clayton Act.

[18]*United States v. Loew's, Inc.,* 371 U.S. 38 (1962).

[19]Ibid., at 48.

[20]*Theater Enterprises, Inc. v. Paramount, Film Distributing,* 346 U.S. 537 (1954).

[21]Ibid., at 540–541.

6

The Other
Exhibition Windows

As alluded to in the history section in Chapter 2, broadcast television was the first new telecommunication technology and service to appear on the scene and to become a new exhibition window for theatrical films after their domestic and international runs. While the major studios first boycotted this new technology as a threat to their protected position in theatrical exhibition, they soon came to understand that television broadcasting, both network and syndication, provided a fertile ground for subsequent runs after the movie had exhausted its theatrical potential.

They came to establish a special exhibition window for network television, usually two to three years after the theatrical run. Syndication to local television stations would occur after the movies no longer had network earning power. As new succeeding technologies, such as pay cable, VCR, pay-per-view, and now fiber-optic video-on-demand have arrived, the studios welcome them with open arms and adjust their exhibition sequence accordingly to maximize the present value of profits across the many new exhibition windows. While this process of "windowing" has generated much attention, it really is not new in the truest sense since, prior to the advent of television, the second and subsequent theatrical exhibition runs constituted the same type of "windowing" process.

Most important is the underlying economic theory behind "windowing," which is really an application of the second-degree price discrimination model explained in Appendix A. According to this theory, the firm with substantial market power can maximize profits by segmenting consumers into clearly distinct groupings, with different elasticities of demand, and charging them their "reservation price," that is, the highest price that they would be willing and able to pay for this product rather than just the single equilibrium price that the firm would normally determine under the standard theory of monopoly pricing. In this way, the monopolist/oligopolist would confiscate consumer surplus (the difference between the highest price and actual price) from each segment of demand and turn it into producer's surplus (e.g., excess profits). This process of segmentation of demand would occur so long as price[1] exceeded MC, that is the net addition to revenues exceeded the net addition to cost. While such price discrimination clearly works to the overall benefit of powerful firms by bolstering their excess profits, there is an added benefit to consumers in the sense that output for the industry is greatly increased from what it would be under the single-price monopoly situation. A whole new group of consumers would now be able to purchase product at reasonable prices, whereas they had been excluded before due to a high monopoly type price. In short, price discrimination would clearly improve society's allocation of scarce resources.

As noted above, for such price discrimination to work effectively, there must be clearly identifiable classes of customers with different elasticities and no arbitrage between the customer classes. In the context of the motion picture industry, the customer classes correspond to the different exhibition windows and the profit maximizing objective of the distributor is to sequence these windows according to whichever customer class is willing to pay the next highest price (or net contribution to revenue). This situation is depicted in Figure 6-1. Each quantity segment corresponds to a different exhibition window. The sequential order is theatrical exhibition (both domestic and international) followed by VCR, pay-per-view, pay cable,

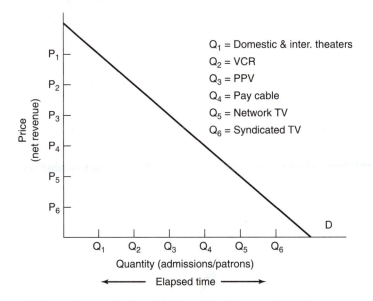

FIGURE 6-1 "Windowing Model" for Motion Pictures

network TV, and syndication.[2] When video-on-demand is fully operational in the next millennium, it can be expected to move to the front of the line, perhaps even challenging theatrical exhibition as the primary exhibition window and "launching pad."

One key difference between this application and the price discrimination model in its purest sense is the importance of time as the critical vehicle for separating out the customer classes in product space. The amount of time clearance between windows will be very important (as it was between first and second theatrical runs before the arrival of television) and geographical clearance between countries is also crucial, as well as prevention of piracy/leakage between windows. The price/net revenue factor is also related to time in the sense that the shorter the elapsed time since theatrical release, the greater the value to the household and the higher the price that will be paid.

While some movie patrons must see a new release the first week it debuts, others are willing to wait until it reaches the VCR or PPV markets and pay a lower household price.[3] As one moves sequentially across the different windows, the net contribution to distribution revenue falls and the films are most likely to be sold to the different windows as parts of groups. The direct contribution by viewers becomes unclear as advertiser support replaces viewer payment in the broadcast realm.

The goal of the profit maximizing distributor is to determine the optimal sequencing of windows and also the optimal time within a window and clearance between the windows.[4] As long as there is no widespread leakage between windows, the sequencing of windows can be maintained and flourish. It should be noted that a window may move to the front of the sequence either because its net contribution to revenues per household is higher (e.g., PPV) or its total contribution to revenues is higher (e.g., VCRs). It is the balancing act that is maintained between the high profit per household technologies and the high penetration technologies that is the key to maximizing profits for the distributor. Also, the degree of market power and bargaining strength by the distributor in each window will also affect its overall financial contribution and place in line.

The emergence of multiple exhibition windows also complicates other aspects of the production/distribution process. Since each window is populated with consumers of different demographic and psychographic makeup, this means that the average movie will have differential levels of popularity as it moves throughout the windowing process. For example, the moviegoing patron is known to be somewhat younger than the average television viewer while those that frequent video stores tend to be more family oriented, and the international viewer prefers certain genres. What this means is that each and every film must be handled somewhat differently, depending on its genre, age orientation, degree of sex and violence, and other factors.

The time spent within a window may be shortened if a movie is not expected to have a favorable reception. This even applies to shortening the first-run theatrical exhibition if the movie is not expected to be favorably reviewed and moving directly into the VCR market. In fact, some low-budget movies now actually bypass the first-run theatrical market entirely. On the other hand, a very popular theatrical launch may cause the distributors to attempt to tap the VCR "sell-through" market direct to consumers rather than rely on VCR rental driven demand.

Another decision involves the production budget, advertising budget, and even casting. It has always been true that well-known actors and actresses are very popular abroad and concessions have been made to include these people in big-budgeted films to appeal to this foreign constituency. Now, with all the new video windows, TV stars and well-known personalities from other entertainment media will be more highly cultivated for these windows. This is not to diminish the marquee value of true movie stars like Arnold Schwartzenegger, Harrison Ford, Jody Foster, Meg Ryan, or the like but simply to imply that former TV stars like John Travolta, Robin Williams, or Ron Howard can also make it big on the silver screen and in the other subsidiary markets. Finally, according to Owen and Wildman,[5] the prevalence of such an elaborate and dynamic windowing process in the United States means that additional funds can be invested upfront in the production budget that will reap financial returns downstream in the windows. This added budgetary flexibility (plus the added richness of the domestic market) has always been a key factor in enhancing the U.S. film in offshore markets and facilitating the worldwide domination that has always characterized the major studios since the 1920s. We will now examine these subsidiary windows in greater depth.

THE TELEVISION NETWORK MARKET

As has been mentioned above, the motion picture distributors made a truce with the television industry in the mid-1950s and began to supply regularly scheduled series and motion pictures shortly thereafter. In the market for regularly scheduled prime-time programs, the major movie distributors have maintained an extraordinary presence, collectively averaging in excess of 40 percent since the mid 1960s (see Table 6-1), with Universal being the dominant supplier for a long time and Warner and Paramount dominating in recent years. The networks themselves historically produced a small percentage of their prime-time programming needs, concentrating primarily on news, sports, and specials rather than entertainment series. The remainder of prime-time series are produced by independent production houses (also known as "packagers"), many of which have market shares comparable to the major film distributors. As Owen originally noted, the major movie companies have no economic advantage in this programming area since the supply industry is monopolistically competitive due to a well-developed rental market for inputs, minimal economies of scale, and easy entry.[6] Given such competitive conditions, the supply industry has been unable to countervail the coordinated monopsony (buying) power of the historic Big 3 networks. The networks understood that their bargaining advantage was greatest in the initial developmental stages of a television show, when the

TABLE 6-1   Network Supplier Market Shares of Prime Time Hours—1995 Fall Schedule

Supplier	Network Hours				Netlets Hours		Total
	ABC	CBS	NBC	Fox	WB	Paramount	
Major Networks (b)							
ABC/Disney-Touchstone	8.0				.5	.5	9.0
CBS		7.5	.5				8.0
NBC			6.0				6.0
Fox	3.0	1.5		4.5			9.0
Total	11.0	9.0	6.5	4.5	.5	.5	32.0
Netlets (b)							
Warner Brothers	2.0	1.5	3.0	1.5	3.0		11.0
Paramount	.5	.5	1.0		.5	2.5	5.0
Total	2.5	2.0	4.0	1.5	3.5	2.5	16.0
Major Movie Co. (c)							
Universal	.5	2.0	1.5	1.0		1.0	6.0
Columbia		1.0	1.5				2.5
Tri-Star		.5	.5	1.0	.5		2.5
Total	.5	2.5	3.0	3.5	.5	1.0	11.0
Independents							
Carsey-Weiner	1.5	1.0	1.0				3.5
Brillstein-Grey		1.0			.5		1.5
Witt-Thomas	.5	.5	.5		.5		2.0
Spelling				2.0	2.0		4.0
New World	1.0						1.0
MTM			1.0		.5		1.5
Dreamworks	1.5	.5					2.0
All Others 7.5							7.5
Total	4.5	2.0	3.5	2.0	3.5		23.0
Grand Total 7.5	18.5	15.5	17.0	11.5	8.0	4.0	82.0

*Fox, Warner Brothers, and Paramount are all major movie company suppliers to other networks.
(a) Excludes movies which have various suppliers each week.
(b) Includes all co-productions with independent suppliers.
(c) Includes all co-productions with non-studio suppliers.
Source: *Broadcasting and Cable,* May 27, 1996, p. 19.

quality of the scripts and pilot are of unknown value and the future success of the program is uncertain.[7] At this stage, venture capital is scarce because the investment is so risky. Once a show becomes a hit and its true value is known, however, it can command a high price on the open market because its parent network cannot risk its being bid away by another network. The same problem occurred in major league sports and the "reserve rule" and other devices were used to tie the players to their teams.

To prevent such competitive bidding, the networks historically developed a series of parallel steps in the buying process which, if commonly followed, would bind series to long-term "option" contracts prior to knowledge being available regarding their ratings popularity; this would enhance their bargaining power relative to their suppliers. This was known as the "step process" of program acquisition. Thus, the networks became profitable in the programming area because they have been able to control both sources of potential profit—profit from uncertainty of program quality and profit from inter-industry coordination. These two sources of power are intricately intertwined. The tight oligopoly structure of the networks acts as a bottleneck which narrows down the number of potential sources of access for program producers. The profit-maximizing incentive for oligopolists to coordinate their behavior inhibits the emergence of significant inter-network competition for programming. The uncertainty over quality, the large number of competing producers, and the scarcity of venture capital made the producers unable to resist this network power. This was the distressing situation that existed for program packages until the arrival of cable opened up more sources of access and created a more competitive network marketplace.

Historically, theatrical movies represented a different species of network programming because specific knowledge exists concerning their value in the theatrical market. This knowledge includes data on the box office gross and rentals accruing to the distributor, as well as the performance of the movie in the various award categories. This information has been shown in previous studies to be an important determinant in explaining the expected rating of these films on prime-time television. The known "quality" of theatrical movies, in reducing the uncertainty and risk to the networks, also enabled the movie companies to demand prices reflecting the marginal worth of their movies. The networks, in turn, were unable to refrain from intense competitive bidding for exclusive rights to these movies as contrasted with their superior position in acquiring television series.

The major movie companies also have more bargaining power because of a much stronger position in the movie industry as producer–distributors than as television series suppliers. As indicated above, the major movie distributors clearly dominate the theatrical movie industry. This highly concentrated market structure enabled these distributors to bargain more effectively with the networks over theatrical movie rental terms.

It should also be recalled that the financial success of theatrical movies historically depended on rentals earned in the domestic and foreign theaters. The sale of network television rights was only a secondary consideration. This is in sharp contrast to the financial requirement of TV program producers to obtain network financing, make the network sale, and remain on the network long enough to create value for the series in the syndication market (their real profit center). In short, the movie companies have a greater independence in their financing and more potential profit centers. This flexibility should translate into greater bargaining strength with the networks over theatrical movie rights. Hence, an interesting paradox prevailed in network negotiations with the major distributors. They had the upper hand in the TV series market but were disadvantaged in the submarket for theatrical rights.

Of course, it still would have been possible for the networks to tacitly agree to hold down prices for movies of known quality. For example, the networks could have established a bidding pool that could designate which one of them was to be "highest" bidder for the next hit movie. But the success of such a price-fixing buying cartel would have required open discussions among the networks and a complex allocation scheme. The risk of antitrust detection would have been very high, which probably explains why network competition has been the rule in this sphere of programming.

Movie companies were able to obtain high and increasing prices for their films since the early 1960s. The prices for theatrical movies were always two to three times higher (for the standard two-hour length of time) than the prices of regularly scheduled programs of comparable quality, offering further evidence that movie producers had greater bargaining leverage than series producers. Movie prices started to rise because of increasing network demand, ratings popularity, and inter-network rivalry for theatrical movies. The average price of a theatrical movie rose from $100,000 for two network runs in 1961 to around $800,000 by the end of 1967. During this period the number of hours of prime-time movies increased from two in 1961 to fourteen in 1968 as each network had at least two movie nights each week.[8] By the mid-1970s, the prices once again skyrocketed due to a shortage of acceptable movies for television. This shortage resulted from the fact that the four-year stockpile of network features amassed during the late 1960s ran out around 1972 or 1973, the trend in the 1970s toward R- and X-rated pictures resulted in a smaller percentage of acceptable features for TV, and the major movie studios, addressing a slight recession in their industry, cut back their output significantly, concentrating their efforts on fewer high budget films.

Around 1966 and 1967, the networks attempted to neutralize the power of the movie distributors and stabilize movie prices by producing their own made-for-television movies (a substitute product) and ABC and CBS entered directly into motion picture production. This vertical integration into the production sphere resulted in some eighty theatrical movies during 1967–1971 and 40 to 50 percent of their yearly requirements of made-for-television movies. The effect of such a large foreclosure of product was devastating and sent a clear message to the movie producers that, hereafter, theatrical movie licensing fees would be stabilized.

Private and public antitrust litigation ensued.[9] The motion picture distributors charged that the television networks were in violation of the *Paramount* decrees (see Chapter 5 for more details) since they had set up a fully integrated market chain through network distribution, ownership, and affiliation with broadcast exhibition outlets, and now production of theatrical movies. These lawsuits had been filed shortly after the FCC had reduced the ability of the networks to co-venture programming with outside packagers (another form of vertical integration) and had forced the networks to abandon one hour of prime-time programming to open the airwaves to independent sources of supply.

The case ended with a consent decree in 1980 that basically ratified the FCC's "Prime-Time Access Rules" and "Financial Interest and Syndication Rules" and limited the ability of the networks to produce in-house television series. Paradoxically, the decrees did not forbid the networks from producing theatrical movies nor from broadcasting them on their own network after the theatrical run.[10] While ABC and CBS had left the theatrical production industry in 1972 because of the lawsuits as well as an inferior product, all three networks reentered into this arena in the late 1970s and early 1980s. To their dismay, they learned a hard lesson. Success in producing hit TV series did not translate into movie production. None of the networks was even moderately successful.

In the meantime, competition for the limited quantity of available theatrical movies once again caused license prices to increase to roughly $2 million per film. To counteract this problem, the networks increased their requirements for made-for-television movies to all-time record levels. While the increased demand for these tailor-made programs naturally increased their prices, they still cost less than half the rental fee for a theatrical movie.

In 1978, the networks once again tried to stabilize the prices of theatrical films by purchasing television rights before the theatrical movie was released, and often before filming was completed.[11] The rationale behind this change in strategy was to obtain commitments by the movie producers at an early stage in the production process when the quality was uncertain, the risk was high, and the television value was indeterminate. In this way, the networks sought to bind themselves to specific producers and thereby reduce inter-network competition over theatrical movies. It was, of course, a risk for the networks because they would be wedded to the flops along with the hits, but one that had been shown to be acceptable and profitable with regularly scheduled programming. Because of the success of this blind bidding strategy and its growing financial dependence on network advances, the movie distributors eventually demanded "escalator" clauses in their licensing contracts to tie network prices more closely to theatrical rentals, thereby negating the network bargaining advantage. By the mid 1980s, the entire point became largely moot as the television networks severely reduced their reliance on theatrical movies since they had been pushed further back in line behind other exhibition windows and the plummeting television ratings of these shopworn movies no longer justified such high license prices. The networks continue to reposition their product line to fill a more unique niche in the burgeoning video market; they now prefer program product, such as made-for-TV movies, that has not been shown in other media and is not generally available on videocassette.

THE PAY TELEVISION MARKET

The development of the pay television market and role of motion picture distribution requires an understanding of the basic structure of television broadcasting. The scarcity of space in the electromagnetic spectrum created a natural limitation on the number of available Very High Frequency (VHF) stations in any local market. The necessity of maintaining a buffer zone (a one-channel separation) between adjacent VHF frequencies and the fact that the FCC decentralized the allocation of VHF frequencies, so that smaller cities would have at least one originating broadcast station, further reduced the number of viable broadcast signals in local markets. On average, there were only three VHF commercial frequencies available in the top 100 markets in the country (which account for over 90 percent of all TV households). Given the overwhelming economic incentive to share programming expenses through "networking," and the necessity for networks to have local affiliates to transmit their programs, there was room for only three national TV networks.[12] When the FCC sought to increase the amount of spectrum space for television by adding on a technically inferior Ultra High Frequency (UHF) band to the existing superior VHF band, it created a surplus of unwanted UHF frequencies and the perpetuation of the tight network oligopoly. With only three national network signals and the incentive (imposed by advertising sponsorship) for maximizing ratings by seeking the lowest common denominator of programming, "minority taste" programming went unfulfilled even though public broadcasting sought to fill the void with their own cultural and educational programming.

One new approach toward solving the lack of diversity inherent in broadcasting was that of pay television. Proponents of pay TV argued that direct consumer payment would make programming more sensitive to viewer's preferences than the current advertiser-supported system of "free" television. The zero-priced television system is inconsistent with an efficient allocation of resources among program types since it does not provide information concerning *intensity of consumer demand*. In a pay TV system, this program inefficiency can be cured since viewers can express the strength of program preferences through a pricing system. Although there were experiments with pay TV scrambled over-the-air on under-utilized UHF stations, with the development of cable television during the 1960s a collection mechanism was now in place for excluding "free riders"—the basic market failure problem associated with over-the-air broadcasting and the reason for advertising support in the first instance.

The FCC was lobbied by the broadcast interests in the late 1960s not to permit pay TV to get a foothold since it was anathema to the "free" system of broadcasting that had developed and threatened to fractionalize the audience and "siphon" programming.[13] According to broadcasters, consumers would thereby suffer a loss of welfare since they would now have to pay directly for programs they formerly received free: the World Series, National Football League, and the Miss America Beauty Pageant were some of the examples of prominent programming that were always cited as being in jeopardy if pay TV caught on. Also, such high preference programming would be unavailable to most people due to their inability to receive cable because they resided in a low population density area. The end result of this controversy was a series of FCC rules that permitted pay TV to exist but restricted its programming to those types that were unavailable from commercial broadcasting. There could be no duplication of broadcast programming whatsoever. The most important program area permitted was that of recent theatrical movies for the time interval between their theatrical run and their appearance on network television.

In 1972, Home Box Office initiated a pay-cable program service consisting of recent uncut, uninterrupted movies, Las Vegas night club acts, and special sporting events. This channel (package) of programming was sold on a monthly subscription basis for about $7 to those areas already wired for cable. Yet, the nationwide development of this alternative form of television would not come until the expensive system of microwave transmission was replaced in 1975 by the new cost-effective satellite-to-dish national transmission system. When the FCC failed to liberalize these restrictive programming rules in 1975, HBO decided to appeal their legality through the courts. Finally, in 1977, in the *Home Box Office* case, the U.S. Court of Appeals declared "null and void" all programming limitations imposed by the FCC on pay cable networks.[14] This Declaration of Independence for pay cable networking meant that they could become full-fledged competitors of the three commercial networks and is generally credited with triggering off what has come to be known as the "cable revolution," with penetration in slightly over two-thirds of American households in 1996.

Such movie-driven "premium" networks as The Movie Channel, Showtime, and Cinemax soon joined HBO, the industry leader, to exploit this new pay cable market.[15] In recent years, several specialty networks have entered by differentiating their product in other dimensions (e.g., Disney, Playboy, American Movie Classics, and Bravo [cultural]) rather than offering the full range of motion pictures and entertainment specials as do the leading networks.

In the development years of the late 1970s, the pay cable networks decided on a conscious policy of *nonexclusive* licensing of theatrical movies. The basic strategy was for each network to present a full movie package, including all the box office hits, to overcome viewers' hesitancy in paying for a product that formerly was provided "free" of charge (albeit with commercials). This meant that for the movie component of the pay cable schedule, usually 80 to 85 percent of the total schedule, all the pay networks were virtually identical since the motion picture distributors would license everyone at approximately the same time. At the cable system level, the local cable monopolist would generally license only a single pay network to avoid programming redundancy. Frequently, the local cable system was a part of a nationwide chain (multiple system operators) that, in turn, was a subsidiary of one of the top pay cable networks. As is true for all such vertical arrangements, there was the incentive for self-preference, and the same linkage that had occurred in motion picture distribution/exhibition began to surface in the pay cable industry. Competition for exclusive access to smaller cable systems would necessarily then turn on nonproduct dimensions such as marketing or the percentage split of the consumer's monthly payment between the network and the local system.

Ironically, in these pre-VCR days, in a few markets, consumers expressed a willingness to buy a multiple number of redundant networks in order to gain more viewing flexibility. Soon most cable systems began offering multiple networks, which meant that there would be competition for local patronage even in vertically integrated systems. HBO set up a sister service, Cinemax, to try to capture the extra business, but the genie could not be put back in the bottle and *product competition* became a new reality. Product competition/differentiation meant having exclusive rights for a period of time to certain movies and, of course, not sharing your entertainment or sports specials. While at first the networks continued licensing box office hits on a nonexclusive basis, less successful movies and all-time classics were licensed exclusively. By 1981, exclusive rights were also obtained for many of the former category as well. It should be noted that the license prices for exclusive rights for a single network were significantly higher than when everyone had equal access and could in a sense "split" the total license fee. Throughout this entire period, HBO and companion service Cinemax collectively dominated this market, with a combined market share ranging over 60 percent, twice the size of Showtime. HBO used its monopsony power to reduce the license prices to the motion picture distributors, paying on a "flat" rental basis rather than the customary "per-subscriber" method. HBO followed a "take it or leave it" bargaining strategy, which, given its strategic position, was reluctantly accepted.

In April 1980, a new and potentially explosive element was introduced into the pay cable industry. Getty Oil, a giant multinational oil company and a partner in the ESPN cable network, announced a joint venture with four of the major motion picture distributors (Fox, Universal, Paramount, and Columbia) to establish a new programming network known as Premiere. The Premiere network was scheduled to begin operations on January 1, 1981 and would offer twelve to fifteen films a month, primarily those of the movie distributor partners. The key provisions in this venture were the exclusivity clause that permitted Premiere to withhold the theatrical films of these four companies for a period of nine months from the other pay cable networks and the "formula" for setting the license prices. The Premiere network felt that only through such a product differentiation plan could it possibly compete with HBO and Showtime. This was the first attempt of the major studios to bypass the distribution buying strength of the entrenched giant of HBO. Having control over the key movie product, they felt they no longer needed others for distribution. This should be a natural in-house activity rather than negotiated out with others.

Immediately HBO and Showtime complained to the Justice Department that such a joint venture represented:

[a] horizontal agreement among competitors to increase prices, a group boycott, and a concerted refusal to deal. The plan is in violation of both the Sherman and Clayton Antitrust Acts and is an obvious at-

tempt by these film companies, fueled by Getty Oil, to force the public and cable industry to pay higher prices for their films.[16]

The Justice Department filed a civil antitrust suit against the Premiere principals in August 1980, and an injunction against the network beginning its operations was granted just before the January 1 starting date. Within a month, the Premiere network folded. However, HBO had learned an important lesson; lacking an assured source of films, it was vulnerable to such an "end around" as Premiere. It decided to become vertically integrated through ownership and long-term contracts to avoid future problems. It established a theatrical film subsidiary called Silver Screens, joined CBS and Columbia in launching a new mini-major production–distribution company called TriStar, and signed long-term exclusive contracts for the full line of theatrical films of Columbia, Orion, and CBS.[17]

To counteract this move, in 1983 the owners of Showtime and The Movie Channel, in conjunction with Warner Brothers, Universal, and Paramount, announced a new joint venture under which the #2 and #3 pay cable networks would be merged together.[18] While the principals claimed that these networks would continue to be run separately and that the motion picture distributors would continue to license their theatrical films on a nonexclusive basis, the Justice Department believed that such an amalgamation at the production stage would increase the likelihood of coordinated behavior, with the possibility of price squeezes on nonintegrated downstream competitors.[19] On the withdrawal of the motion picture companies, Showtime and The Movie Channel were permitted to merge, even though neither company was in danger of financial failure and the resulting concentration of market power greatly exceeded the threshold values of the Department of Justice's "Merger Guidelines" (see Appendix C for more detail on the guidelines). Within months, another small player, Spotlight Network, folded and the newly combined Showtime–The Movie Channel signed a five-year exclusive pact with Paramount Pictures.

Since the execution of the merger, many other exclusive arrangements have taken place. For example, Showtime–TMC locked up Atlantic, Cannon, DeLaurentis and Touchstone. As original contracts expired, there were many changes that ensued. Paramount has shifted over to HBO and, of course, Disney Studios were always exclusive with the Disney Channel. The main point is that while some large studios still have *not* signed these agreements and prefer to negotiate picture by picture for either exclusive or nonexclusive rights, a significant share of the movie supply industry became committed to this form of vertical tying arrangement, and this severely restricts a potential new pay cable distributor from gaining access to a sufficient number of box office hits to offer a service competitive with HBO and the other giants. It should be recalled that there are only about twenty or so box office hits any single year (a severe bottleneck), and pay cable distributors like to have a major hit each month to showcase on the cover of their cable guides. Hence, splitting up the top twenty hits, especially if done through exclusive contracts, doesn't go very far and, not surprisingly, hasn't opened the market to any new entrants. This is a severe deterrent to new full-fledged competition! While HBO–Cinemax and Showtime–The Movie Channel continue to dominate the movie-driven portion of the pay cable market, the market itself has diminished in importance with the arrival and strength of the VCR market whereby consumers can more directly select their own movie lineup.

NEW TECHNOLOGIES

The market for private backyard satellite dishes has developed in recent years as an offshoot and complement to cable technology. While at first cable systems were required to have a ten-foot diameter "dish" (at a cost of nearly $100,000) to receive the satellite transmissions, by 1979 the FCC had totally deregulated dish size requirements, and the cable industry had standardized with the four-and-one-half meter dish (at an initial cost of about $10,000 and later on $5,000). With reception costs significantly reduced, every cable system could now afford to participate in the nationwide satellite delivery system.

As the cable industry continued to develop, more sophisticated television receive-only satellite dishes (TVROs) came on line, and a new unintended use for these TVROs became apparent. In rural areas that were starved for TV signals, individual households could install a slightly cheaper version of the cable dish (for about $2,000 to $3,000) and receive signals from the same satellites as the cable systems. Thus, rural areas that had too low a population density to make cable financially viable could nonetheless participate in the same television phenomenon as their urban counterparts. Hence, the individual household could become a mini-cable system of its own.

While at first advertiser-supported cable services had no objection to the emergence of these backyard satellite dishes, since they increased their nationwide coverage area, the premium channels and especially the industry giant HBO fought bitterly since they represented a "leakage" from the system—nonpaying "customers." HBO became especially enraged when hotels and taverns began installing their own dishes and thereby subverting the system.

The legality of these backyard satellite dishes remained in question. Were these dishes engaged in theft of service (private transmissions) as HBO claimed or rather were these signals of the same class as over-the-air broadcast transmissions and thereby part of the public domain? This issue was finally resolved in the Cable Policy Act of 1984, which formally legalized the right of consumers to *individually* own a backyard TVRO and *freely* receive satellite transmissions, provided that the satellite network did *not* encrypt (scramble) its signal nor set up a marketing system for collecting payments. During 1985, there was an absolute stampede by consumers to purchase their own dishes and take advantage of receiving so many free signals (especially recent movies) for the one-time installation investment of about $3,000. While there were rumors that scrambling was coming, it was conveniently forgotten or downplayed by satellite dish vendors in the euphoria of such a thriving business. Dishes were even being sold in areas passed by cable, causing cable operators to pressure their network suppliers to speed up their scrambling plans. Some 1.5 million dishes were operational by December of 1985.

Scrambling arrived in January of 1986 when HBO and its sister service Cinemax encrypted their signals and announced a $12.95 per month subscription price for the former and a $19.95 packaged price for the combination. Additionally, consumers would need to affix a descrambler box to their dish at a one-time cost of $395. The scrambling issue created significant confusion in the minds of consumers concerning how many (and which) services would eventually be scrambled, how one actually subscribed to a single service or package of services and became "authorized" to receive them, and whether consumers might have to buy several incompatible descrambler boxes.

During this 1986–1987 period of confusion, consumers significantly curtailed their demand for backyard dishes; sales fell by nearly 65 percent compared to the 1985 benchmark and eventually stabilized at about 20,000 units per month. Nevertheless, by mid-1988, some 2 million households in the U.S. (out of 88.6 million total) had backyard satellite dishes and some 500,000 "addressable" descramblers had been sold.[20] With a dozen major cable networks now scrambled and more on the horizon, with standardization of the descrambler technology and continued declines in basic dish prices, and the emergence of "third party" packagers, consumer confusion ended. The industry continues a steady growth path in those rural or outlying areas where cable cannot efficiently serve (some 10 to 15 million U.S. households). Since 1990 the backyard satellite industry has steadily declined as the cost of running cable became affordable in less dense areas. Furthermore, there were early attempts to replace this technology with a direct broadcast system to the home using a more powerful satellite necessitating a smaller, flat rooftop dish. Since 1995, this DBS system has gradually begun to compete with the other technologies, especially for delivery of pay-per-view networks.

The motion picture distributors should profit from the growth of this home satellite industry since it widens the exhibition market for premium pay TV networks like HBO and should eventually translate into higher license prices for theatrical movies. Furthermore, this industry is currently capable of transmitting movies, boxing and wrestling matches, live concerts, and other special event programming on a pay-per-view basis. This means that the viewer orders (by telephone) a particular performance (play) rather than receiving a bundle of films or the like on a monthly basis. This capability is also available on cable if the home converter has an integrated chip that can receive an authorization signal from the cable system headquarters. Only about 30 million cable households currently have "addressable" converters, but as more cable systems are upgraded over the next decade, this new technology may alter the distribution path for theatrical movies. Instead of a nationwide theatrical release, the movies may be premiered on pay-per-view television, thereby yielding an enormous opening night payoff. This may also cause the movie distributors to directly enter this market rather than rely on intermediaries as is current practice, with Request TV and Viewer's Choice being the dominant pay-per-view distributors.

Yet, an even broader industry can now be envisioned. With the development of the fiber to home information superhighway, there is the potentiality in the near future for true video-on-demand, that is, the consumer can order the movie or video program directly from a computer bank, and then download it for play at the consumer's convenience. Whether this new revolutionary approach to movie distribution will eclipse the theatrical market as the new "launching pad" still remains to be seen and will critically depend on the costs of wiring households and latent consumer demand.

THE VIDEOCASSETTE MARKET

Of even greater importance to the motion picture industry than cable has been the videocassette revolution of the past decade. VCR penetration at nearly 80 percent now exceeds cable penetration by nearly 15 percent and has long surpassed the theatrical box office in revenues generated. Ironically, the motion picture industry stalwartly tried to handicap the development of VCRs just a few short years ago in the *Betamax* case by claiming that their use in taping programs violated the copyright protection afforded motion pictures and TV programs.[21] Having lost that fight, they soon realized the potential for home video as another valuable exhibition window for theatrical films.

The main reason for the popularity of the VCR is its versatility; it permits viewers to "time-shift" programming to escape the temporal tyranny of program times dictated by the networks and local stations; it allows playback of home video photography made by compatible portable video cameras; and finally, and most importantly, it allows consumers to access, through purchase or lease, a wide array of prerecorded videocassettes. In essence, the VCR significantly improves consumer sovereignty and provides the diversity of programming that is absent from commercial television. Within this short thirteen-year period, the VCR industry has reached such an advanced stage of maturity that product differentiation according to content types (genres) already appears to satisfy even the narrowest programming taste. Critically, *this industry is still driven by the theatrical motion picture* (over 70 percent share of sales),[22] which explains why the motion picture distributors have taken such a keen interest and dominant position.

The key difference between the VCR, television, and cable related markets is that in VCRs, *the majors act as distributors themselves,* while in the latter two markets, they rely on specialized distributors like CBS, HBO, Viewers Choice, and others. In fact, VCR distribution is very similar to that of magazines, paperback books, and records. The market shares for VCR distributors is given in Table 6-2. It is clear that the major theatrical distributors have transplanted their power into this market.

TABLE 6-2   Domestic Revenues of Home Videocassette Suppliers, 1989–1996 (in $million)

Supplier/Year	1989	1990	1992	1993	1994	1995	1996
Disney	439	634	1025	1250	1600	2000	2200
Warner	562	486	602	763	790	1000	1400
Columbia/TriStar	215	416	696	643	620	500	580
MCA/Universal	246	350	492	631	720	670	750
Paramount	310	376	529	315	430	460	450
LIVE Ent.	106	278	167	141	100	100	100
CBS/Fox	272	221	577	519	650	850	1000
Orion/Nelson	191	173	86	51	65	65	65
MGM/UA	223	203	143	200	—	—	—
Goodtimes	67	45	5	—	475	475	450
New Line	—	—	—	150	200	275	250
Polygram	—	—	6	—	120	140	175
Turner	—	—	23	50	65	110	100
Anchor Bay	—	—	—	—	100	100	115
Republic	—	31	29	50	65	80	85
Vidmark	31	34	59	40	65	100	110
Media	123	50	—	—	—	—	—
Video Treasures	—	52	111	—	—	—	—
Academy	—	—	37	—	—	—	—
Prism	—	—	23	—	—	—	—
Starmaker	—	—	17	—	—	—	—
All Others	305	333	350	405	350	475	370
Total	3,350	3,700	4,977	5,208	6,415	7,400	8,200
CR4	51.2	51.9	58.3	63.1	58.6	61.1	65.2
CR8	79.5	80.5	85.0	85.8	85.5	84.2	86.3
HHI	965.6	961.8	1,151.4	1,271.8	1,223.7	1,287.7	1,380.3

Source: *International Television & Video Almanac* (annual edition); *S&P Industry Surveys: Leisure Time,* March 14, 1991; *Billboard,* January 25, 1997, pp. 81–83.

Yet, their dominance in VCR software is somewhat smaller than in the traditional theatrical market. This is explained by the persistence of a strong group of independent distributors who specialize in non-movie types of videos such as the "How-To" genre (e.g., "Jane Fonda's Workout Book"), music videos, children's, pornographic, and educational.[23] The independents have also been involved in the distribution of "B" quality movies that purposely have a short theatrical run (sometimes none at all) in order to move more quickly through the VCR and other subsidiary markets. It is the insatiable appetite of these subsidiary markets for product that has caused the growth of the independent production industry and led to a record number of movie releases over the last decade.

It should be noted that these market shares are based on sales of cassettes rather than rentals, even though rentals account for the vast majority of consumer transactions. This is due to the "first sale" copyright provision that permits distributors to only collect copyright payments the first time a cassette is sold, not every time it is rented. Thus retail establishments will pay the wholesale price for theatrical movie cassettes but need not share revenues from renting. To capture some of this producer's surplus, the movie distributors charge very high wholesale prices for their cassettes and the retailers mark them up by their customary margins to yield extremely high retail prices that scare away consumer sales and further encourage the rental market. Occasionally, the wholesale price will be lowered after the first ninety days in order to stimulate the "sell through" consumer market.

One interesting difference between the prerecorded videocassette industry and the other subsidiary markets is the partial integration of the cassette distributors into the manufacturing (duplication) stage but not into the wholesale or retail stages. Because of high capital costs, long-term contracts and vertical integration, the tape duplication stage is very concentrated, with a four-firm concentration index fluctuating between 71 to 94 percent since 1984 and the recent merger between the #1 and #3 firms giving industry leader VCA–Technicolor a market share of 40 to 47 percent.[24] Until CBS–Fox (#3) merged with VCA–Technicolor, it and Bell & Howell–Columbia–Paramount (#2) were the only two vertically integrated firms and accounted for roughly a third to a half of the industry's market. Most of the other distributors have long-term exclusive contracts with duplicators, making new significant entry very difficult. On the other hand, the retail stage is extremely competitive with large discount department chains like K-Mart and Sears in competition with grocery chains and individually owned specialty shops. The availability of videocassette movies is now as plentiful as cigarettes, milk and bread.

THE INTERNATIONAL MARKET

Historically, the second most important subsidiary market has been the international market which is the aggregation of some 80 or more trading partners of the United States (see Chapter 10 for more detail). Going as far back as World War I, the American film distributors have dominated this world market for film, later extended to television and most recently to videocassettes.[25] In fact, U.S. control has been so pervasive that charges of "media imperialism" have been leveled. This refers to the same kind of domination of a country's cultural products that the economic imperialists had over their resources and mercantile goods. Most of all, it is a fear of the loss of cultural identity embedded in a weak indigenous production industry that has led many countries to impose economic and institutional barriers to free trade in cultural products.

The reason why U.S. motion picture distributors have been so powerful rests primarily on the relative size and strength of the U.S. market compared to those of other countries. U.S. motion picture and television producers can largely recoup their production costs from the domestic market alone, and given the public goods nature of the mass media[26] and the fact that the greatest expense is the "first-copy" production cost, distribution prices to foreign lands only need cover the incremental expenses. This pricing practice is often mislabeled as "dumping." Prices are based primarily on the strength of a country's demand (demand driven), providing that they cover the incremental costs of distribution for the particular country. Hence, the richer and more populous countries must pay higher prices for the same video product.

Since foreign countries do not have such a well-developed domestic market as the United States, they must either cut back on production costs (with detrimental effects on production values) or charge higher domestic and/or export prices; either strategy puts them at a disadvantage both within their own country and internationally, because the U.S. market had erected noneconomic barriers to imports through their ethnocentric dislike of foreign films, especially those with subtitles or dubbing.

The leading U.S. film distributors have bolstered their economic advantage by developing the most far-flung distribution networks throughout the world—comparable to their extensive domestic networks. This also includes significant ownership of foreign theaters! Furthermore, with the blessings of the U.S. government (under the Webb–Pomerene Act of 1918), the major movie distributors had a formal export cartel in place for nearly forty years that acted as the sole export sales agent for its members. The Motion Pictures Export Association set general export price levels for each country, terms of trade, and guaranteed the smooth functioning of the distribution process.[27] While the Webb–Pomerene Act was eventually repealed, its effect was long-lasting.

The protectionistic response of foreign countries to U.S. dominance has been the erection of traditional and nontraditional trade barriers. These barriers include import quotas, tariffs, strict licensing procedures, limitations of the percentage of screen time for imported films (and TV programs), and the freezing of local currencies from leaving the country (the most recent occurrence is in the European Common Market). In some instances, the U.S. government has been able to reduce these trade barriers as a quid pro quo for more favorable exchange rates or more open trade in other products. Additionally, foreign governments have provided encouragement to indigenous producers through formal subsidies, production prizes, tax breaks, or loans at favorable (or zero) interest rates.

The U.S. response to such foreign government tactics has been to qualify as indigenous producers within the countries, thereby escaping the penalties associated with being importers while enjoying the benefits afforded local companies.[28] This is one reason why Hollywood has experienced "runaway production" over the last ten to twenty years and so-called foreign coproduction has become more prevalent; the other reasons include the attractiveness and mystique of foreign locales and the cheaper costs in filming abroad.

No matter what barriers have been erected, the major motion picture distributors have successfully hurdled them and prospered. With the proliferation of new TV stations and satellite networks throughout the world, due to deregulation and privatization of formerly state-controlled monopolies, the export market, rather than constricting, appears wide open.

NEW BROADCAST WINDOWS

As has been mentioned, the motion picture studios have tight control over the movie product in the domestic and international theatrical markets but only partial control within the other exhibition windows, the strongest being VCRs. While they have grudgingly been forced to deal with strong network buyers in broadcasting, pay cable, and now in pay-per-view, they have always had the secret desire to form their own distribution networks in these exhibition windows and thereby bypass the powerful bottlenecks they encounter. While attempts have been made at times in the past, such as with the Premiere Cable Network or in conjunction with the Showtime–The Movie Channel merger, these have often been rebuffed by antitrust authorities or unreceptive market conditions.

One transplant that has finally taken hold and that may have started a new trend is the movie distributor's attempt to own and operate their own television networks, thereby bypassing the Big Three networks that have historically disadvantaged the studios in the market for regularly scheduled prime-time series. While conditions were unfavorable for new network entry for over thirty years, by the mid-1980s the economic hurdles in starting a network seemed somewhat less daunting.[29] This stimulated the Fox organization to take a chance in 1986 and then their success was followed in 1995 by Paramount and Warner Brothers on a smaller scale. Of course, the mega-merger between ABC and Disney may have set the course for further significant television involvement by the remaining major studios.

The Fox Network Saga

In the mid-1980s, the television networks were in dire financial straits.[30] Industry critics and financial analysts blamed the networks' problems on excessive costs, poor management techniques, and a failure to be innovative with new programming. Beginning in the mid-1980s, as the networks began to institute various cost controls, such as cutting their news staffs, they simultaneously were put into "play" since it was widely believed that their stock prices were undervalued relative to their earning potential. Shortly thereafter, each of them was acquired or reorganized in highly publicized multibillion dollar deals (NBC by General Electric, ABC by Capital Cities, and CBS by Lawrence Tisch) and new corporate managements installed. Each became a subsidiary of a giant U.S. media conglomerate. This corporate reorganization was also rationalized as a defense against unfriendly takeovers by foreign corporations—a strategy that turned out to be clairvoyant when Sony and Mashushita acquired major motion picture studios at the end of the decade and Rupert Murdoch (News Corporation) first purchased Twentieth-Century Fox and then the Metromedia Broadcast Group to act as a foundation for his proposed fourth television network.

Murdoch believed that a new network that was both innovative in its programming and cost-conscious could selectively compete for viewership against the bigger networks. Even in the face of new competition from cable and other services, Fox believed that the timing was right to establish a fourth network since the technological and regulatory handicaps that made network entry so risky before seemed to be lower due to the entrance of many new independent stations in the top 100 markets as potential affiliates and the newfound possibility of using cable outlets as well. Recognizing the hazards of full scale entry, Fox sought to first establish its presence in the weekend prime-time hours. Furthermore, Fox believed that viewers were ready for a more exciting kind of network programming that contrasted with the staleness and predictability of the traditional broadcast networks and was targeted to youth and young adults. The economics of networking seemed irresistible to both Fox and the independent stations; they could both improve their economic position through forming a network partnership.[31]

During its first several years, the audience for Fox programming continued to grow, and its survival was assured. By 1995, it had developed a consistent lineup of successful programs (*Married with Children, Star Trek, Melrose Place,* etc.) across seven nights of the week and established a very successful children's lineup as well. Even to this day, Fox still has not achieved ratings parity with the Big Three, leaving open the question of why Warner Brothers and Paramount would now enter into this crowded, fiercely competitive marketplace.[32] Industry speculation suggests that Paramount and Warners were positioning themselves for the possiblity of a friendly takeover by a giant media conglamerate anxious to have a strong foothold in all kinds of programming.

Understanding the harsh realities of establishing new networks, after six-month planning horizons, both Warner Brothers Television Network and United–Paramount debuted in mid-January 1995. Warner Brothers began with a single night of prime-time programming while Paramount had two nights. As expected, neither network had comparable affiliate clearances to the established networks. By September 1995, UPN had access to 88 percent of the nation's television households while Warner Brothers had only 81 percent. Warner achieved this clearance only after utilizing superstation, WGN, to enter some broadcast markets where no affiliates were available while Paramount was forced to accept secondary affiliation status in many markets, covering some 15 percent of the country, which means that the stations could position the programs in different slots than originally broadcast.[33]

The Paramount network was based around the *Star Trek* franchise program and consisted of hour-long dramatic fare targeted to males, while Warner Brothers utilized half-hour situation comedies to attract a predominantly "yuppie" demographic target. With the exception of *Star Trek,* none of the programs showed acceptable ratings during the abbreviated first season, most earning ratings in the 1 to 3 percent range, which is comparable to that of a basic cable network or an access hour syndicated show. For the next season, Paramount replaced all its shows save *Star Trek,* while Warner Brothers retained its shows, added a second night, and began planning for expansion into the children's market. With widespread losses their first two years of operation, unless their programming achieves acceptable ratings next year, the planned expansion of Paramount to a third night in 1996 may be torpedoed and the fate of these new netlets may be sealed.[34] In fact, during 1996, there were talks about a possible merger between the new networks to provide a stronger, more united, front in affiliates and programs to create a market niche that could be sustainable.

Syndication

The strength of the major studios in supplying prime-time entertainment programming to the networks over the last twenty years or so creates additional benefits in the television syndication industry. After passage of the Financial Interest and Syndication Rules in 1971, the subsidiary syndication rights for network series remained in the hands of the studios, each of which had syndication divisions. In addition to off-network rerun rights, the major studios also had a continuously expanding inventory of old and "classic" films that could be sold in packages to local television stations, cable superstations, and some family oriented "basic" cable networks like USA or The Family Channel.

Beginning in the 1970s, another type of syndicated programs began to catch fire, the first-run talk shows, game shows, and "info-tainment" type fare. These programs were more current than off-network reruns or old movies and they became quite popular during non-network hours of the broadcast day (e.g., mid-morning, late afternoon, and early fringe evening). To keep up with this trend, the movie studios began producing such first-run syndicated programming and, by the 1990s, they were dominating this segment of the syndication industry as well, eclipsed only by King World with its franchise of *Wheel of Fortune, Jeopardy,* and *Oprah Winfrey.*[35]

The prospects for continued studio domination of the syndication exhibition window are somewhat uncertain at the present. While the overall syndication industry continued to grow over the period of the 1980s, the most recent entry of the Warner Brothers and United–Paramount networks has somewhat contricted the open market for all kinds of syndication programming, since each hour of new network programming reduces the demand by these formerly independent stations for syndicated programming. Furthermore, the recent repeal of the Financial Interest and Syndication Rules suggests that the broadcast networks, now including Fox, Paramount, and Warner Brothers, will play a bigger role in off-network syndication in the future as they either produce more prime-time series in-house (the current trend) or they co-venture with independent program packages. Hence, the high and increasing market concentration in the syndication industry, and the market strength of the major movie studios, first noticed in the 1980s, may see some erosion over the next several years.

NOTES

[1]Price and and marginal revenue are coextensive in this context.

[2]For more detail on this point, see the pioneering article, David Waterman, "Pre-recorded Home Video and the Distribution of Theatrical Feature Films," in Eli Noam, ed., *Video Media Competition: Regulation, Economics, and Technology,* New York: Columbia University Press, 1985, Chapter 7.

[3]If the movie theaters were to vary their prices according to how long the film had been at a particular location, a certain group of patrons would undoubtedly pay premium prices to see highly publicized movies their premiere night or opening week.

[4]This is equivalent to maximizing a group of simultaneous demand equations for each exhibition window.

[5]Bruce M. Owen and Steven Wildman, *Video Economics,* Cambridge, MA: Harvard University Press, 1992, Chapter 2.

[6]Bruce Owen, Jack H. Beebe, and Willard G. Manning, *Television Economics,* Lexington, MA: Lexington Books, 1974, Chapter 2.

[7]This entire section comes largely from Barry R. Litman, "The Economics of the Television Market for Theatrical Movies," *Journal of Communications,* 29 (Autumn 1979): 20–33.

[8]Owen, Beebe, and Manning, op. cit.

[9]*Columbia Pictures v. ABC and CBS,* U.S. District Court, Southern District of New York, 1972; *U.S. v. CBS, NBC and ABC,* U.S. District Court, Central District of California, 1974.

[10]For more detail on these decrees, see FCC Network Inquiry Special Staff, *An Analysis of Television Program Production, Acquistion and Distribution,* Washington, DC: GPO, 1980, Chapter 8.

[11]Litman, op. cit.

[12]In fact, the DuMont network realized this economic fact in 1955 and exited from the scene, greatly fortifying ABC with whom it had been fighting for the limited number of affiliates. In 1986, with the greater viability of UHF signals transmitted by cable, Fox Broadcasting established itself as the fourth network, although it broadcasts only two nights per week.

[13]This section comes largely from Barry R. Litman and Suzannah Eun, "The Emerging Oligopoly of Pay TV in the USA," *Telecommunications Policy,* 5 (June 1981): 121–35.

[14]*Home Box Office, Inc. v. Federal Communications Commission,* 567 F. 2d 9 (D.C. Cir. 1977).

[15]A corollary market of advertiser-supported cable networks, such as USA, ESPN, CNN, and MTV, and several 'superstations' emerged and was packaged together by local cable systems and sold as "basic" cable service. The premium channels mentioned have always been sold separately (à la carte).

[16]*Variety,* April 30, 1980, p. 158.

[17]It also established a production unit for producing made-for-cable films, ironically called Premiere Films.

[18]*Wall Street Journal,* 10 June, 1983.

[19]Lawrence White, "Antitrust and Video Markets: The Merger of Showtime and The Movie Channel," in Noam, op. cit., Chapter 11. The post merger Hefindahl–Hirschman Index was approximately 4500 and the change in the index was 400 points.

[20]*Satellite Times,* September 7, 1988, p. 1.

[21]They sought to ban the import of VCRs into the U.S., permit only machines that had a playback (as opposed to a record) mode, and levy a copyright surcharge on all blank tapes sold.

[22]For an historical treatment of this issue see Heikki Hellman and Martti Soramaki, "Economic Concentration in Videocassette Industry: A Cultural Comparison," *Journal of Communication,* 35 (Summer 1985) 122–34.

[23]If one narrowly defined the market as theatrical videos, their control would be approximately equal to that of the theatrical movie market. However, just as movies on television must compete with other entertainment and information programming, so must videocassette recordings.

[24]*Videoweek,* January 1988, p.

[25]This section draws heavily on Thomas Guback, "Hollywood's International Market," in Balio, op. cit. (1985), Chapter 17.

[26]Mass media products possess the "non-rivalry in consumption" attribute of public goods. This means that one person (or one country's consumption of a movie or TV program) does not diminish the utility available for others to consume. On the other hand, with the exception of over-the-air broadcasting, a collection mechanism is available for excluding nonpayers, so the "exclusion" and "free rider" problems of public goods do not apply.

[27]Ibid.

[28]Ibid.

[29]Laurie Thomas and Barry Litman, "Fox Broadcasting Company, Why Now?" *Journal of Broadcasting and Electronic Media,* 35 (Spring 1991): 139–57.

[30]Ibid.

[31]Ibid.

[32]Larry Collette and Barry Litman, "The Strange Economics of New Broadcast Entry: The Case of United Paramount and Warner Brothers Networks," AEJMC Convention paper, Anaheim, CA: August 1996.

[33]Ibid.

[34]Ibid.

[35]Sylvia Chan–Olmstead, "A Structural Analysis of Market Competition in the U.S. Syndication Industry," *Journal of Media Economics,* 4 (Fall 1991): 9–28.

7

Merger Madness

BARRY LITMAN AND ANNE M. HOAG

The movies are bigger than ever. High tech and star-driven wonders like *Jurassic Park, The Lion King,* and *Batman Forever* drove the average cost of making a picture in the mid-1990s to more than 35 million dollars.[1] Add in the average cost of marketing a movie and the total bill grows to more than 50 million dollars,[2] more than double the costs of the typical mid-1980s movie.[3] The big pictures, of course, cost substantially more; the final bill for *Waterworld* exceeded $175 million.[4]

Though press accounts still cite box office receipts as the measure of a movie's success, studios count on a growing number of exhibition and retail windows, such as home video and premium cable, to repay their immense investments. In fact, without these outlets, few major Hollywood pictures would earn a dime. So vital are the secondary markets that the question becomes how important is that first window, the U.S. box office? Though theatrical exhibition is still the single biggest source of revenues for movies, it appears that the segment is losing power as a sales outlet for filmed entertainment. How have competitors in this segment responded to threats from other windows, from changing consumer habits, from producers and distributors?

In the last ten to fifteen years, a variety of investment and operating strategies have emerged in the theatrical exhibition segment. This has led to fundamental alterations in the structure and makeup of the segment. While several former segment leaders have faded from view, others survived and new competitors emerged. This chapter first describes the recent history and current state of the segment in the context of the larger market for filmed entertainment. It reports in case study form the individual competitive responses of theatrical exhibition leaders. Next, the relative success or failure of the leaders' approaches as well as overall theatrical segment investment and operating strategies are analyzed. The chapter concludes with a discussion of the major trends that will mark the future of the segment.

THE U.S. THEATRICAL EXHIBITION SEGMENT

On its face, the U.S. exhibition business seems prosperous. Indeed, a *Variety* report on the 1994 NATO ShoWest, called the industry's mood as "never better."[5] Since July, 1978 when *Star Wars* became the first movie to gross more than $10 million over a weekend, there have been more than 360 repeat occurrences of this feat, the number growing every year. The 1995 box office take was over 5.5 billion dollars,[6] the biggest ever. The number of screens in 1996 exceeded 26,600, an increase in outlets by almost 50 percent from fifteen years before.[7] Revenues and net income for most of the biggest chains have also grown in recent years.

All the major theater circuits publicly declare their optimism for the future of the business. Even outsiders and expert commentators seem confident. One entertainment attorney points out that studios reap $2.50 per theatrical customer but get much less, ten to sixty cents per viewer, from ancillary markets like videocassettes and pay television.[8] Sumner Redstone, who runs Viacom with subsidiaries Paramount and Blockbuster, says that he'll always be an exhibitor at heart.[9] Non-exhibitor Ted Turner has said that the information superhighway is "no threat to a well-run [motion picture theater] industry."[10] Maybe all the hype surrounding digital compression, video-on-demand, interactivity, and multimedia is not worrisome for exhibitors—the habit of "going to the movies" will continue to be the most important way Americans get their filmed entertainment.

Yet, in the midst of optimism, several interesting events are occurring that augur significant change for the historic theater industry. In 1995, for the first time ever, a major studio decided to bypass theatrical release altogether for a major motion picture.[11] Box office figures in dollars are impressive but actual attendance has been flat for the last decade (see Figure 7-1). In 1995, admissions topped 1.26 billion tickets, which was only 4 percent higher than ten years earlier.[12] By contrast, the importance of two other windows has grown astronomically. Figure 7-1 shows the now well-known but nevertheless dramatic rise of pay TV and VCR penetration. Since 1983, pay unit penetration has grown from a quarter of all television households (TVHH) to 45 percent. Even more dramatic has been the rise of the VCR. Since 1983, VCR penetration has grown more than seven times so that by the mid-1990s, it accounts for 77 percent of TVHH.

The market for "filmed entertainment" is comprised of box office, home video, and television. Figure 7-2 shows that total spending at the box office was steady throughout the 1980s and early 1990s. However, growth in total spending on television and home video so enlarged the total pie that the box office share had shrunk rather significantly. As Figure 7-3 shows, in 1983 the total market for filmed entertainment was $9.6 billion. Within ten years it tripled. However, in 1993 (Figure 7-4),

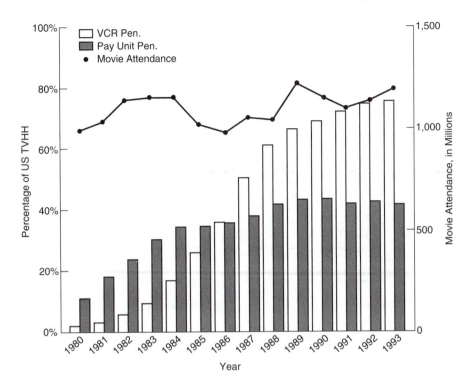

FIGURE 7-1 Growth in "Windows"—VCR and Pay Unit Penetration vs. Movie Attendance

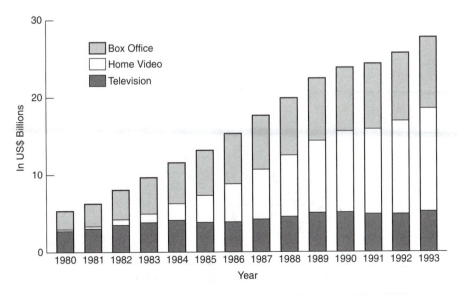

FIGURE 7-2 Total Spending on Filmed Entertainment 1980–1993

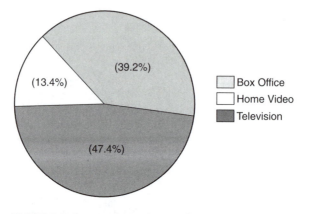

FIGURE 7-3   Market Shares for Filmed Entertainment, 1983—Total Pie: $9.607 Billion

the box office garnered only 18 percent of a $27.7 billion market, while in 1983 that share was a much larger 39 percent.

Increasingly, the theatrical segment is losing the power position as a sales outlet for filmed entertainment. How have competitors within the exhibition segment responded over the last several years? In the last ten years, a variety of investment and operating strategies have emerged. Former segment leaders went into decline or were driven out altogether, others survived, and new competitors emerged. Former top six chains, Plitt, Martin, and Commonwealth, all absorbed by competitors before the end of the 1980s, were replaced by newcomers Carmike, Cinemark, and

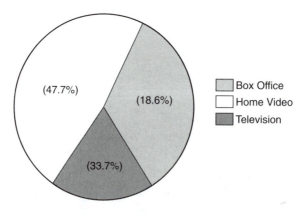

FIGURE 7-4   Market Shares for Filmed Entertainment, 1993—Total Pie: $27.71 Billion

Cineplex–Odeon. Still, the top three circuits of 1983, General Cinema, United Artists, and AMC, were among the six biggest more than ten years later. In a period that introduced so many changes to the competitive landscape for exhibition, the strategic responses of the top firms in the segment provide clues to the future of exhibition. In 1996, the top six theater chains ranked by number of U.S. screens were Carmike, United Artists, AMC, Cinemark, General Cinema, and Cineplex–Odeon. As the accompanying case studies of these companies document, the strategies of the 1980s have given way to new approaches.

STRATEGIC RESPONSES TO EMERGING COMPETITION

In terms of operating strategies, various firms within the segment have attempted to become more efficient and raise revenues with such strategies as multiplexing, clustering locations geographically, installing centralized computer systems to improve management control, implementing marketing and service innovations, and developing non-motion picture revenue streams.

While the formulas for improving operations have remained fairly consistent across the segment throughout the 1980s and 1990s, the investment strategies have not. As Guback[13] and others have identified, through the mid-1980s, concentration, vertical integration, and diversification were the major trends. However, in the second half of the decade, these strategies were abandoned. By the early 1990s all three showed themselves as weak in their ability to provide adequate returns for parent companies or to improve market power.

CONCENTRATION

From 1983 until 1988, change in concentration in the segment was rapid. As Figure 7-5 shows, concentration, expressed as ratios of the top four and top eight operators, increased from less than a fifth of all U.S. screens to almost a third for the top four and from about 25 percent to over 40 percent for the top eight. Outright growth in the number of screens the top eight circuits controlled grew considerably as the total number of U.S. screens grew almost 23 percent in just five years.

A degree of concentration may lead to improved operating efficiencies, but it is a poor strategy for countervailing the bargaining power of distributors. The Paramount decrees require distributors to make deals on a theater-by-theater and market-by-market basis. In addition, market "splits" have been declared illegal and have proven in practice to be ineffective. This means a small chain that may have a significant presence in one market, like Marcus in Milwaukee (198 screens in Wisconsin and Illinois in 1995), actually has as much bilateral market power as the second biggest circuit, United Artists Theatres Circuit (UATC) (2,295 screens in twenty-

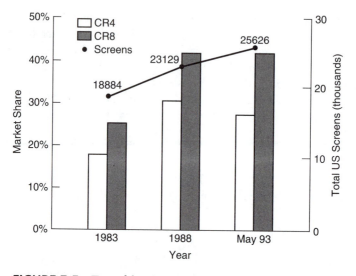

FIGURE 7-5   Trend in Concentration 1983–1993: CR4 and CR8

nine states in 1995), which may operate in the biggest markets, including New York and Los Angeles, but dominates few.

It was no surprise then to find that national concentration declined in the second half of the last decade. Between 1988 and 1993, concentration among the top four dropped below 27 percent and for the top eight, it remained flat (see Figure 7-5). The growth trend in the number of screens of some of the biggest circuits has also turned downward or leveled off. General Cinemas, AMC, Cineplex–Odeon, and UATC have pruned theaters from their all-time highs in the late 1980s and now operate fewer screens.[14] Some analysts envisioned the return of concentration when, in 1995, Cineplex–Odeon and Cinemark announced they would merge to form the largest exhibitor in the world.[15] However, the deal unraveled within a few weeks and no similar deals have since emerged, for the same reasons the strategy was abandoned in the late 1980s.

VERTICAL INTEGRATION

The second trend of the 1980s, vertical integration with producer/distributors, also ran its course. Several studios invested in exhibition in the 1980s. Table 7-1 shows six of the bigger acquisitions.

In Guback's view,[21] the studios believed that integrating forward would allow them to control ticket prices, guarantee outlets for their movies, and improve returns

TABLE 7-1   Vertical Mergers

Year	Circuit	Acquiring Parent
1988	USA Cinemas	TriStar/Columbia
1987	Loews	TriStar/Columbia[16]
1987	Cinamerica (Mann)[18]	Warner Communications & Paramount[17]
1986	Cineplex–Odeon	MCA (49.7% stake)[19]
1986	Famous Players	Paramount
1986	Commonwealth	The Cannon Group[20]

on production investments by keeping all the money from the box office, not just the studio's split, around 50 percent.[22] The flurry of theater buying may also have been driven by a rise in film supply (see Figure 7-6) and the studios' move into exhibition was an attempt to weaken exhibitors' negotiating position. At the same time, however, screen expansion was rapid (see Figure 7-5) so fears of a buyers' market for movies seemed unfounded.

Indeed, in the five years following this buying frenzy, forward integration fell out of fashion. Cannon divested two years after buying. For four vertical relationships that continue, there seem to be limited strategic benefits for the parents. No chain ever had enough screens or geographic coverage to provide guaranteed distribution. There continued to be a glut of screens and plenty of distribution opportunity. Furthermore, the potential to run afoul of the Paramount decision may have been a disincentive to grow: When Barry Diller was head of Twentieth-Century Fox he remarked, "Who wants to be in a business where, if you enhance your leverage, you have to worry that someone will sue you?" An astute if not obvious analysis of the trend was offered by Sumner Redstone, "I think it's irrational ego."[23]

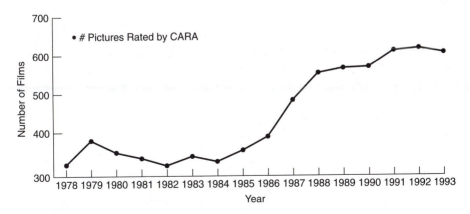

FIGURE 7-6   Motion Picture Supply 1978–1993

With the possible exception of Sony's theaters, whose top managers are unusually customer-oriented and innovative, the vertically integrated exhibition chains have suffered from benign neglect rather than benefiting from the initial promise of strategic synergies. For example, four vertically integrated chains have either shrunk or remained about the same size, shown in Table 7-2.

Financial data that isolates theater operations for all but Cineplex–Odeon are unavailable so it is hard to say whether these chains at least returned adequate profits. In the case of Cineplex–Odeon, the company lost money continuously until 1993, when it finally turned in its first quarterly profit since restructuring in 1990 (see case study).

In the mid-1990s Hollywood studios were still interested in vertical relationships but they ignored exhibition to pursue other windows vigorously. All major and most minor studios are part of some vertical chain involving home video, broadcasting networks, and/or stations such as Viacom, with its ownership of Paramount and Blockbuster, and Disney, which now owns the TV stations and broadcast network of Capital Cities/ABC. Others put more stock in cable networks or MSOs such as Time Warner, which now controls Turner's networks and Castle Rock as well as its own studio, cable networks, and cable systems. Finally, at least one major studio, Columbia, is integrated with an electronics manufacturer, Sony.[25]

The newest, hottest vertical combination is with telephone companies. Even before the passage of the 1996 Telecommunications Act, which permits telephone companies to enter the content business freely, three such relationships had been established: MCI Communications and News Corp.; BellSouth, SBC Communications, Ameritech, and Disney; US West and Time Warner. Meanwhile, Bell Atlantic, Nynex, and Pacific Telesis had pooled $300 million and were looking to acquire programming for their interactive TV systems.[26]

DIVERSIFICATION

Finally, the effort some chains undertook to diversify themselves didn't last either. Not because it did not make sense, however. It appears that in two cases, United Artists and General Cinemas, the sister businesses dumped the chains as nonstrate-

TABLE 7-2   Diversified Holdings

Chain	1988	1994	Change
Loews (Sony)	822	904	+ 82
Cinamerica(Mann)	456	341	−115
Cineplex–Odeon[24]	1272 [1832]	1055 [1630]	−217 [−202]
Famous Players	448	461	+ 13

gic. By 1989, United Artists Entertainment (UAE), parent to the theater circuit, had become not only the biggest theater circuit but also the third largest cable multiple system operator (MSO) in the United States. In the preceding months UAE had acquired hundreds of screens and merged with two other top MSOs. However, this acquisitive behavior, over just a few months, created significant debt. This was one of the reasons Tele-Communications, Inc., (TCI), the nation's largest MSO, which owned more than 50 percent of UAE, took over the company in 1991. Immediately following the merger, TCI spun off the theater circuit. UATC today, is once again a single line business.

General Cinema, the biggest chain in the early 1980s, diversified into retailing, insurance, and publishing, and changed its name to Harcourt General to reflect the new emphasis. It then spun off the theaters in 1993. This single line of business chain is now called GC Companies.

CONCLUSION

The three major exhibition strategies of the mid-1980s, concentration, vertical integration, and diversification, have been practically abandoned. So is anyone interested in investing in exhibition anymore? Well, yes, exhibition chains themselves are closing ranks and making the best of it. New rivals in the exhibition segment have emerged. The two fastest growing, most efficient, and perhaps most profitable circuits of the last decade, Carmike and Cinemark, practically didn't exist ten years ago. They engage almost exclusively in theatrical exhibition. They don't draw attention with flamboyant gimmicks or make splashy deals. But they do attract the attention of investors and analysts with low-glamour, common sense investment and operating strategies that have made them profitable.

The marketplace for filmed entertainment had certainly changed dramatically from the 1980s to the 1990s. The first half of the 1980s saw the rise of strategies like concentration, vertical integration, and diversification as responses to the emergence of competing windows and an increase in both screens and product supply. However, just as rapidly as these trends emerged, they seem to have gone into decline. They didn't work as a means of increasing market power vis à vis distributors or to improve performance in terms of market share or profits. Through the mid-1990s, new competitors and old rivals in the exhibition segment have concentrated on getting "back to basics." The big veteran companies have retrenched, shedding nonstrategic screens and other assets or getting spun off themselves so that they now are primarily dedicated to exhibition. The newer arrivals were dedicated to their core business, exhibition, from the start. Exhibition has thus become an industry of "specialists" dedicated to fine tuning and reviving the moviegoing experience, responding to demographic shifts and building more and more efficiently run theaters.

By the mid-1990s, the top six chains were enjoying a recovery from lean profits or, for some like Cineplex–Odeon and United Artists, a string of annual losses. The entire segment's performance has always hinged to a very large degree on the quality of Hollywood product. Still, exhibitors were managing revenues and costs to the extent that they had control, and between 1990 and 1995 revenue and net income per screen rose, on average, 17 percent and 109 percent respectively. Cineplex–Odeon and United Artists had begun to shore up losses. If concentrating on one single line of business is the future of exhibition, what will be the result for the bigger markets for filmed entertainment? By 1994, another expansion in screens was underway after stagnant growth in the preceding years.[27] In 1995, there was a net increase of 4 percent in U.S. screens, the biggest one-year spurt since 1987, moving total outlets to an all-time high. The idea is to serve smaller niche audiences with efficiently run, strategically located multiplexes. Perhaps these exhibition specialists will be the future and salvation of the exhibition window and theaters will indeed remain the first and most important outlet and launching pad for filmed entertainment in the United States.

CASE STUDIES

Carmike Cinemas

In 1996, Carmike surpassed United Artists to become the largest exhibitor in the United States, a noteworthy feat considering the company barely existed a dozen

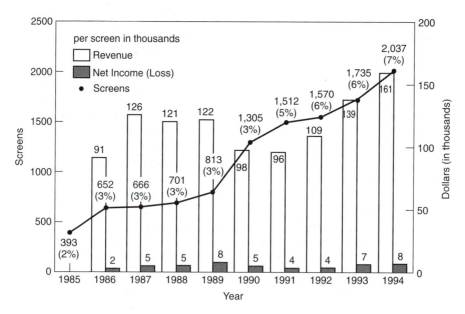

FIGURE 7-7   Carmike Cinemas 1985–1994

years before. The chain was born in 1982 when Carl Patrick, Sr. bought the Martin Theater Chain of Georgia. He renamed it for his two sons, Carl, Jr., and Mike, who now serves as Carmike's president.[28]Though now a public company, the firm retains a family-run flavor, a characteristic that contributes to its success. Initially, the company expanded only in Southern markets, coming to dominate that region—and then primarily only in small and medium-sized markets in which it could maintain a monopoly or clearly dominant position.[29] By the time the company went public in 1986, it had more than doubled the number of screens it operated to more than 650. By the end of the 1980s, Carmike had expanded to over 800 screens, garnering a 4 percent share of the entire market for exhibition in the United States. Throughout the 1980s and into the mid-1990s, Carmike's rapid expansion represented a contrast to other major circuits that were divesting and shrinking in size. In addition to a comparatively aggressive expansion-through-construction plan (300 new screens built between 1982 and 1994), Carmike made purchases of one or a few locations from almost every major circuit; it sometimes bought out entire chains. Since 1982, it has acquired more than 1,600 screens often through major purchases,[30] shown in Table 7-3.

By the 1990s, however, Carmike found that it had exploited much of the opportunity to become the monopoly operator in small and medium-sized Southern markets. It then began to enter bigger markets in which it would be a competitor, aggressively acquiring theaters in the Northeast, Midwest, and West. It also experimented with strategies such as new multiplexes built specifically for second-run.

By 1996, Carmike had become the largest exhibitor with a market share of 8 percent operating 2,367 screens[31] in over thirty states, mostly in the Southeast, Midwest, and West. Sticking to the business it knows, Carmike has shown no interest in nonexhibition diversification or in expanding beyond U.S. markets.

In addition to maintaining an aggressive expansion strategy, Carmike crafts its operating strategies carefully. Keeping ticket prices low, controlling costs and con-

TABLE 7-3

1982	All 265 screens of Martin Theatres, Inc.
1983	All 85 screens of Video Independent Theatres, Inc.
1986	All 209 screens of Essantee Theatres, Inc.
1989	All 116 screens of Consolidated Theatres, Inc.
1990	137 screens from United Artists and Plitt (Cineplex–Odeon, parent)
1991	45 screens from AMC
1992	150 screens from Plitt (Cineplex–Odeon), AMC, and Cinamerica Theatres
1993	All 355 screens of Westwynn Theatres, Inc., of which Carmike had been a part-owner
	All 80 screens of Manos Enterprises
1994	All 176 screens of Cinema World
	48 screens from General Cinema

stantly improving performance are important management goals. Carmike's average ticket price ($3.76 in 1991) was significantly below the national average ($4.75 in 1991). Despite its rapid rate of growth, Carmike's overhead has remained low, at 4 percent of revenue in 1990. Carmike has become expert at controlling construction costs, spending a fraction of what other chains do on construction. This has helped the firm keep capital and borrowing requirements lower, and consequently its total long-term debt is lower, around 144 million dollars in 1994.[32] Before other major chains adopted the innovation, in 1982 Carmike invested in computerizing operations, which permits quick response to ticket and concession sales data.

Attention to these revenue and expense areas has paid off. While revenue per screen is far lower than that of any other top chain, it has been improving in the last few years. In 1994, revenue per screen averaged about $160,000, a 65 percent improvement over the 1990 figure of about $98,000. Carmike may well be the segment's low-cost exhibitor. In 1989 Carmike's "efficiency" ranked higher than any other major chain, a 25 percent cash flow-to-revenue ratio, versus 16 percent for United Artists, 15 percent for GC Companies, 14 percent for AMC, and 9 percent for Cineplex–Odeon.[33]

That efficiency has paved the way for steady and strong performance in earnings. Between 1986 and 1994, Carmike was the only one of the top six chains to keep a positive net income in every year, averaging over $5,000 per screen per year. In the industry recession year of 1990, it was the only top six chain to have a positive net income. Though competitors have performed better in single years, Carmike has the best overall income performance for the last ten years. The twin sets of strategies—for expansion and operating—have produced a financial performance record no other major operator in exhibition can match.

United Artists Theatre Circuit

United Artists Theatre Circuit (UATC) became the largest circuit in the United States in 1985 and retained that distinction for ten years. Of the top American circuits, it is arguably the oldest: UATC calls itself the descendent company of the original United Artists founded in 1926 by Mary Pickford, Douglas Fairbanks, Sam Goldwyn, and Joe Schenck.[34] In the early 1960s it began investing in a new potential exhibition window, cable television. By the late 1980s, it was both the biggest exhibitor and one of the top five cable operators in the United States. However, its cable holdings were clearly the driving force for the company and made it an attractive acquisition for Tele-Communications, Inc. (TCI), the leading cable system operator in the United States. In 1991, TCI acquired the remaining stock it did not already own, then immediately spun off the theatre circuit to former executives of United Artists Entertainment Company (UAE) and other investors.

Before it was spun off, the theatre circuit had been very acquisitive. In 1988 alone, it acquired more than 400 screens in its purchase of the Commonwealth chain.[35] Between the time UATC became the biggest U.S. exhibitor and the time of

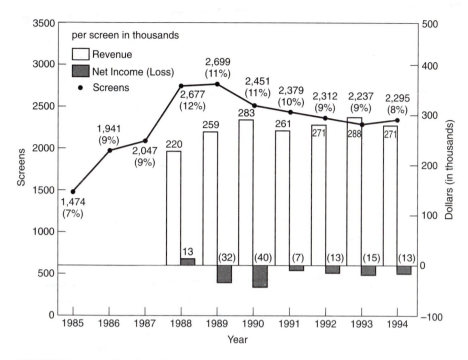

FIGURE 7-8   United Artists 1985–1994

the spin-off, it had expanded by a net of more than 800 screens. The chain grew to its biggest in 1989 when it operated nearly 2,700 screens and held a 12 percent market share. Post-spin-off, UATC adopted a simple operating strategy: prune for efficiency. In 1993, it announced plans to close or sell 17 percent of its screens and has since increased the ratio of screens per location by remodeling, building, or acquiring more multiplexes and disposing of unprofitable single- and twin-screen sites as well as those that did not fit into established geographic "clusters." The firm worked to lower overhead in a variety of ways, such as consolidating management offices and cutting jobs.[36]

The new United Artists is strictly an exhibitor with 100 percent of revenues derived from admissions, concessions, lobby videogames, and some "mall entertainment" game centers adjacent to theaters. Almost all locations are multiscreen, some in freestanding structures, but many are anchor tenants in malls. While many properties are owned, most are leased. It operates in 29 of the top 50 U.S. markets and several smaller U.S. markets where it is a monopoly or dominant exhibitor. Until recently, its operation has almost exclusively been limited to domestic theaters, running just twenty-four screens outside the U.S. In 1994 however, UATC announced it would focus on international expansion, opening theaters in Mexico.[37]

Though cost containment and efficiency are major objectives, UATC continues to act on opportunities to improve its sales. In 1994, the company announced a $250 million expansion to add 900 screens in major metropolitan markets. It built ninety-four new screens and shed over thirty in that year alone. This move is part of an industry-wide wave of expansion. Though many analysts see the United States as over-screened and expansion rates did decline in the late 1980s, there was a surge in 1994 of 4 percent, the biggest one-year gain since 1987.[38]

The chain began experimenting with innovations to offer a more exciting entertainment experience. For example, UATC planned to fit theaters with motion simulation seats[39] and entered the "mall entertainment" business when it opened Starport, a giant, glittery videogame center adjacent to a multiplex in a mall.[40] UATC developed other uses for its theaters at low traffic times, for example, by renting theaters to training companies for seminars. However, the core line of business continues to be exhibition; theaters are never turned over completely to these new revenue streams.

The resulting financial performance indicators are mixed. While revenue per screen increased from $220,000 in 1988 to $271,000 in 1994, the 23 percent growth is the lowest of the top six chains. Net income, or rather loss, per screen hovered between minus 13,000 to 15,000 dollars for the three years ending 1994. However, this is an improvement over 1990 when the chain suffered losses of over $40,000 per screen. One of the major causes of the continued net losses was the cost of servicing a heavy debt burden of over $300 million carried each year since at least 1990. While all of the top six chains have financed expansion with debt, at times UATC's debt exceeded 85 percent of total assets and equity by six-to-one, a risky ratio in an industry where cash flow is customarily low.

United Artists' rapid ascent to top exhibitor in the United States has been quite uneven, to say the least. The chain has not reaped significant benefit from efficiencies associated with its size or clustering strategy. Efforts to improve revenues through innovation have fallen flat. Finally, the spun-off UATC has not yet profited from becoming a single line of business of exhibition, contrary to some of its exhibition-only competitors.

AMC Entertainment

The roots of today's AMC Entertainment are in the Durwood family-owned circuit begun in the 1920s with screens in Kansas and Missouri.[41] The firm experienced tremendous growth in screens throughout the 1980s, expanding 200 percent, from 537 in 1980 to 1,614 in 1990. Unlike competitors who were either expanding or shrinking in size, AMC halted and maintained a steady screen count around 1,600 for the next several years. Into the mid-1990s, AMC continued to pare down non-strategic screens, acquire others, and build new multiplexes, all with a relatively conservative plan compared to several other competitors. AMC clusters its theaters geographically and has a significant market presence in major markets, including

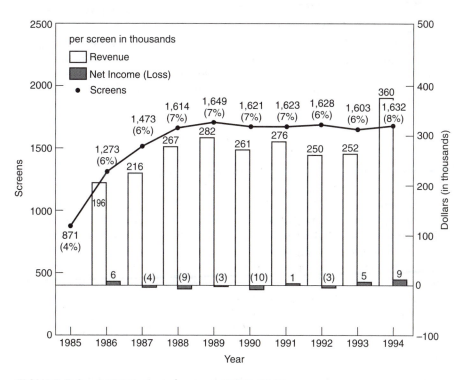

FIGURE 7-9   AMC Entertainment 1985–1994

149 screens in Los Angeles, 142 in Philadelphia, 95 in Detroit, 94 in Miami, 87 in Washington, D.C., 85 in Houston, 75 in Dallas, and 56 in Orlando.[42] It also is a major competitor in medium-sized markets such as Denver (63 screens), St. Louis (47), Kansas City (62), and Tampa (94). There are no small markets with AMC theaters and none with fewer than eight AMC screens.

The operating philosophy of the chain, according to Stanley Durwood, has stressed decentralization,[43] fostering an environment in which local managers are encouraged to assess and respond to local tastes. Moreover, even greater emphasis has been focused on cost containment, both at the theater level in general and administrative overhead. For example, in 1992, field operations were consolidated and one field office eliminated.[44] At the theater level, the company reported that it exceeded its goal of reducing the cost of serving patrons by five percent.[45]

AMC has also experimented broadly with strategies to build brand loyalty by focusing on customer service and concessions. It runs the segment's biggest "frequent guest" program, "Movie Watcher," which awards points toward special screenings, concessions, and prizes to patrons.[46] Like other circuits, AMC focuses on customer convenience, offering advance telephone ticket sales and self-serve credit card box offices. With their motto, "There is a difference," AMC was the first circuit to announce it would outfit all of its screens with digital sound technology.[47]

Despite efforts to improve sales and control costs, financial performance began to pay off only in recent years. From 1987 until 1990, AMC reported consistent losses in the range of 5 million to 16 million dollars each year. Company analysts were quick to note that financial success as well as failure are tied to the uncontrollable quality of films, yet this is true for the entire business and other exhibitors were profitable in those years. Like United Artists, Cineplex–Odeon, and other exhibitors, debt financing in the 1980s became costly. Between 1986 and 1988, long-term debt ballooned from 122 million dollars to over 350 million dollars. It was reduced significantly in 1989 and held steady around 250 million dollars through the mid-1990s. As a percentage of assets, it was still high in 1995, 53 percent. Still, by reining in debt, and with other management controls, net income rose dramatically by 1995 to almost 27 million dollars. This was AMC's third consecutive profitable year and evidence of a sustained turnaround.

The company reports that it plans to continue careful expansion, growth in box office and concession receipts, and is exploring international expansion—a strategy it tested and abandoned in the 1980s. AMC has no plans to diversify into non-exhibition lines of business.

Cinemark USA

In 1995, Cinemark, the fourth largest U.S. exhibitor, announced that it would merge with Cineplex–Odeon, then the sixth biggest, to form the largest U.S. exhibitor. This plan was scuttled within a few weeks because of complications caused by Seagram Company's subsequent takeover of MCA.[48] Despite the speculation that this kind of mega-chain would be the trend for the future as a way for exhibitors to gain market power vis à vis distributors,[49] no similar deals have subsequently emerged.

Before Cinemark attempted this mega-merger, the firm had already acquired a reputation for rapid expansion. It was established in 1985 by Lee Roy Mitchell, an exhibition segment veteran.[50] Within ten years, Cinemark grew faster than any other major circuit, doubling its size times and becoming the fifth largest exhibitor in the United States with over 1,200 screens. Cinemark began by selectively acquiring screens in the West, first in Utah, then more in California and Oregon. Through two separate multiple screen purchases, another cluster was assembled in Texas. By the early 1990s, Cinemark was also building new screens and, by 1992, it was operating 965 screens in 26 states. The biggest growth spurt took place between 1989 and 1991 when the firm grew by more than 60 percent in screens. In 1995, the company operated in three geographic clusters, a group of screens in the north, the "Southern" unit, primarily in Texas, and the East Coast unit. Approximately 60 percent are first-run screens; none are drive-ins.

Mitchell continues to look for expansion opportunities, concentrating on both first-run and dollar-house sub-run theaters in mid-size markets with little existing

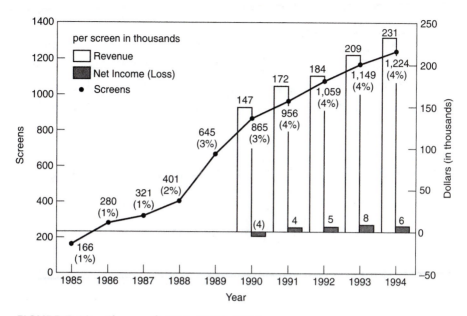

FIGURE 7-10 Cinemark USA 1985–1994

competition.[51] Since opportunities to buy and build screens in these categories are thinning, Cinemark has begun to expand internationally with operations in Mexico and Chile. In addition to the exhibition business, Cinemark's holding company, Cinemark USA, also has small investments in a pizza restaurant chain and a video rental chain, yet one cannot categorize this company by any means as a major conglomerate. Aside from this, Cinemark has no plans to diversify into other lines of business as Mitchell remains optimistic about the future of the theater business.

The financial performance of Cinemark theaters is better than most of the big exhibitors. Revenues per screen are somewhat below average at around $230,000 in 1994, rebounding with positive momentum by 50 percent between 1990 and 1994; this should continue into the future. Cinemark uses debt to finance construction and acquisition and was carrying $180 million in long-term debt in 1994, a remarkable 66 to 1 debt to equity ratio. Despite the burden of servicing this debt, Cinemark's net income per screen ranks among the best, between $4,000 and $8,000. The fact that Cinemark has handed in a consistently positive net income says a great deal for their management skill and business acumen in an arena in which several leaders reported net losses for several years in the 1980s and 1990s.

GC Companies (Harcourt General, General Cinema)

Of all major U.S. exhibitors in the 1980s and 1990s, none has experimented with the concept of diversification more literally and dramatically than General Cinema. But

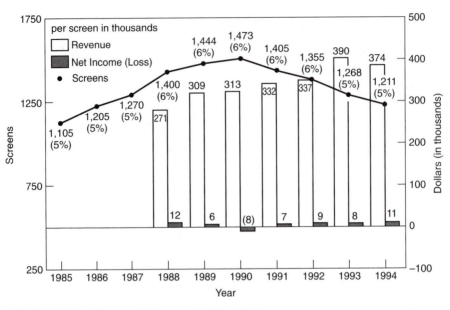

FIGURE 7-11 **General Cinema 1985–1994**

then, General Cinema has maintained a tradition and reputation for pioneer-risk taking. It opened the first drive-in in 1938 and one of the first indoor shopping center theaters in 1951.[52] By 1983, the theater division was the biggest in the United States, operating over 1,000 screens, 5 percent of the U.S. market. Throughout the 1980s, the company followed a conservative strategy of maintenance of market share through internal growth via construction. By 1995, GC's share was slightly lower, around 4.5 percent, though the number of screens it operated had declined 14 percent from the all-time high of 1,473 in 1991. Its most prominent management strategy was to operate greater numbers of multiplexes and stick to the largest twenty-five or thirty U.S. markets where high ticket prices ensure higher revenues per screen. However, most of these are the overbuilt and undoubtedly more competitive markets where no exhibitor can generate the kind of market power that firms like Carmike enjoy in small markets. Making calculated moves, unlike several other major chains, General Cinema managed to avoid both rapid growth with the attendant high costs as well as emergency downsizing and retrenching and its host of losses. The company continues to innovate through such practices as selling advance tickets through Ticketmaster, accepting Mastercard, and offering Taco Bell Express.

The willingness to experiment and take risks spilled over into other endeavors. Rather than focus on exhibition or invest in movie-related diversification like its competitors, GC diversified into other consumer markets. During the 1980s it operated in soft drink bottling, retailing, and insurance. GC owned a Pepsi bottling com-

TABLE 7-4

	% Revenues	% Net Income (not including corporate expenses)
Publishing	27 percent	61 percent
Specialty Retailing	48 percent	34 percent
Insurance	13 percent	18 percent
Theater	12 percent	5 percent

pany that it sold in 1989 for $1.77 billion. The proceeds from this sale enabled GC to acquire the major publisher, Harcourt, Brace and Jovanovich in 1991.[53] In March 1993, the company changed its name to Harcourt General and defined its portfolio of businesses in four categories: publishing, specialty retailing (including 65 percent of The Nieman Marcus Group), insurance, and theater. In the 1992 annual report and 10-K,[54] theater revenues and net income represented only a small fraction of overall revenues and income, shown in Table 7-4.

It was not surprising therefore, that the decision was made to spin off the theaters from the $3 billion-a-year company. In December 1993, GC Companies was created and received an infusion of $65 million in cash from Harcourt General for further upgrade and expansion.[55]

The financial performance of the theater chain both before and after the spin-off was relatively healthy, even if the profits of the giant parent experienced greater fluctuations. GC boasted the highest revenue per screen in the mid-1990s, over $370,000, nearly a 40 percent improvement over six years before. While many chains were suffering annual net losses, GC managed to turn in respectable net income figures of between $7,000 and $11,000 per screen in the early 1990s. Now that GC is again an exhibition-only business, it plans to stick to exhibition.

Cineplex-Odeon

More than any other major theater chain, the 1980s and 1990s rise and fall and rise again of Cineplex–Odeon plays like one of the dramas on its screens. Under the command of a flamboyant visionary, Garth Dabrinsky, the chain started small in Canada in 1979. It grew quickly, expanding both vertically and horizontally to own the fourth largest number of U.S. screens by 1990. It diversified into glamorous nonexhibition businesses, borrowed extravagantly to feed its growth, then subsequently crashed under the heavy load—all in ten years. The firm's initial strategy was to change Canadian theater-going with the multiplex concept. After acquiring one of its two major competitors, the 297-screen Odeon Theaters in 1984 (Famous Players being the other), the company ventured south of the border and began an aggressive acquisition campaign in major American markets,[56] shown in Table 7-5.

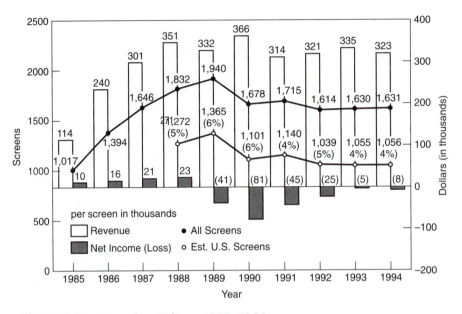

FIGURE 7-12   Cineplex Odeon 1985–1994

In three short years, the chain had become the second largest exhibitor in North America. Additionally, Cineplex–Odeon began to expand internationally, taking on a major position in UK exhibition.

While one of its major exhibition strategies was to stake out as many North American major markets as possible, the second objective was to change the fundamental moviegoing experience to attract an older audience willing to buy higher-priced tickets. Drabinsky spent lavishly to renovate formerly drab theaters. By 1988, Cineplex would spend $2.75 million to build a location, a full million dollars more than the industry average.[57] The renovations included marble floors, wall-to-wall carpets, Dolby and THX sound, and plush seats. The theaters were kept clean; personnel were trained in "Canadian politeness." Concessions were overhauled—real

TABLE 7-5

Year	Chain	# Screens	Purchase Price	Major Markets
1985	Plitt	574	$65 million	Chicago, S.E.US
1986	Septum	48	$7.5 million	Southeast US
	Essaness	41	$14.4 million	Chicago
1987	Neighborhood	80	$21 million	Wash., DC
	SRO	106	$45.5 million	Seattle
	RKO–Century– Warner	97	$179 million	New York
	Walter Reade	11	$32 million	Manhattan

butter on the popcorn, cappuccino, carrot cake, and pizza. All this cost dearly—the annual cost of butter alone added $2 million to annual expenses.[58]

At the same time the chain was expanding horizontally, it became the first in decades to branch out vertically into a wide variety of other movie and entertainment businesses. In 1986, it accepted investment from producer–distributor MCA, which eventually took a 49 percent ownership stake.[59] It controlled a vast real estate empire and owned the largest film lab/postproduction facility outside of Hollywood. Cineplex–Odeon backed a variety of movie productions and made high-profile production deals with industry names like Oliver Stone, Paul Newman, and Robert Redford. It ventured into non-motion picture entertainment, such as live theater, where it spent millions to renovate theaters and back the Canadian production of *Phantom of the Opera,* and invested $85 million in the Universal Studios theme park in Florida.

By 1988, long-term debt had risen to a staggering total of US$685 million. Despite revenues of US$644 million that year, there was a net loss of almost US$80 million. Despite the kudos that Drabinsky earned for single-handedly revitalizing the segment, the firm's two major investors, the Bronfman family and MCA, were not happy. The Bronfman family had invested $20 million in 1982 then boosted its stake further, to 15 percent, in 1988 to support Drabinsky's vision of further expansion and theater luxury.[60] In 1989, doubts emerged about Cineplex–Odeon's aggressive financial reporting and the firm's actual financial health.[61] Dabrinsky attempted to gain control of the firm, failed,[62] and was forced out by the end of the year.

Cineplex–Odeon's new managers immediately set to work to bring costs and assets under control. They sold nonexhibition related enterprises and unprofitable screens and made huge cost cuts, eliminating the corporate jet, limousines, hundreds of jobs, even the symbolic popcorn butter.[63] However losses, attributable in part to the crushing debt, continued to mount after restructuring,[64] as shown in Table 7-6. After receiving $100 million from MCA and Bronfman in 1991,[65] performance began to improve, lenders eased repayment deadlines and some debt was converted to equity.

By 1995, Cineplex–Odeon had shown itself to be a survivor and reported profits in some quarters. In operating its significantly smaller chain of theaters, it developed a decentralized management approach that encouraged local managers to craft strategies that would appeal to local tastes.[66] For example, where the demographics skew

TABLE 7-6

Year	Net Losses in US$millions
1990	135
1991	80
1992	41
1993	7
1994	14

to senior citizens, there are more matinees. Like other top exhibitors, Cineplex–Odeon experimented with service innovations. It introduced the convenience of telephone ticketing,[67] air-popped popcorn for calorie-conscious patrons,[68] and "Operation Popcorn," computerized self-serve concessions.[69]

By the time the planned 1995 merger with Cinemark dissolved, when Bronfman acquired Cineplex–Odeon's other major stockholder, MCA, the number six U.S. exhibitor planned to pursue expansion once again. In 1995, it announced plans for an $11 million 16-screen multiplex at Universal Studios theme park in Florida. However, Cineplex–Odeon sees dwindling North American opportunities and has its sights set on international exhibition.[70]

FIGURE REFERENCES

AMC Entertainment Inc. (1993). *1992 Annual Report.* Kansas City: Author.

AMC Entertainment Inc. (1992). *Third Quarter Report.* Kansas City: Author.

Carmike Cinemas, Inc. (1995). *The 1994 Annual Report.* Columbus, GA: Author.

Cinemark, USA, Inc. (1995). *Form 10-K Annual Report, 1994.* Dallas: Author.

Cineplex–Odeon Corporation. *Annual Report,* 1991, 1992, 1993. Toronto: Author.

Harcourt General (1993). *1992 Annual Report.* Needham, MA: Author.

Litman, B. (1993). "The Motion Picture Entertainment Industry." In *The Structure of American Industry,* pp. 183–216.

Litman, B. (1989). Statement of Barry R. Litman, Professor of Telecommunication, Michigan State University before U.S. Senate Subcommittee.

Magiera, M. (1991, March 4). "Movie chains test brand-building," *Variety,* p. 43.

Motion Picture Association of America, various statistics.

National Association of Theater Owners. *Encyclopedia of Exhibition:* 1989, 1990, 1991–92, 1992–93, 1993–94, 1994–95, 1995–96. North Hollywood: Author.

Standard & Poors. *Industry Surveys.* Various issues, 1988–1995.

Swort, E. General Cinema. *ValueLine,* various reports 1991–1993.

Tele-Communications, Inc. (1992). *Annual Report, 1991.* Denver: Author.

United Artists Entertainment Company (1990). *Annual Report, 1989.* Denver: Author.

United Artists Theatre Circuit, Inc. *Form 10-K Annual Report: 1992, 1993, 1994.* Denver: Author.

Veronis, Suhler & Associates (1994). *The Communications Industry Report, 1989–1993.*

Worldscope/Disclosure Partners (1995). *Company Profiles: Cineplex–Odeon Corporation; Carmike Cinemas, Inc.; AMC Entertainment, Inc.; Harcourt General, Inc.* [CD-ROM Database]. Bridgeport, CT: WDP.

NOTES

[1]Wood, D. (1996, January 3). "Movie Industry Likely to Go on Diet," *Christian Science Monitor,* p. 4.

[2]Shapiro, E. & King. T. (1995, December 21). "Lights! Camera! Checkbooks!" *Wall Street Journal,* pp. B1, B8.

[3]Motion Picture Association of America, various statistics.

[4]Wood, D. (1996, January 3). "Movie Industry Likely to Go on Diet," *Christian Science Monitor,* p. 4.

[5]Klady, L. (1994, March 14). "The Dicey Game of Exhibition," *Variety,* pp. 7–8.

[6]Bannon, L. (1995, December 29). "At the Movies: Revenue Is Up, Ticket Sales Off," *Wall Street Journal,* pp. B1, B13.

[7]National Association of Theater Owners. *Encyclopedia of Exhibition: 1995–96.* North Hollywood: Author.

[8]Gubernick, L. & Schlax (1991, December 9). "Hollywood Blues," *Forbes,* pp. 131–132.

[9]Klady, L. (1994, March 14). "The Dicey Game of Exhibition," *Variety,* pp. 7–8.

[10]Ibid.

[11]Disney's second sequel to the 1989 blockbuster, *Honey I Shrunk the Kids,* was distributed directly to video. This marked the first time a major studio decided to skip the traditional first window of theaters for a quality film with stars and special effects. Formerly, direct to video releases had been produced by small studios on small budgets in the action-adventure or erotic thriller genres. King, T. (1995, May 25). "Disney Plans to Make Live-Action Film for Video Stores, Bypassing Theaters," *Wall Street Journal,* p. B4.

[12]Bannon, L. (1995, December 29). "At the Movies: Revenue Is Up, Ticket Sales Off," *Wall Street Journal,* pp. B1, B13.

[13]Guback, T. (1987). "The Evolution of the Motion Picture Theater Business in the 1980s," *Journal of Communication,* Spring, 1987, 60–77.

[14]Meanwhile, two 1980s startups, Cinemark and Carmike grew rather prodigiously during the period; as will be shown later, their strategies and ownership are similarly structured and quite different from the other major circuits'.

[15]Peers, M. (1995, March 6–12). "Cinemark, Cineplex Merge Ops," *Variety,* p. 22.

[16]In 1995, it owned 946 screens and the ultimate parent was Sony Corp.

[17]Gulf+Western was the parent at the time.

[18]In 1994, the chain's ultimate parents were Viacom, Inc. and Time Warner.

[19]MCA's ultimate parent is Seagram Co., controlled by the Bronfman family. Another branch of the family holds a major stake in Cineplex–Odeon.

[20]Trainor, R. (1988, June). "Let's Get Vertical," *American Film,* pp. 42–48.

[21]Op. Cit.

[22]Harris, K. (1990, July 23). "Squeezing the Customers," *Forbes,* pp. 39–40.

[23]Gubernick, L. (1988, February 8). "Movie Madness," *Forbes,* p. 37–38.

[24]Estimated U. S. screens only, total screens in brackets. Standard & Poors. *Industry Surveys.* Various issues, 1988–1995.

[25]Landro, L. (1995, September 25). "Giants Talk Synergy but Few Make It Work," *Wall Street Journal,* pp. B1, B6.

[26]Ziegler, B. (1995, May 24). "Staid Phone Giants Try Marriage to Hollywood," *Wall Street Journal,* pp. B1, B8; Cauley, L. (1995, September 25). "Weiswasser Named CEO of Disney, Baby Bells Venture," *Wall Street Journal,* p. B5; Cauley, L. (1995, April 18). "Three Baby Bells, Disney Set to Unveil New Video Venture," *Wall Street Journal,* p. B6.

[27]Klady, L. (1995, March 20). "Exhib's Expansion Buoys Distribs," *Variety,* p. 7.

[28]Barrett, W. (1988, August 22). "A Wal-Mart for the Movies," *Forbes,* pp. 60–61.

[29]"Now Playing, Carmike," (1995, March 27). *Forbes,* pp. 160–161.

[30]Carmike Cinemas, Inc. (1995). *The 1994 Annual Report.* Columbus, GA: Author; Barwick, J. (1993, July 26). "Carmike Cinemas Completes Acquisition of Westwynn Theatres," *Business Wire* [CD-ROM Database]; Chaffa, M. (1993, November 22). "Carmike Cinemas Com-

pletes Acquisition of Theatres from Manos Enterprises, Expands into Northeast," *Business Wire* [CD-ROM Database].

[31]Sandler, L. (1996, January 22). "Lights! Camera! Action! Some Analysts Say It's Time to Buy Shares of Carmike Cinemas," *Wall Street Journal*, p. C2.

[32]Carmike Cinemas, Inc. (1995). *The 1994 Annual Report*. Columbus, GA: Author.

[33]Hawkins, C. (1990, July 2). "The Movie Mogul Who Thinks Small," *Businessweek*, p. 37.

[34]United Artists Theatre Circuit, Inc. *Form 10-K Annual Report: 1995*. Denver: Author.

[35]Tusher, W. (1988, August 3). "UA Chain Buying Commonwealth Circuit to Form Midwest Presence," *Variety*, p. 22.

[36]Toumarkine, D. (1993, January 14). UA Circuit Shuts Three Divisions," *Hollywood-Reporter*, p. 6.

[37]Daniels, J. (1994, March 7). "UA Makes Run for the Border," *Hollywood-Reporter*, p. 4.

[38]National Association of Theater Owners. *Encyclopedia of Exhibition: 1995–96*. North Hollywood: Author.

[39]"Theater Chain Has Plans to Jolt Movie Viewers," (1994, August 18). *Wall Street Journal*, p. B1.

[40]Pacelle, M. (1996, January 23). "Malls Add Fun and Games to Attract Shoppers," *Wall Street Journal*, pp. B1, B5.

[41]National Association of Theater Owners. *Encyclopedia of Exhibition: 1994–95*. North Hollywood: Author.

[42]AMC Entertainment Inc. (1993). *1992 Annual Report*. Kansas City: Author.

[43]National Association of Theater Owners. *Encyclopedia of Exhibition: 1994–95*. North Hollywood: Author.

[44]Daniels, J. (1992, June 16). "AMC Field Ops Consolidates," *Hollywood-Reporter*, p. 13.

[45]AMC Entertainment Inc. (1992). *Third Quarter Report*. Kansas City: Author.

[46]Magiera, M. (1991, March 4). "Movie Chains Test Brand-building," *Variety*, p. 43.

[47]"AMC Will Equip 1,700 Movie Screens with Sony Digital Sound Technology," *Wall Street Journal*, (1994, July 28), p. B8.

[48]The Bronfman family controls Seagram and another arm of the family holds a large share of Cineplex–Odeon, as does MCA. "Proposed Cinemark Merger Is Canceled by the Two Firms," *Wall Street Journal*, (1995, May 15), p. C10.

[49]Peers, M. (1995, March 6-12). "Cinemark, Cineplex Merge Ops," *Variety*, p. 22; King, T. and DeSantis, S. (1995, March 3). "Cineplex Odeon Plans to Buy Cinemark, Forming Largest Movie-Theater Chain," *Wall Street Journal*, p. B6.

[50]National Association of Theater Owners. *Encyclopedia of Exhibition: 1992–93*. North Hollywood: Author.

[51]Gubernick, L. (1992, October 12). "Dollar House Mitchell," *Forbes*, pp. 118,121.

[52]Nutile, T. (1993, September 16). "Harcourt General to Spin Off Theaters," *Boston Herald*, Business section, p.

[53]Millman, J. (1991, September 30). "End of a Slog," *Forbes*, p. 180; Putka, G. (1993, March 12). "General Cinema's Makeover Seems a Textbook Success," *Wall Street Journal*, p. B4.

[54]Harcourt General (1993). *1992 Annual Report*. Needham, MA: Author.

[55]Putka, G. (1993, September 16). "Harcourt General Plans to Spin Off Theater Business," *Wall Street Journal*, p. B6.

[56]Trainor, R. (1988, June). "Let's Get Vertical," *American Film*, pp. 42–48.

[57]Trainor, R. (1988, June). "Let's Get Vertical," *American Film*, pp. 42–48.

[58]Gubernick, L. (1992, July 20). "Butterless Popcorn," *Forbes*, pp. 44–45.

[59]Trainor, R. (1988, June). "Let's Get Vertical," *American Film,* pp. 42–48.

[60]Hawkins, C. (1988, October 10). "Umpteen Screens—And Oodles of Debt," *Business Week,* p. 148.

[61]Lathan, K. & Ayscough, S. (1990, January/February). "The Last Emperor," *Film Comment,* pp. 44–48.

[62]Bremner, B.(1989, October 9). "Mogul in Distress," *Business Week,* p. 45.

[63]McMurdy, D. (1991, June 17). "Fade to Black," *MacLean's,* pp. 40–41.

[64]Cineplex–Odeon Corporation. *Annual Report,* 1991, 1992, 1993. Toronto: Author; Worldscope/Disclosure Partners (1995). *Company Profiles: Cineplex–Odeon Corporation* [CD-ROM Database]. Bridgeport, CT: WDP.

[65]Giltenan, E. (1991, April 15). "Pass the Popcorn," *Forbes,* p.

[66]Gubernick, L. (1992, July 20). "Butterless Popcorn," *Forbes,* pp. 44–45.

[67]Magiera, M. (1992, November 30). "Advance Movie Tix Get Big Holiday Push," *Variety,* p. 15.

[68]Vlessing, E. (1994, May 12). "Cineplex Popcorn Airborne," *Hollywood-Reporter,* p. 3.

[69]Petersen, L. (1993, June 28). "Movie Theaters Speed Up Concession Lines," *Brandweek,* p. 17.

[70]Murray, K. (1995, June). "Cineplex–Odeon Parking 5,000-Seater at Uni Fla," *Hollywood-Reporter,* p. 3.

8

The Wages of Synergy

Integration into Broadcast Networking by Warner Brothers, Disney, and Paramount

LARRY COLLETTE

The risks associated with the creation of motion picture products are both historic and well known.[1] Several important factors have amplified these risks throughout the 1990s: The cost of producing feature films has risen dramatically, competition has become stronger, and profit margins have shrunk. Ironically, at the close of 1995, a year in which Hollywood churned out more movies than in its previous twenty-five years, an industry analyst proclaimed "this is the worst time to be producing motion pictures in the history of the business."[2] Amid mounting risks, large entertainment firms have sought more stable ventures in which to invest, leaving motion pictures as merely one subsidiary of their overall enterprise. Indeed for Hollywood's major players, the simpler days when corporate revenues could be tallied based on theatrical receipts and motion picture rentals have long been a thing of the past.[3] These huge, increasingly diversified entertainment-based firms continue to extend their corporate reaches well beyond traditional film industry boundaries, their portfolios now bursting with assets ranging from multimedia to theme parks.

The established patterns of horizontal integration across different media industries and vertical integration within the motion picture industry have highlighted the adaptive strategies of the motion picture companies over time. Yet, during the 1990s the search for successful business combinations has taken on even greater urgency amid a changing media marketplace. As a result, the siren songs of integration, merger, and synergies have proven irresistible to many companies within the industry.

One area of recent activity and emerging importance has been broadcast television networking. Contrary to predictions of the inevitable demise of over-the-air networks, these networks appear to have a strategic place in the overall business plans of some large companies. Several motion picture companies, no longer content in their roles as major suppliers of programming for the television industry, have moved into over-the-air network TV business themselves.

In 1995 Disney acquired Capital Cities/ABC for $19 billion, while only a few months before both Paramount (in association with ChrisCraft) and Warner Brothers launched new networks in an attempt to become significant competitors with the Big Four networks. The timing of these maneuvers by Disney, Paramount, and Time Warner, coming as they do amid a good deal of market uncertainty, suggests an urgency in adopting a strategy for the future.

This chapter examines these three major motion picture companies, Warner Brothers, Disney, and Paramount, in light of their recent integration activities, and those of their parent corporations, into the broadcast network television segment of the market. These media corporations, Time Warner Inc., the Disney Co., and Viacom International, Inc., rank among the top four media–entertainment companies in the world and together have revenues of nearly $49 billion.[4] These diversified companies provide an excellent illustration of how industry conduct has been influenced by the changing industry structure. By examining the adaptive strategies of these companies in a specific market segment we can explore the implications of an evolving market for the overall corporate picture.

THE SHIFTING LANDSCAPE

Companies that have long dominated the production and distribution sectors of the U.S. entertainment industry face formidable challenges in today's rapidly changing communications environment. The transformations of the media landscape, due to rapid advances in technology and changes in government regulation, herald an unsettling period of disequilibrium within the entertainment marketplace. Long-term, perhaps the most convulsive of these transformations is the expected convergence of information and entertainment services onto switched, broadband networks, which will eventually reshape the relationships between consumers, distributors, and producers.[5]

During an interim period, sharper, more immediate impacts are likely to be felt from telephone company entry into video services as permitted by the Telecommunications Act of 1996, and the expiration of a variety of rules that previously maintained Hollywood's dominance in producing content for television. Despite a general atmosphere of uncertainty, the motion picture companies that historically have been agile in adapting to new technologies and weathering periodic squalls are positioning themselves for the future in a number of ways.[6]

THE INTEGRATION OF GIANTS

The potential benefits derived from vertical integration by a company include: the attainment of real economies in production, reduced costs of arm's length transactions, and the advantages gained in product differentiation.[7] In the entertainment industry, vertical integration has serious implications because the competitive positions of nonintegrated companies can suffer and barriers to entry are often raised with this integration. A flurry of merger activity in recent years has led to increased integration between production and distribution levels in the entertainment industry. These mergers have resulted from budgeting decisions that represent an alternative to internal company investment and have primarily been based on scale economies.[8]

The defining events in the recent histories of Warner Bros., Paramount, and Disney have been a series of mergers resulting in the creation of their present media conglomerates. Time Inc.'s takeover of Warner Communications and that of Paramount Communications by Viacom International Inc., perhaps as noteworthy for the tumultuous processes involved, resulted in dramatic reshaping of those two companies.[9] The more recent Disney–ABC merger, albeit a more placid picture, offers an intriguing story of industry finance and the pursuit of business synergies. In the case of Time and Viacom it was a tale of "outlets in search of content," for Disney it was largely "content in search of outlets." Taken together, they speak to the current pressures on entertainment companies to integrate across both distribution and production levels. A summary of the recent merger activities carrying implications for these companies' ventures into television is presented below.

Time Warner

Time magazine was conceived and Time Inc. formed in 1922, coincidentally, the very same year Warner Bros. opened its first film studio on the West coast. Sixty-seven years later, the companies, born and developed in far different media cultures, were joined in a merger that created (at the time) the largest entertainment–media company in the world.

In the mid-1980s it became clear that Time Inc. was plagued by notable shortcomings as it positioned for the future. To begin with, its magazine publishing division, then a major portion of corporate profits, had little growth potential and was very susceptible to wide swings in the economy. This suggested an urgent need to further diversify the company into a variety of ventures. Yet, prior attempts to diversify the company across industries such as newspapers, television stations, and forest products had yielded frustratingly slim results and seemed to signal caution.

The one area of diversification that was fruitful resulted from ventures into cable television and premium cable services (Home Box Office and Cinemax); so fruitful, in fact, that by 1988 the revenues of the video division ($1.9 billion) had nearly reached parity with those of the magazine division ($2.1 billion).[10] Even though the company had secured its position in exhibition and distribution of video through its cable systems and premium cable channels (Home Box Office and Cinemax), the company still did not own any video entertainment of its own.

Each increasingly expensive program had to be obtained on the open market from Hollywood motion picture companies, many of which resented HBO's virtual lock on the pay cable marketplace. Some of these companies, 20th-Century Fox, Paramount, MCA, and Columbia had tried unsuccessfully to circumvent HBO's near-monopsony power by creating their own pay cable channel, Premiere, in 1980. These plans were thwarted in a federal district court in large part from Justice Department intervention. Nevertheless, this episode exposed HBO's vulnerability in relying on outside suppliers for content, as those studios accounted for over half of the best movie products on the network.[11] On a broader plane, this also pointed to the critical void in Time Inc.'s entire corporate structure. As a consequence of not being vertically integrated backwards into production, the company lacked any video or film entertainment copyrights of its own. This made companies already involved in film and video production an attractive prospect for an alliance of some sort.

Also, as the industry moved toward the 1990s, companies that surrounded Time Inc. were becoming increasingly diversified and media markets were now being defined by their global scope. A push towards corporate "bigness" had fueled the growth of rival entertainment companies with international clout such as News Corp. and a variety of formidable foreign competitors. At the same time, for entertainment companies like Time, increased size carried the benefit of allowing risks to be apportioned across a wider corporate base. This was a very important consideration for any firm desiring entry into such a risk-laden market as the creation of filmed entertainment products (a factor equally important to Viacom in its later acquisition bid for Paramount). Importantly, increased company size could be an effective tool for fending off unwelcome acquisition threats at a time when such threats were becoming endemic in the industry.

Warner Communications seemed an attractive partner because its worldwide distribution systems and active production units (Warner Studios, Warner Bros. Television, and Lorimar Television) offered assets Time Inc. urgently needed. A combined company meshed with the strategic goals of integrating into production and ownership of content, increasing Time Inc.'s global reach, and expanding its overall media presence. In 1989, following various stock maneuverings and a bitter legal battle averting a threatened takeover by Paramount, the $14 billion buyout of Warner Entertainment, the last of the leverage deals of the "eighties takeover binge" was completed.[12]

With the takeover completed, Time Warner became the world's largest entertainment company, but was saddled with an enormous debt that would sap corporate revenues over the next two years. In 1992, the company entered into a strategic alliance with the Toshiba Corp. and C. Itochu & Co., bringing a needed cash infusion of $1 billion in exchange for a 12.5 percent of a newly formed Time Warner Entertainment (TWE) partnership. The new unit, TWE, consisted of the film and cable businesses and the cable programming unit, HBO Inc.[13] Time Warner continued to seek additional partners as a way to recapitalize the company and in further hopes of increased synergies. In spring of 1993, US West, a Regional Bell Operating Company (RBOC), acquired a 25.51 percent interest in TWE for a reported $2.5 billion.[14] This strategic alliance was designed to "leapfrog" Time Warner ahead of competitors in the creation of full service networks, while US West would have access to the rich library of Time Warner offerings for its own distribution platforms.[15] However, this left Time Warner with only a 63 percent share of the unit, until a 1995 stock conversion of Toshiba and Itochu shares allowed Time Warner to attain 75 percent ownership of TWE (see endnote 13).

In the fall of 1995, Time Warner announced yet another major move, an $8 billion stock swap agreement to acquire Turner Broadcasting Systems. TBS possessed a vast array of cable channels, production units, extensive film and television libraries, and other properties.[16] A merger would give Time Warner the major presence in basic cable that it lacked and dramatically expand its content holdings. On October 10, 1996, following a Federal Trade Commission consent decree, approval by the Federal Communications Commission, the resolution of a legal challenge by US West, and shareholders' final approval, the merger was completed. Partial plans for integrating the two companies began to unfold in the following weeks: consolidation under Warner Bros. of the two companies' film and animation libraries, combining animation production efforts, folding Turner Pictures projects into Warner Bros., and coalescing the consumer products divisions.[17]

Viacom

Paramount Pictures, whose roots extend back to 1914, was originally formed out of an amalgam of regional film exchanges that created the first national distributor for feature films.[18] One of the original majors, Paramount throughout its history has been a leading producer and distributor in the motion picture industry. What is presently Viacom International was organized in 1986 to acquire the "old" Viacom Int., a company created in the early 1970s from CBS assets spun off when FCC rules foreclosed network participation in program syndication and cable system ownership. The original Viacom gradually acquired properties that ranged from television stations to cable systems. For the most part the company moved cautiously, but eventually entered into the cable network business and limited production through Nickelodeon in 1979. With its 1985 acquisition of MTV from Time Warner, the company expanded its cable networks and acquired what proved to be one of the company's most valuable franchises.

In the early 1990s the "new" Viacom, under Chairman Sumner Redstone, used MTV and Nickelodeon as primary engines for growth. The networks appealed to younger audiences and created a branded identity that successfully differentiated them from all other distribution outlets. Trading on these brand names, these networks enriched corporate coffers to such an extent that by 1992 half of corporate profits and revenues were traceable to the cable networks.[19] One Viacom executive boasted that, in 1993, the MTV networks had themselves generated more operating profit than the network operations of CBS, ABC, and NBC combined.[20]

Yet, over the same period, profits from other Viacom divisions had proven unreliable. For example, the entertainment division reeled from a slump in the syndication market as previously inflated prices dropped precipitously and the revenues from prior contracts such as *The Cosby Show,* first shopped around in 1988, began to tail off. Coupled with this was an advertising drought that gripped the company's radio and TV stations and represented a further drain. Also, the growth curve for cable television had flattened out as that industry entered its "mature stage" with very few areas left to be wired and subscriber penetration rates slowing. Revenue from Viacom's cable operations would be further threatened by the increased regulations brought about by the 1992 Cable Act. In addition, despite advertising revenues from Viacom's cable networks appearing robust in light of the current market, the other network revenue stream, that generated by subscriber growth, seemed certain to stagnate. It appeared the company had to look outside itself for growth opportunities.

Despite the ambitions of its chairman, Viacom had neither the size nor the range of assets necessary to compete with companies such as Time Warner and News Corp.[21] As with Time Inc., Viacom lacked a strong presence in producing and controlling original content. Once again, an entertainment company with a studio seemed the essential asset to round out a corporate portfolio. This addition could insure a constant supply of motion pictures and television shows for distribution over the company's outlets and increase the breadth of its corporate holdings. It was determined that Paramount Communications, with its Paramount Pictures and Paramount Television, was the most attractive prospect. A merger of Viacom and Paramount took place in 1994 after a prolonged battle with QVC and its Chairman, Barry Diller, over control of Paramount. Once again the fate of a large media merger was decided by the Delaware court. With a ruling in its favor, on March 11, 1994 Viacom International Inc. acquired a majority of the outstanding shares of Paramount by tender offer. On July 7 Paramount Communications became a wholly owned subsidiary of Viacom, and on January 3, 1995, Paramount Communications was merged into Viacom International.[22] In September of 1994 Viacom also merged with Blockbuster Entertainment Corp., the largest retailer of video products.

Disney

In April, 1954 Walt Disney became the first studio executive to strike a deal with a television network to produce an original television series.[23] That program, *Disneyland,* alone accounted for nearly one half of ABC's advertising billing that year. This casual romance helped to secure the future marriage of all Hollywood studios with the television networks. Most importantly, this new arrangement provided a viable means for meeting the expenses associated with keeping Disney's motion picture studio fully productive. From the studio's perspective, the series, and its various iterations over the years, was both an entertainment program and a vehicle for relentless cross-promotion of Disney's other ventures, feature films and theme parks. Disney pioneered this cross-promotional edge, much sought after in today's market, and it was part of a strategy ingrained in the corporate culture early on.

Disney's television involvement was primarily in producing content and recycling its motion pictures for later use on TV. Its distribution resources were limited to a single independent Los Angeles station, KCAL and The Disney Channel, begun as a premium channel but now increasingly shifted to the basic tier. The cable channel was also used as a vehicle for promoting other aspects of the Disney product line. For example, every time a new animated feature debuted in theaters, a special, *The Making of* _____ (*Beauty and the Beast, The Lion King,* etc.) was repeatedly shown. After a theatrical run had long been completed and the videocassette market fully tapped, Disney eventually moved the film onto its cable outlet as a programming centerpiece, a process that allowed the company to make efficient use of a single product while enjoying returns across a number of windows, all controlled by the company. Each subsequent use in this windowing process allowed the company to further spread costs and risks across a wider field. This will be discussed further in a later section.

For the over-the-air TV market, distributed to a mass audience and under regulatory scrutiny for its content, Disney offered a franchise name in "family entertainment," deftly cultivated through the years. In his message to stockholders in the Disney 1995 Annual Report, Chairman Michael Eisner wrote:

> We are fundamentally an operating company, operating the Disney brand all over the world, maintaining it, improving it, promoting it and advertising it with taste. Our time must be spent insuring that the Brand never slides, that we innovate the Brand, experiment and play with it, but never diminish it. Others will try to change it, from outside and within. We must resist.[24]

Even with a myriad of copyrights to exploit, Disney, this "Brand," still required a distribution mechanism to bring it to the audience. In 1995, Disney revenue was up 20 percent ($12.11 billion) as compared to 1994 ($10.01 billion), with filmed entertainment contributing $6 billion, or more than the theme parks and resorts and consumer products divisions combined.[25] Yet, within that $6 billion, a significant amount came from a single source, *The Lion King,* then in video release and international theatrical distribution. Across the corporation, continued losses with Euro Disney, the abandonment of a planned new park in Virginia, a weak performance in live action films, all indicated limited growth potential given the company's current position.

A network seemed a good fit to complement Disney's present structure and provided a much needed avenue for growth. Capital Cities–ABC became the choice. Eisner had worked for ABC from 1966 to 1976 and later at Paramount helped to develop the programming (*Happy Days,* etc.) that propelled that perennial third-ranked network to number one.[26] Disney paid a premium for an existing network, thus avoiding the pitfalls Warner Bros. and Paramount would face in their attempts to establish the WB network and UPN respectively.[27] The acquisition of ABC allowed Disney immediate entry in networking, and eliminated the uncertainty and high start-up costs of creating a new network from scratch. With its very profitable ABC owned and operated stations, an affiliate base of over 200 stations intact, network operations secured, and business components established, this network amounted to a "turnkey" arrangement. The newly configured Disney company's business segments included:

Creative content—in the production of live-action and animated motion pictures for distribution to theatrical, home video, and television markets, and the production and distribution of original television programming; the licensing of company names, characters, and properties; development and marketing of educational and entertainment software and audio products; producer of live plays, and publisher of newspapers, books, and periodicals.

Broadcasting and Cable—ABC TV and ABC radio networks, owned and operated stations, production and distribution of ESPN and The Disney Channel.

Theme Parks and Resorts—Walt Disney World and properties, Disneyland, Tokyo Disneyland, and Disney Sports Enterprises.

Corporate Activities and Other—equity shares in Euro Disney, A&E, and Lifetime cable networks.

The historic identity and entrenched market position that ABC had developed over the decades seemed to translate into immediate economic advantage. However, these advantages came at a steep price, even for the deep-pocketed Disney Company, which swallowed $12 billion in loans to buy Capital Cities–ABC. One year after the deal, the company was paying close to $700 million a year in interest on debt and, under the rules of corporate accounting, would be taking a $450 million a year charge against earnings until the year 2036.[28]

BARRIERS TO ENTRY IN BROADCAST NETWORKING

For newcomers, like Paramount (UPN) and Warner Bros. (WB), the barriers to entry created by economies of scale and the imperatives of vertical integration within the television industry can be formidable obstacles. To achieve these economies of scale and become competitive both UPN and WB needed to create a truly nationwide distribution system. At the outset this was a problem due to the scarcity of independents, making it difficult to gain a foothold in the marketplace. It was highly unlikely that another network's affiliate would be so attracted to UPN's and WB's limited program schedule—two nights a week—that it would forsake affiliation status with one of the Big Four. Therefore, independent stations were counted on to furnish the critical base needed to form a new broadcast network. Yet, the number of markets with independents and the total number of independents had shrunk, a result of Fox Broadcasting's entry some years before and a now slowed pace in newly licensed independent stations. In 1994, 275 licenses were held by independents, 63 percent of which were in top 50 markets, nearly one in five of these stations were not yet on the air at a time when the two networks were seeking affiliates.[29] This meant 223 on-air stations were in theory "available," or roughly the number that each historic network already had in their fold. A sizable portion of these independents were also weaker UHF stations. Importantly, these 223 independent stations were not evenly distributed across TV markets; those in the mid-sized and smaller markets were few, making a nationwide network a very difficult proposition. This scarcity was magnified by the simultaneous entry of two new networks competing to sign these rare stations as affiliates.

At launch in January 1995, UPN claimed 96 affiliates covering 79 percent of the country, but nearly a third of UPN program clearances and 13 percent of its coverage were "out-of-pattern" secondary clearances.[30] Faced with the shrinking number of pure independents, UPN implemented a backup plan to use these secondary affiliates. These sorts of clearances reduced the efficiencies associated with networking and made ad placement uneven for national sponsors. Also, some of these secondary affiliates carried only a portion of the network's two night program offerings.

Warner Bros. started with only forty-three affiliates and was forced to use superstation WGN's cable satellite coverage to boost its coverage area to 72 percent of the country. This "hybrid network" was necessary again because of the scarcity of independents in many television markets and the superstation accounted for 18 percent coverage in markets without WB affiliates. This coverage proved vital because WB had particular problems gaining affiliates in smaller markets, signing only twelve affiliates in TV markets number 51 to 200. However, such a hybrid configuration left the network vulnerable to actions of large cable MSOs (multiple system operators) that could exclude the superstation from system lineups and, in effect, cut the network's lifeline.[31]

Taken together, the UPN and WB difficulties suggest there was insufficient capacity in the way of independent stations needed to create a viable over-the-air network. The situation improved somewhat with gains in affiliates for both networks over the next two seasons as more nights of programming were offered by the networks. In 1996 UPN claimed 151 affiliates, while WB had broadcast affiliates in 90 markets.[32] However, some affiliates carried only a portion of network offerings such as *WB! Kids,* the children's programming service, or UPN's *StarTrek Voyager.*

The continued reliance on secondary affiliates in some markets and the lack of any affiliates in others persisted as problems.

In the summer of 1996, Warner Bros. announced the WeB cable channel, a de facto cable network aimed at providing WB network programs in smaller markets where WB had few affiliates.[33] Under this plan MSOs would get a share of advertising revenues based on the percentage of the DMA (Designated Market Area) coverage the MSO delivered for WeB. This strategy would give system owners an incentive and equity stake in the channel, and shore up smaller markets, lessening the reliance on WGN. Unlike Paramount, which owns a chain of broadcast stations, Time Warner lacked stations of its own and had instead partnered with Tribune stations. The WeB channel gives Warner Bros. an "O&O" type presence in the exhibition stage, albeit a rather small one.

MOTIVATIONS FOR MARKET ENTRY INTO BROADCAST NETWORKING

Given the current state of the marketplace, there appear to be three important motivations driving the Warner Bros., Paramount, and Disney entry into broadcast networking. These primary motivations are interrelated in nature and suggest larger trends at work within an evolving entertainment industry.

1. Securing a mass distribution outlet for programming products as the relationship between motion picture companies and the major broadcast networks enters a transition phase;
2. Expanding the synergies arising from windowing, cross-promotion, and branding of content across a wider variety of distribution methods;
3. Establishing a network brand identity to differentiate it from an expected flood of competing sources and to provide a direct entry path into the lucrative O&O aspects of television networking.

Motivation 1—Securing a Mass Distribution Outlet

An Early Frost

In the late 1950s, the motion picture industry's aversion to television ended with recognition of television's potential value as a steady revenue stream, TV being an eager outlet for original products generated by the studios. Operating under a changing economic imperative, the major studios followed Disney's lead and became the primary suppliers of television programming products. In time, the studios' television divisions and film divisions became inseparable because of joint costs and shared revenues across these operations. As production increasingly became the domain of the motion picture industry, network attempts to produce more of their own programming were greeted with hostility and legal action.[34] The network domination of both the distribution and exhibition stages in television became *the* issue. The oligopoly power wielded by the networks appeared to tip the balance of power appreciably toward them, leaving the studios to bargain from an unaccustomed, inferior position. Yet, the stinging lessons of the Paramount case, which prohibited integration across production, distribution, and exhibition, were still fresh in the minds of movie studio executives. This provided impetus to their legal actions against the networks. However, it was the intervention of the Justice Department and a subsequent consent decree that ultimately eliminated the lawsuits. This underscores the general atmosphere surrounding the issue of programming and access to the airwaves that has colored the relationship between Hollywood and the TV industry through much of its history.

As suppliers of the premiere programming for the TV industry, with most substitutes acknowledged to be inferior, it might seem that the motion picture companies enjoyed a strategic position. In a truly competitive market, they might, for example, play one network against the others to some advantage in reaching licensing agreements for popular programs. However, in these classic oligopoly-versus-oligopoly confrontations, the network bottleneck still represented a formidable force. The networks recognized that cooperative restraint secured the greatest economic rewards and extravagant risk-taking and "throwing money" at studios could come back to haunt them. Within this tight network oligopoly, the step process of program acquisition kept prices in line and forced producers into long-term contracts that assured their operating at a deficit in producing programs.[35]

A Changing Climate

The Financial Interest and Syndication Rules, "fin–syn," were adopted in the early 1970s by the FCC and limited network ownership of programming and participation in their aftermarket syndication. With the relaxation of these rules in 1991 and their eventual removal in 1995, network in-house production units began producing an increased number of network programs as part of their desire for greater self-sufficiency. There are now powerful incentives for networks to increase their own production of content. By adopting such an integration strategy networks could attempt to rein in program costs and utilize their existing distribution outlets as "launch pads" for their own content to be sold in aftermarkets. The revenues from sales of these other broadcast rights should be sufficient to induce networks to produce more or have an interest in more programs carried on their networks. Also, the elimination of the FCC's Prime Time Access Rules (PTAR III) in the top 50 markets, which had forbidden the networks to program more than three of the four prime-time hours, will open more time slots for network programming. This further suggests stronger network incentives to own more of their programming.

In addition, the Big Four networks began negotiating for a larger share of some programming that is being produced by outside companies.[36] Though the networks contribute more towards up-front production costs, the lucrative back-end revenues in the syndication market are shared under these deals. Historically, the monies generated through syndication have been the TV industry equivalent of owning the rights to a blockbuster feature film. This revenue had been a major incentive for program producers to play along with the network's game.

The increased power given to network gatekeepers could have serious implications for motion picture companies lacking an over-the-air outlet of their own. In theory, the Big Four networks could give preference to their own programs, to the exclusion of products from outsiders. Facing a suddenly constricted market, program producers may opt for an alternative system to distribute their goods, such as cable or direct broadcast satellite. However, all other means of distribution remain inferior options to the national networks in terms of reach and, therefore, potential revenues. Those media companies not vertically integrated forward could be disadvantaged by having to strike deals with the over-the-air oligopsony networks that stand controlling the gate.

A large entertainment company assures a means to distribute its programming by having a network at its disposal. Thus, owning a network offers a hedge against any squeezes by the other networks in the future. This is vital for companies that have developed enormous production capacity such as Warner Bros., Paramount, and Disney. Part of this production capacity is demonstrated by the number and percentage of prime-time programs produced for the Big Four networks in the 1990s. As can be seen in Table 8-1, these three companies played an important role in one-third of all programs on the Big Four primetime schedules from 1990–1991 to 1996–1997. Even though the supply of programming to the networks has long been considered unconcentrated and competitive, these three producers contributed a sizable portion.[37] Time Warner's production companies have dominated the TV

TABLE 8-1   Prime-Time Programs on Big Four Networks from Disney, Paramount, and Warner Bros.

	Disney	Paramount	Warner	Total	Percentage of Programs
1996–97	4	8	14	26	27%
1995–96	7	9	18	34	36%
1994–95	8	7	12	27	29%
1993–94	9	8	15	32	39%
1992–93	8	9	15	32	31%
1991–92	10	8	14	32	32%
1990–91	6	9	18	33	35%
Total	52*	58**	106***	216	33% average

*includes Disney, Touchstone TV, and coproduction partnerships
**includes Paramount, Viacom, and Spelling Prods. (beginning 1994), and coproduction partnerships
***includes Warner Bros., Lorimar TV, Witt Thomas (beginning 1995), and coproduction partnerships

Sources: *Broadcasting and Cable*, May 27, 1996; Barry Monush, *International Television and Video Almanac*. New York: Quigley, 1991–1996.

market for ten consecutive years, placing the most programs on primetime schedules, including the popular hits *E.R., Murphy Brown,* and *Friends.* Over the same
period Disney (Disney, Touchstone TV) and Paramount (Paramount, Viacom,
Spelling) have also been very important producers for the major networks.

Perhaps a harbinger of things to come, in the 1996 season Warner Bros. inserted
seven of its own programs (3.5 hours) on the WB network, accounting for half of the
network's seven-hour schedule. Drawing on its own resources, the new network
provides an additional outlet for the company's content and opens up a range of
possibilities for the future. In the 1996–1997 season Paramount programs also accounted for 2.5 hours of the total of six hours offered on UPN, while Disney placed
four programs (2 hours) on ABC's prime-time schedule.

Given the changes in network rules, Warner, Paramount, or Disney may elect to
take on more programming risks through their networks in hopes of generating
higher payoffs somewhere down the road. Having their own networks insures a captive name brand distribution for programs they produce and buy both domestically
and internationally. These networks provide the valuable "shelf space" in a crowded
media market for products not licensed by others. In a newly evolved video marketplace a network may represent something akin to what the theatrical market is now
for motion pictures in later exhibition windows.

Children's Programming

Although more attention is usually given to prime-time programs, children's
programming has become a lucrative source of income for broadcast networks.[38]
Program production costs are lower, programs can be strip syndicated, and repeated
more often. The advertising market for children's TV has proven fairly durable even
amid ratings declines as more participants enter the market. In 1995, despite an
overall weakened advertising market, the broadcast networks still realized double
digit gains in revenue from the children's market.[39]

All three companies, Disney, Warner Brothers, and Paramount (through
Viacom's Nickelodeon) have strengths in children's programming content. Time
Warner and Disney own many hours of storehoused children's programming from
years of production activity and continue to be active in production. However, when
Fox Broadcasting canceled Disney's afternoon block of animated programs in the
mid-1990s, it highlighted Disney's vulnerability when it came to mass distribution
of children's content. The acquisition of ABC provides Disney with a secure outlet
in this important market segment.

For WB its greatest success as a network thus far has been in the children's
programming market where it doubled advertising billings across one year's time.[40]
Like Disney, Warner Bros. enjoys a historic association with animation, and the
acquisition of Hanna–Barbera in the Turner merger further strengthens that facet.
UPN planned to expand its UPN Kids Network on Sunday to two hours in 1997 and
both WB and UPN planned to add a two-hour afternoon block.

Motivation 2—Expanding Synergies

In today's Hollywood, the act of creation has been largely redefined and goes well beyond what simply appears on any screen. In current terms, creation is most likely to involve the development of exploitable branded products, whose earnings potential extends into every conceivable distribution market from videogames to pay-per-view. The emphasis is placed on creation of a "copyright" that can be exploited across exhibition windows and into other markets.

Internal Windows

Within the television industry the first copy costs of general interest, mass-distributed programming are quite high. The greater the audience for this programming, the lower is the cost per consumer. Hence, the desire to achieve greater economies has driven entertainment companies to seek more audience mileage from their created products across more "internal windows" controlled by the company. In terms of existing copyrights and the ability to synergistically create copyrights that complement strategies in television, Disney, Time Warner, and Viacom are very well positioned. These companies can peddle a wide variety of offerings in both the domestic and international marketplace. For example, Time Warner's film and television library, the world's largest, includes 6,000 feature films, 28,500 television titles, 6,500 episodes of animation and 600 "classic" animated shorts.[41] Importantly, this content can also be utilized over the numerous Time Warner distribution outlets such as TNT or the Cartoon Channel. In addition to products in the can, Time Warner production units can churn out a great deal of content to be utilized over Time Warner cable networks and the WB Network (see Appendix). The opportunities for the internal "windowing" of content across the company's television options include pay cable, basic cable, and over-the-air broadcast channels, and are unrivaled in the industry. Disney and Viacom can also take advantage of these opportunities across their outlets with their extensive libraries. For example, *The Lion King,* already a hit in theaters, on videocassette, and cable, aired on ABC during the November 1996 sweeps period and drew high ratings.

According to Redstone, the latest version of Viacom has as its goal to be a "software-driven global media powerhouse" that would control and distribute movies, television shows, books, magazine, videos, toys, and videogames.[42] With Viacom Productions, Paramount Television, and Spelling Entertainment now in its fold, Viacom is a vertically integrated giant with interests in all levels of video entertainment.

It seems unlikely that companies will achieve, or even wish to achieve, a level of total self-sufficiency enabling them to ignore outside vendors. The uncertainty of audience tastes and the risks associated with programming tend to be countervailing forces here. Despite the promises of synergy, major pitfalls can exist in production and distribution integration when it comes to windowing.[43] For example, Disney gains no advantage by airing a movie on ABC that was a dismal flop at the box office. Indeed, the liability of a box office failure may be magnified across each subsequent outlet. Clearly, programs of inferior quality will damage any distribution network's identity and revenues. Also, as producers selling only to their own distribution outlets, Disney, Warner Bros., and Paramount could not take advantage of the multiple bidders in the marketplace that generate higher prices for superior programming products.[44] Therefore, the best approach to integration is one that strikes a balance between self-sufficiency and allows the company to take advantage of the marketplace.

External Windows

The syndication market in video entertainment is an important aftermarket, representing the largest external window (outside company use) for these entertainment products. In the mid-1990s the major historic networks are growing more active in some aspects of the syndication market. Viacom and Time Warner, too, are major participants in the current off-network syndication and motion picture syndication industry. Warner Bros. Domestic Television Distribution and Warner Bros. International Television hold thousands of hours of syndication offerings ranging from *Murphy Brown* to 330 hours of *Dallas*. Similarly, Viacom's Paramount Television, Viacom International, and Spelling Television (78 percent owned) syndicate a catalog ranging from *The Cosby Show* to *Beverly Hills 90210*. In this new environment, it would be possible for a company like Time Warner or Viacom to be competing against itself in the syndication business through new agreements with an established network.

The demise of the Prime Time Access Rules does suggest a possible fogging of this external window. A studio with a network might be tempted to offer its own affiliates the better off-network programs that it controls. Using this subtle form of "network compensation" a network could attempt to secure its affiliate base and offer stronger lead-ins for its own network offerings by "cream skimming" its syndication catalog. For example, reruns of the popular Warner Bros.-produced series *Friends* were sold in 1996 to seven stations in major markets owned by the Tribune Co., all key WB affiliates.[45] Also, once exclusive rights expire in 2001, WTBS, owned by Time Warner, will carry the program on cable, extending the window even farther. From the company's perspective this may be viewed as synergistic progression but it may also bring into question possible allocative inefficiencies that may result from a few large companies wielding such market power. For the outside producer wishing to sell programming to a network's affiliate or a station competing with that affiliate (desiring that same content) this may be seen as a kind of foreclosure.

However, such favored treatment given to affiliates on a large scale does seem improbable. This drastic scenario is unlikely because producers are strongly motivated to sell to the highest bidder in the market. Nevertheless, when viewed in the broader context of the overall corporate goals of maximizing audience, thus reducing costs, and reaping rewards that come in other ventures, such a scheme may seem tenable to some.

Cross-Promotion

In addition to traditional sources of revenue, Disney, Paramount, and Time Warner have revenue streams available to them in so-called ancillary markets. These companies are already practiced in the product tie-ins that now are commonplace in the film industry. For example, Disney, Time Warner, and Viacom can market their TV-related products and characters through their own retail outlets and in licensing and merchandising arrangements. With their own broadcast networks these companies can exert greater control over cross-promotion and merchandising opportunities that may exist for other aspects of their enterprise. For example, past collaborations among Viacom divisions have resulted in film promotions of Paramount products on Nick at Nite and MTV and Blockbuster in-store promotions for MTV Video Music Awards.

Motivation 3—Branding a Network

There is no doubt that viewing shares of over-the-air network affiliates have declined appreciably as new entrants such as cable have fractionalized the existing audience.[46] However, the anticipated wave of competing channels delivering content over multiple platforms will increase this effect sharply and make the current marketplace seem sparse by comparison. As this trend persists, it will further complicate matters for all new entrants trying to differentiate themselves amid an increased stream of television competitors. This heightens the urgency in establishing a network distribution presence that allows a company to cut through the increased media clutter. Companies that delay entrance into a market segment will suffer in their attempts to establish an identity and gain market share in the crowded, more competitive market. Those late entrants, obliged to play catch-up, may be forced to operate at the margins of the market or find specialty niches that allow their survival. Starting a network of any kind from a dead stop amid such a race promises to be quite problematic. Attempting to start a national over-the-air network, capable of reaching a mass audience, in such a race, may be unthinkable.

An important advantage wielded by the networks, as important as their pervasive reach, is the brand-name identity established within the competitive market. The network as a programming entity is itself an important name-brand asset in product differentiation. Similar to the "being there first" advantage enjoyed by companies such as HBO, which continues to reign supreme in premium cable service, creating an early foothold is vital. The ability to differentiate programming products from those of new competitors is especially vital during this interim period. The distinguishing marks of the major historic networks have largely depended on programming supplied by others, primarily, the major studios. It is here that companies like Disney, Paramount, and Warner Bros. enjoy a strategic advantage in creating a network identity. Operating in an environment that encourages self-sufficiency, the brand name becomes even more vital. Those companies possessing control over creation and distribution of product seem far better positioned. As discussed previously, a wider distribution stance during this interim period is especially important to large producers like Paramount, Disney, and Warner Bros. These companies already have familiar and established identities in other aspects of the industry and sought to establish one in broadcast networking.

The greatest economic bonanza for the broadcast networks comes from their very profitable Owned and Operated stations (O&Os). These stations have remained cash cows even as networks have declined in the ratings; profit margins above 50 percent are fairly common.[47] In their role as flagships for the networks, O&Os enjoy a high profile in the advertising market and the prestige of a steady stream of attractive network quality programming. The entry paths into the profitable O&O business are limited. New entrants must either buy an existing network with its O&Os or start a new network to which its own stations can be attached. The value and the prestige of stations owned and operated by a successful network can be expected to rise through time, subject to the continued good fortune of the network itself. Time Warner does not own any stations, Disney acquired ABC's, and the Paramount Stations Group has ten large market stations, eight of which are now UPN affiliates (see Table 8-2). For Paramount the stakes here are the greatest. Among the most integrated companies in television, Paramount's gamble in networking may eventually pay its greatest dividends with its stations group. Also, the promise of standard digital television, with its ability to squeeze multiple channels out of each station's 6 Mhz channel allocation, would likely increase the value of O&O stations.

CONCLUSION

Over the short run, the vertical integration into broadcast networking has been a bumpy road for all three companies involved. Over its first six months, UPN lost $67.1 million and Chris-Craft Industries (which bore the upfront costs, hence most economic risk) predicted continued losses of $150 over the first two years of the network.[48] Time Warner lost an estimated $33 million on WB in its first six months and the yearly loss was calculated to be around $75 million.[49] For the fiscal year

TABLE 8-2   The Paramount Stations Group

WPSG-57	Philadelphia	UPN
WSBK-38	Boston	UPN
WDCA-20	Washington	UPN
KTXA-21	Dallas	UPN
WKBD-50	Detroit	UPN
WUPA-69	Atlanta	UPN
KTXH-20	Houston	UPN
WBFS-33	Miami	UPN
KMOV-4 St.	Louis	CBS
WVIT-30	Hartford	NBC

Source: Paramount homepage: http://www.Paramount.com/homestations2.html

ending September 30, 1996, amid a ratings decline for ABC, Disney's broadcasting division reported 4 percent yearly growth with $6.2 billion in revenue. However, this growth was due mostly to strong increases in advertising and subscriber revenue from ESPN.[50] While these reports suggest the immediate returns from networking have been nonexistent or scant, the long-run implications of the movements into over-the-air networking are much more important.

The changes occurring in the entertainment industry make operating in the short term while deciding upon a strategy for the long run all the more problematic. These decisions reflect a pattern of necessary readjustment for all media companies positioning for the future. The search and desire for greater self-sufficiency and the synergies sought from vertical integration are driving these large media companies today. In such a light, it should be remembered that over-the-air networking is one portion of the overall strategies.

Disney with ABC has created an immediate presence in broadcast networking that should eventually allow it to take advantage of the historic strengths in production combined with an established distribution entity. At the same time, changes in network rules will allow them to pursue opportunities in new areas. On the other hand, the outlook for UPN and WB in their present form is less optimistic when viewed in this market segment alone. In September of 1995, executives from WB and UPN met to briefly to discuss a possible merger that never occurred, perhaps suggesting a recognition that the market may not accommodate two new networks at this time. Yet, with their deep-pocketed corporate parents, incremental gains in audience share, success in specialty markets like children's programs, and future opportunities arising from integration, these new ventures may prove successful.

For today's motion pictures studios, now part of large diversified companies such as Disney, Viacom, and Time Warner, there is a new imperative. These companies must be positioned to spread the risks of new ventures across a wider, much more diverse playing field. This adaptive strategy includes greater ownership and control of resources such as content and, equally important, a means to distribute that content. A broadcast network that insures an outlet for a company's media content and diversifies the opportunities into other markets needing branded products is vital.

APPENDIX

Resources in the content domain held by Time Warner as of November 1996:
Warner Bros. Studios—a large studio that has recently produced blockbusters such as *Maverick, Batman Forever,* and *Twister.*

Warner Bros. Television—the leading supplier of prime-time network programming for nine consecutive years, having placed twenty-one series on the 1995 fall television season schedule. The division produces *E.R.* and *Friends.*

Telepictures Productions—a production unit that creates and produces TV programming primarily for the first-run syndication marketplace.

Witt-Thomas Productions—under exclusive long-term contract to produce films and TV programming for Warner Bros. Past credits include *The Golden Girls* and *The John Larroquette Show.*

HBO Pictures and HBO Showcase—producer of original motion pictures for use primarily over the pay cable outlet.

HBO Independent Productions—produces original comedy programming and series for broadcast and cable, productions include *Martin.*

HBO Downtown Productions—creator of specialty programming for cable and CD-ROM outlets.

HBO Sports—live action sports such as boxing and Wimbledon tennis and behind-the-scenes shows such as *Inside the NFL* and *Real Sports with Bryant Gumbel.*

Warner Television Animation—one of the largest suppliers of animated programming, having a catalog of over 3,500 cartoons. Active in production of new product, including *Steven Spielberg Presents Animaniacs.*

Hanna-Barbera Cartoons—founded in 1957 and acquired by Turner in 1991. Studio has produced over 3,000 half-hour programs including *The Flintstones* and *The Jetsons.*

Turner Pictures—an L.A.-based motion picture company started in 1994, with production of six movies expected in 1996. In fall 1996 it was announced that this division and its projects would be integrated into Warner Bros.

Castle Rock Entertainment—A TBS subsidiary since 1993, in its nine-year existence its film and TV productions have included *When Harry Met Sally, City Slickers,* and *The American President* and television's *Seinfeld.*

New Line Cinema—acquired by TBS in 1994, a leading independent producer and distributor of theatrical films. Products have included *The Mask* and *Hoop Dreams.* Turner Original Productions—a nonfiction development and production unit that under TBS had supplied its networks and businesses.

Turner Sports—live sports programming produced for Turner outlets TNT and TBS Superstation.

Warner Bros. Domestic Pay TV, Cable & Network Features—responsible for the sale and marketing of already produced features, series, and miniseries to interactive, pay-per-view, pay cable, basic cable, and broadcast networks.

Warner Bros. Domestic Television Distribution—responsible for first-run and off-network syndication of more than 7,600 hours of programming.

Turner Program Services—domestic syndication of first-run and off-network programs such as *The World of National Geographic* and *The Wonder Years.*

NOTES

[1]Suzanne M. Donahue, *American Film Distribution: The Changing Marketplace.* (Ann Arbor, MI: UMI Research Press, 1987) and Barry R. Litman, "The Motion Picture Entertainment Industry." In Walter S. Adams, (ed.) *The Structure of American Industry,* 8th ed. (New York: MacMillan, 1990), 183–216.

[2]Eben Shapiro and Thomas R. King, "Lights! Camera! Checkbooks! Costs Menace Movie Makers," *Wall Street Journal,* Dec. 21, 1995, B1,B8.

[3]David J. Londoner, "The Changing Economics of Entertainment." In Tino Balio, (ed.) *The American Film Industry,* 2nd ed. (Madison, WI: University of Wisconsin Press, 1985), 603–623.

[4]"Global 50," *Variety,* Sept. 1, 1996, 40.

[5]George Gilder, *Life After Television: The Coming Transformation of Media and American Life,* 2nd ed. (New York: Norton, 1994), and Thomas F. Baldwin, D. Stevens McVoy and Charles Seinfield, *Convergence: Integrating Media, Information & Communication.* (Thousand Oaks, CA: Sage, 1996).

[6]Janet Wasko, *Hollywood in the Information Age: Beyond the Silver Screen,* (Austin, TX: University of Texas Press, 1995).

[7]Richard Caves, *American Industry: Structure, Conduct, Performance.* (Englewood Cliffs, NJ: Prentice-Hall, 1982), 40–41.

[8]Gary W. Ozanich and Michael Wirth, "Mergers and Acquisitions: An Overview." In Allison Alexander, James Owers, and Rod Carveth (eds.), *Media Economics: Theory and Practice.* Hillsdale, NJ: Erlbaum, 1993), 115–134.

[9]Both Time Inc. and Viacom engaged in prolonged legal battles in which their respective mergers were eventually decided in the Delaware Supreme Court.

[10]Bill Saporito, "The Inside Story of Time Warner," *Fortune,* November 20, 1989, 164.

[11]Thomas Baldwin and D. Stevens McVoy, *Cable Communication.* (Englewood Cliffs, NJ: Prentice-Hall, 1983), 134.

[12]Jonathan R. Laing, "Coming Attraction: Bad Scene behind It, Time Warner is Wired for Growth," *Barron's,* June 22, 1992, 8, 27.

[13]On Sept. 1, 1995 both Itochu and Toshiba exchanged their interests in TWE for equity in Time Warner Inc. The companies had the option of receiving either 7 million shares of Time Warner stock and $10 million or 8 million shares of stock. This secured 75 percent ownership of TWE for Time Warner, with US West holding the remaining shares.

[14]"Time Warner Sees Synergy in Partnership," *The Wall Street Journal,* May 18, 1993, B1.

[15]This coupling would prove frustrating for Time Warner because US West had in reality gained more control over Time Warner cable systems than expected. Under terms of the Modified Final Judgment that broke up AT&T, these systems were now legally regarded as part of a Baby Bell, which gave US West veto power regarding key aspects of the systems operations. The most fractious disagreement came over Time Warner's announced plans to acquire Turner Broadcasting Systems in 1995. US West held that this plan, which would lead to sole ownership of Turner cable channels, would place Time Warner into competition with channels it already owned with US West. The Delaware court eventually ruled in favor of Time Warner and the merger was allowed.

[16]Michael O'Neal, "The Unlikely Mogul," *Business Week,* December 11, 1995, 86.

[17]"Time Warner Inc. Closes Merger with Turner Broadcasting System," Time Warner press release, October 10, 1996, available online at: http://pathfinder.com/@@oa490gc AARnbkul/Corp/officialword/merger/newmerger.html

[18]Tino Balio, *The American Film Industry,* 2nd ed. (Madison, WI: University of Wisconsin Press, 1985), 117.

[19]Mark Landler and Geoffrey Smith, "The MTV Tycoon," *Business Week,* Sept. 21, 1992, 56–62.

[20]John Battelle, "Viacom Doesn't Suck," *Wired,* April, 1995, 1–12.

[21]Landler and Smith, 58.

[22]Viacom Securities Exchange Commission Filing, Form 10-K. December 31, 1995, p. 3.

[23]Sydney Head and Christopher Sterling, *Broadcasting in America,* 5th ed. (Boston: Houghton Mifflin, 1987), 91. In addition, ABC had earlier loaned Walt Disney $500,000 toward the building of the Disneyland theme park.

[24]Disney Annual Report, 1995. Disney Corp., "Message from Chiarman," available online at: http://www.disney. com/investors/annual/yir.html

[25]Disney Annual Report, 1995.

[26]For a discussion of this period see Barry R. Litman, "The Television Networks, Competition and Program Diversity," *Journal of Broadcasting,* 2 1979, 393–410.

[27]Details of these costs are contained in Eric Schmuckler, "The Fifth Wheels," *MediaWeek,* October 23, 1995, 9–10. These high start-up costs of creating new networks, United Paramount Network (UPN) and the WB Network, were evidenced by the expected loss of nearly $100 million each in their first year.

[28]Christopher Byron, "A Year and 19 Billion Later, Questions Remain in Disney/Cap Cities Merger," *MSNBC,* Oct. 28, available at: http://www.msnbc.com/news/37355.asp

[29]Larry Collette and Barry R. Litman, "The Strange Economics of New Broadcast Network Entry: The Case of United Paramount and Warner Brothers," paper presented to the annual meeting of the Association for Education in Journalism and Mass Communication, Anaheim, August 1996. Also, further indicating this shortage of independents, UPN's network included new stations in New Orleans and Waco, Texas not yet on the air when the network began.

[30]David Tobenkin, "New Players Get Ready to Roll," *Broadcasting & Cable,* Jan. 2, 1995, 30–33.

[31]For example, in fall 1996 TCI was said to be considering dropping WGN from the lineup on all its systems because of a price dispute with Tribune Co. On the other hand, WGN is secure on those systems carrying the superstation that are owned by Time Warner. This pro-

vides testimony to the necessity of horizontal integration in creating these "hybrid networks."

[32]"UPN, The Facts," Viacom, November, 1996. Available online at: http://www.viacom.com /x/prodbyunitl.html?unit_id=30, and "The Warner Brothers Affiliates," 1996 UTV, http:// TVNet.com/TV /US/Networks/WB.html

[33]Greg Spring, "WeB Cable Forms Initial Partnerships," *Electronic Media,* September 16, 1996, 1, 30.

[34]Barry R. Litman, "The Changing Role of the Television Networks." In Allison Alexander, James Owers, and Rod Carveth (eds.), *Media Economics: Theory and Practice* (Hillsdale, NJ: Erlbaum, 1993), 225–244.

[35]Litman, 1979.

[36]Richard Zoglin, "Network Crazy!" *Time,* January 16, 1995, 68–72.

[37]Bruce W. Owen and Steven S. Wildman, *Video Economics* (Cambridge, MA: Harvard University Press, 1992).

[38]Sylvia Chan–Olmstead, "From Sesame Street to Wall Street: An Analysis of Market Competition in Commercial Children's Television," *Journal of Broadcasting & Electronic Media* 1, (Winter 1996): 30–44.

[39]Steve McClellan, "Cable on a Roll in Kids Upfront," *Broadcasting & Cable,* February 12, 1996, 12.

[40]McClellan, "Cable on a Roll," 12.

[41]"Time Inc. Closes."

[42]"Redstone Says 'New ' Viacom to Emphasize Software Strength," *Publishers Weekly,* July 18, 1994, 12.

[43]Laura Landro, "Giants Talk Synergy But Few Make It Work," *The Wall Street Journal,* September 25, 1995, B1, B6.

[44]Elizabeth Jensen, "What's Up, Doc? Vertical Integration," *The Wall Street Journal,* October 16, 1995, B1.

[45]Elizabeth Jensen, "New Market Rules Help Make 'Friends' Quick Syndication Hit," *The Wall Street Journal,* January 15, 1996, B1, B3.

[46]Wilson Dizard, *Old Media, New Media.* (New York: Longman, 1994).

[47]Joseph R. Dominick, Barry L. Sherman, and Gary A. Copeland, *Broadcasting/Cable and Beyond,* 2nd ed. (New York: McGraw-Hill, 1993), 112.

[48]"UPN Loss to $67.1 Million for Half-Year," *Electronic Media,* July 24, 1995, 30.

[49]Thomas Tyrer, "WB, UPN Explore Merger," *Electronic Media,* September 18, 1995, 1.

[50]Disney Fourth Quarter Report, 1996. Disney Corp. available at: www.disney.com/investor/ earnings/q496.html

9

Consumer Selection
of Motion Pictures

Indra De Silva

Once limited to the theater and network television, movies are now the staple of the multibillion dollar home video industry that includes videocassette, cable TV, pay cable, pay-per-view, video-on-demand, and laser disc. The typical moviegoer is now presented with an unprecedented array of windows from which to choose when and where to see a movie. Industry estimates of consumer acceptance of these windows show consumers are well aware of the choices and use them in a selective fashion that has not so far greatly altered conventional theater attendance habits.

While the industry attempts to understand movie audience behavior with a commercial interest and keep the findings to themselves, academic researchers concentrated more on the aesthetic aspects of the medium than its audiences.[1] Only over the last ten to fifteen years did an emergence of serious interest surface among media scholars to study movie audiences from a communication and economic perspective.[2] Yet, they fell far behind the amount of audience studies done on, say, television, radio, or newspapers. The lack of such research, argue Litman and Kohl, "is largely traceable to the proprietary nature of financial data in the industry and the fact that certain creative/artistic elements in film making are so complex (and subtle) that they remain beyond even the most sophisticated content analysis attempts to quantify them."[3]

Academic research on movie attendance, however, concentrated mainly on two broad but essential research questions: (1) Why do people *choose to go to movies* from among the wide array of entertainment options? and, (2) Why and how *is a particular movie selected* over all the other movies available at a given time and place? There are two dominant research approaches that sought to answer these questions. One is identified as the communication theory approach and the other as the economic/business approach. The communication theory approach uses social/psychological theories to explain why people choose to go to movies and why a particular movie is selected. This approach looks at the *individual* motives for movie attendance. The economic/business approach, on the other hand, studies the economics of the industry to explain movie attendance among a *group* of people as a precursor to financial success of the movies. This line of research looks at various elements of the supply side of the industry. While it acknowledges the effects of such demand factors as *price, income, quality of the product,* and available *substitutes* on the moviegoing habit of groups of people, the economic/business approach primarily focuses on the institutional factors affecting the entire vertical system of supply of films.[4] As such, the economic/business approach has concentrated largely on the question of why a particular movie is chosen over the other movies than why people select movies as an entertainment option. Interestingly, both approaches test the basic concept of movie consumption (which is, in fact, demand in action) and share many of the same variables in their analysis. But they differ on the data sources and manner in which they test hypotheses. The communication approach uses attitudinal survey research, whereas the economic approach examines the forces of the marketplace and uses aggregate data from industry and trade sources.

As such, the goal of this chapter is to attempt to converge the two approaches to find common ground, theoretically and methodologically, to explain movie attendance behavior. To do so, this chapter will look into the selection process consumers now use in watching motion pictures in theaters and other windows, such as home video and pay-per-view. Specifically, this chapter provides empirical evidence of the movie selection process that attempts to answer the question: What factors have the most influence when consumers are deciding which movie to see? The research is approached from the demand side using household data.

SAMPLE AND DATA COLLECTION

The sample for this study was drawn from the general public[5] to represent a cross section of the moviegoing population. The telephone survey method was employed to collect data.[6] Random digit dialing, using the local LATA prefixes, was used to select and reach the sample.[7] Although most of the questions were derived from previous studies and information gathered from two focus group sessions, two pilot studies were conducted to refine the survey instrument on small samples from the target population.

VARIABLE SELECTION

As the two statistical models in the present study deal with estimating theater attendance and video rentals, two dependent variables have been used. The first dependent variable (labeled as MOVIE#) estimates the average monthly movie theater attendance of the respondents. The use of this variable as a criterion variable in multiple regression requires assignment of approximate values to the variable by the researcher. For example, if a respondent attends one or more movies per month, the actual number is recorded and used. However, if the respondent's attendance frequency is less than once a month, the value was then classified in one of the appropriate categories (i.e., "Once about every two to six months" or "about once a year"). To approximate a value that would be isomorphic to the real values of these two categories, .5 and .1 were assigned to the first and second categories, respectively. Naturally, those who said they "never" go to movies received a true 0. Part of this measurement procedure was adopted from the Motion Picture Association of America's (MPAA) survey instruments. Given the sporadic nature of theater attendance among the older public, this seems to be the closest one can get to measure attendance on a continuum.

Twenty-two independent variables were used in this study as predictors to explain theater attendance and video rental patterns. Twelve of them were related to creative and promotional aspects of movies.[8] The remaining ten variables were used to measure demographics and price factors. As the research objectives for this study emerged from economic and communications research and industry analyses described in various other chapters, an effort was made to accommodate all the possible variables suggested by the appropriate theories and industry findings. Unfortunately there is no reliable and valid way to measure certain variables from the demand side using attitudinal household data. For example, the variables pertinent to the scheduling and release pattern of the movies, such as the importance of release pattern, number of screens, or the impact of production budgets, are impossible to operationalize meaningfully using household data without drastically changing the research design. The following section further elaborates the independent variables with their theoretical expectations.

CREATIVE AND PROMOTIONAL VARIABLES

The importance of Stars, Director, Story Type, MPAA Ratings, Critical Reviews, Theater Previews, Previously Known Story, Word-of-Mouth Advertising, winning or nominations for Awards such as Oscar or Golden Globe, Advertising in the Media, Star appearances on TV Talk Shows, and the movie being a Sequel, are the variables that were used as creative and promotional predictor variables of movie attendance and video rental.[9] The importance of each of these variables to the audiences was measured on the basis of self-reports. Respondents were asked to rate how important each of these factors was to them when they decide which movie to see. The rating scale ranged from 0 to 10 where 0 = "Not Important at All" and 10 = "Very Important."

The first variable from the creative sphere is "Stars." This variable is expected to estimate the importance of a star or stars on the attendance decisions. While the conventional wisdom always tends to attribute a movie's success to the star power, the actual contribution of "superstars" has changed from time to time. For example, Litman found that the presence of a Star had no significant impact on rental revenues, but Litman and Kohl found that the Star actors and top directors were significantly related to financial success.[10] Austin[11] also asserts the significance of popular stars on attendance but argues that stars alone are rarely an important factor in attendance decisions. The ever-increasing market value of "superstars" also indicates the faith the industry has in the stars. The presence of Stars, therefore, were expected to have a significant positive impact on attendance decisions.

Both economic and communications research recognizes the importance of a reputable director on financial success and attendance decisions. Economic research goes beyond the simple reputation of the director to his or her ability to blend all the creative aspects of a movie, including the director's reputation in industry circles, to obtain outside financing for a film project.[12] While it is difficult to measure such attributes of a director from the audience's perspective, only the importance of the director to the moviegoer on the attendance decision was considered here.

In their last testing of the Litman model, Litman and Kohl[13] used fifteen categories to describe the story type or genres (STORYTYPE), e.g., Drama, Comedy, Action Adventure, and so on. The economic research measures the impact of each different genre category on rental revenues. However, testing the importance of each specific genre category from the demand side creates some problems since there are no established categories.[14] As such, it is difficult to develop reliable measures to assess the importance of each genre type to the audiences as they often have difficulty identifying the proper genre except for some overwhelmingly obvious categories such as Comedy, Western, or Science Fiction. This research, then, measured the *perceived importance of genres* on attendance in general, not for *a* specific genre.

The MPAA rating (RATINGS)—G, PG, PG-13, R, NC-17—generally is an indicator of the degree of sexual content, violence, and harsh language in a movie. Past research and industry preferences suggest the largest audience appeal for PG and PG-13 movies, while the R, X, and "Not-Rated" movies scare off the audiences.[15] Similar to the genre variable economic research also measures the importance of individual rating types on revenues. Again, our research measured the importance of the overall concept of ratings and not the likes or dislikes of specific rating types.

The recent success of movies that were adaptations of, or based on, a previously known story (PRESTORY) that is familiar to the public shows the positive impact the familiarity of the story line has on attendance. As Litman and Kohl[16] noted, the movies based on known stories (e.g., successful plays, novels, TV shows, cartoons, etc.,) have a built-in advantage over those that start from scratch. The successes of *The Fugitive* (TV Show), *Schindler's List* (Book and the subject—Holocaust), and many Scott Turow and Stephen King films suggest the importance of the known story in attracting audiences. They also give a head start in marketing and promotions as audiences already possess some knowledge about the story line.

The last variable associated with the creative aspect is the "sequel" (the attractive power of a movie that is a sequel of one that the audience has seen and liked). While the economic approach puts sequels under the same category of a "previously known story/idea," sequel was measured in this study as a separate variable.

Litman and Kohl regarded advertising and publicity as the key to luring the avid movigoer into the theaters to begin the important word-of-mouth campaign. However, they were not able to include either one of these variables in their models due to the practical problems associated with measuring them from the supply side. The inclusion of this variable through the survey approach may then provide some insights to their effects on attendance decisions. Two separate variables were measured, one for advertising in the media and the other for the importance of other people's recommendations (labeled: ADVERTISING and WORDOFM, respectively).

Theater previews (PREVIEWS) have also been excluded in economic research. Austin[17] considers theater previews, or "trailers," as a form of advertising that addresses an already interested group, and he includes them in his "zoom model" under the broad category of "Advertising and Publicity." Winning or having been nominated for major awards, such as an Oscar or Golden Globe (AWARDS), is considered by Litman and Kohl[18] to be a key advertising/publicity tool. The financial significance of this variable is well recognized even in the trade circles. For example, *Advertising Age* recently observed that "Oscar nominations and eventual Academy Award win—can as much as double a film's box-office business and provides strong mainstream appeal for 'art-house' pictures."[19] Litman and Kohl[20] only included the nomination or winning of an Oscar in Best Picture, Best Actor, and Best Actress categories and found that the nomination to one of these categories is significantly related to rental revenues. This research attempts to take the awards factor one step forward and includes not only Oscars but also other recognitions such as the Golden Globe, as these awards also receive increased media attention and subsequent publicity.

Appearances of stars on television talk shows, such as *The Today Show, The Tonight Show,* or *Late Night With David Letterman* (TVPROMOS), is a new variable included in this study to assess the publicity value of star appearances on TV talk shows on attendance. In recent years this has become such a crucial publicity event that some studios book their big stars in more than one show in the same week to coincide with the release dates. This is certainly not as important as Awards on the attendance decisions but may be of interest if this factor is at least registering in the audiences' radar.

DEMOGRAPHIC, MEDIA, AND ECONOMIC VARIABLES

Seven demographic variables have been used as predictor variables. Age (AGE), level of education (EDULEVEL), and income (INCOME) were measured using the same categories used by the annual MPAA surveys and other standard measurement procedures used in mass media research. Three binary[21] (dummy) variables were used for marital status (MARITAL), respondent's gender (GENDER), and absence or presence of children under sixteen in the household (CHILDREN). The total number in the household (HHHEADS) was included as a continuous variable.

In addition to the demographics, several price and media related variables were also included as possible predictor and grouping variables. They included: subscription to cable television (CATVSUB), respondent's willingness to attend more movies if the admission prices were lower (ADMSN$), number of movie channels subscribed to (PREMIUM#), the total cost for a movie outing (MOVICOST), and an estimate of the percentage of movies seen in the theaters out of all movies seen during the past six months (PERCENTAGE). The inclusion of some of the media penetration/usage variables, such as the number of movies watched on premium channels, pay-per-view availability, usage, and frequency of usage, were included primarily for descriptive purposes.

Additional questions were included primarily to compare video rental behavior with theater attendance and to measure audience perceptions about the home video window. Four open-ended questions, adopted from Austin's research, were used to measure what attracted the viewers to their last movie seen in a theater and the last movie seen on video.[22] Additional open-ended items were included to explore what the audiences most and least like about theater attendance and video rental.

The expected relationships between independent and dependent variables were largely governed by: (1) the theoretical suggestions; (2) the current industry structure; and (3) the specific window (movie or video) the variable is used to explain. As such, the expected relationships will be discussed with the results.

TELEPHONE SURVEY OUTCOME

Table 9-1 presents the outcome of the telephone survey results and the completion rates. A total of 845 telephone numbers were made with 490 successful contacts. Of

TABLE 9-1 Telephone Survey Results

	Frequency	Percentage
Completions	366	58.7
Refusals	76	12.2
No Answer[1]	181	29.1
Ineligibles[2]	174	—
Excusions[3]	48	—
Total	845	

[1]No Answer, Answering Machines, Call Backs, Busy Signal, Language Barrier.
[2]Disconnects, Not in Service, Business.
[3]Respondents who hadn't seen a movie in a theater or on video in previous six months.

the 490 eligible respondents that were contacted, 414 (84.5 percent) agreed to take part in the survey while 76 (15.5 percent) refused. However, 48 of the 414 respondents who agreed to take part in the survey said they haven't seen a movie either in a theater or rented one on video during the past six months. As such, their interviews were not continued, so the effective sample size was 366 (414 – 48). As expected from a sample of random digit dialing, a large amount of numbers (181) were either not yet assigned, disconnected, or assigned to business or government establishments. The final 58.7 percent response rate of all households contacted is in the higher end for a telephone survey and might be attributed to the higher concentration of college students in some of the area prefixes in the sample.

THE RESULTS

Sample Demographics

Table 9-2 presents the summary statistics of major demographic variables. The population distribution for major demographic variables presented in Table 9-2 are based on recent national census data. The sample seems to comprise about 4 percent more females than the actual population it is expected to represent. About one-fifth of the sample was sixteen to twenty years old and the age grouping of sixteen to twenty-nine-year-olds accounted for slightly over one half (51.4 percent) of the sample. The age categories used in this study were adopted from the MPAA's annual motion picture attendance survey. Overall, the sample seems somewhat skewed toward youth, higher education, and income categories, yet it represents the characteristics of the population it is drawn from.

Movie Attendance Patterns: An Overview

Using theater attendance frequency as the criterion, the movie industry categorizes moviegoers in four broad groups: *Frequent* (those who attend at least one movie per month); *Occasional* (those who attend at least one movie in two to six months); *Infrequent* (those who attend less than once in six months); and *Never* (those who reported not going to the movies at all).[23] When the same criterion was employed, this study found the majority of the respondents self-reported to be "frequent" moviegoers (54.3 percent), about 30 percent "occasional," and 8.2 percent "infrequent." Only 7.4 percent of the respondents reported that they "never" go to the theaters to see movies. Nonetheless, those who never go to a theater to see a movie were kept in the sample because subsequent probing found this group uses other windows, specifically home video, to see movies. The average adult frequents a theater slightly more than once a month (Mean = 1.3). A little more than one half of those surveyed (52.7 percent) attend movies one to four times a month.

The overall average attendance, however, appears to disguise the specific movie attendance habits. A closer look at the different demographic subgroups

TABLE 9-2 Sample Demographics

Variable	Percent (N = 366)	Population Frequency	Distribution*	
Gender				
Male	44%	160	48%	
Female	56%	206	52%	
Marital Status				
Single	59%	216	51%	
Married/Living Together	41%	150	49%	
Children Under 16 in Household				
Yes	28.7%	105		
No	71.3%	261		
Age				
16–20	20.5%	75	15–19	11.2%
21–24	22.4%	82	20–24	14.4%
25–29	08.5%	31	25–34	22.1%
30–39	18.6%	68	35–44	19.7%
40–49	16.1%	59	45–54	12.3%
50–59	05.7%	21	55–64	8.8%
60 or over	08.2%	30	65 >	11.5%
Income				
under $15,000	30.3%	111	under $15,000	21.3%
$15,001–$25,000	11.7%	43	$15,001–$25,000	16.7%
$25,001–$35,000	12.6%	46	$25,001–$35,000	16.2%
$35,001–$45,000	10.7%	39	$35,001–$50,000	19.8%
$45,001–$55.000	09.3%	34	$50,001–above	26.0%
$55,001–$65,000	05.7%	21		
$65,001 and above	12.0%	44		
Refused	07.7%	28		
Education				
Less than high school	01.1%	4	15.7%	
High school completed	10.7%	39	27.6%	
Some college	51.9%	190	24.1%	
College graduate	21.6%	79	14.5%	
Post graduate	14.8%	54	10.2%	
Associate degree	—	—	7.9%	

	Mean	Median	Std Dev
Number of children	1.9	2.0	.99
Number in household	2.89	2.0	1.57

*Based on 1992 census data.

TABLE 9-3   Overall Average Movie Attendance Habits: Significant Differences Between Demographic Subgroups

Group	Group Means	T-value	df	Alpha
Single / Married	1.51 / 0.90	4.95	360	.001
Age: 16–29 / 30 and Over	1.58 / 0.92	5.18	350	.001
With Children / Without	.99 / 1.37	2.89	244	.01
Subscribe to Pay TV / Do Not	1.62 / 1.14	2.55	117	.01

showed that these groups significantly deviate from the average attending habits. For example, those who were single attend movies significantly more often than their married (or living together) counterparts (Table 9-3). As expected, age makes a significant difference in movie attendance as well. Those who were in the sixteen to twenty-nine year age category attend significantly more movies than people thirty years or older (Table 9-3). It is no surprise then that the movie industry estimates show this age group (sixteen to twenty-nine) accounts for nearly one half of total domestic movie attendance.[24] Also as expected, those who have children living with them go to the movies significantly less often than those without children (Table 9-3).

Further differences were also present with regard to the subscription of premium cable channels. Those who subscribe to premium cable channels (particularly movie channels such as HBO, TMC, or Cinemax) tend to frequent movies significantly more than those who do not (Table 9-3). Although the cable TV subscribers, VCR/Laser Disc owners, and males tend to go to the movies more often than their respective counterparts (Group Means: 1.36/1.21; 1.35/1.21; 1.39/1.28, respectively), the differences were simply due to chance than to a statistically meaningful regularity.

Importance of Creative and Marketing Factors on Movie Attendance

Table 9-4 presents the importance assigned to creative and marketing variables on individual and collective movie attending decisions by the respondents.[25] Variables are listed in order of their importance to the entire sample with corresponding means and standard deviations. Subsequent columns show the respective mean values for four demographic subgroups and the results of significance tests (t-tests) to assess the group differences.

As seen in Table 9-4, story type topped the list and the first six variables received above average ratings. Also evident is the mixture of creative and marketing factors in the rankings. What is more important and interesting, however, are the significant differences found between the subgroups. For example, although it is in

TABLE 9-4 Importance of Creative and Marketing Factors on Movie Attendance

(Scale: 0 = Not Important at All; 10 = Very Important)

Factor	Ttl Sample Mean (SD)	Gender M/F	Marital Mrd/Sgl	Children Yes/No	Age 16–29/30>
1. STORYTYPE	8.39 (1.44)	**8.18/8.54**	**8.57/8.26**	8.57/8.32	**8.10/8.69**
2. WORDOFM	7.44 (1.71)	7.44/7.44	7.75/7.23	7.77/7.31	7.22/7.67
3. STARS	7.05 (2.11)	7.07/7.02	6.97/7.10	6.98/7.08	7.15/6.93
4. PREVIEWS	6.57 (1.82)	6.42/6.68	6.42/6.68	**6.91/6.43**	6.73/6.39
5. REVIEWS	5.81 (2.31)	5.61/5.98	**6.27/5.50**	**6.34/5.60**	**5.21/6.46**
6. ADVERTISING	5.73 (2.01)	5.93/5.58	5.65/5.80	5.89/5.68	5.90/5.55
7. SEQUEL	4.87 (2.40)	4.81/4.91	4.97/4.80	5.05/4.80	4.68/5.07
8. PRE-STORY	4.79 (2.27)	4.70/4.86	**5.07/4.60**	4.79/4.79	**4.40/5.20**
9. AWARDS	4.41 (2.42)	4.56/4.30	**4.71/4.20**	4.52/4.37	4.18/4.66
10. TVPROMS	4.10 (2.25)	3.94/4.14	**3.77/4.25**	3.86/4.16	**4.38/3.71**
11. RATINGS	3.80 (2.96)	**3.46/4.06**	**4.67/3.20**	**6.17/2.84**	**3.08/4.56**
12. DIRECTOR	3.77 (2.53)	4.01/3.58	3.65/3.85	3.53/3.87	3.85/3.68
Group Sizes	366	160/206	150/216	105/261	188/178

Bold type indicates the mean differences that are significant at a: .05.
All two-tailed tests.

the lower end of the list, the importance of MPAA ratings significantly differs from group to group. As evident from the group means, older, married, and females with children found MPAA ratings significantly more important in their movie attending decisions than their respective counterparts. Likewise, those who were married also found story type, other people's recommendations (word-of-mouth), critical reviews in the media, winning or nomination for awards, such as the Oscar and Golden Globe, and the movie being based on a previously known story as significantly more important than those who were not married. We found evidence to the effect that the importance of creative and marketing variables were related to demographic and other lifestyle factors. Correspondingly, "the young," "the single," and "the ones without children" were willing to place a lesser value on these factors than their respective counterparts. The empirical evidence simply shows how indiscriminate the young moviegoer is.

The Social Context of Movie Attendance

An important factor in movie attendance is the social context in which it takes place. Only a very small minority (5 percent) goes to the movies alone. For the vast majority it is a social activity. Most young adults (sixteen to twenty-four) go to the movies with friends or a date, and for those who are thirty years or above, going to the movies is a family activity. The social appeal of moviegoing goes beyond doing something with family and friends. For some, it also means being part of an "unknown" crowd. For example, a majority (53 percent) cited "going out" or "being in the crowd" as the most important reason for going to the theater to see a movie.

The social nature of going to the movies appears to cost the audiences dearly. On the average, it cost them more than twelve dollars to go out to see a movie (mean $12.46; standard deviation = $7.70). The average, however, tends to conceal the details as different subgroups spend well above the average. Naturally, the cost is a function of the magnitude of the social ties. As social ties grow, so does the cost. Those who were married, for example, spend twice as much as those who are single for a movie outing ($24.19 vs. $12.16; t = 4.42; df = 333; a = .001; two-tailed test). Similarly, those who are thirty years or older spend $21.50 for a movie outing compared to the $12.80 the "younger" spend (t = 4.47; df = 287; a = .001; two-tailed). Larger differences also exist between those who have children living with them and with those who do not ($25.89 vs. $13.64; t = 8.03; df = 112; a = .001; two-tailed test).

The significance of the price factor emerged elsewhere in the study as well. For example, the high ticket and concession prices kept a large number of audiences away from the theaters, (Table 9-5). A vast majority (75 percent) would go to the movies "more often" if the ticket prices were lower. It seems reasonable, therefore, to believe that it is mostly the high costs and other "inconveniences" associated with going to the theater, not the movie quality itself, that keeps the majority away from the theaters. It also explains why the adults, as a group, are more cautious when it comes to theater attendance decisions. For those who are older the consequences are more expensive and time-consuming than for the younger audiences who have more time, fewer social obligations and, above all, are likely to get cheaper admission prices as well.

What then do the movies offer to outweigh and overcome the audience's antipathy? Our findings appear to shed some light on this area. When asked to single out the most important reason for going to a theater, more than 95 percent of the audi-

TABLE 9-5   Least Like about Going to a Theater to See a Movie

(N = 339)	Frequency	Percentage
Price (admission and concession)	153	45.1%
Noise (people talking, rudeness)	64	18.9%
Comfort (uncomfortable seats, sticky floors)	35	10.3%
Crowds	32	9.4%
Logistics (finding a sitter, parking)	18	5.3%
Having to go out	14	4.1%
None	10	2.9%
Other (previews, show times, etc.)	13	3.9%

ences agreed on four major reasons: escape (43.8 percent); technical superiority (31.7 percent); to see it now (10.3 percent); and the theater atmosphere (9.1 percent) (Table 9-6). The "escape" represents such reasons as "need to go out," "to relax," "to unwind," "to get away from kids," and "to get away from daily routine." Technical reasons include the "big screen," "superior sound quality," and the "lifelike" experience only the theater can offer. About 10 percent of the audiences go to the theaters because they want to see the movies "now" or see it "before the others see it." About the same number of respondents like the theater "atmosphere" in which they can be "among the crowds." These patrons, to use an economic phrase, perceive a degree of utility from the theater going experience that offsets the inconveniences (efforts) and costs (admission and other) of watching a movie in a theater.

A rather qualitative measure, adopted from Austin's research, was applied to look into the reasons surrounding the selection of a specific movie. A large majority of those who have seen a movie (81.2 percent) during the past six months did remember the movie by name. Table 9-7 presents the reasons that attracted audiences to the movie they have last seen. While the list contains more than ten reasons, most of the audiences apparently agree on a few reasons. Among them, the "stars," "story line" (the plot), and the "story type" (genres) contributed to about 50 percent of the attendance while advertising and publicity related factors accounted for about 25 percent of the attendance. The obvious limitation of this measure is its exclusive reliance on the *last* movie attended, which may or may not be a typical movie. For example, the measure can be largely skewed if an "event like" movie, such as *Jurassic Park,* dominated the theaters during the period the measurements were taken.

The Other Windows: Watching Movies at Home

Cable television was universally available in the sampled universe and the subscription rate stood at 83 percent. About 30 percent of the cable subscribers also subscribed to at least one of the premium movie channels (HBO, TMC, Cinemax,

TABLE 9-6 Most Important Reason for Going to a Theater

	Frequency	Percentage
Escape (relax, unwind, get away)	145	43.8%
Technical (big screen, sound quality)	105	31.7%
To see it now	34	10.3%
Theater atmosphere (being in the crowd)	30	9.1%
None	7	2.1%
Not on video	4	1.2%
Other	6	1.8%

(N = 331)

TABLE 9-7   Factors Attracted to the last Movie/Video

What Attracted to the Last . . .	Video		Theater	
	Frequency	Percentage	Frequency	Percentage
Star	65	29.3%	60	22.0%
Ads/Promos/Reviews/Previews	16	7.2%	50	18.3%
Story line	33	14.9%	47	17.2%
Someone took/Wanted to see	11	5.0%	27	9.9%
Story type	18	4.9%	25	9.2%
Kids wanted to see	18	4.9%	20	7.3%
Recommendations	19	5.2%	14	5.1%
Awards/Nominations	0	0%	8	2.9%
Knew the story	5	2.3%	6	2.2%
Sequel/FX/Prequel	5	2.3%	5	1.8%
Director	4	1.8%	6	1.8%
Other	4	1.8%	5	4.0%
See again	16	7.2%	NA	NA
Attractive cover	4	1.8%	NA	NA
Missed at the theater	2	.9%	NA	NA
	(N = 222)		(N = 273)	

Showtime, or Disney), and premium channel subscribers watch an average of 6.7 movies on these channels per month.

While a large majority of the cable households (82.3 percent) do have access to pay-per-view (PPV) services, requesting movies on PPV was not a popular activity. Only 14 percent of the PPV accessible households had ever requested and paid for a movie on PPV and 80 percent of those who did did so only less than once a month.

Conversely, home video is the most popular window for the movies. An overwhelming majority of the households have a VCR (86.1 percent) and a small percentage of those VCR households (3.6 percent) were also equipped with a laser disc player. The average monthly rental of 4.1 videos was more than three times as much as the average theater attendance of 1.3 per month. The average household audience for a rented movie stands at 3.3 people.

An interesting feature of the video audience is that it does not apparently overlap with the theater audience. A large majority (84.2 percent) of the video renters "rarely" or "never" rented the movies already seen in a theater. If these two were independent audiences, what is the impact of the traditional theater on the home video or vice versa? The answer is that home video is becoming a substitute window for the traditional theater. Nearly one half of the respondents did say they wait for the video rather than going to the theater "always" or "almost always" and an additional third (33.9 percent) did so "about half the time." In addition, the majority of the moviegoers (56.2 percent) would rent the video instead of going to the theater if a movie were released on video simultaneously with the theater release. Under such a circumstance they would be willing to pay a higher rental fee for such an early release than what they pay now. These estimates reveal that home video has undoubtedly become the largest window for the movies according to penetration and usage levels but, more importantly, how people perceive it as an independent exhibition window for the movies.

There are some noticeable similarities and differences between the theater and the home video windows in their appeal to the audiences. The reasons that attract audiences to the theater were more or less the same for video as well (Table 9-7). One noticeable difference is the impact advertising and publicity strategies have on the two windows. While advertising and promotional factors were the second biggest attraction for theater attendance, only 7 percent of the video rental decisions were affected by those factors (Table 9-7). This seems quite normal because, unlike the theater release, the video release hardly has advertising budgets or promotional strategies built into it.[26] Moreover, the effects of reviews largely dry out by the time the video hits the stores. This finding also explains the recent attempts by the industry to narrow the passage of time between the theatrical and the video releases to benefit from the spillover effects of advertising and other promotions initially done for the theatrical release.

Why has the home video become such an attractive alternative to going to the cinema? The answer is simply the *price* and *convenience*. Virtually all video renters (91.5 percent), prefer to rent because watching at home is much more convenient and far less expensive (Table 9-8). Home video is convenient because it allows audiences to "watch it at the convenience of home," and "at a convenient time," and "watch it without leaving home." And renting a movie is cheaper because the audience can avoid high ticket and concession prices. This may be the reason why only 36 percent of the movies seen by the sample respondents occurred in a theater. The traditional theater has now clearly become a less important movie window than it was five or ten years ago, rather it is now perceived by industry insiders as a "launching pad" for the other windows.

Results of Multivariate Analyses

The multivariate analyses supplement the findings presented up to this point with more sophisticated statistical procedures that assess the *collective* impact of the independent variables on theater attendance and video rental. Two separate sets of multivariate equations have been estimated—one for movie attendance and the other for video rental.

To set the stage for this complex analysis, it is useful to examine the simple correlations between the dependent variables and the independent variables. Table 9-9 presents simple correlations for the entire set of independent variables with the two dependent variables, theater attendance and video rental.[27] The direction of the relationship between independent and dependent variables needs to be discussed at

TABLE 9-8 Most Important Reason for Renting a Movie

	Frequency	Percentage
Convenience	181	59.3%
Price	98	32.1%
Watch what missed in theater	11	3.6%
Watch again	6	2.0%
Other (family event, bad theaters)	9	3.0%

(N = 305)

this point as their expectations vary from one dependent measure to the other. As seen in Table 9-9, only four of the twelve movie quality and marketing variables (Director, Storytype, Reviews, and Awards) were significantly correlated with theater attendance (MOVIE#).

Three of the other independent variables, marital status, having children in the household, and age, were significantly negatively correlated with theater attendance. Their negative relationship with movie attendance is within the range of theoretical expectations as an older, married populace with children tends to attend movies less frequently than their respective counterparts. Although not statistically significant in this simple analysis, the cost of going to the movies (MOVICOST), willingness to go to the movies if admission prices were lower (ADMSN$), and the number of people in the household (HHHEADS) have the correct signs and are approaching empirical significance. No a priori direction had been expected for the variable household income. Income was found to be negatively correlated with theater attendance but showed a positive correlation with video rental, suggesting the higher the income the lower the theater attendance but, consequently, the higher the video rental. This is a somewhat awkward relationship given the fact that going to the theater to see a movie is the more expensive option between the two.

Age is also significantly negatively correlated with video rentals, but the relationship is weaker than it is with movie attendance. While there is no a priori direction for this relationship, it is reasonable to expect a positive relationship between age and video rental as the price and time sensitive older population may find it more convenient and less expensive to rent than to go to the theater. As expected, theater attendance percentage (PERCENTAGE) shows a strong significantly negative correlation with video rentals. Although not significant, unlike with theater attendance, marital status was positively correlated with video rentals, suggesting a tendency among the married to rely more on the home video window than on theaters for their movie viewing.

A salient factor in the correlations are the very weak associations among the twelve movie quality and marketing variables and video rental patterns. Not only do they lack significance, their correlation coefficients were considerably low, in many instances reaching near zero correlations. On the contrary, demographic and economic variables were more strongly related to video rentals, with some relationships gaining statistical significance.

Regression Analysis Results for Theater Attendance

While the simple correlations provide some useful information about the relationships between the independent and the dependent variables, the bivariate nature of simple correlations does not allow one to assess the *collective* impact of the independent variables on the criterion measure. As such, the multiple regression procedure was used to better understand how the independent variables collectively fit together to explain the variance in theater attendance. Table 9-9 presents various summary statistics for the variables used in regression analyses.

The regression equations listed in Table 9-10 present the results obtained using the same set of variables but in different variable and sample configurations to assess the models that best fit statistically yet are theoretically meaningful. Equation 1 was estimated using a partial sample of 301 cases with missing values remaining untreated, including all 21 independent variables. Equation 2 has been estimated using all the variables in equation 1 but the missing values for the variables income (28 cases), movie cost (31 cases), and size of the household (9 cases) were substituted by their respective averages.[28] The second equation, (Table 9-10) with the missing values treated, provides a slightly better statistical fit as it explains about 2 percent more variance in the dependent measure ($R^2 = .2069$ vs. $R^2 = .1871$).

Equation 3 is similar to equation 2 but was estimated without the factor income. Although income was found to be a significant predictor for theater attendance (as seen in equations 1 and 2), it appears to highly intercorrelated with several other predictor variables, suggesting potential multicollinearity problems, i.e., lack of independence among the "independent variables."[29] Income was thus excluded from subsequent estimates and the results, as it turned out, seem to be a good compromise (Equation 3). Although equation 3 resulted in a model with smaller R^2, a new variable, "Awards," which lost its significance earlier, reentered the equation as a significant predictor.

Equation 4 was estimated by regressing only the 12 variables that deal with movie quality and marketing factors, leaving demographic and economic predictors out. This equation presents some very interesting results. The new equation has a lower statistical fit as it only explains about 15 percent of the observed variability ($R^2 = .1483$), compared to the preceding models, which is not unusual given the evidence of impact of other predictor variables like age and marital status. Nevertheless, the new equation resulted in a model with three new statistically significant theoretically sound variables (story type, reviews, and ratings). Although the statistical fit was lower, this equation provides some useful information relevant to our understanding of movie attendance. As discussed earlier in this chapter, the importance of these three variables significantly differs from group to group (i.e., married to single, young to old, and households with and without children) when group dif-

TABLE 9-9   Sample Statistics for Variables in Regression Analyses (N = 366 unless otherwise stated)

Variable	Mean	Std Dev	Skewness	Correlation with Movie#	Vidrent
Movie#	1.26	1.27	2.07	——	.089
Videorent	4.12	3.95	1.80	.089	——
Stars	7.05	2.11	−1.05	.088	.007
Director	3.77	2.53	.33	.204**	.010
Storytype	8.39	1.44	−1.37	.108a	.006
Ratings	3.80	2.96	.45	.062	.033
Reviews	5.82	2.31	−1.03	.129a	.025
Previews	6.57	1.82	1.03	.091	.051
Prestory	4.79	2.27	−.07	.009	.006
Wordofm	7.44	1.72	−1.34	.029	.001
Awards	4.41	2.42	.16	.175*	.001
Advertising	5.74	2.00	−.76	.160*ab	.028
TVpromos	4.06	2.25	.04	.072	.044
Sequel	4.87	2.40	−0.14	.008	.035
Percentage	35.89	34.33	0.80	——	−.501**
Movicost	12.46	7.70	1.33	−.070	.267a
HHHeads	2.89	1.57	1.15	.008	.319**
Age	3.37	1.89	.35	−.222**	−.135*
Edu. Level	3.38	.90	.30	−.003	.134
Income	3.24	2.14	.57	−.033	.036
Binary Variables					
Admsn$	.75	na	na	.082	.121
Marital	.41	na	na	−.200**	.117
Children	.29	na	na	−.111a	.249**

For those variables that are continuous and polynomial, the means, standard deviations, and degree of skewness are presented. For binary (dummy) variables, only the means are presented to be used as proportions as standard deviation and skewness are not meaningful with such variables.

*Significant at .01. **Significant at .001.
aBecame significant after mean substitutions.
bLost significance after mean substitutions.

ferences were estimated using t-tests. Intrinsically, when the importance of these variables was assessed collectively in regression analysis, the group differences (impact of demographic variables) appear to prevent these variables entering the equation as significant factors.

The fifth and the final equation in this section is similar to equation 3 but uses a logarithmic transformation (base 10) of the dependent measure.[30] The equation with the transformed criterion measure achieved a statistical fit equal to that of equation 2 even without the income factor. In terms of the number of variables in the equation,

TABLE 9-10   Regression Equations for Movie Attendance

Dependent Variable: Average Monthly Theater Attendance

Ind Variable	Nonstandardized Beta Coefficients				
	Eqn 1	Eqn 2	Eqn 3	Eqn 4	Eqn 5
Director	.0761*	.1272*	.0903*	.1055*	.1078*
Reviews	.0869*	.0958*	.0963*	.1231*	.0194*
Advertising	.0784*	.0673*	.0952*	.0696*	.0270*
Awards	.0543*	.0843	.0610*	.0537*	.0319*
Storytype	.0663	.0776	.0671	.0943*	.0805
Previews	.0611	.0516	.0740	.0735*	.0396
Ratings	.0187	.0294	.0280	.0362*	.0072
Age	−.1354*	−.1344*	−.1848*	——	−.0660*
Marital Status	−.6406*	−.6948*	−.5610*	——	−.2225*
Income	.1557*	.1749*	——	——	——
Constant	1.07	1.13	1.63	1.39	−.188
R^2	**.1871**	**.2069**	**.1753**	**.1483**	**.2064**
Adj R^2	.1677	.1935	.1615	.1316	.1929
F (sig)	9.63 (001)	15.47 (001)	12.71 (001)	8.90 (001)	12.11 (001)
Std Error	1.09	1.14	1.16	1.18	.372
N	301	366	366	366	366

Equation 2: Missing values substituted with mean values.
Equation 3: Regressed without the independent variable "income."
Equation 4: Regressed with only the creative and marketing variables.
Equation 5: Logarithmic transformation (base 10) of the dependent variable.

*Significant at .05 or greater.

Variables not significant at .05 level in any of the above equations: stars, previews, prestory, wordofm, tvpromos, sequel, movicost, admsn$, children, hhheads, edulevel.

both equations 3 and 5 have the same variables, while the latter has a better statistical fit of almost 21 percent of the variability explained ($R^2 = .2064$) when the dependent measure is "straightened out" with log transformation, thus making it a better model.

Some other interesting things happened when we moved from the simpler to more complex statistical analysis. For example, while the children factor was negatively but significantly related with movie attendance in correlation analysis, its significance disappeared in combination with other variables and did not enter into any of the equations. It may be possible that the children factor can work both ways. Although having young children put an additional burden on going to the theater (as it is necessary to find a sitter and other logistics), the children that are relatively older may be a factor that attracts parents to the theaters, thus offsetting the negative impact. This is also evident from the responses given to one of the open-ended items in the survey for which 7.7 percent cited "kids wanted to see" as the reason for going to the last movie.

Three variables, MPAA ratings, theater previews, and advertising, which were not significant in correlation analysis, but appear to share their variances with demographic factors, did enter into the model in the absence of demographics (equation 4). What is quite noticeable is the entry of more or less the same set of variables in all equations under different sample and variable configurations. This indicates the robustness of the estimation process.

In looking at all five equations collectively, there were four creative variables, director, reviews, advertising, and awards, and two demographic variables, age and marital status, that always related significantly to theater attendance. This was true even when the sample and the variable configurations were altered, indicating their strong association with theater attendance.

In all five models, the entire set of independent variables was linearly related to the dependent variable as all the F values were all significant at .001.[31] The statistical fit (R^2) ranged from .1483 to .2069, meaning between 15 percent to 21 percent of the observed variability in theater attendance can be explained by the variables: director, reviews, advertising, awards, story type, previews, MPAA ratings, age, and marital status. While there is no such thing as good, best, or optimal R^2, it can be viewed as a measure of the explanatory power of a regression equation. Provided theoretically sound variables were included, R^2 is one statistic that can be used to evaluate the "goodness" of an estimated regression equation.[32] However, as R^2 is greatly affected by the individual household data sources used to estimate the regression equations of this study, 15 to 21 percent of explained variance provides encouraging results and is certainly within the standard range of acceptability of similar communication studies.

Regression Analysis Results for Video Rental

Regression equations listed in Table 9-11 present the results for video rental patterns. The same set of independent variables, plus a new predictor variable (proportion of movies seen in the theaters over the past six months, PERCENTAGE), was used to estimate these equations in which the dependent variable was the average monthly video rentals (VIDEORENT). Income was also a significant factor in video rentals but was excluded from subsequent analysis due to its known multicollinearity problems. As noted elsewhere in this chapter, the theoretical justifications for the inclusion of these variables come from their usage to explain theater attendance—consumption of the same product (i.e., movies) but via a different medium.

Similar to the previous analysis, three equations were estimated, one without treating the missing values and the other with missing values substituted with mean values.[33]

Equation 1 in Table 9-11 shows the five variables that are significant when all the variables, including income, were entered using the standard Stepwise method. The equation was estimated using a partial sample (n = 301) as missing values remain untreated. Equation 2 was estimated without income and equation 3 with the

TABLE 9-11   Regression Equations for Video Rental

Dependent Variable: Average Monthly Video Rental

Ind Variable	Nonstandardized Beta Coefficients		
	Eqn 1	Eqn 2	Eqn 3
Age	−.5331*	−.3224*	−.4910*
Percentage	−.0485*	−.0465*	−.0504*
Children	.2962*	.2655*	.3052*
Movicost	.0948*	.0599*	.0726
Income	.2950*	——	——
Constant	6.25	5.36	6.90
R^2	**.3210**	**.3003**	**.2746**
Adj R^2	.3094	.2916	.2665
F (sig)	27.70 (001)	27.87 (001)	33.87 (001)
Std Error	3.14	3.12	3.39
N	301	301	366

Equation 2: Without income, missing values untreated.
Equation 3: Without income, missing values treated.

*Significant at .05 or greater.
Variables not entered to at least one of the equations: all 12 creative and marketing variables, admsn$, hhheads, edulevel.

same variables as equation 2 but with missing values substituted with mean values. Once the missing cases were included, "movicost" lost its significance and did not enter the equation. It also lowered the explained variance by about 2.5 percent. All the other variables were still significant but no new variables entered the model.

What was obvious at the outset is the insignificance of all the creative and marketing variables in all three equations. Although the extremely low correlation coefficients between video rental and all the creative and marketing variables had indicated this outcome, it was surprising to see that none were significant.

Age still remained a significant factor in explaining video rental. However, it was somewhat surprising to see a negative coefficient for age, because it seems reasonable to expect people to rely more on the convenient home video window as they grow older. Unlike the movie attendance equations, marital status, however, was not a significant predictor for video rentals. This seems quite logical as watching a video takes place at home, thus eliminating the need to go out, which is more appealing to the married. As expected, "percentage" had a negative coefficient, suggesting a relatively low tendency toward video rentals among those who attend theaters more. The children factor (having children in the household) entered into the video rental equation with a positive coefficient, suggesting that households with children tend to rent more than non-children households. The significance of "movicost" also suggests that for those who have to spend more for a movie outing, home video provides a less expensive alternative. Again, the importance of both of these variables was not surprising as the early results found "price" and "convenience" were overwhelmingly attractive reasons for renting rather than going to the theater.

The statistical fits (R^2) of theses' equations range from .2746 to .3210, which was about 10 percent more than the equations estimated to explain theater attendance. The most important variable in explaining video rental was theater attendance percentage, which alone explained about 17 percent of the variance in video rental.

CONCLUSIONS

The average adult goes to the movies about once a month. If the industry classifications were to be used, about one half of the respondents are "frequent" moviegoers. To a large extent, the sample statistics closely match the attendance habits found by the industry research and some prior studies.[34] For example, age, education, and marital status significantly influence theater attendance habits as the young, single, and college educated tend to go to the movies more often than their respective counterparts. Consistent with what the industry has noted lately, there seems to be an upward swing in attendance among older demographic segments. For example, the average attendance rate of those who are fifty to fifty-nine years of age ranked only behind the young adults (sixteen to twenty-four age category). However, as the differences did not attain statistical significance, it seems premature to conclude that this is a trend or just an aberration. Likewise, the tendency among males to frequent theaters more often than females shows no statistically significant regularity as well.

Determinants of Theater Attendance

In looking at the results of the collective impact of predictor variables on theater attendance, several findings are worth noting. In all five regression equations five variables, Director, Advertising, Reviews, Age, and, Marital Status were always significantly related to attendance, even under different sample conditions and variable configurations. "Awards" was significant only under different sample size. Storytype, Previews, and Ratings attained significance only when creative and marketing variables were entered without demographic variables. Among all the demographic variables included, Age and Marital Status were the only ones to attain significance.

Age emerged as the most important predictor of attendance and the first variable to enter the equation, explaining about 6 percent of the variability. The negative coefficient of Age suggests an inverse relationship between age and theater attendance and confirms the known association that exists between the young and movie attendance. The strong relationship between age and attendance is also evident from the group t-test results. As bivariate analysis indicates, the young moviegoers not only dominate attendance, but are also quite indifferent to the quality of the movies in their selection process. For example, factors such as the story type, critical reviews, and ratings seem to matter less for them than to older audiences. Instead, their attendance decisions are largely influenced by advertising and promotional factors.

Marital status, a binary variable that is significant in all equations, was able to add 4 percent to the explained variance. The negative coefficients of marital status tell us that being married decreases the number of movies seen by the families compared to their single counterparts. Similar to age, marital status is also associated with other factors that influence attendance decisions. As group t-test results revealed, the married audiences place a significantly higher value on factors such as story type, word-of-mouth advertising, and awards and ratings in their decisions to attend movies.

The importance of advertising and promotional factors on attendance seems overwhelming. Of the six advertising and publicity related variables included (Advertising, Reviews, Previews, Awards, Word-of-Mouth, and TV Promotions), four variables were significantly related to attendance decision. The most prominent were the paid advertising in the media and critical reviews. In all the equations estimated, advertising was the most important variable besides age. In terms of explanatory power, advertising is equal to marital status, which added 4 percent to the explained variance. The significance of critical reviews is consistent and added about 2 percent to the statistical fit. The Awards (nomination or winning of major awards) is also a significant contributor to attendance decisions as it entered all but one equation. Theater previews, a new variable that was adopted from Austin's model, is as important as reviews, but its entry was conditional. Previews entered as a significant predictor of attendance in the absence of demographic factors, suggesting its appeal to the specific demographic sectors. The insignificance of word-of-mouth is quite surprising given its reputation as the most effective form of "advertising" for movie attendance and the rank it earned as the second most important factor affecting attendance decisions. Another new promotional variable attempted for the first time, TV Promos, (appearance of movie stars on television programs like *The Tonight Show* or the *Late Show*) did not gain significance in any of the equations. Perhaps its popularity is not yet widespread or established, or it may not have been measured comprehensively enough.

Despite their wide recognition as important factors affecting attendance, this is the first time practically *all* advertising and publicity related factors were included in a multivariate predictive model to explain theater attendance. Consequently, the significance of four advertising and publicity related variables uncovers some new information and confirms some of the early findings of communication and economic research. The strong relationship between attendance and advertising, together with the significance of theater previews, provides empirical evidence to show filmgoers' reliance on outside sources for information to help them with decision-making. The regression results, together with the results of bivariate analysis, show that advertising and promotional factors have an overwhelming impact on attendance decisions. Based on this, it make sense that the industry is spending as much to advertise and promote a movie as to make one. The advertising budgets, for example, have more than doubled to an average of $20 million over the past ten years—apparently to fulfill the moviegoers' thirst for information. As Litman and Kohl noted, advertising serves a dual purpose. First it lures the avid moviegoer to the theater and then it helps build the word-of-mouth campaign. Our data suggest that the advertising and promotional monies are well spent and help meet the aforementioned goals.

Overall, the creative variables fared very weakly in regression equations. For example, from the five creative variables included (Stars, Director, Storytype, Sequel, and Pre-Story), only the Director entered in all five equations. Story type (genre) attained significance only in the absence of demographics. Each of these two variables added 2 to 3.5 percent to the explained variability in attendance. The significance of Director seems more consistent as it entered in all five equations, suggesting the familiarity of the director does matter in attendance decisions. Quite interestingly, the importance of the director did not gain much support in individual ranking of important factors on attendance. Yet, director attained significance in all equations. On the contrary, STARS was ranked as the third most important factor in attendance decisions and was the most cited reason that attracted filmgoers to their last movie. Still, Stars didn't attain significance in any of the equations. Perhaps, the nature of being a star is too subjective or abstract to measured or defined.

Video Rental

While the results discussed in the preceding sections tend to help explain movie attendance and reconfirm some of the early results, the most revealing findings are the ones that shed light on the viewing that takes place outside the traditional theater.

Among the three leading delivery channels that compete with each other to bring movies to living rooms (pay cable, pay-per-view, and home videocassette), home video has emerged as the indisputable winner. Despite the heavy concentration of young, educated, and high income households in the sample, the popularity of both pay cable and pay-per-view seems minimal. Less than one-fourth of all the households subscribe to at least one pay cable channel and, even among the cable subscribers, the subscription rate for premium channels only goes up to 29 percent. Pay-per-view fared even worse. Although it is largely accessible, with availability to over 80 percent of the households, only 14 percent of them have ever ordered and paid for a movie on pay-per-view. The lukewarm acceptance of pay cable and pay-per-view seems to justify the recent industry decision to give home video the exclusive four to five week window before making the movies available to pay cable and pay-per-view. It appears that the industry is simply, and correctly, responding to the signals it receives from the market to maximize profits by "determining the optimal sequencing and time clearance for each successive exhibition window."[35]

With an 86 percent penetration rate[36] and average rental of over four cassettes per month, home video is undoubtedly the most widely used exhibition window for the movies. Eighty-five percent of the households with a VCR rent two or more tapes a month and virtually all VCR households rent at least one movie per month. According to industry classifications, these statistics reveal that the VCR has turned more than 80 percent of the nation's households into "frequent" movie viewers. A technology that started as a time-shifting device for the avid TV viewer eventually became the primary means for preselling movies. The mere size of the home video audience attests to this. For example, the average audience of 2.9 persons per each video rental,[37] taken together with the industry estimates of 4.5 billion videos rented last year, put the audience size for home video over the 10 billion mark. This is even more than double the size of the audience the movie industry had enjoyed during its heyday in the late 1940s when weekly attendance levels reached 90 million and were more than ten times greater than the number of tickets sold annually for the last three decades.

As is evident from these results, home video's huge success can be largely attributed to two factors: price and convenience. Audiences perceive home video as the least expensive and most convenient window to see movies. But price and convenience are only half the story and tend to overlook the role played by the industry to bring home video to its current popularity. It is the classical "invisible hand" that put the private interest of the industry with the interests of individuals to create the current situation. For example, as the financial significance of home video increased, the industry responded by gradually shortening the clearance time between theater and video—sometimes to the point that the video is released when the movie is still in its first theatrical run—and shifting the clearance sequence from pay-per-view to home video. As a result, home video has become the first exhibition window outside the theater to offer movies in such a short time to more than 80 million of the nation's households. Neither pay cable nor pay-per-view has given such an appealing opportunity to such a large populace before. Moreover, unlike pay cable or pay-per-view, home video does not select titles; each and every movie is guaranteed to come on video sooner, not later. The movies that did well in the theaters come sooner to reap the benefits of successful theater performances and word-of-mouth publicity. The movies that did not do well also come sooner to recoup whatever they can from the video market before they completely fade away from people's minds. As a result, about one half of the audience now "always" or "almost always" wait for the video to see the movies. Furthermore, more than one half the audience would rent the video rather than going to the theater if the option were offered to them by simultaneously releasing movies to theater and on video. And a majority is willing to pay more for such an early rental opportunity. The specific factors that influence video rental will be the focus of the following discussion.

Determinants of Video Rental

Quite surprisingly none of the twelve creative or promotional variables included in regression analysis are significantly related to video rental patterns. However, the insignificance of marketing related variables can be attributed to the virtual absence of advertising efforts to promote video releases by the movie industry. In fact, information on new video releases is only publicized through in-store advertising and on videos themselves (similar to theater "trailers") that only expose them to the already committed renter. Only Disney titles and "mega-hits" that are meant for the sell-through market use some TV advertising and product tie-in promotions. Still, they are quite limited and nominal compared to the big promotions for the initial theatrical release, which in 1996 averaged $20 million. As such, it probably is the absence of easily identifiable advertising and promotional strategies that made these variables insignificant.

The insignificance of creative variables, such as the Storytype, Stars, or Director depicts the indiscriminant renter who appears to relax his or her standards when renting a movie compared with going to the theater. Naturally, the relatively lower financial risks involved with renting (the average rental is around $2 per video compared to the average $5 admission per person plus concession prices) and the low involvement associated with renting (logistics involved such as finding a sitter, leaving home) seem to explain why the renters apparently place a lower value on creative factors when it comes to renting. In fact, these findings suggest that the moviegoers may have developed two different standards for the two exhibition windows: the "try anything" attitude for the videos and "play cautious" attitude for going to the theaters (conceivably based on the cost and involvement). A bad rental choice, therefore, is financially more tolerable and the "opportunity cost" can be minimized by turning the VCR off—much easier task than leaving the theater, especially when the movie is often the center of the planned activities for the evening.

The four variables that are significant seem to clearly explain the dynamics of the home video market. Percentage of movies seen in the theaters emerged as an important predictor of video rental, which alone explained about 17 percent of the variance in video rental. As expected, the negative coefficient of the percentage suggests an inverse relationship between theater attendance and video rental. This relationship appears to indicate that home video, unlike pay cable or pay-per-view, is gaining acceptance from moviegoers as a *substitute* to theater attendance, an indication that suggests possible audience shift from the theaters. However, the use of this variable as a predictor of video rental should be somewhat cautious as this seems to be an endogenous variable. The strength of "Percentage" may be overblown to an extent, since all the respondents that do not attend movies but do rent them were given 100 percent.

The second variable to enter the equation was Movicost—the average cost for a movie outing. It added about 5 percent to the explained variance and is positively related with video rental, suggesting that rental is more popular among those who have to spend more at the theater. Naturally families with children fall into this category. As correlation results indicate, households with children also go to the movies less but rent more videos. Therefore, as expected, Children is significantly positively related to video rental. The significance of Children suggests that home video serves as a better (cheaper and convenient) way to see movies for families.

The significantly negative relationship between age and video rental is somewhat surprising given its similar relationship with theater attendance. It seems logical to expect a positive relationship that suggests a higher rental tendency among older people since renting is more convenient than theater attendance. However, if home video is emerging as a substitute for the theater window for *all* the moviegoers, the negative relationship appears to be the correct direction. However, further research with larger, more representative samples will be needed to find the proper direction of the relationship between these two factors.

What are the implications of this enormous success of home video for theater attendance? The results of this study show that home video has greatly enhanced accessibility to the movies and consequently increased the net audience to an unprecedented level. While it is almost impossible to dissect the video audience into its root components, the data, however, seem to suggest some identifiable trends. First, it is clear that the moviegoers did not totally desert the theaters to flock to the video stores. It is more likely that moviegoers became more selective in their theater attendance in the face of the video alternative. As such, it is likely that the growth of the video audience will eventually emerge at a cost to theater. However, it will be a while until the true impact of audience erosion might show up in attendance figures and a link can be established. The process would also be a rather slow one as neither the industry nor the moviegoers apparently want to totally abandon the theater. Yet, as the industry continues to shorten the clearance time between theater and video as a measure of profit maximization and viewers, on the other hand, continue to acquire better viewing facilities (stereo VCR, big screen TV) as measures to optimize the benefits, home video is likely to affect the theater attendance levels that have remained quite stable since the 1960s.

Interestingly, unlike the early days of TV, when the industry fought tooth and nail to hold the audiences defecting to TV, the current shift seems to be carefully orchestrated by the industry through timely clearance and proper sequencing of home video releases. In fact, a financially strong home video window, which appears to have no strong seasonal bias like the movies, will have a tendency to solve some complex distribution problems as studios may be able to avoid fiercely competitive release dates of summer and Christmas. Finally, after everything is said and done, the distributors will be the ultimate winners as the new exhibition windows constantly enlarge the net audience for the movies. A significant change for a industry that enters its second century.

NOTES

[1]Bruce A. Austin, "Film Attendance: Why College Students Choose to See Their Most Recent Film," *Journal of Popular Film and Television,* 9:1981.
[2]See: Bruce A. Austin, "Rating the Movies." *Journal of Popular Film and Television* 7: 4, (1981) 384–399; "Film Attendance: Why College Students Choose to See Their Most Recent

Film," *Journal of Popular Film and Television* 9: (1981b) 43–49; "A Factor Analytic Study of Attitudes toward Motion Pictures," *Journal of Social Psychology* 117: (1982) 211–217; "But Why This Movie?" *Boxoffice* (February, 16–18, 1984); "Motivations for Movie Attendance," *Boxoffice* (October, 13–16, 1984); *Immediate Seating: A Look at Movie Audiences.* Belmont, California: Wadsworth (1989) and Barry R. Litman, "Predicting TV Ratings for Theatrical Movies," *Journalism Quarterly* 53: (1979) Autumn, pp. 590–594: 694; "Decision Making in Film Industry: The Influence of the TV Market," *Journal of Communication* 32: Summer, (1982) 32–52; "Predicting Success of Theatrical Movies: An Empirical Study." *Journal of Popular Culture* 16: Spring, (1983) 159–75; Barry R. Litman and Linda Kohl, "Predicting Financial Success of Motion Pictures: The '80s Experience," *Journal of Media Economics* (Fall 1989): 35–50.

[3]Litman & Kohl, op. cit.

[4]Litman, 1989, op, cit.

[5]Residents of East Lansing (Michigan) Local Access Transport Area (LATA) that includes: East Lansing, Lansing, Okemos, Holt, Mason, and Grand Ledge.

[6]Professional telephone interviewers reached the sample in interviewing sessions that stretched to a seven day period to allow time for maximum number of call-backs to assure the data quality by increasing the response rate. Interviewing took place between 6:00 p.m. and 9:30 p.m., on weekdays and on weekends interviewing began at noon and ended at 6:00 p.m. Interviewers were directed to call each number, a minimum of four times.

[7]While random digit dialing is one of the most comprehensive methods for selecting a random sample of telephone numbers, a large number of the numbers generated by this method tend to be invalid because some phones have been disconnected, some numbers generated have not yet been assigned, and for other reasons, such as the numbers assigned for businesses and commercial establishments. The adverse effects of this drawback are, however, not on data quality but on time and money.

[8]Litman and Kohl, op. cit.

[9]Some of these variables have been used in previous studies though they were measured using nonsurvey methods. See Litman, 1989, op. cit.

[10]Litman, 1983, op. cit., and Litman & Khol, 1989, op. cit.

[11]Austin, 1989, op. cit.

[12]Litman, 1989, op. cit.

[13]Litman & Khol, 1989, op. cit.

[14]Austin, 1991, op. cit.

[15]Litman, 1983, 1989, op. cit.

[16]Litman, 1989, op. cit.

[17]Austin, 1991, op. cit.

[18]Litman & Khol, 1989, op. cit.

[19]*Advertising Age Fax*, February 9, 1994.

[20]Litman & Khol, 1989, op. cit.

[21]Binary variables are those categorical variables that provide only two choices, "yes" or "no." They are frequently used to describe demographic and other business environmental conditions.

[22]Austin, 1989, op. cit.

[23]International *Television & Video Almanac.* (New York: Quigley Publishing Company, 1992).

[24]MPAA 1992, ibid.

[25]The twelve variables listed in Table 9-4 are broadly divided into two groups adopting Litman's (1989) and Austin's (1991) classifications as **"creative"** [STARS, DIRECTOR, STORYTYP, PRESTORY, SEQUEL, REVIEWS, RATINGS] and **"marketing"** [WORDOFM, PREVIEWS, ADVTSNG, AWARDS, and TVPROMOS].

[26]Except for most of the Disney movies and "mega-hit" titles such as *Jurassic Park, Independence Day,* or *Twister,* where the video release is primarily intended for the sell-through market with low unit prices.

[27]These simple correlations were obtained without any treatment to the missing values. As missing values will be substituted for regression analysis, the strengths and the significance levels of the present relationships may change as missing value treatments effectively change the sample composition.

[28]Extreme care was taken to see whether the missing values were random or take an identifiable pattern. To find this out, the sample was first divided into two groups—those observations with missing data on INCOME and MOVICOST (the two variables with largest number of missing cases) and those with complete data—and the distribution of the dependent measure (MOVIE#) was examined using t-tests. The results found no statistically significant differences between the groups, thus confirming the randomness in missing values.

[29]The problem with collinear variables is that they provide very similar information and may weaker each other when used in conjunction, hence it is difficult to separate out the effects of individual variables. However, it is quite premature to exclude a variable as collinear on the basis of simple correlation results, as they might have different effects in the presence of other variables. [Two sophisticated diagnostic tests (Tolerance and Variance Inflation Factor [VIF] and Eigenvalues and Condition Indexes) show the true nature of multicollinearity in the context of other predictor variables and suggest that income, in fact, seems to share an unacceptable amount of its variance with age and marital status.]

[30]The log transformation is a result of a series of tests performed to check the linearity of the continuous variables. A casewise residual test performed under Subprogram Regression of SPSS revealed a slight departure of the dependent variable from normality (this may be due to the way in which values were assigned to the dependent measure, which created a large number of cases for two values). Under these circumstances, SPSS suggests the transformation of either the dependent or independent variables, or both, to approximate normality (SPSS, 1990). All three transformations were attempted and only the transformation of the dependent measure resulted in an improvement in the statistical fit. As the distribution of the variable has a positive skew, the log transformation appears to be the most appropriate.

[31]The F is a test of the null hypothesis that $e_1=e_2=e_3=e_4....e_n=0$.

[32]Johnson, Johnson, & Buse, 1987.

[33]Normality test performed on the dependent variable revealed it to have a fairly normal distribution, therefore there was no need for transformation. Entry techniques and assumption checks used in these equations were similar to the ones used in theater attendance analysis.

[34]Austin, 1989, op. cit.; Quigley, 1992, op. cit.

[35]Litman & Kohl, 1989, op. cit.

[36]Close to the 88 percent penetration rate the industry had predicted by the year 1995.

[37]This is the weighted average after discounting for possible fraternities and sororities in the sample by trimming the top 10 percent of the cases. The sample average is 3.3 per/HH.

10

Predicting Financial Success of Motion Pictures

The Early '90s Experience

BARRY LITMAN AND HOEKYUN AHN

Movies are ubiquitous today. "They are seen in many places other than theaters, most often, in people's homes on television monitors, via pay-per-view, home video systems, premium channels, networks, local television stations, and a herd of cable channels; but also in airplanes, hospitals, schools, universities, prisons, even in dentists' chairs. The major Hollywood corporations are often involved in all of these activities, all around the world," as Wasko observed. "It becomes increasingly difficult to distinguish the motion picture industry from other media and entertainment industries. Hollywood, indeed, is one of the focal points of the culture industry, and no longer as merely involved in the traditional production, distribution, and exhibition of movies. Thanks to technological developments, commercial motivations, and globalization trends, Hollywood has moved beyond the silver screen."[1]

Indeed, popular films often initiate or continue an endless chain of other cultural products through merchandising. "A film concept or character often leads to a television show, with possible spin-offs, videogames, and records. Merchandising and marketing efforts also include toys, games, trading cards, soap products, cereals, theme park rides, coloring books, magazines, and even how-the-movie-was-made books." Consider how "Roger Rabbit, the movie, becomes Roger Rabbit, the cartoon, then Roger Rabbit, the video, and so on."[2]

Despite these new developments and increased significance of the ancillary markets, at the heart of such transnational conglomerate businesses is theatrical release. Not only does the box office come first in the chain of windows, but it tends to determine the performance of motion pictures in the subsequent markets. Thus, the box office plays a critical role as the "gateway" of financial success for theatrical motion pictures. In fact, theatrical performance has been shown in previous studies to be an important determinant in explaining the expected rating of these films on prime-time television.[3] Thus, theatrical performance of films can be considered as the "quality" of the film and its impact continues to spread throughout home video sell-through and rentals, pay-per-view, network television, and other subsidiary markets, including cable television and syndication. In essence, "theaters are the goose, even if pay-per-view is the golden egg."[4]

Well aware of the significance of box office performance, a number of students in film and communication as well as Hollywood itself have tried to formulate the golden rules for financial success of motion pictures. Thus far, however, Hollywood seems to believe only one rule, namely, that there are no hard-and-fast rules in the motion picture industry. To some analysts, "Hollywood is the land of hunch and the wild guess,"[5] and the most fundamental difficulty facing Hollywood decision-makers is the uncertainty of product demand.[6] The motion picture industry, for some observers, is the riskiest business since its product is art that has several qualities that make it a less-than-ideal object of commerce. "No one can tell you what a movie is going to do in the marketplace until the film opens in a darkened theater and sparks fly up between the screen and the audience,"[7] observed Jack Valenti, president of the Motion Picture Association of America. "Although it is fairly easy to gauge the market for an art (say movies) in general, it is nearly impossible to do so for a particular artistic product. Everyone knows that people love to see good movies; nobody knows which movies will be considered good by enough people to make them profitable."[8] Not surprisingly, trade journals of the motion picture industry are replete with examples, statements, anecdotes, and experiences that prove such wisdom.

The demand uncertainty makes the production of films a business of constant risk-taking. With no assurance that the public will buy their product, film producers today invest about $35 million to make a typical motion picture and perhaps another $16 million to market it.[9] Imagine if you built a skyscraper and the day it was finished, you found that no one liked it. So you tore it down. Thus, it is quite understandable that Hollywood would fall back on reliable formulas that have worked in the past—Die Hard on a train, Die Hard on a ship, Die Hard on a bus, Die Hard on an airplane.[10] An idea that is creative must survive a tortuous process of assembling money, scripts, production facilities, actors, and distribution arrangements before it is realized on film. Even once the process is finished, an industry rule of thumb suggests that seven out of ten Hollywood feature movies end up in the red. Rosen observed, "It is often argued that the attempt to predict audience behavior or reaction is essentially futile. Taste and preference are claimed to be highly variable; fads are by definition, short lived. And movie audiences are nothing if not faddish. Thus, it is further claimed that even the popularity of well-established genres or stars is not sufficient to allow robust predictions."[11] In sum, excellence is a fragile substance.

Furthermore, the unpredictability of audience behavior is exacerbated by the complexity of variables affecting the success or failure of the release of any film. Numerous variables influence the fate of a film in the marketplace. "Time of year, competition from other films, alternative leisure activities, weather and economic conditions, advertising, critical reviews, subject matter, network, pay and cable TV, theater location, and demographics all contribute to the level of a film's performance. Some of these variables affect, in particular, the opening phase, which in turn determines the next stage. Other variables have more of an impact on the longevity of a theatrical run, in spite of a healthy launch. In all cases, most of these variables cannot be predicted, at least not early enough to influence the release strategy."[12]

Despite the growth in interest in examining the movies and the almost exponential increase in books and articles on the subject of movies since the 1960s,[13] the uncertainty and unpredictability associated with investments in the motion picture industry remain the same today and scholarly research continues to remain underdeveloped. And that was the paradoxical underlying motive for Litman fifteen years ago.[14] Since Litman's first attempt to quantify this conventional wisdom, little has been done in this area.

THE PSYCHOLOGICAL APPROACH AND THE ECONOMIC APPROACH

Traditionally, there have been two distinct research approaches attempting to shed light on those factors underlying motion picture attendance and thus financial success. The psychological approach focuses on individual moviegoers' decisions to first attend movies among the vast array of entertainment options and second to select particular movies. While traditional marketing researchers have relied heavily on demographic profiles, the psychological approach found that demographic data alone were not sufficient to shed some light on consumer behavior. Incorporating consumers' various psychological dimensions with demographic elements, the latter typically tries to connect such variables as interests, opinions, need, values, attitudes, and personality traits with the consumer decision-making process in the demand side of the motion picture industry.

Since Blumler and Katz's 1974 landmark collection of uses and gratifications, *The Uses of Mass Communications,* a growing body of research has addressed how audiences' media consumption patterns are related to the gratifications people report from various media. The uses and gratifications line of research espouses the idea that audience members are active in selecting and processing media content. Uses and gratifications approaches have in common the assumptions that (1) audiences are active, (2) media use is goal directed, (3) media use fulfills a wide range of gratifications, and (4) the gratifications audiences report can be due to media content, the practice of exposure in and of itself, or the social situation in which media–audience interaction takes place.[15] Within this tradition, a group of communication theorists have been able to explain the film audience's fundamental "uses and gratifications" associated with the consumption of theatrical films.

Palmgreen and Lawrence conducted a survey among 486 college students to measure gratifications sought from moviegoing and theatrical movie avoidances.[16] They also measured frequency of movie attendance, movie dependency, and frequency of discussing movies with others. The strongest predictor for gratifications sought and frequency of movie attendance was "mood control/enhancement," followed by "entertainment," and "social utility (i.e., moviegoing as a social event)." Movie dependency was found to be strongly correlated with frequency of attendance. On the other hand, Palmgreen and Lawrence found that avoidance motives played a more significant role, relative to gratifications sought, in influencing movie attendance than they did in affecting related dependency on movies. In addition, both "specific content (i.e., obscene language, explicit sex, violence)" and "general content (i.e., objectionable thematic characteristics of movies as a whole)" showed significant negative correlations with movie attendance, although the magnitude of the coefficients was somewhat low. While movie prices, another potential factor, failed to emerge clearly on any of the avoidance factors, they were significant negative predictor for movie attendance.[17]

Similarly, in a telephone survey of 150 respondents, Knapp and Sherman found that the best predictor of film attendance was "having friends interested in movies."[18] Other significant variables included interest in hiking, disinterest in radio listening, perceived importance of a college education, and the willingness to pay extra for quality television.

The psychological approach has been most enhanced by the collective work of Austin, who has integrated movie consumption within the framework of the "uses and gratifications" approach and "diffusion of innovation" model. For Austin, consumers purposefully select and attend to media and content, as opposed to other leisure time pursuits, to satisfy innate needs. They choose among various movie options according to a sequential process of acquiring knowledge, which leads to persuasion and eventually decision.[19]

In a survey of 493 college students, Austin investigated several psychological motives sought out by movie attendance at theatrical motion pictures, and the relationship between such motives and frequency of attendance, pattern of moviegoing, and respondents' demographic variables.[20] Factor analysis of the motivation items identified seven motives for movie attendance among which motives such as "learning and information," "forget and escape," "enjoyment and pleasure," and "learning about self" were found significantly different within three different attendance groups, while motives such as "pass time," "behavioral resources," and "relieve loneliness" did not turn out to be significantly different. Regression analysis showed that 25.5 percent of variance in frequency of movie attendance was accounted for by enjoyment and pleasure, learning about self, age, and moviegoing pattern. The first two motives were found to positively predict frequency of attendance, while age was negatively related. Moviegoing in streaks was associated with less frequent movie attendance.[21]

The economic approach, on the other hand, is premised more on the economic factors that influence collective movie attendance decisions. It takes advantage of group data for a collection of individual films and pays special attention to the supply side of the motion picture industry. Studies employing the economic approach focus on the institutional factors that flow along the decision process within the entire vertical system of the motion picture industry. Thus, just as critical in affecting the bottom line as the content of the film itself are the process of film financing, scheduling, timing, advertising, and publicity as well as the degree of competition among films.[22] Here, while direct audience measurement is absent,[23] audience response is assessed through the dependent variable, either theatrical movie rentals accruing to the distributor or box office grosses. In other words, rather than asking about frequency of movie attendance employed in the psychological approach, the economic approach is "ground-based," making use of solid market data and strongly implies the aggregated influence of the film audience through "voting by viewing."

Under this approach, Garrison studied the impact of film content on rentals released by Columbia between 1966 and 1968.[24] Film content was measured by type of picture, plot, public awareness, sexual emphasis, production values, and author's subjective ratings of the creative personnel, and so forth. While his twelve-variable equation provided by regression analysis of over thirty factors accounted for 72.7 percent of the variation in box office revenue, the Garrison study invited wide criticism on the methodology employed.[25]

Simonet criticized Garrison's method of subjective ratings, but he partially confirmed the Garrison study. Using a sample of seventy-three top grossing films released between 1928 and 1972, Simonet employed a similar regression analysis of theatrical rentals with a number of production variables.[26] The past box office record of the director and producer of the film were the two significant variables that positively predicted the financial success of a film. Together with actors and writers, these variables accounted for half of the variance in distributor rentals.

However, both studies have been under criticism. Kindem has argued that "neither Garrison nor Simonet isolated consumer demand for movie stars as an independent variable, and the variables they do select confuse causes with effects."[27] As a result, Kindem concluded that although Garrison's and Simonet's studies clearly lend support to the *auteur* theory of filmmaking, the notion that the director, or author, of the film is the controlling force, "bankable stars" still remain a critical factor securing and protecting production investments, differentiating movie products, and thereby ensuring the ultimate box office success.

Litman resolved this seemingly futile dispute in a study on the economic symbiosis between the film and television industries.[28] He incorporated those fragmented variables into three critical areas that will affect financial success of motion pictures: the creative sphere, the scheduling and release pattern, and the marketing effort. The creative sphere is composed of the content and source of the story itself, production decisions including budget and director, and MPAA rating. The scheduling and release pattern of a film included involvement with major studios, the timing of release, and various release strategies. Marketing effort included variables such as Academy award nomination and winning, critics' reviews, and advertising intensity. With a sample of 155 films released between 1972 and 1979, Litman found that Academy Awards, critics' ratings, newspaper advertising, Christmas release, and production expenses were some of the variables that had a significantly positive impact on theatrical rentals. Interestingly, MPAA ratings and subject matter were largely irrelevant as predictors of financial success for theatrical movies. Furthermore, the inclusion of highly paid superstars in the cast added no additional revenues over and above their contribution to the quality of the picture itself.

Following this, Litman and Kohl then replicated the 1982 Litman baseline model with a sample of 697 films released from 1981 to 1986.[29] Not only did they modify the categories of variables in the previous study conducted by Litman to accommodate environmental changes, but they also added a few more variables such as well-known ideas, country of origin, and annual Herfindahl–Hirschman Index of market shares, all of which were significantly associated with theatrical rentals.

This new set of data from the 1980s suggested several changes in results from the 1982 "baseline" study that dealt with films released in the 1970s. Horror and comedy were no longer found to have a significant impact on theatrical rentals. Christmas release failed to retain its significant impact, while the summer release has increased in its relative importance. Academy Awards became an insignificant predictor for financial success, and the production budget, top directors, and stars decreased in importance from the original study. In addition, the importance of being a major distributor's film decreased, while access to a large number of screens still retained its significance as a predictor of financial success.

An interesting study from the economic approach was done by Wyatt.[30] Using a sample of 512 motion pictures released between 1983 and 1986 that grossed more than one million dollars at the box office, Wyatt has sought to explain how some major studios succeeded in garnering more box office rentals in the 1980s. The most interesting feature in Wyatt's study is the application of product differentiation concept to predicting commercial success of motion pictures. He defined the differentiation, as applied to motion pictures, as "high-concept picture: a film which relies heavily upon a surface stylishness and extensive marketing."[31] Wyatt argues that high concept films are significant as a differentiated product since they are marked as distinct from other films through their design and packaging. As a form of product differentiation, high concept films operate through two channels: an emphasis on screen style and integration with marketing and merchandising. High concept was operationalized through three facets: the style of the films, the links to merchandising and licensing, and the repetition through either remakes, sequels, or series. A binary variable equaling one was assigned to those films merchandised through soundtracks, book tie-ins, posters, and toys. Likewise, a binary variable was set to one if the film was a remake, sequel, or part of a series. Wyatt found that Paramount has been the most financially successful studio of the 1980s, since the studio produced the most high concept films.

Even if Wyatt's conceptualization of high concept is not new and revolutionary, his work has some important implications. Considering the significant role of marketing, drastically increased advertising and marketing expenditures, and the difficulty in obtaining such data, Wyatt showed that the economic concept of product differentiation could add some more explanatory power to the attempts to explain motion picture success, and merchandising could be used as a component of, or a proxy for, marketing expenditures. The problem, however, lies in his operationalization of high concept in general, and the style in particular. Wyatt did not explain very well why films such as *Top Gun, Flashdance,* and *American Gigolo* constituted the high concept film, but others did not. The style as an element of high concept, however subjectively defined, seems to lie in the viewer's mind, not in the researcher's.

Another interesting and major study within this approach in more recent years was conducted by Sochay.[32] His study represents the latest replication of the Litman model. Using 263 films released between October 1987 and October 1989, Sochay attempted to derive a model that would predict two interrelated dependent variables: the traditional theatrical rentals and the length of run. It was found that many independent variables had similar impacts on each of these two constructs, suggesting a multidimensional construct of film performance. Sochay also introduced a new independent variable, concentration ratio, to measure the impact of competition on financial performance of motion pictures, which enriched the explanatory power of his model. "The idea behind this variable is that each film faces differing levels of competition depending on the competitive strength of the film market on a weekly basis," and that the performance of a film is "partially dependent on the strength of the film it competes against."[33] Despite the inclusion of a new significant independent variable, however, the overall explanatory power ($R^2 = .38$) of his equations for theatrical rentals remained roughly the same as the results obtained by Litman and Litman and Kohl due mainly to the omission of key independent variables such as production budget and advertising intensity.

The major findings in previous studies are summarized in Table 10-1. There appear to be some patterns in these studies. First, all the major studies covered films released in the 1970s and 1980s. Although stochastic, the last three studies in Table 10-1 cover the whole period of the 1980s from 1981 to 1989. Second, all three studies covering the 1980s produced somewhat low explanatory power of their equations, with R^2 ranging from .300–.458. This shows the complexities of the subject matter and difficulties in data gathering. Finally, there exist some variations in their findings depending on the time covered in each study. It suggests the movie audiences' changing taste even in the relatively short period of time over the last decade.

TABLE 10-1   Findings of Major Studies (authors, year, and sample periods in parentheses)

Independent Variables	Litman 1982 (1972–1978)	Litman & Kohl 1989 (1981–1986)	Wyatt 1991 (1983–1986)	Sochay 1994 (1987–1989)
Production Budget	*	*	*	–
Critics' Ratings	*	*	*	*
Number of Screens	*	*	–	*
Advertising Intensity	*	–	–	–
Competitive Forces	–	– * (HHI)	–	– * (CR4, CR10)
Superstar Actor	3	*	*	*
Top Director	3	3	3	3
Oscar Awards	*	*	*	*
Major Release	*	*	–	3
Sequel	–	*	*	–
Summer	–	*	*	*
Christmas	*	3	3	*
Easter	–	3	–	3
Merchandising	–	–	*	–
Tie-ins	–	–	*	–
MPAA G	3	3	3	3
MPAA PG	3	3	3	3
MPAA PG13	3	3	3	3
MPAA R	3	3	3	– *
Sci-Fi/Fantasy	*	*	*	3
Comedy	*	*	*	*
Horror	*	3	*	3
Drama	3	– *	3	3
N	155	697	512	263
R^2	.558	.312 – .384	.446 – .458	.325 – .380
Adjusted R^2	.524	.300 – .368	.423 – .436	.304 – .360

*Significant.   3 Insignificant.   – Not included in the study.   Negative sign (–) before asterisk means negative effect on dependent variable.

The fundamental difference between the psychological approach and the economic approach lies not in the presence or absence of observation on film audiences, but in the purpose of observation on audiences. The former tries to reveal the causes or motivations of film attendance by asking audiences after viewing their psychological needs, and "explain" film attendance. The underlying purpose of the psychological approach is not "predicting," but "explaining" audience behavior. The psychological approach does not aim to find the linking objective between audiences' psychological needs and their gratifications, nor does it answer the question of what kinds of films would fulfill such needs. The economic approach assumes that movies are mass culture products since they are designed to please the average taste of an undifferentiated audience, and that there are some utility and entertainment values in attending motion pictures. It only attempts to uncover the ingredients of film success and ultimately "predict" film performance in the future.

As Blowers pointed out, Litman and others' economic approach is "clearly innovative to the problem of audience research, revealing many of the variables which play a part in a film's ultimate commercial success."[34] The present study, using recent data on films released in the early 1990s, attempts to replicate the early Litman models of the 1970s and 1980s because they had the advantage of focusing on individual films, incorporated the broad series of factors affecting the different stages in the industry, and were based on objective measurements of industry factors.

METHOD

The sample for this study was drawn from *Variety*'s annual reports of "Top 100 Total Box Office Gross Films" that were released between 1993 and 1995. Thus, our sample is somewhat different from most previous studies that investigated films with $1 million or more rentals in the domestic theatrical market. In addition, unlike most previous research, the dependent variable here is box office gross, as opposed to theatrical rentals accruing to the distributor. Another important difference is that the dependent variable will be estimated in two separate markets: domestic and foreign. The domestic market is composed of the United States and Canada. Although it seems almost impossible to collect reliable data on each separate market of the whole foreign market, a separate equation will be estimated and compared with the domestic market. We will also estimate the worldwide market with total box office gross, which constitutes box office gross from foreign markets added together with that from the domestic markets.

Although this study covers the top 100 films each year between 1993 and 1995, our sample contains 241 films because several films every year were carried over from the previous years and only the first half of 1995 data were available at the time. Blockbusters usually collect a considerable amount of box office gross even in the following years after initial release and tend to retain a spot in the top 100 lists, thereby reducing the total number of eligible films for the study. A few foreign films also were excluded from the sample due to the unavailability of key variables such as the number of screens, production budget, and competition intensity. These films were included in the top 100 lists largely because of box office revenues in foreign countries, and domestic box office gross for those films is negligible.

In many cases, it is necessary to standardize the dependent variables by taking account of the impact of rising admission prices on box office grosses; the dependent variables of the present study were not adjusted for two reasons. First, the sample covers a very short time period between 1993 and 1995. Second, and more importantly, the admission prices remained virtually the same during this period: $4.143 in 1993, $4.178 in 1994, and $4.35 in 1995.[35]

INDEPENDENT VARIABLES

The film business operates fundamentally in the triple-tiered vertical motion picture industry. The opportunities and risks start with the production decision, but they are more created and enhanced by distributors and exhibitors. Indeed, the triad of production–distribution–exhibition grew organically, each needing the other two to function smoothly and profitably. The choice of independent variables for the present study closely follows the sequential vertical stages of decision-making in the industry, proceeding from production through distribution to exhibition.

Production Stage

The major decisions at the production stage have much to do with the so-called creative sphere. The creative sphere refers to the total effort extended in making a film and all choices concerning the various creative aspects. The initial starting point of the production stage is the melding together of the right script, actors, and director with the right theme and appropriate amount and treatment of commercial appeals factors such as sex and violence.

Content Categories

Every film was placed into ten content categories that were mutually exclusive and exhaustive of each other. The categories include: action/adventure, children/family, comedy, documentary, drama, horror, musical, mystery/suspense, science fiction/fantasy, and Western. Binary variables were used to represent the different categories. Science fiction has been found positively correlated to box office performance in Litman and Litman and Kohl, but not in Sochay. Drama has been found negatively correlated in Litman and Kohl and Sochay. (See Table 10-1.)

MPAA Rating

Another element considered important in the creative sphere is the rating assigned by the Motion Picture Association of America (MPAA). The motion picture industry first established a voluntary code in 1968 and modified it later to the current rating system as a means of giving advance information to movie audiences about the theme and treatment of films. There were six possible rating categories, each operationalized with a binary variable: G, PG, PG-13, R, NC-17, NR. These ratings suggest and help to assess the degree of sexual content, violence, and strident language within the sample of movies. Since G, PG and PG-13 rated movies have the largest audience potential, previous research suggested that such movies should be positively related to commercial success in box office while R, X, and NR films should be negatively correlated.[36] Litman indicated that PG rating was the most desirable for a film because the film was not as limited by age restrictions as an "R" film nor stuck with the Walt Disney label that accompanies "G" rated pictures.[37] In fact, filmmakers handed a G rating regularly insert profanity to graduate to PG. Mall owners often put it in their leasing contract that theaters cannot show X or NC-17 films, and many newspapers refuse to carry even the most discreet advertising for such pictures. It is no surprise, therefore, that all studio contracts with directors insist that their films receive a rating below NC-17.[38] Medved supported this reasoning with his analysis of 1,010 films released between 1983 and 1989.[39] He found that G films have the highest median box office gross followed in order by PG, PG-13, and R. However, none of the previous research has supported a significant relationship between MPAA rating and box office gross. Interestingly, while Austin's "forbidden fruit" theory[40] concerning the appeal of restricted films has never found any empirical support, the motion picture industry shows its undying faith that R rated films, are the most profitable by releasing R rated films most often in the 1970s.[41]

Superstar Actors and Directors

Another measure of film content involves a binary variable for the presence or absence of any box office superstars in the cast of the films. The presence of superstars was determined by checking if the cast contained any of the Top 10 box office stars for the two years prior to the film's release. To measure the effect of the star's notoriety on box office gross for particular films, it is necessary to exclude the current year's box office champs. The lists of Top 10 money-making stars are based on the poll of theater exhibitors conducted for the *International Motion Picture Almanac* (1990–1995).

Since there is no listing for directors corresponding to the Top 10 box office stars, a different measure for "greatness" was used. If a director won, or was nominated for, an Academy Award for Best Director during any of the five years prior to the year his or her film was in the sample, he or she would be considered a superstar director.

While the 1982 Litman study found no significant relation between the presence of superstar actor and box office rentals, the 1989 Litman and Kohl and the Sochay studies found that the presence of a superstar in the cast had significant impact on film rentals. Sochay suggests that besides the positive effect on theatrical success, the presence of a superstar makes subsequent marketing campaigns in the later distribution windows easier to develop thanks to the recognizable star's notoriety. Kindem[42] and Balio[43] have shown the significant contribution of movie stars to the performance of theatrical films in their treatise on Hollywood's star system in a broader historical context as well as an empirical sense.

Production Budget

The production cost of the average feature made by the major studios increased from about $400,000 in 1941 to $2.2 million in 1972 to $35 million in 1995. The recent increase in production budget is largely attributed to inflated star salaries and exorbitant costs for dazzling special effects—from the digitalized characters of *Toy Story* to the exploding jet skis of *Waterworld*. Of course, blockbusters can flop, but studios feel safer with big budget films. Most low-budget films do not catch fire at the box office, and the moviegoers do not find them sufficiently different from what is available on television.[44]

To the extent that budget expenditures lead to greater production value, they should increase a film's entertainment value and hence its probability of box office success. Budget expenditures would enhance entertainment value by bringing more diverse and state-of-the-art techniques for production (e.g., special effects), more exotic locales, and more popular stars and directors, more lavish sets and clothing in the film.

Production budgets are the most difficult data to obtain. In many cases, the actual production cost data are considered confidential and unavailable for research purposes. Only the 1982 Litman's and the 1989 Litman and Kohl's studies were able to include such data in the past research and they found significant impact on theatrical rentals.

Production cost data were abstracted from various issues of *Variety, Hollywood Reporter,* and newspapers. Another source was Entertainment Data, Inc. (EDI), which compiles and reports financial data on motion pictures including weekly box office figures. This combined and cross-validated data set provided production budget information for 200 films (83 percent) out of 241 films in the sample. For the remaining 41 films whose budget data were not available from any of these sources, due mainly to their relatively small production expenses, production budgets for each film were estimated through the ordinary least square (OLS) regression of other important independent variables.[45]

Critical Reviews

To measure the impact of critical film reviews on box office success, information on critics' reviews was collected and averaged together from three nationally recognized sources that use a rating system based on a five-star scale.[46] Their numerical rankings range from five stars (masterpiece) to one star (poor). The 1982 Litman study found that each additional star had a significant positive impact on theatrical rentals.[47] The 1989 Litman and Kohl study also found the same impact in their second research.[48] Sochay confirmed the previous findings in his 1994 study.[49]

Distribution Stage

The second critical area that can determine theatrical movie success is the scheduling and release pattern. The secret of success in previous years was to have the film released by a major distributor. Involvement with a major distributor includes a production loan, either from a bank with favorable terms or internally financed by the major distributor itself, and ensures preferential access to the best theaters during the most favorable times.

Release by Major Distributor

A significant change has drastically altered the distribution stage of the motion picture industry during the 1980s and early 1990s. A "second string" of large distributors, known as mini-majors, has grown much stronger so that these mini-majors, including Buena Vista, Orion, TriStar, and DeLaurentis can perform the same quality distribution as the majors. To capture this major distributor effect, binary variables have been assigned to each film according to the classification system of whether they were distributed by the majors or the independents. Six major distributors include Disney, Warner Brothers, Sony/Columbia, Paramount, Twentieth-Century Fox, United Artists/MGM, and Universal.

Litman found a major release had a significant positive impact on a film's theatrical rentals released in the 1970s . Litman and Kohl confirmed Litman's earlier findings with the market clout of major distributors in their 1989 replication study, but this effect had been moderated. Sochay did not find the presence of a major distributor to have a significant impact, suggesting that mini-majors and the independents had gained market clout in the distribution stage recently.

Release Dates

A second critical decision in the distribution stage involves the release date. There are three peak periods for motion picture attendance: the holiday season surrounding Christmas (November and December), the summer season between Memorial Day and Labor Day (May through August), and the Easter season (March and April). For the films released at each of these peaks, binary variables were assigned and expected to have a significant positive impact on box office success as compared to films released in off-peak periods. Christmas release has been found significant in the studies by Litman[50] and Sochay,[51] while summer release has been found significant in most recent work by Litman and Kohl,[52] Goldberg,[53] and Sochay.[54]

Pattern of Release

The final consideration in the distribution stage involves the pattern of release. The key is to obtain as wide a national release pattern with as many screens as are available. While such a national release pattern formerly was the exclusive reserve of the major studios, the mini-majors now are fully capable of releases to 1,000 or more screens. This variable measured the mean number of screens for the first two weeks of release for each film. The data for the number of screens come from *Variety*. Many previous studies, including Litman, Litman and Kohl, and Sochay found that the pattern of release had a significant positive impact on theatrical rentals.[55]

Exhibition Stage

Competitive Forces

As Sochay pointed out, "no film operates in a vacuum."[56] Rather, each film competes for the consumer's entertainment dollar with other films released concurrently or carried over from a previous time. Thus, its success or failure is highly dependent on the strength of competitive forces in the marketplace. Indeed, nothing was scheduled to compete directly with *Jurassic Park* on the second week of June in 1993.[57] To estimate this influence, an independent variable was measured. Top 8 film concentration ratio (CR8) is weekly concentration of box office revenues for the top 8 films compiled from weekly editions of *Variety*. This variable was derived by taking the revenues accruing to the top 8 films each week as a percentage of total film revenues for the week in question. The resulting ratio represents the competitive forces in the film marketplace that each individual film faced in its release week. The ratio was measured for the first two weeks of release and averaged. If each particular film had been in the top 8, its revenues were excluded from the numerator of the ratio and the revenues of the ninth film was included to fill in the opening slot due to the exclusion of the film in question. Litman and Kohl first introduced in the 1989 study the influence of market forces as an environmental factor by using Herfindahl–Hirschman Index of market shares.[58] Sochay refined the concept by using top 4 film concentration ratio (CR4) and top 10 film concentration ratio (CR10). He found them to have negative impact on both theatrical rentals and the length of run.[59]

Academy Awards

One area that analysts often have ignored in the realm of marketing is the competition for Oscar nominations and awards. The main target of the promotional efforts of the Oscar hopefuls is the members of the Academy of Motion Picture Arts and Sciences who are courted by lavish ads in *Daily Variety* and *The Hollywood Reporter,* special screenings, gifts of soundtrack albums, expensive promotional materials sent to their homes, and saturation screenings on cable television. Studios, producers, distributors, and even talent themselves spend an amount that totals hundreds of thousands of dollars every year.[60] In return, the competitors anticipate reaping substantial additional box office revenue—and stars increased compensation for their future movie appearances—from the receipt of Oscar nominations and awards. Industry estimates have put the value of a best picture award in the range of $10 to $30 million and that of a best actor or actress at from $3 to $8 million.[61] In Levy's study, the cash value of the Oscar Best Picture award has been estimated as ranging from $5 to $30 million dollars.[62]

Winning an Oscar has pervasive and universal effects. Indeed, Levy asserts in a comprehensive study of Oscar awards during the 1927–1985 period that the highest goal of every studio in Hollywood is to get nominations and win the Best Picture award since the Oscar award plays a crucial role in bringing in major rewards in the film industry: money, prestige, and power.[63] Levy found that, since the mid-1930s, there has been a strong correlation between the Oscar winners and the blockbusters—that is, between artistic and commercial success. The Best Picture award can produce a bigger draw, particularly for audiences who would not have gone to see the movie had it not won an Oscar. Litman, Litman and Kohl, and Sochay confirmed that the Academy awards had a significant positive impact on theatrical rentals.[64]

RESULTS

A brief summary of the sample for this study seems necessary to better understand and discuss results of our analysis. It should be noted that the sample from "Top 100 Box Office Gross Films" inherently is skewed toward the big budget, box office hits. It is also reflected in the fact that 85 percent of the 241 films in our sample were released by the seven major distributors, leaving only 15 percent in the top 100 lists for mini-majors and independents (see Table 10-2). In addition, the top 3 studios (leaders) in terms of advertising expenditures in 1995 are responsible for about half of the films (51 percent). The average production costs of the sample are $31.4 million, while the adjusted costs show a conservative measure of production costs with a mean of $30.7 million. This fact roughly matches the industry statistics released by various sources. According to Motion Picture Association of America (MPAA) and *International Motion Picture Almanac,* the cost of a feature film averaged $29.9 million in 1993 and $34.3 in 1994.[65] *The New York Times* reported that the average expenditure for production in 1995 was $35 million.[66]

The sample statistics also show that box office gross in the domestic market averaged $51 million, while $1 million more per film was collected from the foreign markets. This fact also confirms general observations in trade journals that have been reporting that since 1992 foreign markets began to account for slightly more than 50 percent of total box office gross. The mean of total box office revenues exceeded $100 million.

TABLE 10-2   Summary of Sample

Variable	Cases	Mean	Std. Dev.	Min	Max
Majors	241	.85477	.35306	0	1
Leaders	241	.55602	.49789	0	1
Domestic	241	51.24	46.41	4.8	337.8
Foreign	237	52.27	68.01	0	530.3
Total	241	102.65	109.76	21.7	868.1
Cost ($mil.)	200	31.38	21.14	1	175
Adjusted Cost	241	30.67	19.78	1	175
Running Time	241	110.6	18.9	69	195
Screen	239	1669.9	620.0	7.5	2867.5
CR8	238	61.11	9.47	30.6	86.5
Reviews	241	3.13	.67	1	4.67
Summer	241	.39419	.48969	0	1
Christmas	241	.17842	.38367	0	1
Easter	241	.14523	.35306	0	1
MPAA G	241	.05394	.22637	0	1
MPAA PG	241	.26141	.44032	0	1
MPAA PG-13	241	.26556	.44255	0	1
MPAA R	241	.37344	.48473	0	1

TABLE 10-3   Correlation Matrix

	Domestic	Foreign	Total	Cost	Reviews	Screen	CR8	Star	Oscar	Summer	Christmas	Easter	Sci-Fi	MPAA-G	MPAA-PG	PG13	MPAA-R
Domestic	1.0000																
Foreign	.8416	1.0000															
Total	.9427	.9736	1.0000														
Cost	.3683	.4222	.4165	1.0000													
Reviews	.2938	.2335	.2684	-.0184	1.0000												
Screen	.3666	.3058	.3440	.5093	-.2532	1.0000											
CR8	-.2267	-.2204	-.2320	.0540	.0448	-.2067	1.0000										
Star	.2248	.2046	.2214	.3873	.0451	.1612	.0394	1.0000									
Oscar	.1979	.1954	.2044	-.0463	.3787	-.2600	.0883	.0592	1.0000								
Summer	.2651	.1984	.2346	.3603	.0359	.2367	.3864	.1267	-.0254	1.0000							
Christmas	.0332	.0802	.0636	-.0272	.1843	.0053	-.0142	.1084	.0442	-.3743	1.0000						
Easter	-.1361	-.1349	-.1409	-.2286	-.1566	-.0923	-.2451	-.1756	-.0661	-.3291	-.1868	1.0000					
Sci-Fi	.1179	.1777	.1596	.2700	-.0474	.1676	-.0705	.1495	-.0783	.0418	.0009	-.0661	1.0000				
MPAA-G	.1467	.1223	.1376	-.0802	.2592	.0564	.0155	-.1008	.0096	.0487	.0457	-.0385	.0096	1.0000			
MPAA-PG	-.0401	-.1425	-.1050	-.1167	-.1085	.0386	.2205	.0052	-.1307	.0467	.0290	.0628	-.0934	-.1396	1.0000		
PG-13	.0789	.0729	.0784	.0979	.0120	.0554	-.0317	.0583	-.0188	.1060	-.0220	-.0207	.1304	-.1396	-.3605	1.0000	
MPAA-R	-.0408	.0533	.0157	.1079	-.0161	-.0250	-.1472	.0301	.1254	-.1188	.0176	-.0068	-.0109	-.1789	-.4619	-.4619	1.0000

(obs = 235)

The average film had the running time of 110 minutes and was presented at 1,670 screens for the first two weeks of release. Among 241 films in the sample, 39.4 percent were released in the summer season, 17.8 percent in the Christmas season, and 14.5 percent in the Easter season. PG and PG-13 each constituted 26 percent of the sample and R-rated films occupied 37 percent. In terms of likelihood, therefore, R rating was found to have a higher comparative probability of being included in the top 100 list, which confirms the Hollywood faith in such rating in a sense, but suggests nothing about the relative profitability of the R rating.

The correlational analysis indicated that production costs, reviews, the number of screens, the presence of superstars, the Oscar Best Picture award, the summer season, science fiction, and G-rated films were all positively related with each of three dependent variables: domestic, foreign, and worldwide box office gross (see Table 10-3). As expected, competitive forces measured by concentration ratio (CR8) and the Easter season were negatively correlated with all three dependent variables.

Interestingly, unlike all previous studies, the Christmas release showed virtually no strong correlation with any of these variables, whereas an Easter release was negatively correlated. As expected, MPAA ratings also suggested no consistent patterns with respect to box office gross.

The regression equations listed in Table 10-4 represent the final "best fit" after initial screening of different groups of independent variables through correlational analysis. The regression analysis in Table 10-4 illustrates that our equations explain 45.9 percent of total variance in domestic box office gross and 44.1 percent in worldwide.

As consistently found in the previous studies by Litman, Litman and Kohl, Austin, Wyatt, and Sochay, none of the MPAA ratings are significantly related to box office gross. Contrary to the 1989 Litman and Kohl study, however, no film genre could enter the equation. Science fiction–fantasy, which was found to be significant in the Litman and Kohl study, but not in the Sochay study, failed to retain its significance in predicting financial success of theatrical films. These findings suggest that films of any content category and MPAA rating can become blockbusters, and financial success lies more with execution than with any foolproof content formula. It may also imply that any content area once achieving success can become saturated until it approaches the average and no longer is differentially important.

Another interesting finding is that there is interaction between the Christmas season and family–children films. Neither of these two binary variables by itself was a significant predictor, as revealed in previous studies and confirmed by the present study, but family–children's films released in the Christmas season turned out to be significant at least for domestic and worldwide box office gross. Such films are predicted to increase domestic box office gross by $34.6 million and worldwide by $75.9 million. Thus, while the Christmas release does not guarantee financial success, select films that fit into the seasonal sentiment may have a good chance to perform very well. The summer season, which generally accounts for 40 percent of

**TABLE 10-4   Regression of Box Office Gross
(nonstandardized coefficients)**

Independent Variables	Dependent Variables	
	Domestic Gross	Worldwide Gross
COST	.38254*	1.49551**
REVIEWS	19.39725**	39.64378**
SCREEN	.01982**	.03711**
CR8	−1.69710**	−3.90414**
STAR	8.49935	13.03995
OSCAR	39.40593**	96.19216**
MAJORS	−4.25815	−19.45512
SUMMER	26.88411**	52.41079**
MPAA PG	7.48703	6.186814
CHRISTMAS*FAMILY	34.61009**	75.92744*
Constant	35.57675	92.92928
N	238	238
R^2	.4594	.4410
Adj R^2	.4356	.4164
F (10, 227)	19.29	17.91
Prob > F	.0000	.0000

*$p < .05$, two-tailed.   **$p < .01$, two-tailed.

all box office receipts,[67] even retains greater prominence since Litman and Kohl, and Sochay have found the same with films released in the 1980s.

Top directors and superstar actors failed to retain their significance as a predictor for commercial success. The insignificance of the top director variable is consistent with most recent studies by Litman and Kohl, Wyatt, and Sochay. A surprise is the failure for the star variable to maintain its positive impact on financial success at the box office in both domestic and worldwide box office gross.

The release by the major studios was not a significant predictor for the financial success of films. Although this binary variable is intricately intertwined with other key variables, such as production budget and the release pattern, it was found significant in the 1982 Litman study that analyzed films released in the 1970s. But Litman and Kohl found that the positive effect of the major release lessened in the early 1980s and Sochay confirmed the decline in the impact of major distribution in the late 1980s. In our regression here, major distribution was in fact negatively correlated with financial success, but it was not statistically significant. It suggests very strong performance by the mini-majors and large independents. Indeed, they have been able to do a better job at obtaining screens for their releases in recent years.

Not all categories of the Academy Awards are important predictors for financial success. The only significant category was winning or being nominated for the Oscar Best Picture, which was predicted to increase box office gross by \$39 million in the domestic market.

Not surprisingly, production costs were found to be a significant predictor, as they have been consistently in the previous research. The regression of box office gross shows that holding other variables constant, one additional million dollars are predicted to collect \$0.38 million from the domestic box offices and \$1.5 million from worldwide. This finding indirectly suggests that the foreign markets tend to respond more favorably to the increase in the production budget and that it brings in even more financial rewards for the film producers. It also conforms to the fact that revenues from foreign box offices began to exceed the domestic markets in the early 1990s.

With the increased production and release, competition between films becomes intense. Theaters are crowed with movies, and those that do not sell bundles of tickets right from the start see themselves being converted early to home video. In our regression analysis, a 1 percent increase in the top 8 film concentration ratio is predicted to decrease the domestic box office gross by \$1.7 million and the worldwide sales by \$3.9 million. Thus, the competitive forces at the marketplace not only have significant impact on films' fortunes at the box office, but also will determine their fate and performance in the subsidiary windows.

As expected and previously proven, the critical reviews continue to be significantly related to film success, but the question of whether this variable represents an additional information source for moviegoers or serves as a proxy for film "quality" is still unresolved.

With the increase in the number of films produced in the early 1990s, competition for screens is becoming more intense and theater owners' clout is growing. Access to a large number of screens still remains a key factor linked to financial success, as proven in the previous research. The major studios collectively have taken a quantum leap in the number of wide releases. In 1994, there were 130 films that played in at least 800 theaters and in 1995 the number of wide release has risen to 153. The 130 wide releases accounted for \$4.9 billion (94 percent) of \$5.2 billion theatrical revenues.[68] The regression result explains why the distributors strive to have more screens for their films. One hundred additional screens are predicted to increase the domestic box office gross by approximately \$2 million, holding other factors constant.

Another pair of dependent variables to be examined are box office returns from the domestic and worldwide markets: the domestic return simply represents domestic box office gross less production costs divided by production costs in the percentage form $\left(\dfrac{\text{domestic box office} - \text{costs}}{\text{costs}} \times 100 \right)$ and the worldwide return represents total box office gross less production costs divided by production costs $\left(\dfrac{\text{worldwide box office} - \text{costs}}{\text{costs}} \times 100 \right)$. Perhaps these two measures are more important and relevant to the production decision-making process since they suggest some degree of profitability and efficiency in the motion picture industry. The return ratios are of particular significance when the industry suffers from the multiple threats of flat domestic box office revenues, soaring production and marketing costs, and heightened competition. These equations accounted for 41 percent of total variance in the domestic returns and 36 percent in the worldwide returns (see Table 10-5).

A main difference from the regression analysis of box office gross came with the cost variable. The inclusion of the squared term of production costs produced a more precise measure of the relationship between the cost and the return. The positive sign on the squared cost ($COST^2$) suggests that the production cost has an interesting characteristic of a diminishing effect model. The returns on the production budgets will decrease initially to some point, but they will begin to increase beyond that bottom point. This finding implies that, not very surprisingly, small and big budget films will enjoy higher returns to their production investment whereas the mid-range budget films will have lower returns. The quadratic relationship between the production cost and theatrical returns holds true in the domestic markets as well as the worldwide markets.

TABLE 10-5 Regression of Box Office Returns (nonstandardized coefficients)

Independent Variables	Dependent Variables	
	Domestic Return	Worldwide Return
COST	-10.72788^{**}	-18.72683^{**}
$COST^2$	$.05280^{**}$	$.09582^{**}$
REVIEWS	59.44802^{**}	119.10810^{**}
SCREEN	$.04628^{*}$	$.08264$
CR8	-3.37077^{**}	-7.69797^{*}
STAR	30.91857	64.90839
OSCAR	179.51460^{**}	532.70180^{**}
MAJORS	-45.24629	-282.77280^{**}
SUMMER	77.06683^{**}	167.53730^{*}
MPAA PG	-1.65135	-62.17835
CHRISTMAS*FAMILY	139.58260^{*}	578.22920^{**}
Constant	305.3497^{**}	859.28080^{**}
N	238	238
R^2	$.4129$	$.3610$
Adj R^2	$.3843$	$.3299$
F (11, 226)	14.45	11.61
Prob > F	$.0000$	$.0000$

*p < .05, two-tailed. **p < .01, two-tailed.

The findings here confirm the two conventional stratagems employed by various studios.[69] The first school maintains that Hollywood should focus on what it does best: making potential blockbusters irrespective of cost. Since there is a fundamental need for people to experience group entertainment outside their home, it further argues, a big budget film will attract more people by bringing in superstars, spectaculars, and special effects, thereby differentiating it from television programs or ordinary movies. The second school contends that the only realistic strategy is to focus on "edgy" pictures costing under $20 million. Let the story be the star, says this school of thought—pay the writers and filmmakers, not the superstars. When it comes to profitability, it may turn out to be risky to accommodate both strong audience appeals and economic reality with the mid-range projects.

A very surprising result in the regression of box office returns is the performance of the major distributors. The films released by the major studios are no longer an advantage for box office returns from worldwide markets. The coefficient on the worldwide return shows a very significant negative correlation between the major-distributed films and their return ratios. It was discovered that such films would suffer much lower returns compared to films distributed by others. The regression analysis clearly shows that the majors were outperformed by mini-majors and independent studios in terms of box office returns, and that the major studios made inefficient investment decisions to the extent that this measure of returns reflects the efficiency. However, it is not clear whether this finding reveals a transient decline of the majors in the early 1990s or an early symptom of a new wave in the motion picture industry.

Another interesting finding is the impact of the number of screens on the box office returns. Even if it still held its positive effect on the domestic returns, the significance was reduced and it disappeared in the worldwide returns.

The competition in the marketplace was found to have a negative impact on the returns as well. A 1 percent increase in the top 8 film concentration ratio is predicted to decrease the domestic returns by 3.4 percent and the worldwide returns by 7.7 percent, other things being equal.

The independent variables such as STAR and MPAA ratings did not have any significant relationship with the box office returns. On the other hand, the critical reviews, the Academy Awards, the summer release, and children–family films in the Christmas season were all found to have significant positive relation with both dependent variables. For example, the summer release is predicted to return 77 percent more in the domestic markets and 168 percent more in the worldwide markets than release in other seasons.

DISCUSSION

Despite the biggest draw in history, the motion picture industry today sees profit margins shrinking down to 14 to 15 percent.[70] The skyrocketing costs of producing and marketing motion pictures have become a huge threat to the industry. In the past six years, studio marketing costs have ballooned by 92 percent, top star salaries have doubled, and production costs have seen significant double-digit growth, while domestic box office has increased by 9 percent. Part of the problem is also the growing number of movie releases from the major companies. MPAA member companies produced and released 212 films in 1995, an increase of 45 pictures from 1994.[71] The competition has led to costly advertising campaigns. International theatrical, worldwide videocassette sales, and television revenues have experienced considerably better expansion but still fall short of the hefty strides in the debit column. It becomes more dangerous to take risks, so the studios are likely to produce more predictable films and ones that are similar to those that have already been hits, while trying to cut back budgets for office space, newspaper subscriptions, and creative and technical personnel. Ironically this austerity psychology tends not to affect costs for stars.

Successful movies have to move people. The nature of the uncertainty about audience preferences necessitates the development of an often vague "audience image" that governs much of the decision-making in the economic stages of the movie business. Our attempt here is not so much to make golden rules for film success as to help understand the intricate interaction between movie audiences and producers. Also, we hope our findings to be some help in reducing the uncertainty associated with production, distribution, and exhibition decisions in the motion picture business. The utility is not in duplicating reality, but in providing enough road signs and benchmarks to help one at least not get lost, even if one does not always reach one's destination.[72]

Of course, any film's ultimate success should take into account ancillary income from video and worldwide television fares that can take years to amortize. Apparently, theatrical performance itself increasingly becomes the important independent factor that will determine the financial opportunities of films in these subsequent windows. The industry rule of thumb suggests that, if a movie grosses $50 millions, it will likely sell 200,000 videocassettes. It is further assumed that a top feature film will be rented five or more times per week,[73] adding additional revenues for the motion picture. A rough estimation in the industry is that ancillary markets account for 20 percent of a film's income. Thus, a simultaneous equation model and multiple stage estimation would produce much richer insights for this area of research. To explore further the relationship between decision-making and windowing processes would be extremely valuable and desirable, but it would be possible only when reliable and comprehensive data on subsidiary windows are available. Data on pay-per-view buy rates, home video sell-through and rentals, premium cable channels, and network ratings on a per title basis are necessary for the ideal research framework. Regrettably, however, the proprietary nature of these data is a formidable obstacle for further research.

The increasing importance of, and dependence on, international markets poses another problem. The top 100 films worldwide rang in with $9.15 billion in 1995 box office of which the international markets accounted for $4.99 billion (54.8 percent). While domestic growth was modest, international grosses ballooned by 16.5 percent.[74] There are a number of pictures whose substantial international performances exceed their very good North American results or make up for a shortfall in North America. The majors see the best growth markets as Mexico, Taiwan, South Korea, Indonesia, and India.[75]

The rising value of overseas markets for filmed entertainment is a boon for film producers, but it poses a significant challenge as well. On the one hand, the international markets enable the producers not only to compensate deficits in the domestic market through overseas box offices but also to tap into new opportunities for production budget sources. Now, it is not uncommon for foreign media companies to take partnership in coproducing films with Hollywood studios. Furthermore, foreign locales provide not only for exotics but also for more favorable economic conditions for film producers to cope with the incessantly increasing production expenditures.

On the other hand, the international markets bring in a challenge for the researchers as well as producers. While international distribution has grown from an easy way to earn extra profits into an economic necessity, international markets have virtually no constants and tend to defy conventional wisdom. For every picture that fits some particular logic, there is always an anomaly since the international markets are composed of a lot of culturally diverse and economically distinct countries. Due to the heterogeneity, "exceptions are the rule in foreign box offices"[76] and studios do not have a recipe for overseas success. Researchers, too, face similar difficulties with regard to data collection. The estimation of foreign box office gross and return would not be very fruitful unless the researcher obtains in the international contexts such key variables as the number of screens and competitive forces. Nonetheless, our regression analyses of worldwide box office gross and return should shed some light, even if indirectly, on the financial performance of films in the foreign markets.

NOTES

[1] J. Wasko, *Hollywood in the information age: Beyond the silver screen* (Cambridge, UK: Polity Press, 1994), p .4.

[2] *Ibid.*

[3] R. Taylor, "Television movie audiences and movie awards: A statistical study," *Journal of Broadcasting*, 18 (1974), pp. 181–186; R. Taylor, "Television movies: Directors win audiences," *Journal of Broadcasting*, 20 (1976), pp. 495–500; B. Litman, "The economics of the television market for theatrical movies," *Journal of Communication*, 29, 4 (1979), pp. 20–33.

[4] J. Wasko, *op. cit.*

[5] W. Dizard, *Old media, new media: Mass communications in the information age* (New York: Longman, 1994), p. 129.

[6] B. R. Litman, "Predicting success of theatrical movies: An empirical study," *Journal of Popular Culture*, 16, 4 (1983), pp. 159–175; J. Dominick, "Film economics and film content:

1964–1983," in B. Austin, *Current research in film: Audiences, economics, and law*, vol. 3, Ablex, 1987, pp. 136–153.

[7]Jack Valenti, "Motion pictures and their impact on sciety in the year 2000," speech given at the Midwest Research Institute, Kansas City, April 25, 1978, p. 7.

[8]D. Prindle, *Risky business: The political economy of Hollywood* (Boulder, CO: Westview, 1993), p. 4.

[9]D. Lieberman, "Owners play key role in consolidation," *USA Today*, 1995, pp. B1–B2.

[10]A. Marks, "The Color of Money," *The Christian Science Monitor*, 1995, pp. 11–10.

[11]D. Rosen, *Off-Hollywood: The making and marketing of Independent films* (New York: Grove Weidenfeld, 1990), p. 282.

[12]*Ibid.*, p. 284.

[13]G. Jowett and J. Linton, *Movies as mass communication* (Newbury Park, CA: Sage, 1989).

[14]B. Litman, "Decision-making in the film industry: The influence of the TV market," *Journal of Communication*, 32 (1982), pp. 33–52.

[15]K. Rosengren, L. Wener, and P. Palmgreen, *Media gratifications research: Current perspectives* (Newbury Park, CA: Sage, 1985).

[16]P. Palmgreen and P. Lawrence, "Avoidances, gratifications, and consumption of theatrical films: The rest of the story" in B. Austin, *Current research in film: Audiences, economics, and law*, vol. 5 (Norwood, NJ: Ablex, 1991), pp. 39–55.

[17]*Ibid.*, p. 48

[18]S. Knapp and B. Sherman, "Motion picture attendance: A market segmentation approach," in B. Austin, *Current research in film: Audiences, economics, and law*, vol. 2 (Norwood, NJ: Ablex, 1986), p. 43.

[19]B. Austin, "Motivations for movie attendance," *Communication Quarterly*, 34, 2 (1986), pp. 115–126; B. Austin, "The film industry, its audience, and new communications technology" in B. Austin, *Current Research in Film*, vol. 2 (Norwood, NJ: Ablex, 1986), pp. 80–116; B. Austin, *Immediate seating: A look at movie attendance* (Belmont, CA: Wadsworth, 1989).

[20]B. Austin, "Motivations for movie attendance," *Communication Quarterly*, 34, 2 (1986), pp. 115–126.

[21]*Ibid.*, p. 123

[22]B. R. Litman and L. S. Kohl, "Predicting financial success of motion pictures: The '80s experience," *Journal of Media Economics*, 2 (1989), pp. 35–50.

[23]G. Blowers, "Psychological approaches to film audience research: A critique" in B. Austin, *Current research in film: Audiences, economics, and law*, vol. 5 (Norwood, NJ: Ablex, 1991), pp. 56–67.

[24]L. Garrison, *Decision processes in motion picture production: A study of uncertainty*, Ph.D. dissertation, Stanford University, 1971.

[25]See, for example, G. Kindem, "Hollywood's movie star system: A historical overview," in G. Kindem, *The American movie industry* (Carbondale, IL: Southern Illinois University Press, 1982), pp. 79–93.

[26]T. Simonet, *Regression analysis of prior experience of key production personnel as predictors of revenues from high grossing motion pictures in American release* (Philadelphia: Temple University Press, 1977).

[27]G. Kindem, "Hollywood's movie star system: A historical overview" in G. Kindem, *The American movie industry* (Carbondale, IL: Southern Illinois University Press, 1982), p. 92.

[28]B. Litman, "Decision-making in the film industry: The influence of the TV market," *Journal of Communication*, 32 (1982), pp. 33–52.

[29]B. R. Litman and L. S. Kohl, "Predicting financial success of motion pictures: The '80s experience," *Journal of Media Economics*, 2 (1989), pp. 35–50.

[30]J. Wyatt, "High concept, product differentiation, and the contemporary U.S. film industry," in B. Austin, *Current research in film: Audiences, economics, and law*, vol. 5 (Norwood, NJ: Ablex, 1991), pp. 86–105.

[31]*Ibid.*

[32]S. Sochay, "Predicting the performance of motion pictures," *Journal of Media Economics*, 7, 4 (1994), pp. 1–20.

[33]*Ibid.*, p. 9.

[34]G. Blowers, *op. cit.*, pp. 60–61.

[35]*International motion picture almanac* (New York: Quigley, 1994–1996).

[36]C. Musun, *The marketing of motion pictures* (Los Angeles: Chris Musun Co., 1969).

[37]B. R. Litman, "Predicting success of theatrical movies: An empirical study," *Journal of Popular Culture*, 16, 4 (1983), pp. 159–175.

[38]Hollywood still gives NC-17 low rating, *Variety*, January 10–16, 1994, pp. 1, 44.

[39]M. Medved, *Hollywood vs. America* (New York: Harper Collins, 1992).

[40]B. Austin, "G-PG-R-X: The purpose, promise, and performance of the movie rating system," *Journal of Arts Management and Law*, 12, 2 (1982), pp. 51–74.

[41]J. Izod, *Hollywood and the box office 1895–1986* (New York: Columbia University Press, 1988).

[42]G. Kindem, *op. cit.*

[43]T. Balio, "Stars in business: The founding of United Artists," in T. Balio, *The American film industry* (Madison, WI: The University of Wisconsin Press, 1985), pp. 153–172.

[44]J. Phillips, "Film conglomerate blockbusters: International appeal and product homogenization," in G. Kindem, *The American movie industry: The business of motion pictures* (Carbondale, IL: Southern Illinois University Press, 1982), pp. 325–335.

[45]StataCorp., *Stata Statistical Software: Release 5.0* (College Station, TX: Stata Corporation, 1997).

[46]L. Maltin, *Movie and video guide, 1996 edition* (New York: Signet Books, 1995); M. Martin & M. Porter, *Video movie guide 1996* (New York: Ballantine Books, 1995); R. Castell, *Blockbuster Video guide to movies and videos 1996* (New York: Dell Publishing, 1995).

[47]B. R. Litman, "Predicting success of theatrical movies: An empirical study," *Journal of Popular Culture*, 16, 4 (1983), pp. 159–175.

[48]B. R. Litman and L. S. Kohl, "Predicting financial success of motion pictures: The '80s experience," *Journal of Media Economics*, 2 (1989), pp. 35–50.

[49]S. Sochay, *op. cit.*

[50]B. Litman, "Decision-making in the film industry: The influence of the TV market," *Journal of Communication*, 32 (1982), pp. 33–52; B. R. Litman, "Predicting success of theatrical movies: An empirical study," *Journal of Popular Culture*, 16, 4 (1983), pp. 159–175.

[51]S. Sochay, *op. cit.*

[52]B. Litman and L. Kohl, 1989.

[53]F. Goldberg, *Motion picture marketing and distribution* (Boston: Focal Press, 1991).

[54]S. Sochay, *op. cit.*

[55]Litman, 1982; Litman and Kohl, 1989; S. Sochay, 1994.

[56]S. Sochay, *op. cit.*, p. 9.

[57]T. King, "Studios fear a glut of summer movies will crowd out films lacking big stars," *The Wall Street Journal*, 1993, p. B1.

[58]Litman, 1989.

[59]Sochay, *op. cit.*

[60]G. Jowett and J. Linton, *op. cit.*

[61]J. Dodds and M. Holbrook, "What's an Oscar worth? An empirical estimation of the effects of nominations and awards on movie distribution and revenues," in B. Austin, *Current research in film*, vol. 4, (Norwood, NJ: Ablex, 1988).

[62]E. Levy, *And the winner is. . . : The history and politics of the Oscar awards* (New York: Ungar, 1987).

[63]*Ibid.*

[64]B. Litman, 1982; B. Litman and L. Kohl, 1989; S. Sochay, 1994.

[65]*International motion picture almanac* (New York: Quigley, 1996); *Variety*, March 13–19, 1995, p. 5. Although direct comparison is not possible since our sample covers three years between 1993 and 1995, this comparison reveals that MPAA and trade sources tend to focus on big budget films for the estimation.

[66]R. Abelson, "The shell game of Hollywood 'net profits,'" *New York Times*, 1996, pp. C1, C4.

[67]T. King, "Studios fear a glut of summer movies will crowd out films lacking big stars," *The Wall Street Journal*, 1993, p. B1.

[68]L. Klady, "Hollywood lays an egg," *Variety*, December 11–17, 1995, pp. 1, 102.

[69]P. Bart, "Studios in search for Seven percent solution," *Variety*, October 23–29, 1995, pp. 1, 5.

[70]D. Wood, "Movie industry likely to go on diet," *The Christian Science Monitor*, 1996, p. 4.

[71]L. Klady, "Hollywood suffers severe sell shock," *Variety*, March 11–17, 1996, p. 9.

[72]D. Rosen, *op. cit.*, p. 284

[73]J. Wasko, *op. cit.*

[74]L. Klady, "B.O. with a vengeance: $9.1 billion worldwide," *Variety*, February 19–25, 1996, p. 1.

[75]D. Groves, "Jumbo B.O. bucks found o'seas in '93," *Variety*, January 17–23, 1994, p. 13.

[76]L. Klady, "Exceptions are the rule in foreign B.O.," *Variety*, November 14–20, 1994, p. 7.

11

The Story of Censorship and the American Film Industry

License to Kill, License to Lust

ERIK LUNDE

Since the very beginnings of the theatrical exhibition of moving images, there has been continual public and private debate about the suitability of the content in legitimate films, both in the U.S. and international cinema, particularly in reference to so-called graphic sequences, erotic and/or violent. The special power of what critic Robert Warshow termed the "immediate experience" was initially felt, according to some observers, by the individuals who attended the first presentation of the *Lumiere Picture Show,* which was directed by the brothers Louis and Auguste Lumiere and screened in Paris on December 28, 1895. The *Picture Show* contained a series of short documentary episodes featuring typical daily activities photographed outdoors—a kind of home movie or video. In one such episode entitled "Arrival of a Train," early audiences were startled by the image of a moving train that seemed to be coming directly at them when, in fact, the front portion innocently exited the right side of the frame. And, with the introduction of "story" films in the early 1900s, such as Edwin S. Porter's celebrated *The Great Train Robbery* (1903), audiences were even more amazed at the "violent" content of some narratives. Porter's film, the first U.S. Western, featured what quickly become standard fare, fisticuffs, a saloon sequence, a chase, and gunplay. At one point, an outlaw throws the body of a fireman off the moving train after besting him in a fist fight; at another, a fleeing passenger is shot to death; the story ends with the traditional gunfight during which some bandits, among others, are killed. Besides these "shocking" events, most of the screenings of the famous film ended with what *Premiere* magazine (January, 1991) identified as one of the "Ten Shots That Shook the World": an outlaw points his six-shooter at the audience and unloads all the chambers at his "hapless" victims.[1] Indeed, *The Great Train Robbery* presented such a vivid, detailed portrayal of a train robbery that it was condemned by some as a reenactment or "how to" film, that is, "how to rob a train," open to imitation by any miscreants who might be exposed to it.[2]

But some early images also invited commentary for their "erotic" nature. One of the most famous sequences in an early Thomas Edison "peepshow" (on a Vitascope) was entitled *The Kiss*: It featured two rather stout actors, John Rice and May Irwin, "bussing" one another in a reenactment of their climactic scene from the current Broadway production entitled *The Widow Jones*.[3] What seems today to be the most proper and restrained romantic behavior was labeled "obscene" by some in 1896! And so the debate over what should be the limitations of this new art form had begun, both in America and abroad.

Indeed, the controversy over the question of censorship was central to all art forms of the nineteenth century and earlier, whether in print or visual form. And, certainly, the history of still photography, which preceded the history of film by almost sixty years, had raised questions about the suitability of content. But there was something else introduced by the Lumieres. If the early pioneers, inventor/artists as they were, could actually capture and preserve images of real people behaving in a realistic fashion, as seemed possible with the moving image, the filmmakers had discovered one approach to immorality: A human life could, in this sense, endure beyond death. But, as well, the "immoral" behavior of human beings, especially in their most nefarious activities, at least according to the rather superficial Victorian social code of the day, could be documented, namely their propensity to engage in animalistic, passionate acts—a bodily embrace or a murder!

In the United States, these early images, which to the contemporary eye seem so innocuous, would provide the impetus for the call to censor inappropriate visual material, a question still not settled in 1997, of course. Indeed, the introduction of a new labeling criterion for television programs suggests that no one has fully resolved the debate over objectionable content in legitimate visual entertainment. In a democratic culture, there will always be individuals or groups, often with institutional sponsorship, who will object to the content of any art form, whether in literature or live theater or any of the other seven arts. But, since the theatrical film is the primary unique art form pioneered throughout the twentieth century (not to neglect the impact of radio and television drama), it has consistently highlighted the debate over censorship during the past one hundred years. For many years, films were regarded by some as a "lesser" form of entertainment, appealing to base impulses in audiences and incapable of stirring spectators to "higher" ground. And early filmmakers felt that they had a certain license to exploit controversy in order to market their films. Just as barkers tried to beckon potential audiences into sideshows at circuses or carnivals to witness the "forbidden," so filmmakers endeavored to lure individuals into the "dark," to view their dazzling and shocking images. So a D. W. Griffith in his landmark epic, *Intolerance* (1916)—his next feature after the pioneering *The Birth of a Nation* (1915)—included risqué sequences featuring a Temple of Love where female performers danced about in revealing, flimsy outfits, and a Charlie Chaplin in his classic comic short, *Easy Street* (1916) included a sequence involving a dope addict about to shoot himself "up" with a "loaded" syringe. These were startling twists for the time. And, after World War I, with the coming of the 1920s, artists in all forms of expression exhibited the new, "looser" values of the Jazz Age—when talk of Sigmund Freud's ideas about sex was very much of the moment—and this at a time when films were rapidly becoming a sophisticated mass entertainment form. Theda Bara had already become notorious as the first vamp, marking a star fully identified as a sex symbol. And, during the twenties, other such stars became renowned for their romantic *personas,* including the Latin lover Rudolf Valentino, who appeared in such "hot" vehicles as *The Sheik* (1921), *Blood and Sand* (1922), and *The Son of the Sheik* (1926). Greta Garbo and John Gilbert were famous for heating up the screen in a film like *The Flesh and the Devil* (1926). Even in a serious and high profile World War I drama from the late silent era, William Wellman's powerful *Wings* (1927), a nurse played by Clara Bow (as Mary Preston), the famous "It" girl, at one point exchanges her uniform for a flapper's outfit, a shimmering cocktail dress, in an attempt to intrigue the aviator/hero, played by Buddy Rogers (as Jack Powell), now on "R & R" in Paris. She is "discovered" by the military police in a bedroom with Rogers, now innocently passed out from too much alcohol: Bow is disciplined for her improper behavior by being sent home from the front—but not before she portrayed the sexy side of a "girl next door."

In response to such imagery, various individuals, civic groups, religious organizations and official institutions attempted to restrict the content of film narratives, whether documentary or fictional, from the earliest days of the silent film. Hence the history of censorship of films is virtually as old as the history of film itself. The push for some form of external control over motion pictures has endured throughout the twentieth century. Proponents for film censorship have often cited their concerns for the family and its set of morals while opponents of film censorship have often cited the freedom of expression guaranteed in the First Amendment. For instance, after representatives of the NAACP picketed theaters screening *The Birth of a Nation* (1915) because of its alleged racist content, Griffith responded with a pamphlet entitled "The Rise and Fall of Free Speech in America": He argued that the "pictorial press [moving pictures] claims the same constitutional freedom as the printed press."[4] Beginning with the first minimal censorship code adopted in Chicago in 1907, various municipalities and states throughout the land inaugurated boards of censorship in one form or another. By 1922, six state governments had censorship regulations: Pennsylvania was the first entry in 1911, followed by Ohio (1913), Kansas (1914), Maryland (1916), Florida (1921) and Virginia (1922).[5] As well, through licensing and zoning ordinances, city governments always had the power to threaten the survival of theaters if there were a public outcry over the content of their exhibition schedule. In connection with the Motion Picture Patents Company, the National Board of Review was established in 1908: The Board attempted to bring some order out of the chaos of censorship codes by granting a seal of approval to "decent" films. When the film "trust" was "busted" in 1915, the National Board lost much of its effectiveness.

When feature length films began to replace "shorts" as the staple for exhibitors, beginning with the success of *The Birth of a Nation* in 1915, the calls for some form of national censorship increased both in intensity and breadth. In the early 1920s, several notorious scandals rocked Hollywood, including the Fatty Arbuckle affair, which involved the death of a young woman, the unsolved murder of Director William Desmond Taylor, and the mysterious death of actor Wallace Reid amid charges of drug abuse. In response to the sullied reputation of the film business—a kind of "Hollywood Babylon," indeed—the newly emerging studios united in 1922 to form the Motion Picture Producers and Distributors of America (later, the Motion Picture Association of America) and appointed a man of government and hitherto unvarnished reputation, Postmaster General Will Hays, to head it, in much the same fashion as the baseball owners had appointed a distinguished jurist, Kenesaw Mountain Landis, to "clean up" the game after the notorious Black Sox scandal of 1919—when the World Series was fixed—became public knowledge. During the 1920s, the Hays office published a list of "Don'ts and Be Carefuls" in an attempt to circumscribe presumably salacious content in U.S. mainstream films. But the Hays office, for all its ballyhoo, had trouble enforcing its credo, especially after the 1927 release of the first "talkie," *The Jazz Singer,* signaled the birth of a new era. A new system of censorship seemed necessary, and the Hollywood Production Code, adopted in 1930, was the answer. As one of the drafters of the Code, Martin Quigley, said in his book, *Decency in Motion Pictures* (1937), "with the introduction of the spoken word into motion pictures . . . the problem of the moral and social significance became magnified in extent and in degree."[6]

Hence the emergence of the "talkies" as the standard product by 1929 solidified the push for a stricter form of industry driven censorship. One cause of this intensified concern was the growing popularity of the gangster film genre. In the early 1930s, three renowned examples of the gangster genre were released, Mervyn LeRoy's *Little Caesar* (1930), with Edward G. Robinson, William Wellman's *The Public Enemy* (1931), with James Cagney, and Howard Hawks's *Scarface* (1932), with Paul Muni. All three classics, which have endured as powerhouse narratives, exploited the advantages of sound: They included the "new" sound effects featuring the gunfire of various kinds of "gats" and snappy dialogue pumped up with sexual innuendoes. As well, the kind of high quality imagery associated with the silent era persisted in these films. For instance, *Scarface*, produced by industrialist Howard Hughes, contained several provocative violent and romantic images that would soon become taboo in the Hollywood industry. The bonding of the gangster hero, Tony Camonte (Paul Muni), with his sister, Cesca (Anne Dvorak), with a subtext of incestuous passion, would be considered too blatant to many, and the success of Tony, who defies all authority figures until he is gunned down at the end, would be considered too subversive. Tony boldly defined his credo for success with the lines, "do it first, do it yourself, keep on doing it."

As well, the audacious Mae West's salty dialogue in such films as *She Done Him Wrong* and *I'm No Angel* raised troubling concerns for the Hays Office. West both appeared in and scripted these films; they were released by Paramount in 1933.

There were other reasons behind the push for both the adoption and enforcement of a stricter system of censorship. For one thing, the industry leaders wanted to control censorship themselves in order to prevent the supervision of an agency of the federal government. The Payne Fund Studies, the results of which were popularized in Henry James Forman's *Our Movie Made Children,* published in 1933, raised serious questions about the impact of films on the behavior of children. As well, national Prohibition was still in force (it was repealed in 1933), and the adoption of the Code represented an attempt to control potential dens of iniquity, movie theaters, just as Prohibitionists wanted to shut down saloons, among other things. Hence, the paternalistic Progressive desire to "clean up" America, to do "good" for those who may not know any better, characterized some forces behind the Code. This was also symptomatic of Progressive reformers who supported the New Deal in 1933. The push for the Code would represent a curious blend of benign authoritarianism and democracy.

Martin Quigley's principal co-author of the draft of the Hollywood Production Code, as accepted by Hays office in 1930, was Daniel A. Lord, a Jesuit priest who was a member of the faculty of St. Louis University. Quigley himself was a prominent member of the Catholic Church, a layman who was the publisher of the *Exhibitors Herald-World.* According to an excellent article by Stephen Vaughn, "Morality and Entertainment," another prominent layman, Joseph L. Breen, also contributed to the draft (in addition to others). However, while the Catholics were instrumental in the writing of the Code, this vital document also drew on the list of the "Don'ts and Be Carefuls" publicized by the Hays Office in the 1920s. And, while the drafters may have been motivated by a touch of anti-Semitism (this is uncertain) in response to the Jewish faith of many Hollywood titans, many of the same individuals, however reluctantly, would embrace the Code by 1934. Certainly, the Code also represented the concerns of many mainstream Protestant leaders. In many ways, therefore, the Code was, as Vaughn persuasively argues, "an attempt to bind movies to Judeo-Christian morality."[7] In this sense, the Code was responsive to more universal concerns than some detractors might assert.

The Code was revealing in its attempt to define "motion pictures" as a new, universal art form, the most democratic of the arts. And it also argued that film had a greater reach and power than the other performing arts. Hence, the Code celebrated and sponsored the special impact of motion pictures. It was, in one sense, a public relations document. In a kind of preamble, the Code confessed that producers "know that the motion picture within its own field of entertainment may be directly responsible for spiritual or moral progress, for higher types of social life, and for much correct thinking." Quigley would later argue that the "function of art is to ennoble. . . . *There is a grave difference between a presentation of what is wrong when the effect is only to acquaint the audience with the wrong and a presentation of wrong which encourages approval.*"[8] The Code distinguished between censorship of literature and censorship of film, pressing for a stricter enforcement of the latter. For instance, according to the Code, a "book describes; a film vividly presents; . . . a book reaches the mind through words merely; a film reaches the eyes and ears through the reproduction of actual events." In a further comparison between the image and the word, the Code asserted that "newspapers present by description, films by actual presentation; . . . newspapers are after the fact and present things as having taken place; the film gives the events in the process of enactment and with the apparent reality of life." Furthermore, the Code stressed that "everything possible in a play is not possible in a film," because of the "larger audience of the film, and its consequential mixed character. Psychologically the larger the audience, the lower the moral mass resistance to suggestion."[9]

Among the limitations on vulgar or immoral content, the Code highlighted violent crime and sexual activity. In response to the gangster film, it argued that "'Crimes Against the Law' . . . shall never be presented in a way as to throw sympathy with the crime or to inspire others with a desire for imitation." For instance, in reference to "murder," the Code specified that "brutal killings are not to be presented in detail." As well, "*Methods of crime* should not be explicitly presented," and "*illegal drug traffic* must never be shown." In a resonance with Prohibition, the Code stated that the "*use of liquor* will not be [generally] shown." In reference to sexual activities, the Code specified that the "sanctity of the institution of marriage and the home shall be upheld"; "adultery . . . must not be explicitly treated, or justified"; "excessive and lustful kissing . . . are not to be shown"; "*Seduction or Rape* . . . should never be more than suggested." Also, the Code forbade "obscenity," "profanity," "*complete nudity*," and the treatment of "*white-slavery*." It prohibited certain kinds of dances, particularly those suggesting "sexual action or indecent passion." Sensitive to the policies of an apartheid South, the Code asserted that "*miscegenation* . . . is forbidden." As well, in keeping with the religious convictions of its authors, the Code specified that no "episode may throw *ridicule* on any religious faith," and, in conformity with basic national traditions, the Code patriotically stated that the "*use of the Flag* . . . shall be consistently respectful."[10]

Partially as a result of the threat of an economic boycott made by the prominent Catholic organization known as the Legion of Decency, founded in April 1934, the Production Code Administration was established in the same year. Joseph Breen was appointed its head, a position he held until 1954, when he resigned and was replaced by Geoffrey Shurlock. And, periodically, to keep current with the social climate, the MPAA would amend the Code. The Breen office monitored a project in several stages, from preproduction through postproduction, from script approval to a final screening of the finished film print before its release. Any film failing to meet the criteria of the Breen office would not receive the official Production Code Seal of Approval. This meant that most film exhibitors, whether studio owned or not, would not screen the film. A film without a Seal would not be generally marketable. If a studio were not fully cooperative in connection with a particular film, it could be subject to a fine. Since the Major Five Studios—MGM, Warners, RKO, Paramount, Twentieth Century-Fox—and the Little Three—Universal, Columbia, and United Artists—all belonged to the Association, the chance of any uncooperative film-maker receiving the financing to make a major film was virtually negligible. Of course, there was always a chance that a film independently made might buck the Code; this would become more possible in the 1950s and beyond.

The Code, as it reads in 1997, initially appears to be excessively restrictive; it is fully understandable why genuine *auteurs* like a William Wyler, an Orson Welles, and an Alfred Hitchcock, would find the Code almost incompatible with their at-tempts to render narratives of a creative and original mode. And, certainly, as Gerald Mast and Bruce Kawin indicate, the manner in which the Code was sometimes en-forced subjected the Breen office to well-justified ridicule, particularly in matters of legitimate romantic relationships when even married couples were often restricted to twin or "Hollywood" beds, such as Nick and Nora Charles (Myrna Loy and Wil-liam Powell) in the engaging *Thin Man* series—the first of which was released in 1934.[11] Howard Zieff's *House Calls,* released in 1978, makes good fun of these earlier restrictions on lovemaking when the protagonists, played so nicely by Walter Matthau and Glenda Jackson, attempt to kiss and embrace on a bed with each keep-ing a foot on the floor.

But, as Leonard Leff and Jerold Simmons make clear in their excellent history of the Production Code, *The Dame in the Kimono* (1990), the Code was never as repressive as it may have read. In fact, according to Leff and Simmons, Joseph Breen and his fellow censors loved film and were willing to compromise on the matter of so-called objectionable dialogue and imagery. Often, the Breen people worked with liaison officials assigned by the studios, like Luigi Luraschi of Para-mount. In essence, the principal concern of Breen and his cohorts was to convince the producers and studio heads to comply with the objectives of a self-regulated industry, to provide works of popular culture for a mass audience presumably con-cerned with basic communal values—and hence, to avoid the number one fear of those in authority, the curse of federal government regulation. It was certainly diffi-cult enough for the Breen office to work with state and municipal censorship offi-cials.[12]

If the Code were as oppressive or inhibiting as some of its detractors have claimed, the Studio years would have yielded a consistently meager output of sig-nificant films, but, of course, such was not the case at all. Indeed, during every year of the Code's "heyday," great films were produced and released, even, in some cases, from "B" units of the studios—this at a time when films were never more popular or more massively produced. In the 1930s, the studios sometimes turned out more than 700 theatrical films a year; in 1938 alone, more than 80,000,000 single admission tickets were sold weekly—and this in a country of a population of

130,000,000 or so. Great screwball comedies, like Frank Capra's *It Happened One Night* (1934) and Gregory La Cava's *My Man Godfrey* (1936), flourished. Most film historians mark 1939 as the greatest year of Hollywood releases, citing such films as *Stagecoach, Gone with the Wind, Wuthering Heights, The Wizard of Oz,* and *Mr. Smith Goes to Washington,* among others. And, at a later date, the Breen office even "green lighted" some *film noir* classics (usually with a *femme fatale*), such as John Huston's *The Maltese Falcon* (1941), Billy Wilder's *Double Indemnity* (1944), and Howard Hawks's *The Big Sleep* (1946)—after, in some cases, considerable wrangling.

Part of this was possible because filmmakers learned how to play "tricks"—which mature audiences well understood—to communicate essential information. For instance, in Orson Welles's classic *Citizen Kane* (1941), a standard signifier, the fireplace, is utilized to alert the audience about the status of passion in Charles Foster Kane's May/December marriage to his second wife, Susan Alexander (Dorothy Comingore). Early in their married life in the castle Xanadu, when Kane (Orson Welles) is conversing with Susan in the Great Hall, he stands in front of a fire blazing in a monumental fireplace. But, later, when the marriage is deteriorating as Kane gets older, Kane visits Susan as she is working on one of her puzzles in front of the fireplace, and the fire is out, as presumably the passion is spent. Audiences readily picked up on these signals. Also, the compromise with the Breen people often insured the high quality of many film narratives. Part of the process of these compromises involved the way in which filmmakers would plan "forbidden" sequences and then, under threat of the Code office, would abandon their ambitions but, at least, settle for something less prurient but still suggestive enough for the purpose at hand. Again, according to Robert Carringer, Orson Welles, while making *Citizen Kane,* actually shot a sequence in a brothel, and, later, while eliminating this episode in the final version, Welles was still permitted to include a rather daring celebratory "show stopper" featuring chorines dressed in revealing outfits, at least by the standards of the time of the narrative, the 1890s, when the sight of a naked ankle was a source of much excitement![13]

Even during the height of the Breen office's power, there were frequent tussles with various dissenting producers, who challenged and even defied the Code. Among the most daring performers who struggled to retain her risqué dialogue was Mae West, in such a vehicle as *Belle of the Nineties* (1934), and one of the most famous cases involved the last lines of producer David Selznick's *Gone with the Wind* (1939). Selznick fought successfully for the inclusion of the word *damn* in Rhett Butler's final response to Scarlett O'Hara's entreaties, "Frankly, my dear, I don't give a damn!" (Clark Gable speaking to Vivian Leigh). The film was released to universal acclaim.

By the end of World War II, the Breen office would find its authority under more relentless attack than ever before, and, by the 1950s, some producers, directors, and exhibitors became openly defiant. One of the most famous cases involved Otto Preminger's *The Moon Is Blue* (1953), which Preminger successfully released without the Production Seal: among other things, the Breen office had objected to such words as *pregnant, mistress,* and *virgin,* which remained intact in the dialogue.[14] Later, Preminger successfully released his adaptation of the Nelson Algren novel, *The Man with the Golden Arm* (1955)—again in open defiance of the Code office, which objected to the way the theme of drug addiction was introduced. Howard Hughes would cause some trouble again with such films as *The French Line* (1954), as he had with his earlier *The Outlaw* (1943). And, in a further push for realism, an Elia Kazan would fight for the preservation of content in such films as the adaptation of Tennessee Williams's play *A Streetcar Named Desire* (1951) and *Baby Doll* (1956). Breen even relented and permitted a "cop-killing" that occurs at the end of William Wyler's *The Detective* (1951).[15]

Other film *auteurs,* in a subtle fashion, could undermine the intentions of the Code. Alfred Hitchcock was a master at this game. As Gerald Mast and Bruce Kawin have stressed, Alfred Hitchcock's *Rear Window* (1954) represented a wonderful subversion of the Code.[16] For instance, the film's treatment of a male protagonist addicted to voyeurism, in which the audience participates, clearly did not resonate with the spirit of the Code. As well, a Miss Torso, a professional dancer presumably on the "make," dances about her apartment in a most provocative way— both before the open window and on the balcony and often dressed in "short-shorts" for all male gazers to see and enjoy. What had happened to the Code's restrictions on suggestive dancing? The male hero, L. B. Jefferies (James Stewart), has suffered a broken leg sustained during an attempt to take a daring photograph at a race track. His leg is encased in a full length rigid plaster cast . Hence, when his gorgeous fiancée, Lisa Freemont (Grace Kelly), periodically visits him, there is really nothing he can do about lovemaking, even when she spends a Friday night dressed in a most attractive nightgown. Partially to alleviate his sexual frustrations, Jeff looks out of the window to observe the various activities of the neighbors in his Greenwich Village apartment complex; and, subsequently, Jeff thinks that he has detected enough evidence to implicate one of his neighbors, Lars Thorwald (Raymond Burr), in the murder of his wife. As an aid, Jeff utilizes a large telephoto lens to enable him to watch Thorwald more carefully: periodically, the lens suggestively rests on Jeff's lap, as a kind of substitute for his phallus. And, toward the end of the film, Jeff temporarily wards off the attacking culprit by setting off flashbulbs aimed at Thorwald: before the altercation, the flashbulb fixture rests suggestively on Jeff's lap, and one reading of the exploding bulbs is "naughty" indeed: they represent sexual climaxes denied the confined Jeff. Adding to the joke is that, at the end of the narrative, Jeff will be further restricted to abstention as, now, both his legs are encased. And, while the Breen office had some objections to the content of the film, it let all this pass—and more—however knowingly and unknowingly. The master had triumphed again.

Later, Hitchcock, who, in various interviews, confessed that there was always a sexual subtext to his films, would be especially proud of how he ended his magnificent thriller *North by Northwest* (1959): A train, on which Cary Grant (as Roger

Thornhill) is "bedding" his new wife Eva Marie Saint (as Eve) in their sleeping compartment, passes, like a phallus, into a vaginal tunnel. Subsequently, Hitchcock's enduring horror film, *Psycho,* released in 1960, would deeply trouble representatives of the Code office, with special attention to the famous shower sequence, when a naked Janet Leigh (as Marion Crane) is stabbed to death by an unknown assailant as she is relaxing in a motel after a long day's drive. Leigh's nudity is really never fully displayed, but the location, a bathroom, and the graphic and shocking nature of the attack clearly violated the spirit of the Code. But, as Stephen Rebello notes in his *The Making of Psycho,* Hitchcock had to make only a few cuts under the pressure of the Code office, now headed by Geoffrey Shurlock.[17] Times were clearly on the march! As well, the shower sequence is filled with suggestive sexual nuances. The showerhead has "phallic" tendencies as it rains down its essence on an initially joyous Marion (Leigh), and the attack itself appears like a rape: In one clip, the sharply pointed knife even enters Crane's body just above the unseen vaginal area.

Changes in censorship policies and practices were virtually inevitable in this era. The 1940s, 1950s, and early 1960s were difficult years for the U.S. film industry. In 1948, in the landmark *U.S. v. Paramount* decision, the Supreme Court sided with the government, and, under the authority of antitrust legislation, directed the studios to divest themselves of their theatrical chains. While the divestiture took some time to complete, eventually the studios would no longer directly control the films exhibitors would choose to screen. In a sense, all the theaters were now technically independent. Also, by the early 1950s, television began to replace the theatrical film as the most encompassing form of mass entertainment in the United States. At first resisting television programming by trying to attract audiences with such technologies as the three-dimensional print or wide screen processes like Cinemascope or Cinerama, the leaders of the industry eventually succumbed and cooperated with the networks, which, of course, provided a new outlet for vast archives of film prints. Because of television, the audience for the theatrical film began to decline dramatically—to about 30 million single ticket admissions a week by the end of the decade; dozens of neighborhood theaters closed.

As well, from the 1940s onward, films from abroad, which often, under more flexible national standards, contained "controversial" and "unacceptable" content, from the perspective of both the Breen office and other groups, were marketed more boldly than ever before, including Vittorio De Sica's *The Bicycle Thief* (1948), with its depiction of extreme poverty, and Robert Rossellini's *The Miracle* (1948), which was viewed by some as "sacrilegious." An attempt to block *The Miracle* in the state of New York led to the Supreme Court decision of 1952 (*Burstyn v. Wilson*) whereby the Court ruled that, as an art form, films were protected in their content by the First Amendment. By the later 1950s and 1960s, most urban locales featured "art" and/or revival theaters that screened such international films as Roger Vadim's *And God Created Woman* (1956) (with Brigitte Bardot), Ingmar Bergman's Bergman's *Wild Strawberries* (1957), and Frederico Fellini's *La Dolce Vita* (1960).

because of court findings spelled the beginning of the end of the major era of censorship of motion pictures. And while the tension between directors and their studio superiors over the final cut remains to this day, the movement away from an industry-wide sanctioned censorship was irreversible. To its credit, the Shurlock office (Shurlock would resign in 1968) even "green lighted" a crucial sequence in Sidney Lumet's powerful *The Pawnbroker* (1965) wherein a female character briefly exposes her breasts. The 1966 release of Mike Nichols's superior adaptation of Edward Albee's *Who's Afraid of Virginia Woolf,* with its string of obscenities kept intact, marked the end of the effectiveness of the Code Administration. The impact of the live theater on film fare was complete. It now seemed ridiculous to censure "real talk."

Also, partially because of the Civil Rights movement, the Vietnam War and the emergence of a counterculture, the era of the 1960s and 1970s would unleash a freedom hitherto unknown in the U.S. film industry. And so the Code would even succumb, to be replaced by the Rating system in 1968, sponsored by a new industry leader and spokesman, Jack Valenti. But there was no assurance that better films would be the result.

Film as illusion had given way to a kind of documentary realism. No longer would filmmakers be restricted from including naked performers, profanities, or realistic violence in their work. Indeed, theatrical audiences not only would become accustomed to "real" human talk and "real" human behavior, but they would expect or even demand it. As in some romantic novels, the explicit love scene was almost obligatory. At times, such sequences would seem natural in the story line, while, at others, the sequences would seem artificially inserted. But such was the price of the new found liberty. And the pressure on even major stars to disrobe periodically—to many a performer's embarrassment—was on (sometimes "body doubles" were used)! Some viewers would even welcome a kind of self-imposed restraint as filmmakers resisted the pressure to exploit their new license if they did not need to. Just a nice kiss might express all that was needed—witness the recently released romantic comedy *One Fine Day* (1996), starring George Clooney and Michelle Pfeiffer, and directed so charmingly by Michael Hoffman. These same viewers sometimes observed that, in vintage films, there was a kind of grace now missing from contemporary cinema. But there are few who, while mourning the demise of the efficiency of the old studio system, would simultaneously issue a call for the restoration of the Code.

To demonstrate different artistic treatments of adult romantic relationships in two similar story lines—one created under the aegis of the Code and the other long after its demise, a comparison between two enduring films, William Wyler's classic *The Best Years of Our Lives* (1946) and Hal Ashby's *Coming Home* (1978 and rated "R"), is instructive. Both narratives treat the story of veterans adjusting to postwar domestic life. And both films showcase a bedroom sequence featuring the iron commitment of a female character to her wounded male partner. In Wyler's film, Homer Parrish (Harold Russell), a World War II veteran who has lost his hands in a fire on his ship, invites his fiancée, Wilma Cameron (Cathy O'Donnell), to help him un-dress for bed. Homer, still much in love with his "girl next door," has been avoiding Wilma so that he will not become a burden. A fully dressed Wilma helps remove Homer's hooks tied to a harness, buttons up his pajama top, and tucks him into bed, cementing her declaration of love with a tender kiss. Homer, with his doubts re-moved, responds positively at last; as Wilma turns out the light and leaves, the audi-ence knows that the two are now partners for life. The film ends appropriately with Wilma and Homer's wedding, which is staged at Wilma's house.

In *Coming Home,* Sally Hyde's (Jane Fonda's) husband Bob (Bruce Dern) is still fighting in Vietnam while she volunteers at a veteran's hospital in 1968. There, after some initial tension, she gradually falls for Luke Martin (John Voight), a Viet-nam veteran paralyzed below the waist. Luke has been fulfilling his sexual needs with expert "call girls," but, after he stages a much publicized protest by chaining his wheelchair to the gates of a Marine depot, Sally boldly announces that she wants to spend the night with him. The subsequent lovemaking sequence, without the restric-tions of the Code, features both partners undressed in bed while engaged in an ex-plicit form of oral sex. After this signal night, both Sally and Luke are emotionally bonded and, despite the adulterous nature of their affair, achieve a rare moment of romantic bliss. Sadly, this will be inevitably disrupted when Bob comes home. Both sequences are central to their film narratives, and both are powerful. And it is essen-tial to be fair to Ashby here: He included such a graphic sequence to demonstrate how Sally could achieve an orgasm with the physically challenged Luke, something she was unable to enjoy in an earlier encounter with her husband. But, in some ways, the Wyler sequence, with its restraint, achieves a poetry and lyricism not possible in the Ashby sequence, which is spiced up with a realistic soundtrack punctuated with the passionate sounds of the excited lovers. Greater freedom does not necessarily make greater art.

Stanley Kubrick's evolving career highlighted how the transformation of what was permissible in legitimate films in these transitional years of the1960s and 1970s could affect the treatment of controversial material. For instance, when Kubrick brought Vladimir Nakobov's famous novel *Lolita* to the screen in 1962, he had to eliminate some of the erotic material, under pressure from Shurlock's Code Admin-istration. However, in his brilliant spoof of the possibility of a nuclear holocaust, the classic *Dr. Strangelove, or How I Learned to Stop Worrying and Love the Bomb,* which was released two years later, Kubrick, while still avoiding any explicit sexual sequences, incorporated many audacious verbal and visual sexual references. For instance, at the beginning of the film, a sequence featuring a B-52 bomber being refueled by a tanker in mid-air is photographed in such a way as to suggest an act of copulation between the aircraft: the fuel line is a symbolical phallus, and the two "mates" bob up and down to the tune of "Try a Little Tenderness." Late in the film, when Major "King" Kong straddles a bomb on its descent toward a Russian target, the nuclear device appears like a giant phallus lodged between the pilot's legs. Ironi-cally, when the bomb hits the ground, it sets off a Doomsday Machine, which will presumably destroy all life on earth. The resulting mushroom clouds present a visual rendering of the bursts of joy emanating from the ecstatic mating of two heterosexually driven machines—the masculine bomb and the feminine Doomsday machine—a "strange" form of "love" indeed![20] But, with the full license accorded in 1971, Kubrick could now treat the Anthony Burgess novel, *A Clockwork Orange,* to the limit. The narrative provides a commentary on the attempts of future government agencies to condition the behavior of criminals. Kubrick fills his film with images of frontal female nudity, abusive violence, and rape scenes. In one sequence, a gang of three members, led by the "hero," Alex (Malcolm McDowell), breaks into the affluent home of a prominent writer and brutally rapes his wife while compelling him to look on, all to the tune of "Singing in the Rain." This sequence, tough to look at, is photographed in explicit detail. Kubrick no longer had to rely on the subterfuge of machines making love but now had the license to display naked human beings in erotic, albeit brutal embrace.

In the pivotal year of 1967—positioned between the virtual end of the Code and the introduction of the Rating system—famed director Arthur Penn demonstrated in the classic *Bonnie and Clyde* how cinematic artists could press the "envelope" in their work. The film posits the images of the real 1930s gangster duo, Bonnie Parker and Clyde Barrow, as representatives of 1960s youthful radicals defying the "Establishment." Early in the film, when Clyde (Warren Beatty) is trying to impress Bonnie (Faye Dunaway), he holds a revolver belt high in a very suggestive manner; Bonnie touches it tentatively as she might his male organ in sexual play. As she does so, a match, like an erect phallus, bobs up and down in Clyde's mouth. Ironically, because Clyde is suffering from impotence, the gun substitutes for his inability to achieve consummation. Later, during a partially botched attempt to rob a Kansas bank, Clyde kills a bank teller who jumps on the running board of the escaping car. In a shocking image, a close-up of the teller's face virtually explodes in all its bloodiness on the screen. These images serve Penn's and his collaborators' purposes. Penn wants to stress how, in an emotional sense, Clyde replaces his sexual inadequacy with his skill at gunplay. And, in the scene with the bank teller, Penn demonstrates the terrible price of Clyde's capers, and, hence, separates the audience from too close an identification with the male protagonist.

At this point, the influence of the "blue" or blatantly pornographic film heritage on legitimate films—however marginal—should be acknowledged, from the silent days to the 1960s and 1970s, with the release of such films as *Deep Throat* (1973) and *The Devil in Miss Jones* (1973). Even a director of pornographic films like Russ Meyer went legitimate: In 1970, Twentieth Century-Fox, under the leadership of Richard Zanuck, bankrolled and released Meyer's *Beyond the Valley of the Dolls,* which was scripted by both Meyer and a then little known film critic named Roger Ebert! In their work, entitled *Playboy's Sex in Cinema* (1970), Arthur Knight and Hollis Alpert stated that the "films of 1970 would thus seem to have reached the ultimate phase of the liberating process as we have described it in *Playboy* over the past five years. Complete frontal nudity, both male and female, is no longer taboo;

nor is its presence now confined to low-budget exploitation shockers."[21] They cited Mike Nichols's *Catch-22* (1970) and Ken Russell's *Women in Love* (1969), among others . As Knight and Alpert asserted, "it is almost impossible to find a picture other than from the Disney studios that didn't include . . . at least one graphic bed sequence."[22] In this period, other so-called legitimate films like Vilgot Sjoman's *I Am Curious (Yellow)* (1968) and Bernardo Bertolucci's *Last Tango in Paris* (1973), with Marlon Brando, contained several explicit sequences that were blatantly pornographic, whatever the artistic intentions of the creators.

In cases involving such films as these, various Supreme Court decisions over the years widened the latitude of obscenity permissible in a motion picture. In this spirit, according to Edward de Grazia and Roger K. Newman's *Banned Films* (1982), the 1970 report of the President's Commission on Obscenity and Pornography urged the repeal of laws "prohibiting the sale, exhibition and distribution of obscene materials," while expressing reservations about uncontrolled availability of such materials to minors and the unsolicited mailings of "obscene" documents. However, in the *Miller v. California* case of 1973, the Burger Court, in a 5–4 decision, drew back somewhat on earlier, more libertarian stances, citing, among other things, local, "contemporary community standards" as the determinant as to whether a given "work . . . appeals to the prurient interest." Despite the somewhat more limiting conditions of the *Miller* findings, which have since served as a kind of benchmark, nothing as powerful as the Production Code Administration had once been could really prevent mainstream filmmakers from taking risks anymore.[23]

The 1960s marked the emergence of Sidney Poiter as a major American star whose *persona* as a dignified and brilliant African American reflected the impact of the Civil Rights movement on the film industry. For many years, especially prior to World War II, the characters of African Americans in mainstream films had been relegated to Sambo-like, servile images, partially in deference to the apartheid policies of the South—consider the slave played by Butterfly McQueen in *Gone With the Wind*. However, this began to change in the 1940s and 1950s—witness *The Jackie Robinson Story,* starring Robinson himself in 1950. But, in his seminal 1967 films, *To Sir, with Love* and *In the Heat of the Night,* Sidney Poitier profiled a new kind of African American character: a powerful, professional black hero, so shrewd that he could outwit and overcome oppressive white folks. Poitier and others were achieving and overcoming—at long last.

And with the full demise of the Code, a different kind of Black film was introduced, the genre known as the Black exploitation or "blaxploitation" film, beginning with such works as Melvin Van Peebles's *Sweet Sweetback's Baad Asssss Song* (1970) and Ossie Davis's *Cotton Comes to Harlem* (1970). These and subsequent films like Gordon Parks's *Shaft* (1971) and Gordon Parks, Jr.'s *Super-Fly* (1972) reflected the growing militancy expressed by young urban Black leaders in the 1960s, like a Stokely Carmichael who helped popularize the expression "Black power." The narratives of such films, usually fashioned by Black filmmakers, often featured strong-minded Black male protagonists, sometimes detectives, termed by

Daniel Leab "Superspade" heroes, who openly disdained white racism, identified with the culture of the ghetto, and countered violence with violence. This genre, which had died out by 1975 or so, readily included many excessively violent and erotic images, the appearance of which would have been impossible just a few years earlier. The tradition of these films resurfaced later in the work of such Black film-makers as Spike Lee and John Singleton. As well, other, more "genteel" films of the 1970s, like Martin Ritt's *Sounder* (1972) and John Badham's *Bingo Long Travelling All-Stars & Motor Kings* (1976), powerfully and enduringly evoked the heritage of Black Americans who lived and worked in the segregated South of the 1930s.[24]

While there had always been enormous disagreement over the issue of censor-ship, most individuals, inside and outside the film industry, agreed on one thing: that the exposure of children to film should somehow be monitored. In this case, the question was not over control of a film's content but rather over who should be permitted to see the film. In terms of censorship, the Classification and Rating Ad-ministration (CARA), which officially replaced the PCA in 1968, was much more satisfactory. The original Rating system established a series of designations that have changed somewhat over the years: "G" meant that the film could be viewed by all; "M" designated films for "mature" audiences; "R" films were "restricted" to audiences of eighteen years of age or older, unless accompanied by an adult; "X" films were "restricted" solely to audiences eighteen or older. Later, the "M" cat-egory would be replaced by the "PG" designation (initially "GP"), standing for "pa-rental guidance"; this meant that parents were warned against some "unsuitable" material; the age for the "R" rating was lowered to seventeen. In 1984, as a result of the furor over some torture sequences in Steven Spielberg's *Indiana Jones and the Temple of Doom*, a "PG-13" rating was added, deeming some films as "inappropri-ate" for children under thirteen; and, in 1990, the "X" rating was changed to "NC-17," standing for "no children" under seventeen.[25]

While there is no question that the current system is infinitely superior to the confining regulations of the Production Code, some filmmakers have objected to the Ratings as a new form of censorship. To this day, filmmakers often must eliminate more explicit materials, just to receive an "R" rating, preferable to an "X" rating, or, after 1990, the "NC-17" rating. Filmmakers, of course, much prefer the "R" rating because many legitimate theaters either would not exhibit "X" films on principle or would avoid such films because they were "cursed" and therefore hard to market. As an example, in order to qualify for an "R" rating for the theatrical release of his *Color of Night* (1994), director Richard Rush eliminated some sequences featuring gay lovemaking between two principal female characters, played by Jane March and Leslie Anne Warren, and a sequence involving partial frontal male nudity of the protagonist, played by Bruce Willis. But, thanks to video, Rush was able to release the video version as a "director's cut," which restored the excised footage. Of course, how much these restored cuts added to the power of the film is open to question. All of this suggested that a new politics had arrived with the demise of the Code in 1968, the "Rating" game.

Three films in which Jack Nicholson either starred or had a prominent part, Dennis Hopper's *Easy Rider* (1969), Bob Rafelson's *Five Easy Pieces* (1970), and Mike Nichols's *Carnal Knowledge* (1971), showcased the new freedom—as Nichols's landmark *The Graduate* had in 1967. *Easy Rider* featured various characters who openly smoked marijuana; *Five Easy Pieces* etched a Nicholson character (Bobby Dupea) who frequently defied any semblance of authority, private or commercial; in *Carnal Knowledge,* Nicholson (as Jonathan) experimented with different forms of sexual behavior throughout his adult years. In *Carnal Knowledge,* aggressive females were identified as "ball-busters." Certainly, these films were provocative but hardly uplifting. All of them did reflect quite accurately the experimental and protest nature of the 1960s.[26]

With the flowering of the Hollywood Renaissance, marking the rise of a new group of well-trained *auteurs* in the 1970s, the scope of possibilities was much widened.[27] The new filmmakers were determined to test the limits of permissible content as never before. And, in doing so, they initiated the rebirth of the U.S. film, driving up box office receipts and rekindling universal interest, in the era when each film was "green lighted" by a "deal," unlike the system of the old studios. A Martin Scorsese would incorporate startling images of violence and domestic abuse in such films as *Taxi Driver* (1976) and *Raging Bull* (1980), both starring Robert De Niro; a Francis Ford Coppola would include innovative images of violence and nudity in his powerful reformulation of the gangster genre in *The Godfather* (1972) and *The Godfather—Part II* (1974); a Peter Bogdanovich would bring Larry McMurtry's *The Last Picture Show* (1971) to the screen, with some of its explicit sex scenes intact; an Alan Pakula would treat government and corporate secrecy and corruption in such films as *Klute* (1971), *The Parallax View* (1974), *All the President's Men* (1976), and *Rollover* (1981); a Steven Spielberg would offer the first of many box office smashes, *Jaws*, in 1975, a film filled with gory visual details involving characters attacked by sharks. During this period, even directors from abroad, like a Roman Polanski, could examine with abandon themes of corruption and sexual abuse in the brilliant *Chinatown* (1974), his take on the *film noir* genre with a story line set in Los Angeles of 1937 and a detective hero played, once again, by Jack Nicholson. In *Nashville* (1975), an ironic treatment of the American Bicentennial, a Robert Altman would feature a striptease—from top to bottom—and an assassination in a brilliant series of provocative segments drawn from the U.S. music industry. A John Badham, in *Saturday Night Fever* (1977), would feature two rapes of the same young woman. In such films as *Annie Hall* (1977) and *Manhattan* (1979), a Woody Allen would capture shifting U.S. mores with frank, adult dialogue between the sexes, as did a Paul Mazurski in *An Unmarried Woman* (1978). A Lawrence Kasdan, in *Body Heat* (1981)—another variation of *film noir*—included a number of explicit, powerful love scenes. These films, as well, were demanding on their audiences as they were stylishly made, interlaced with shrewd and subtle imagery. And none of these films could have been made as audaciously or as creatively during the Code years, yet all played well in U.S. theaters. They were serious, artistic, entertaining and well accepted. And they stretched the limits, often receiving an "R" rating as a result. Even the release of the popular mythic or comic book films toward the end of the decade, beginning with George Lucas's *Star Wars* in 1977, did not diminish the possibilities for U.S. filmmakers in subsequent years.

The coming of cable and video in the 1970s and 1980s signaled a new era. Today, the term "anything goes" characterizes the endless variety of choices open to the adult customer. On cable, the *Playboy* channel, featuring "soft porn," has been available as a premium option for years. Home Box Office or HBO has prided itself on broadcasting uncut, uninterrupted feature films and has, on occasion, run "specials" crossing the line into a kind of pornography. For many years, video stores have set aside an "adult" display of pornographic films. And future possibilities with computer access to the "net" and the availability of films on CD-ROM discs seem infinite. With so much explicit material available for the price of a few dollars, prominent feature films, regardless of how many verbal obscenities and graphic images they might contain, may seem tame compared to other options. Of course, this means that legitimate filmmakers may be able to exploit the "family" market, and this has certainly happened, as witnessed with the remarkable revival of wonderful animated features produced under the auspices of the Disney studios. But, as well, filmmakers have felt both compelled and persuaded to include "enticing" sequences in their stories, simply to compete with the "adult" market. In recent years, as well, the so-called lesbian/gay and other independent films have influenced mainstream commercial films as well.

And some legitimate films have aggressively played with themes of male and female sexual fantasies and the encounters they lead to. Adrian Lyne's thrille*r Fatal Attraction* (1987) features an extremely graphic and almost violent sequence involving a brief affair between characters portrayed by the notable performers Glen Close and Michael Douglas. Even the growing cadre of women directors has gotten into the act. In the youth oriented film, *Fast Times at Ridgemont High* (1982), director Amy Heckerling spiced up the film with several sequences featuring female nudity (primarily involving one of the stars, Jennifer Jason Leigh) and promiscuous behavior. And Jane Cameron's splendid *The Piano* (1993) features several nude sequences of the protagonists (played by Holly Hunter and Harvey Keitel) having an affair.

In recent years, female nudity is so much on display that it evokes little comment. In Michael Caton-Jones's charming *Doc Hollywood* (1991), starring Michael J. Fox, the lovely young actress, Julie Warner, at one point simply emerges naked out of a lake in Fox's full view and walks right by him, announcing boldly that there is nothing she has to offer that Fox, as a physician, has not seen before. That she will become Fox's love interest is not surprising! And this film is rated "PG-13." Also, nude sequences are no guarantee of box office success. *Showgirls* (1996) was an attempt by a legitimate *auteur,* Paul Verhoeven, to exploit the female nudity and the live "nudie" shows available in U.S. metropolitan areas: The film featured several women who participated in striptease shows and employed such techniques as "lap dancing" and working the "pole." Despite the abundance of lovely naked actresses, the film was universally condemned by serious critics and did not do very well—and not because of its "NC-17" rating! Even a legitimate and admired star like Demi Moore, while paid very well for portraying a stripper in Andrew Bergman's *Striptease* (1996), could not save the film from a disappointing take at the box office. At best, the response to such films was blasé: no longer would they be regarded as a sensational product, playing on male fantasies.

Furthermore, in the 1970s, 1980s, and 1990s, many filmmakers were now free to unleash astonishing and brilliantly realized images of explosive violence, regardless of the "R" rating they might receive—particularly in some blockbuster adventure and detective yarns. Both Penn's *Bonnie and Clyde* (1967) and Sam Peckinpah's *The Wild Bunch* (1969) can be credited with introducing stylized violence into the legitimate film. *Bonnie and Clyde* ends with the virtual execution of Bonnie and Clyde as they are ambushed by a Texas ranger and his deputies outside Arcadia, Louisiana. The bodies of the two gangsters, as they are pumped full of seemingly endless rounds of ammunition, writhe and turn about in slow motion: Bonnie's gyrations have sexual connotations. And, in Peckinpah's film, many of the principals die gruesomely but almost poetically, again in slow motion.

Clint Eastwood first created the character of Harry Callahan in *Dirty Harry* (1971), directed by Don Siegel: In this film and its sequels, *Magnum Force* (1973), *The Enforcer* (1976), *Sudden Impact* (1983), and *The Dead Pool* (1988), Harry used any means available—legitimate and illegitimate—to clean up the streets. Civil liberty policies simply coddled criminals: The vigilante as police officer was glorified. The Dirty Harry vehicles, as engaging as they are on one level, contained stark, startling images of violence, the deaths of both the innocent and the corrupt. Horror films like John Carpenter's *Halloween* (1978) and science fiction vehicles like Ridley Scott's brilliant *Blade Runner* (1982) embellished terrifying sequences with violent imagery. In the stylish and entertaining *Die Hard* series, featuring a New York policeman (Bruce Willis as John McClane), who almost single-handedly must overcome a determined group of "high tech" terrorists, various characters suffered an endless array of gruesome deaths. For instance, in Rennie Harlin's *Die Hard 2* (1990), during a fight sequence in the snow, Willis terminated one culprit by stabbing him in the eye with an icicle. By the 1980s, both Sylvester Stallone and Arnold Schwarzenneger became world-renowned as action heroes in adventure films which, while sometimes hugely entertaining, contained large doses of violence. For instance, Stallone's third "Rambo" film, *Rambo III* (1988), directed by Peter Macdonald, featured several stunning sequences involving the Soviet occupation of Afghanistan, but they were sometimes offset by an endless litany of "enemies" suffering violent deaths at the hands of the obsessed hero, at least to some viewers. And Schwarzenneger's exciting "Terminator" films, *The Terminator* (1984) and *Terminator 2: Judgment Day* (1991), as skillfully directed as they are by James Cameron, sometimes seemed to suffer the same fate—again, at least to some.

Certainly, film artists were absolutely right to exploit their freedom to incorporate any images—no matter how violent—that they felt essential to the visual enrichment of their work, especially in the action/adventure drama. And these artists were intent on rendering realistic images of dead bodies and of the ritual of tragic deaths. But some of the violence in such films, as professionally made as they were, seemed gratuitous: It added to the fireworks of the adventure narrative but served little to propel the story forward. Some viewers were surfeited with unwelcome images of body parts, fiery deaths, endless car wrecks, gouged out eyes, grotesque corpses, and the like. Indeed, some of these films could boast the advantage of new technology provided by computer generated images, but the cost of these special effects and the involvement of so many stuntpeople could push production budgets into the nine figure range. The compulsion to serve up violence for violence's sake seemed overwhelming at times. Where was the restraint?

But, at other times, images of violence clearly served artistic purposes, in such films as Paul Verhoeven's powerful *Robocop* (1987), whose hero (Peter Weller) is tragically haunted by his half-man and half-machine state of being as he becomes a force of destruction for good, or Timothy Burton's dazzling *Batman* (1989), whose dark hero (Michael Keaton) must think and behave like a criminal in order to apprehend the miscreants. And, certainly, the new realism of violence was powerful in narratives treating combat in Vietnam. Oliver Stone's spellbinding *Platoon* (1986) presented searing images of death and destruction—both of U.S. soldiers and their victims—and thus demonstrated the tragic results of misconceived U.S. military operations in the jungles of Vietnam. The images of decapitated heads of Vietcong soldiers toward the end of Francis Ford Coppola's *Apocalypse Now* (1979) offered testimony of the bankruptcy of the U.S. policies in Vietnam.

Again, many scripts have been peppered with endless profanities—witness Nancy Dowd's screenplay for *Slap Shot* in 1977—so many of them that contemporary viewers may wonder if filmmakers, again, simply utilize such language for its own sake. While no one could dispute that folks in the workplace will often speak in a less than elegant fashion, one could also wonder if the abundance of obscenities in contemporary scripts matched reality.

As well, the repercussions from forays into traditional Biblical terrain remain controversial. Representatives from the religious right protested the release of Martin Scorsese's less than literal take on the Christ story, *The Last Temptation of Christ*, released in 1988. To the credit of the U.S. film industry and many exhibitors, the film did play throughout the country, but its box office potential was presumably affected by this kind of rejection, which, some have argued, was encouraged by the conservative climate characterized by the Reagan presidency. Many critics have characterized Scorsese's film as an art film representing the vision of a great American *auteur*, however special that vision may have been.

In the spirit of a Scorsese, any fair-minded observer, reviewing the story of censorship and the U.S. film industry since the first flickering images were exhibited in the 1890s, might properly salute the role of individual *auteurs*—such as an American master director like the celebrated Hitchcock or a renowned producer like David Selznick—who, while generally cooperating with the Code Administration Office, continually tested and pushed back the limits on content and so made the eventual liberation of a later day possible. Even "captains" of the industry like a Darryl Zanuck, who was chief of production at Twentieth-Century Fox from 1935 to 1956, demonstrated at times an extraordinarily creative leadership and so helped define a new latitude. Zanuck sponsored such enduring and socially provocative films as *The Grapes of Wrath* (1940), *Tobacco Road* (1940), *How Green Was My Valley* (1941), *Gentlemen's Agreement* (1948), *Pinky* (1949), *Twelve O'Clock High* (1950), *The Day the Earth Stood Still* (1951), and *Viva Zapata!* (1952). In a wonderful 1954 memo to producer Jerry Wald, Zanuck demonstrated the kind of professional, balanced approach to censorship that represented the best qualities of the studio era, qualities that eventually would insure a more permissive attitude. Zanuck simultaneously paid tribute to Joseph Breen's essentially rational administration of the Code while condemning unreasonable pressures from outside agencies. Said Zanuck:

> *I have been associated, as you know, with many controversial pictures and I have had many fights with the Breen . . . Office and with other outside censorship groups. It is my belief that the Code protected me far more than it ever harmed me. . . .*
>
> *When you can get by with* From Here to Eternity *and* A Streetcar Named Desire *and have them both turn out to be box-office hits then I fail to see what all the furor is all about.*
>
> *What infuriates me is the pressure groups and censorship groups both here and abroad. This is where we should carry our fight.*[28]

Today, many Americans regard the principles of the First Amendment as sacrosanct: To them, perhaps even more so than to Zanuck, the concept of censorship in any form is anathema. And, yet, for much of the century, at least until the late 1960s, the theatrical film had been subject to censorship of one form or another. So the dilemma remains, at least for earlier films. Given the reality of censorship, what imagery that could have been powerful, uplifting or provocative had been left out? What had obstructed the flow of artistic expression from the filmmakers to their audience? And, in recent years, for serious viewers, any suggestion that a legitimate film has somehow been cut, edited, or otherwise transformed by "invisible" powers before it is broadcast is automatically offensive. There are many individuals who will simply refuse to watch a theatrical film broadcast on a network, not only because of the inevitable packaging under censorship prescriptions but, also, because of the endless interruptions by commercials that destroy the special power of such a kinetic art form. Hence, if such viewers miss a film screened, they welcome films broadcast uncut and uninterrupted on premium cable channels like Home Box Office or, thanks to the videotape revolution, on tape. And, of course, there is, once again, always the compunction not to miss films when first run at the theater.

And there is always one succinct answer to those concerned with unseemly or unwelcome content: abstention—simply do not attend the theater or purchase a television set. But such an alternative has never seemed terribly realistic, because of what Alfred Hitchcock defined as the need to "go out." But, of course, any viewer can be selective, given the abundance of available reviews covering the content of new releases. An intelligent decision is called for. Many daring souls are always willing to expose themselves to a new cinematic experience—or, then, again, simply to reject the option altogether, a kind of self-imposed censorship.

Hopefully, in a democratic culture, filmmakers would be continually willing to experiment and find the financial support they need—even in this day of huge entertainment conglomerates. All of this is tenuous, of course, but what in filmmaking heritage has ever been secure? And, despite and, perhaps, at times, even because of censorship standards, the first century of filmmaking has produced far greater glories than failures: It has been a remarkable ride.[29]

NOTES

[1]Stephen Harvey, "Ten Shots That Shook the World," *Premiere* (Winter, 1991), 20.
[2]Charles Musser, *Before the Nickelodeon: Edwin S. Porter and the Edison Manufacturing Company* (Berkeley, CA: University of California Press, 1991), 257–258.
[3]Gerald Mast and Bruce Kawin, *A Short History of the Movies,* 6th Ed. (Boston, MA: Allyn and Bacon, 1996), 27.
[4]D. W. Griffith, "The Rise and Fall of Free Speech in America," (1916), excerpts found in Harry M. Geduld, Ed., *Focus on D. W. Griffith* (Englewood Cliffs, NJ: Prentice-Hall, 1971), 43.
[5]Ira H. Carmen, *Movies, Censorship, and the Law* (Ann Arbor, MI: The University of Michigan Press, 1996).
[6]Martin Quigley, *Decency in Motion Pictures* (New York, NY: The MacMillan Publishers, 1937), 17–18.
[7]Stephen Vaughn, "Morality and Entertainment: The Origins of the Motion Picture Production Code," *The Journal of American History* (June 1990), 77: 39.
[8]Quigley, 9, 11.
[9]"Motion Picture Production Code," found in Leonard J. Leff and Jerold L. Simmons, *The Dame in the Kimono: Hollywood, Censorship, and the Production Code from the 1920s to the 1960s* (New York: Grove Weidenfeld, 1990), 289.
[10]Ibid., 284–286.
[11]Mast and Kawin, 244.
[12]Leff and Simmons.
[13]Robert L. Carringer, *The Making of Citizen Kane* (Berkeley, CA: The University of California Press, 1985), 28–29; also, see Frank Brady, *Citizen Welles: A Biography of Orson Welles* (New York: Charles Scribner's Sons, 1989).
[14]Daphne Merkin, "Now, Voyeur," *Premiere* (Winter, 1991), 111–112.
[15]Leff and Simmons.
[16]Mast and Kawin, 326–329.
[17]Stephen Rebello, *Alfred Hiitchcock and the Making of Psycho* (New York: Dembner Books, 1990), 146.
[18]Arthur Knight and Hollis Alpert, "The History of Sex in the Cinema: Part Nine: The Forties, War and Peace in Hollywood," *Playboy* (August 1966), 154.

[19]Robert Sklar, *Movie-Made American: A Cultural History of the Movies,* revised and updated, (New York: Vintage Books, 1994), 262–266.

[20]Mast and Kawin, 491–492.

[21]Arthur Knight and Hollis Alpert, *Playboy's Sex in the Cinema, 1970* (Chicago, IL: A Playboy Press Book, 1971), 9.

[22]Knight and Alpert, 10.

[23]Edward de Grazia and Roger K. Newman, *Banned Films: Movies, Censors and the First Amendment* (New York: R. R. Bowker, 1982), 129–135.

[24]See Daniel J. Leab, *From Sambo to SUPERSPADE: The Black Experience in Motion Pictures* (Boston, MA: Houghton Mifflin Company, 1975); John Belton, *American Cinema/ American Culture* (McGraw-Hill, 1994), 291–295; David Cook, *A History of Narrative Film,* 3rd Ed., (New York: W. W. Norton), 930; Louis Giannetti and Scott Eyman, *Flashback: A Brief History of Film*, 3rd Ed., (Englewood Cliffs, NJ: Prentice-Hall, 1996), 393–395.

[25]Mast and Kawin, 469.

[26]Seth Cagin and Philip Dray, *Hollywood Films of the Seventies: Sex, Drugs, Violence, Rock 'n' Roll and Politics* (New York: Harper & Row, 1984).

[27]See Diane Jacobs, *Hollywood Renaissance* (New York: A Delta Book, 1980).

[28]Darryl F. Zanuck to Jerry Wald, February 23, 1954, found in Rudy Behlmer, Ed., *Memo from Darryl L. Zanuck: The Golden Years at Twentieth-Century Fox* (New York: Grove Press, 1993), 247–248.

[29]The author would like to thank Gary Hoppenstand and Douglas Noverr for sharing their special insights on this subject. Other important sources consulted for this study include Gregory Black, *Hollywood Censored: Morality Codes, Catholics, and the Movies* (Cambridge, England: Cambridge University Press, 1994); Francis G. Couvares, Ed., *Movie Censorship and American Culture* (Washington, DC: Smithsonian Institution Press, 1996); Gerald Gardner, T*he Censorship Papers: Movie Censorship Letters from the Hays Office, 1934–1968* (New York: Dodd, Mead, 1987); Ephraim Katz, *The Film Encyclopedia,* 2nd Ed., (New York: HarperCollins, 1994); Leonard Maltin, *1997 Movie & Video Guide* (New York: Penguin, 1996); Gerald Mast, Ed., *The Movies in Our Midst: Documents in the Cultural History of America* (Chicago, IL: The University of Chicago Press, 1982); Murray Schumach, *The Face on the Cutting Room Floor: The Story of Movie and Television Censorship* (New York: William Morrow & Co., 1964); Alexander Walker, *Sex in the Movies* (Baltimore, MD: Penguin Books, 1968).

12

Hollywood and the Business of Making Movies

The Relationship between Film Content and Economic Factors

GARY HOPPENSTAND

It is not surprising that the United States has dominated the international film industry over the past century. After all, both the movies and America embrace similar metaphors. Both concern themselves with the perceived realization of dreams. The American Dream has been well stated by many historians and cultural anthropologists as a compelling argument for our existence as a nation and as a rationale for our work ethic. Hollywood, of course, is in the business of making and selling dreams, on the proverbial silver screen and off. According to Hortense Powdermaker, motion pictures are an art *and* an industry.[1] Art and business need not be incompatible, and as the film industry in America has demonstrated throughout the twentieth century, movies as art and movies as business can achieve both critical and commercial success. Indeed, Hollywood is a sophisticated dream factory that is in the business of manufacturing escapist fare that is solely dependent on the continuing interest of an audience willing to buy the celluloid fantasies that are offered for sale.

This chapter, then, will examine that important relationship between the art of motion pictures and the business of motion pictures. Historically, the evolution of this relationship will be traced from the earliest years of commercial filmmaking, when the film industry began to define its audience in order to better develop a profitable commodity known as movies. Early motion picture technology and exhibition practices will be briefly surveyed, in order to illustrate how most of the major advancements in filmmaking during this period were dynamically linked to economic factors and marketing strategies. The creation of Hollywood itself, as the industrial center of the movie business, will also be discussed, as will the creation of two early film business practices—the star system and the studio system—that, to this day, still exert a great influence on the way movies are made and promoted. Hollywood's response to the growing threat of television in the 1950s will be reviewed, specifically as to how this threat led to experimentation with wide screen projection techniques and with big budget film productions. Next, the role of two present-day Hollywood marketing strategies, known as "Film Environment" and "Film Narrative Cycle," will be analyzed in blockbuster films such as *Star Wars* (1977) and *Jurassic Park* (1993), in order to discover how these practices currently affect the way in which movie content is affected by the sophisticated process of selling movies. Finally, the contemporary economic state of commercial filmmaking will be addressed, using Clive Barker's horror film *Nightbreed* (1990) as an illustration of the practice of "Film Saturation," and it will be argued that with the creation of each new technological venue for film exhibition—from video, to pay television, to interactive computer software—the financial strength of Hollywood will be assured well into the next century.

DISCOVERING AN AUDIENCE: THE EARLY YEARS OF COMMERCIAL FILM

Technology has always determined the way film is marketed. In fact, being the first of the electronic mass media (that would later include radio and television), it was also the first to be wholly dependent on technology for its production and distribution. From the start, people who made these "primitive" films quickly discovered that there was money to be made in celluloid. As Robert Sklar states in *Movie-Made America: A Cultural History of American Movies*, early movie viewers "took hungrily to the movies and turned, by their nickels, an instrument of science and amusement into the first mass entertainment medium."[2] Sklar reports that around the turn of the twentieth century, U.S. filmmakers noted that sex could attract a working class audience to the movies. The Edison company, for example, produced *Tenderloin at Night* (1899) and *How They Do Things on the Bowery* (1902), which featured stories about "loose women" stealing money from drugged "country rubes."[3] It was an important discovery for the fledgling film industry, the idea that the content of a movie could have a dramatic impact on how well or how poorly that movie sold tickets.

The most significant marketing discovery during this earliest period of commercial filmmaking was the development and use of the film projection system. Film historians Gerald Mast and Bruce F. Kawin state that Major Woodville Latham and his two sons invented a failed prototype of the motion picture camera and projector in 1895. In France, the Lumière brothers created a more practical movie camera that was less bulky than a model developed earlier by Thomas Edison, and they shot a film with this equipment entitled *Workers Leaving the Lumière Factory* in 1895, later exhibiting this motion picture in private screenings to scientists and friends. Mast and Kawin claim that the first movie theater opened to the "paying public" on December 28, 1895 in the basement of the Grand Café in Paris.[4] Prior to the invention of the movie projector, the exhibition of film clips was limited to a single viewer at a time. Devices such as the kinetoscope or mutoscope offered film clips that could only be viewed by one person at any given time. Although these devices were profitable for their era (since they capitalized on audience fascination with the novelty of simple, moving images), the makers of these films soon figured out that it was more profitable when moving images were projected on a screen for mass viewing. When an audience of one hundred people seated at a nickelodeon could view a single film exhibited on a single projection, the cost for film manufacturing and distribution became more cost-effective. Prior to the use of film projection, one hundred kinetoscopes and one hundred loops of film were required to generate the same income that one film screening provided. In addition, by freeing film exhibition from the kinetoscope, this offered more flexibility for early movie audiences. One hundred kinetoscopes required a great deal of room, yet a film could be projected most anywhere.

Indeed, the development of film projection opened up new areas of film marketing. Since its inception during the late nineteenth century, motion pictures were embraced by the immigrant and working classes in America. During the first two decades of the twentieth century, the demographics of the typical filmgoing audience substantially shifted from the immigrant and working classes to the middle class. With this shift, fundamental notions about how movies should be marketed also changed significantly. For the new middle-class audience, filmmakers discovered that the exhibition venue was as important as the movie itself in selling the motion picture experience. Though the nickelodeon proved successful in attracting the immigrant filmgoer, because they were generally located in the poorer, working-class neighborhoods of large cities, they failed to attract the more affluent middle-class audience. In 1914, with the opening of the Strand Theater—the first of the great movie palaces—in New York City, it was discovered that the middle class relished these elegant, even opulent, movie theaters, as much as they relished the movies they saw there. Other notable movie palaces followed, including the Rialto in 1916, the Rivoli in 1917, and the Capital in 1919, with each new theater outdoing its predecessor in its seating capacity and in its use of extravagant decor. When the doors swung open on the Roxy in 1927, this magnificent establishment could seat sixty-two hundred patrons, a far cry from the nickelodeon's mere one hundred seats.[5]

Thus, by attracting the middle class (who had more money and leisure time to spend at the movies) to motion pictures, by increasing the numbers and the seating capacities of theaters, and by making the ritual of movie attendance a social "event," the profitability of film production and distribution soared throughout the 1920s in America. As filmmaking technology became more standardized during the decade between 1910 and 1920, and as the business practices of movie production were being established and refined, two important events occurred that helped to shape the way commercial narrative movies were packaged and sold. The first of these important developments was the creation of the "star system," a practice by which movies were promoted by using well-known film actors. The second development was the establishment of the Hollywood "studio system," where films were mass-produced by a specialized labor force in much the same way as an automobile factory mass produced cars.

Early filmmakers were continually searching for newer and better ways to sell their product. Part of this marketing strategy involved the development of longer, multireeled narrative films. It was noted that certain formulaic stories—such as comedy, or romantic melodrama, or the Western—attracted the interest of potential filmgoers. With the technical invention of multireel movies (which allowed narrative film to escape the highly limiting confines of a ten-minute single reel), motion pictures began to be promoted, in large part, by the stories they told. Before 1910, U.S. movie producers were shooting multireel films. Unfortunately, because the distribution system of the period was geared exclusively to single-reel movies, early multireel films, such as Vitagraph's *The Life of Moses* (1909–1910), were exhibited in separate installments. In 1911, Vitagraph released a three-reel movie, *Vanity Fair,* that was exhibited entirely at a single viewing. Shortly thereafter, the feature film in America began dominating the theatrical venues,[6] because they sold more tickets at the theaters than did short films alone.

Another major discovery made by the fledgling movie industry was that people went to movies to see certain actors. Since silent film was a powerful visual medium, it made perfect sense that the moviegoing audience would be drawn to the most visible element in motion pictures: the larger-than-life actor or actress who brought the movies to life. Eventually, film producers began advertising their motion pictures around these movie celebrities, developing elaborate publicity schemes for their most popular actors and actresses, both on and off the screen. Indeed, the Hollywood star system was developed as one of the earliest successful marketing schemes. Film historians Richard Maltby and Ian Craven report that Hollywood created an entire "publicity machine" to support the promotion of stars in their motion pictures. Maltby and Craven state, "The publicity machine at its height assumed almost the status of a peripheral industry in its own right. There were about 20 fan magazines in the United States in the late 1930s, with circulations between 200,000 and one million. *Photoplay, Modern Screen,* and *Shadowland* regularly reached the most devoted quarter of the weekly movie audience. 'Gossip' was a requirement of the industry. . . ."[7] Indeed, the star system continues to influence the way motion pictures today are produced.

Films made prior to 1910 did not promote actors. Biograph Pictures, in fact, did not even provide screen credits for their performers, an indication of the value then placed on actors as screen personalities by movie producers. Instead, Biograph identified their performers by the characters they played (e.g., "Little Mary") or as symbolic ambassadors of the company (e.g., the "Biograph Girl").[8] In 1910, Carl Laemmle—who was one of the first movie producers to recognize the drawing power of screen personalities—in a now famous marketing ploy, lured the Biograph Girl, Florence Lawrence, away from Biograph to his own production company and advertised her as starring in his next picture. Commercial success always bred imitation in the motion picture business, and by 1919, the star system was a popular business practice with a number of filmmaking companies. Mary Pickford ("America's sweetheart") and Charlie Chaplin (the "Little Tramp") were among the most popular movie celebrities of their time, and they benefited greatly from their star status (each making nearly a million dollar salary, which is an astronomical amount even today).[9]

Aside from the development of the motion picture camera and projector, no other single technological innovation changed the way films were made and marketed more than did the use of sound in movies. Although the technology of synchronic sound and image projection can be traced back to the inception of moviemaking, the potential for sound movies was not fully realized until August 6, 1926, with the Warner Brothers' release of *Don Juan,* starring John Barrymore and directed by Alan Crosland. *Don Juan* featured a pre-recorded musical score that was played on Vitaphone disc. This film was accompanied by various sound "shorts," including a speech given by Will Hays, chief of the Motion Picture Producers and Distributors of America, that announced the beginning of the sound era in movies. With the premiere of the most famous early sound motion picture, *The Jazz Singer,* on October 5, 1927, starring Al Jolson and directed by Alan Crosland, even though this movie only had a few scenes of sound dialogue, it proclaimed in no uncertain terms the advent of sound film. Indeed, the popularity of this new technological advancement literally changed the film industry overnight, as other studios scrambled to produce their own "talkies."[10]

The industry's initial conversion to sound pictures, at first, was not without its problems. As Kristin Thompson and David Bordwell state in their book, *Film History: An Introduction:*

Filmmakers and technical workers struggled to cope with the unfamiliar, often clumsy, new technology. Microphones were insensitive and hard to move; it was difficult to mix sound tracks; and scenes frequently had to be shot by multiple cameras in soundproof booths.[11]

Stories of the period abound in Hollywood about actors who had once enjoyed success in silent pictures, and yet who, with the transition to sound movies, found themselves out of work because their voices did not record well in the new sound film. Also, camera movement became static. At the height of the silent era, the camera moved freely, but during the early sound period, sound technology impeded the camera, restricting its maneuverability and locking the screen image in standard shots not dissimilar to traditional theatrical stagings. Audience demand, however, insured that sound pictures became the standard of the industry.

MOVIE FACTORIES: HOLLYWOOD'S STUDIO SYSTEM

The film industry's decision to locate itself in sunny California was motivated by smart business thinking. In other regions of this country, weather could play a major role in the making of movies (or, more precisely, in the unmaking of movies). The winter season in the East, North, and Midwest areas of the United States, for example, could severely restrict the shooting of film outdoors, while unpredictable rain and humidity in the South (e.g., Florida) could play havoc with tight film schedules. The Hollywood area insured year-round filming, since adverse weather conditions were minimized. Robert Sklar notes the other advantages associated with Hollywood—"it provided a unique physical environment: in close proximity to one another were mountains, desert, a city and a sea. Within an hour or two of downtown Los Angles one could find a location resembling almost any conceivable scene one might want to use—factory or farm, jungle or snowy peak."[12]

Thus, supported by a nearly perfect climate for filmmaking, the emerging film studios in California settled down during the early decades of the twentieth century to the serious business of manufacturing their celluloid fantasies. In fact, the movie industry mirrored the development of its counterpart in the heavy industry fields. At about the same time that Henry Ford was perfecting his assembly-line system for the mass production of automobiles, Hollywood filmmakers were perfecting the studio system for the mass production of motion pictures. Many films made before the studio era were inefficient models of production. Sometimes the same individual directed, edited, and starred in a particular film. Perhaps this person also designed the sets and made the costumes as well. Thus, the time it required to make the movie often could not be predicted, and the overall quality of the movie was equally unpredictable. Sklar notes that, during this period, the only motion picture companies large enough to support a division of labor system were Edison and Biograph. Filmmakers tended to be cameramen who sold their movies to film manufacturing companies, or who established their own production companies.[13]

Any free-market capitalist will tell you that the way to improve profitability in a manufacturing economy, like Detroit or Hollywood, is to increase productivity while lowering production costs. The studio system, as a business that manufactured motion pictures, used division of labor as an important method for improving productivity. Instead of working as a "jack-of-all-trades," the employee in the studio system was a specialist. People were hired to do one thing. Film editors were hired to edit films; cameramen to operate the film cameras; scriptwriters to develop the stories; actors to perform the roles of the characters in the stories; and directors to manage the entire production. Obviously, the evolution of a specialized labor force under the studio system dramatically increased the number of films that were made, but it also increased the quality of these films as well. If all a worker is required to do is edit film, over time that worker becomes a good editor. The studio system, in fact, produced some of the finest motion pictures ever made. The year 1939, considered by many film historians to be the height of the Hollywood studio system, saw the release of classics such as *Gone with the Wind, The Wizard of Oz,* and *Stagecoach.*

FIGHTING THE SMALL SCREEN: THE BUSINESS OF 1950'S FILM TECHNOLOGY

One of the greatest economic threats to Hollywood emerged during the 1950s, with the encroaching dominance of commercial television in America. Like radio, the great advantage television had over motion pictures was that it offered "free" entertainment. After the consumer's initial investment in the receiver set, corporate sponsorship of TV shows provided U.S. audiences with the same escapist fare that proved popular at the movie theaters; action, drama, comedy, and variety could all be enjoyed at home, free of charge. Television audiences proved more than willing to tolerate commercial interruptions in order to watch their favorite programming. As the unit cost of TV sets came down, as the technology of individual TV sets improved both sound and picture reception, and as the broadcast quality of television production improved, America fully embraced this new electronic medium with a passion that has not waned in over forty years. Growing numbers of people now began to stay at home to view this strange little box, to enjoy the Westerns, crime dramas, and comedies that they used to go to the movie theaters to watch.

The greatest casualties of this growing love affair with TV were the movies. In 1929, weekly attendance at motion picture theaters in America was at its height, at ninety-five million viewers. At this moment in time, movies were *the* most popular form of entertainment. During World War II, film attendance dropped to eighty-five million a week, but following the war—from 1945 to 1948—attendance rose back up to ninety million a week. In 1950, at the beginning of the decade when movies were dealt a near-mortal blow by television, weekly attendance at theaters dropped to sixty million, and in 1953, dropped again to forty-six million. The leanest years for Hollywood were the 1960s and 1970s, when weekly theatrical attendance fell below twenty million.[14] Today, film attendance has risen back to an average of twenty million theatergoers per week, but it has been a hard-fought battle for Hollywood, this life-and-death struggle with television, a heated contest in which the film industry was forced to explore a number of innovative technological and marketing options in order to better compete with TV's increasing dominance of the U.S. entertainment market.

The film industry challenged television in several crucial areas, such as exploiting the technological and production limitations of the TV medium. Indeed, throughout the 1950s, Hollywood thought they could lure viewers back to the movie theater by promoting the one great advantage that movies had over television at the time: the size and quality of the picture being viewed. Early television was broadcast in black and white, the picture quality was less than perfect, and the size of the TV screen was decidedly tiny when compared to the theatrical screen. Hollywood experimented with wide screen techniques in films such as *Fox Follies of 1929* (1929) and *Kismet* (1930), but felt no pressing need to pursue this technology, because of the cost involved for theater owners to convert their theaters and because filmmakers were more interested in spending their production budgets on sound pictures. During the 1950s, desperate to find a strategy to combat this new and persistent adversary called television, the film industry thought they could capitalize on TV's weakness by producing movies that expanded the size of the projected image. For the religious epic, *The Robe* (1953), Twentieth Century-Fox developed an anamorphic lens system—called CinemaScope—that, when attached to the motion picture camera, compacted the images being filmed. These images were then uncompacted for viewing via a special lens attached to the projector. The end result of this innovation was that CinemaScope dramatically widened the projected image of movies. Prior to CinemaScope, the film screen was basically a square (possessing an aspect ratio of 1.33:1). CinemaScope offered a projected image that had an aspect ratio of 2.35:1, nearly doubling the image's width over the previous industry standard.[15]

Other so-called wide screen techniques were also offered as a marketing ploy to lure the public back to the movie theater. In 1952, a wide screen projection system, called Cinerama (which utilized three synchronized 35mm film projectors to show an image, with an aspect ratio of 2.5:1, on a curved screen) was exhibited in New York in the film, *This Is Cinerama*. The first narrative film that was released in Cinerama was *The Wonderful World of the Brothers Grimm* (1962), directed by Henry Levin and George Pal. However, this process proved to be too costly and technologically too unwieldy, and it fell by the wayside in the late 1960s. A more successful wide screen technology was Todd-AO, which was introduced in the musical, *Oklahoma* (1955), and also used successfully in the popular travel adventure, *Around the World in Eighty Days* (1956). This technique shot the picture using 65mm film and projected the picture from a 70mm print; its advantage over CinemaScope was that it provided a consistently sharp, projected image that did not have the edge distortion commonly found in CinemaScope movies. Super Panavision, another wide screen technique, also used a 65mm film negative, while Ultra-Panavision 70 could project an image with an aspect ratio of 2.75:1, as illustrated in the 1962 epic film, *Lawrence of Arabia*, directed by the master of the movie epic, David Lean.[16]

By developing wide screen exhibition in the 1950s to attract the attention of moviegoers, Hollywood also produced big budget spectaculars to fill that wide screen. Early commercial television could not compete with the film industry's budgetary resources. Hollywood well understood that TV was limited to production settings that were relatively intimate and contemporary in nature. Hollywood subsequently chose to make sprawling historical epics that featured the proverbial casts of thousands in order to provide a product that television could not offer. Biblical epics, such as *Samson and Delilah* (1949), became a popular staple, as well as remakes such as *Quo Vadis?* (1951). Other popular big budget wide screen productions included *Raintree County* (1957), *Spartacus* (1960), and *El Cid* (1961), among many others. In terms of critical respect and box office popularity, the movie epic reached its zenith in *Ben-Hur* (1959), a film based on the Lew Wallace novel and on the earlier 1926 silent film. Directed by William Wyler and starring Charlton Heston, the 1959 version of *Ben-Hur* won eleven Academy awards, more than any other film made before or since. A few short years later, however, the Hollywood historical epic (and Hollywood itself) was dealt a mortal blow. The most expensive movie ever made up to that point, *Cleopatra* (1963), nearly bankrupted its studio because of cost overruns generated by its lavish production and by untimely halts in production due to Elizabeth Taylor's illness. At a whopping 243 minutes viewing time, *Cleopatra* did so poorly at the box office that it virtually ended Hollywood's fascination with extravagant historical epics.

In addition to the use of wide screen motion pictures, filmmakers in the 1950s also experimented with the special visual effects process known as 3-D (or "stereoscopic cinema"). Early 3-D films included *Bwana Devil* (1952), *House of Wax* (1953), and *Kiss Me Kate* (1953). The problems, however, commonly associated with the 3-D process were that it was expensive to film and distribute, and that it required its audience to view the film wearing cumbersome 3-D glasses. Consequently, because of the process's high costs, filmmakers employing 3-D tended to skimp on their production budgets in other areas. 3-D movies generally did not feature major actors or actresses, or indulge in lavish sets, and they quickly became synonymous with low quality filmmaking. In a couple of years, 3-D was dropped by the movie industry as an unprofitable venture.

A more successful innovation during this period was the drive-in theater, which was an attempt by the industry to unite America's growing love affair with their cars with a new and exciting venue for watching motion pictures. John Belton argues that the shift in population in America from cities to the suburbs also accounted for the popularity of drive-ins. As Belton notes, "Drive-ins adapted themselves as much as possible to the needs of the postwar generation. Instead of hiring a babysitter, dressing up, driving into town, and hunting for a parking space (or paying to put the car in a parking lot), couples with young children took the kids along with them to the drive-in (usually at no extra cost)."[17] The proliferation of drive-ins in America ultimately led to a significant change in the content of low budget films. In the 1930s and 1940s, the Hollywood "B" movie was made with the Saturday afternoon matinee in mind. These low budget productions included serial films, which were exhibited in installments over a number of weeks (and even months). Younger adolescents under the age of sixteen were the primary audience of "B" movies, and the Western dominated this market. In the 1950s, as drive-ins sprang up across the country, the "B" picture industry adapted to its new audience, which included older teenagers who had access to the family car. Instead of horse operas, science fiction films became the standard "B" movie fare at drive-ins. The most popular example of this new genre of low budget motion pictures included the alien invasion films—such as *The Thing (From Another World)* (1951) and *Invasion of the Body Snatchers* (1956), which were reflective of the invasion paranoia that gripped America during the earliest years of the Cold War era. Unlike the earlier pre-World War II "B" movies, the postwar drive-in films included content that attracted this older, teenage audience. The 1950s low budget picture often employed elements of sexual titillation or more graphic representations of violence, those things that could lure eighteen-year-old Billy to the drive-in without necessarily shocking Billy's parents.

Because Hollywood could not defeat the young upstart called television, by the mid-1950s the film industry began selling and developing programming for TV. The Disney studios created a weekly television show called *Disneyland,* a number of the major studios—Columbia, Warner Brothers, M/G/M, and others—sold the broadcast rights to their archives of older feature films. The studios also began producing their own shows, including "M-G-M Parade," and "Twentieth Century-Fox Theater."[18] As filmmaking entered the 1960s, television's impact on the industry became more apparent. Feature films started looking like television shows. Hollywood even started soliciting their creative talent from television. One of the most influential filmmakers to have gotten his start in television was John Cassavetes. His work in TV during the 1950s provided him with the training he needed to make the jump to feature motion pictures. *Shadows* (1960), a black-and-white film shot in 16mm on location in New York City, was Cassavetes's directorial debut, and it heralded a new emphasis in moviemaking on realism that remained popular through the 1960s.

HIGH CONCEPT: CONTEMPORARY MARKETING PRACTICES

By the mid-1970s, marketing began to play an even larger role in the making of big budget films than it had in the past. Justin Wyatt calls this increased emphasis on the relationship between marketing and movie production (in both the film and television industries) "high concept." Wyatt defines high concept as "a form of narrative which is highly marketable. This marketability might be based on stars, the match between a star and a premise, or a subject matter which is fashionable."[19] Wyatt goes on to claim, "In practice, the locus of this marketability and concept in the contemporary industry is the 'pitch.' In fact, in order to pitch a project succinctly the film must be high concept; consider Steven Spielberg's comment: 'If a person can tell me the idea in 25 words or less, it's going to make a pretty good movie. I like ideas, especially movie ideas, that you can hold in your hands."[20] Wyatt argues that the first high concept film to be made in Hollywood was Spielberg's *Jaws* (1975), and that high concept motion pictures include films as diverse as *Star Wars* (1977), *Caddyshack* (1980), *The Terminator* (1984), and *Ghostbusters* (1984).[21]

A survey of films made since the release of George Lucas's *Star Wars* in 1977 illustrates how the economic and business aspects of contemporary filmmaking have had a significant impact on the content of motion pictures. There are three ways to approach the analysis of this impact. The first can be defined as "Film Environment," or the method by which filmmakers attempt to create an entire environment (or landscape) of movie marketing and merchandising techniques that basically function as an emotional and psychological reinforcement of the filmgoing experience. *Star Wars* offers an excellent example of how the creation of a Film Environment can greatly assist the way in which a movie is promoted. The second approach can be defined as "Film Narrative Cycle," or the method by which the film industry "cannibalizes" previously successful story forms and repackages them as a new cinematic product. Steven Spielberg's *Jurassic Park* (1993) nicely illustrates how this narrative cycle process works to create box-office success. The third way of looking at how film content is affected by economic practices can be defined as "Film Saturation," or the method by which the filmmaker can sell his movie to audiences outside of the movie theater. Clive Barker's *Nightbreed* (1990) shows how additional exhibition venues—such as foreign distribution, pay television, and the videotape market—rather than harming the earning potential of a particular motion picture, instead generate new revenues that insure the prosperity of today's film industry and allow greater risk-taking among those filmmakers who are not sure that their movie will be a box office smash.

Many successful contemporary marketing practices began with *Star Wars,* arguably the most important movie made over the past twenty years. Not only is *Star Wars* the first popular film to combine both a wide screen technique with a Dolby noise reduction system (thus emphasizing the film's great strength—its special visual and sound effects), but it is also the first modern film to utilize an extremely sophisticated marketing approach, which can be called the Film Environment. Proper manipulation of the Film Environment creates audience demand before a particular movie is released, and then it reinforces the audience's enjoyment of the movie, after the film has been viewed.

Prior to *Star Wars,* a movie was typically promoted prior to its release with advertising trailers (thus termed because they originally "trailed" after a feature film) that were shown a week or more in advance of the film's theatrical release. Occasionally, these trailers—also known as previews or "coming attractions"— were quite inventive, as seen in Alfred Hitchcock's amusing tour of the Bates's house in the well-known trailer to *Psycho* (1960). But, more often, they tended (and still tend) to be fairly standard in format: a brief film of several minutes duration that provides an assortment of cinematic highlights of the motion picture being advertised. For many years, the trailer proved to be perhaps the most successful method of advertising future movies, but this was because the Hollywood studio system did not pursue more aggressive marketing strategies.

Throughout the 1930s and 1940s, the major film studios wanted to produce as many films a year as they could, and in this way they made their profits by the sheer volume of movies released. The motion picture industry relied on "vertical integration," which John Belton defines as an monopolistic economy "in which the studios own production facilities, distribution outlets, and theaters . . . [and] control every level of the marketplace from the top down, from production to exhibition."[22]

With the financial deterioration of the major studios during the 1950s, 1960s, and 1970s, and with the end of studio ownership of motion picture theaters, what had worked in the past as the industry's standard advertising strategy—the movie trailer—no longer proved as successful. Under the vertical integration system, both good and bad movies were profitable, because the studios owned their own movie theaters and could always exhibit both the good and the bad without fear of competition. When the studio's monopoly of theatrical ownership was finally broken by the U.S. Supreme Court in the 1948 Paramount decision,[23] a system evolved in which theater owners (and corporate chains of theaters) competitively bid for the right to exhibit first-run movies. The key strategy, then, in exploiting this new method of film distribution was to generate audience demand for a particular movie, even before the movie was viewed by the general public. Advertising trailers alone did not prove adequate in helping to create this demand.

Enter George Lucas, one of the new film-school generation of directors, which also included Francis Ford Coppola and Martin Scorsese. Lucas, the critically acclaimed director of *American Graffiti* (1973), wanted to develop a science fiction movie in the tradition of the "Flash Gordon" Saturday matinee serials of the 1930s and 1940s. In fact, he initially wanted to remake "Flash Gordon," but when he learned that it would be too expensive and cumbersome dealing with the owners of the "Flash Gordon" property, he decided to make his own space opera story. One of Lucas's greatest strengths as a filmmaker was his understanding of what his audience wanted to see at the movies. In both subject and production values, many motion pictures in the 1960s and early 1970s typically did not offer simple escapism as their fare. Lucas wanted to return audiences to movies of a more innocent era, the era of the "B" movie serials, when fantasy and escapist cinematic fare were at their height. Ultimately, Lucas created in *Star Wars* a film that began the high concept, special-effects boom in filmmaking that has waxed throughout the 1980s and 1990s. *Star Wars'* success also led to the establishment of a major special effects studio, Industrial Light and Magic, which, subsequently, has had a significant role in the production of many of Hollywood's big budget, special effects-driven movies. Most important, however, is the fact that *Star Wars* redefined the contemporary filmgoing audience, emphasizing the importance industry-wide of the adolescent viewer in a way that had never been done before. For better or worse, the new major theatrical audience for movies was sixteen years old and younger, and this major demographic shift in viewers' ages ultimately led to more films geared to a younger audience. Since *Star Wars,* a number of major film releases deemphasized plotting and literate dialogue, while emphasizing special effects and gratuitous violence.

When George Lucas was making *Star Wars,* his $10 million dollar production budget was limiting, especially since he intended to spend a good deal of this budget on special effects and sets that he had to construct from scratch. In the past, as noted earlier, filmmakers had traditionally promoted their new films by advertising the stars appearing in these films, but Lucas's movie did not feature "name" actors or actresses in the lead roles. (The only famous actor cast in *Star Wars* was Sir Alec Guinness, but he was not one of the three principals in the story.) Lucas knew that he had to create audience demand, and do it in a way that had not been fully explored in the past by other filmmakers. Not that he threw out traditional marketing strategies. The film trailer developed for *Star Wars,* for example, was visually stylistic, teasing a potential viewership starving for adventure and escapism to attend the theatrical opening. But Lucas understood that he had to develop new methods to create an audience for his movie, and these new methods led to his invention of the concept of Film Environment, a practice that has been closely imitated since. In fact, addressing Lucas's savvy regarding the initial handling of *Star Wars* merchandising, an article entitled "The Force Is Back," which appeared in the February 10, 1997 issue of *Time,* reports that because of his box office success with *American Graffiti,* Lucas was able to renegotiate successfully his contract with Fox, not for additional money to direct the film but for exclusive rights to *Star Wars* sequels and licensing.[24]

Lucas's first step in creating a Film Environment for *Star Wars* was to "write" and pitch a novelization of the film, releasing the book well before the movie's theatrical opening. Lucas wrote in the Introduction to a recent republication of the novelization:

> In December 1976, Ballantine Books published a paperback novel called Star Wars: From the Adventures of Luke Skywalker. *The book was ghostwritten by Alan Dean Foster from my screenplay of the film. The cover painting was a piece of early conceptual art by Ralph McQuarrie. In small type on the back cover were the words* Soon to be a spectacular motion picture from Twentieth Century Fox.[25]

Of course, novels had always played an important role in filmmaking; purchasing the rights to a particular popular best-seller was usually a competitive affair in Hollywood, and many great books made good films, as illustrated by Margaret Mitchell's *Gone with the Wind,* and the novel's successful translation to the David O. Selznick 1939 box office hit. Novelizations of film scripts also appeared as early as the 1960s, but these were always published after the film's release. Lucas's inventive use of the novelization helped to build an audience for *Star Wars* well before the movie's theatrical opening. In addition, Lucas successfully promoted his novelization so that it became a national best-seller. Best-sellers were frequently made into popular films, but these were movies that were based on books already released to the general public, not the other way around. Lucas turned the positive advertising spin that his novelization received for being a national paperback best-seller into promotion for a movie yet to be seen by the public.

When *Star Wars* finally opened theatrically, Lucas's strategy was to limit the movie's national opening to fewer theaters. He understood one of the basic advertising rules of the movie industry: that the single most important factor in a movie's commercial success is good word-of-mouth praise from the viewers. Whenever possible, Lucas selected theaters best suited to exhibit his special effects-driven movie. These theaters generally were the largest in the area and possessed the largest screens and finest sound systems. Those who attended the opening of *Star Wars* were justifiably impressed by the film's wide-screen showing that greatly enhanced the visual special effects, and by the Dolby noise reduction system that greatly enhanced the sound special effects. Lucas made sure that this tremendously positive audience response made the national news, thus generating a demand in those film venues that had previously overlooked booking the movie at their theaters. When *Star Wars* was ready for a wider national release, by tactful manipulation of the movie's early exhibition, George Lucas had the number one all-time box office hit.

Part of Lucas's overall marketing strategy, however, was to bring the *Star Wars* audience back for a second and a third viewing. The second element of Lucas's creation of a Film Environment involved the reinforcement of the motion picture experience, so that people would be compelled to return to the theaters to see the movie again and again. One way in which this occurred was to target the adolescent audience by developing an entire *Star Wars* "action figure" line of toys. Youngsters could then reenact their favorite moments in the movie, which would keep the theatrical memory fresh in their minds and motivate them to review the film. *Star Wars,* in fact, invented the action figure market, which has grown over the past two decades to become one of the most important merchandising dimensions of both film and television. Today, the action figure market has become so powerful in children's television programming that it is not uncommon to design the action figure toy line first, and then develop the animated programming to sell the toys. Lucas retained the merchandising rights for his film, which was perhaps the single smartest business move he made among many intelligent business decisions. Though *Star Wars* ended up grossing a staggering $322 million dollars (plus), it is rumored to have grossed an astronomical $4 billion dollars from its licensing fees for toys, clothing, and other movie-related merchandise.[26]

In addition to the toy market, Lucas courted the comic book readership by licensing a comic book adaptation of *Star Wars* (the comic book series continued to invent new episodes in the Star Wars saga, even before the release of the second Star Wars film, *The Empire Strikes Back,* in 1980). The music soundtrack to *Star Wars* was slickly produced and released as a two-record set, becoming veteran composer John Williams's breakthrough hit. Music scoring of films had always been an important element of motion pictures, appearing even in the silent era when scores were written for the musical accompaniment of silent pictures. Musical soundtrack records have been commonly marketed in the past, but it was *Star Wars* that dramatically emphasized the role of the musical soundtrack in explaining and reinforcing the aesthetic appeal of film. When people listened to the complete film score on two records, and when they read the elaborate liner notes written for the album by John Williams, this encouraged film viewers to return to the theaters to see the movie once more.

Toys, comic books, the music soundtrack—these and many more strategic marketing ploys (including videogames and theme park rides)—established George Lucas's Film Environment for *Star Wars,* a complete economic landscape that continues to exert a tremendous influences on audiences to this day. Amazingly, the twentieth anniversary re-release of *Star Wars* draws the same long lines of expectant viewers as it did during its initial release. Indeed, this is an entire generation of filmgoers raised in the *Star Wars* Film Environment, weaned on *Star Wars* toys and the books, nurtured on *Star Wars* TV computer games, and cultivated on *Star Wars* clothes. Lucas's science fiction fairy tale invented, and then targeted, a responsive adolescent audience in 1977, and this audience has literally grown up with a movie that has become a more powerful cinematic icon of youth than even *The Wizard of Oz* (1939). The February 14, 1997 issue of *Entertainment Weekly* reported that the weekend opening for the re-release of *Star Wars* grossed an amazing $35.9 million at the box office, which was the largest weekend opening ever for a film opening in January[27] (and this for a film that is twenty years old and has had a widespread video and television release). Lucas, ever the skilled huckster, in fact, recently promoted the boxed video set of the three Star Wars movies by warning potential buyers that this would be the last opportunity to own *Star Wars* this century; shortly thereafter, he re-released the trilogy, especially advertising the digital re-mastering of the three films, as well as some added special effects footage. And for the re-release of these movies, Lucas has even more effectively saturated the television and print media, promoting the film with a greater vigor than he did the first time around. Listed among his recent merchandising triumphs is a $2 billion *Star Wars* marketing agreement with PepsiCo.[28]

As George Lucas and many other successful filmmakers know, the film business is fundamentally a conservative business. Since movie production costs typically run into the millions of dollars (with some current high concept productions costing as much as $150 million dollars or more), producers are strongly motivated by conservative investment practices in making their "product." Most commercial movie producers do not want to be innovative or "cutting edge." They do not want to be forward-looking, to be the first with an outrageously new concept for a motion picture. Instead, filmmakers tend to look backwards at past box office hits as a guideline for the development of new movie properties. When a particular story proves itself to be popular, film producers think that this past popularity can be repeated in the latest motion picture. This process of repackaging and reselling what was once successful to a new audience can be regarded as Hollywood's manipulation of the Film Narrative Cycle. The dominating influence of the Film Narrative Cycle in the film industry explains why there are so many sequels made to popular films—as illustrated by the "Rocky" series, the "Friday the 13th" series, the "Nightmare on Elm Street" series, and many, many others. The Film Narrative Cycle also explains why, when a particular type of movie (such as the James Bond spy thrillers of the 1960s) becomes popular, so many other similar types of motion pictures are subsequently made (including, as an illustration, the Bond knock-offs *Our Man*

Flint (1966) and *In Like Flint* (1967), starring James Coburn as the Cold War super spy, and the popular Matt Helm movies, starring Dean Martin as the American James Bond).

The Narrative Cycle itself extends even beyond the film industry and explains the evolution in narrative films of certain popular story formulas, such as domestic melodrama, or horror, or the Western. In fact, the movie Western offers a good illustration of how the Narrative Cycle crossed over from the print mass media to the movies. The earliest form of print entertainment in America was the mass-produced hardcover book, and the publishing industry in this country during the early decades of the 1800s was looking to develop its own body of fiction, rather than just "stealing" popular books from British authors and reprinting them in the United States. Early U.S. publishers noted that readers were fascinated with tales of the frontier. Indian massacres and abductions made front page headlines in the newspapers of the time (and also were an integral part of that era's folklore, as seen in the proliferation of "captivity narratives"). Thus, early authors of the frontier, such as James Fenimore Cooper and Robert Montgomery Bird, found commercial success in their writing. When the U.S. dime novel developed in the 1860s as the latest and cheapest print medium, the editors and authors of the dime novels looked to the past for their ideas and discovered the frontier story. When the U.S. pulp magazines evolved from the dime novels, the frontier adventure (now the Western) was among the first and most popular type of pulp magazine published. When story radio was launched as a commercial broadcast industry, early radio producers looked backward to the dime novels and the pulps and found the Western. Some of the earliest story radio programs, such as the *Lone Ranger,* were Westerns. And when commercial television rose from the ashes of commercial story radio, early television producers took the Western with them into television production. Popular Western radio programs, including the *Lone Ranger* and *Gunsmoke,* became popular television Westerns. Early filmmakers, in search of narrative formulas to make their pictures, also discovered the Western. One of the earliest narrative films in America—Edwin S. Porter's *The Great Train Robbery* (1903)—was, of course, a Western.

All of this is by way of illustrating how the Film Narrative Cycle operates in contemporary film production, including the making of today's high concept, blockbuster movies. Arguably the most successful high concept film, *Jurassic Park,* reveals the pervasiveness of the Film Narrative Cycle, beginning with the origins of *Jurassic Park* as a best-selling novel. Michael Crichton is the author of the novel, *Jurassic Park* (1990), and his success as a best-selling writer is well known. What is not so well-known is the fact that, in a number of his more popular stories, Crichton borrows from past great literary works, rewriting these classic stories for a contemporary audience. *The Terminal Man* (1972), for example, is Crichton's reworking of Mary Shelley's gothic thriller, *Frankenstein. Eaters of the Dead* (1976) is Crichton's reworking of the Old English epic adventure, *Beowulf,* while *Congo* (1980) is his updating of H. Rider Haggard's *King Solomon's Mines.* For *Jurassic Park,* Crichton turned to the one of the most popular adventure novels ever published, Arthur Conan Doyle's *The Lost World* (1912), the story of the discovery of a remote land in South America by an intrepid group of explorers where dinosaurs still roam. Crichton makes obvious his debt to Arthur Conan Doyle by titling his own 1995 sequel to *Jurassic Park* after Doyle's original novel. Crichton's prosperity as a best-selling writer is due, in part, to his ability to utilize the Narrative Cycle in his own fiction, to identify those stories from the past that can be successfully adapted for a modern-day readership.

Crichton was approached by Steven Spielberg about the filming of *Jurassic Park* when they were both working on Crichton's script, *E.R.—Emergency Room.* Crichton remembers being pleased with Spielberg's interest in his book, noting "From my point of view, I'd been lifting weights in my little office for however many years it was, trying to do an extremely difficult thing—which was to make a dinosaur story that really worked, that wasn't *One Million Years B.C.*"[29] Spielberg himself was originally drawn to Crichton's book because of his lifelong fascination with dinosaurs. His cultural experience as a filmmaker for the *Jurassic Park* project was shaped by earlier dinosaur movies he loved as a child. Spielberg states:

> *Most of them [dinosaur movies] were awful, but each one had some good parts. Gorgo had the mama dinosaur coming after her baby who was stuck in a circus. The Beast from 20,000 Fathoms was a really good yarn with some great architectural destruction. Godzilla, of course, was the most masterful of all the dinosaur movies because it made you believe it was really happening . . . I never thought I wanted to do a dinosaur movie better than anyone else's, but I did want my dinosaur movie to be the most realistic of them all.[30]*

As *Jurassic Park* was being made into a motion picture, both Crichton and Spielberg brought with them to the project an extensive narrative history of dinosaur movies. This narrative history provided the filmmakers with concrete examples of what worked in the past for film audiences (e.g., the "architectural destruction" in *The Beast from 20,000 Fathoms* for Spielberg) and what did not work (e.g., *One Million Years B.C.* for Crichton). The tremendous popularity of *Jurassic Park* guaranteed that Spielberg's movie would take its place among the great Hollywood dinosaur movies, that his film would become the latest proof that this genre still appeals to contemporary moviegoers. It also guaranteed that Crichton's sequel, *The Lost World,* would be made as a successful high concept property. With Spielberg once more directing, *The Lost World* became a top box office draw during the summer of 1997.

In addition to Film Environment and Film Narrative Cycle, Film Saturation plays a significant part in the making of today's motion pictures. With the introduction of every new film exhibition technology—from pay TV to VHS—Hollywood has frequently sounded the alarm about possible damage to box office income. The film industry warned that pay TV would encourage people to stay at home to view recently released major motion pictures, rather than going to the movie theater. Contrary to this line of reasoning, however, was the fact that as the variety of motion picture venues has diversified, the production of so-called first-run movies has financially benefited as a result. People continued to go to the theaters to view first-run films, but they also included movie videos and cable television as part of their leisure time entertainment behavior.

A good example of this new, more flexible attitude regarding the risks involved in producing and marketing contemporary movies can be seen in the horror films made by writer/director Clive Barker. Barker began his professional career writing and acting in Britain's *avant garde* theater. He broke into writing in spectacular fashion with the publication in 1984 and 1985 of his six-volume Books of Blood anthology, which brought him an international reputation and following. Barker decided to try his hand at filmmaking, and in 1987 released the horror film, *Hellraiser,* which he wrote and directed (and which was based on his own short novel, *The Hellbound Heart*). *Hellraiser* did well enough at the box office that Barker was encouraged to try again at making another movie. In fact, he intended the modestly financed *Hellraiser* to be a "showreel," as proof that he could turn a profit in his directorial debut, making a commercially successful film on a limited budget.[31]

For the second movie he would write and direct, *Nightbreed* (1990), Barker decided to take a gamble. Like *Hellraiser, Nightbreed* would be a horror film that was based on another Barker short novel, *Cabal.* With his second foray into filmmaking, he was given a substantially larger budget. As Barker states in an interview at the time *Nightbreed* was being made, *"Nightbreed* now has an $11 million budget. For me, the jump from a $2 million movie [*Hellraiser*] to an $11 million movie is a big one. What we have here is a big, complicated project. The *Star Wars* of horror movies is what we promised."[32] . . . What he delivered, however, was something the studio executives did not anticipate.

Nightbreed did not offer the "traditional" type of horror story, as is found in the popular "Friday the 13th" series or the "Nightmare on Elm Street" series. The social role of evil and the identification of the antagonists in these films are clearly defined. There is no doubt in the audience's mind that Jason or Freddy Krueger are the monsters, and that they will kill the required number of victims in each new sequel, so that the typical adolescent viewer's need for violent entertainment will be adequately satisfied. In *Nightbreed,* Barker wrote a horror story in which the monsters are the good guys instead of the bad guys; humans—a serial killer psychiatrist and a small town sheriff, among others—are the evil ones. *Nightbreed* basically tells the story of a Moses figure who leads a band of persecuted monsters away from human contact to safety. When he completed the project, Barker reported that the studio executives were unpleasantly surprised by the final product, commenting "How do we sell this thing—the monsters are the good guys!"[33]

Nightbreed, in fact, did not make back its production costs in its theatrical release, but the film eventually proved to be profitable. After its disappointing premiere, it earned a solid income from the second-run release at the discount multiplex theaters. It made money from its overseas distribution, from its sale for videotape, and from its sale to HBO and other premium cable television channels. When all the receipts were tallied, *Nightbreed* ended up generating a profit. What *Nightbreed* (and many other films) demonstrated was that even though the movie industry initially feared these new marketing venues as potential threats to box office income, they actually have served to support those movies which otherwise had a disappointing first-run take. Filmmakers like Clive Barker know that multiple film markets provide them with a certain degree of financial security, a type of economic safety net. They allow creative people working in the industry the opportunity to take some risks in the making of their movies. They also allow these filmmakers a greater degree of creative control. For the video release of Clive Barker's recent film, *Lord of Illusions* (1995), Barker restored film footage that was edited from the motion picture's theatrical release, calling this repackaged video his "director's cut."

Discounting the revenue generated by merchandising, a look at the top three moneymakers for 1996 reveals how much these additional exhibition venues contribute to a movie's overall earning power. The number one box office hit, *Independence Day,* took in a whopping $306.2 million in domestic gross. It took in an even larger $474.4 million in foreign gross, and a healthy $252 million in video gross, for a grand total of $1,032,600. Domestic box office accounted for only about one-third of *Independence Day*'s total take. The year's number two film, *Twister,* made $241.7 million at domestic theaters, $251.6 million at foreign theaters, and $107.9 million in video, for a total gross take of $601.2 million. Again, the theatrical release of *Twister* only generated a little over one-third of the movie's total income. The number three motion picture of 1996, *Mission: Impossible,* made $181 million domestic box office, $271.7 million foreign box office, and $91.8 million from video, for a total gross figure of $544.5 million. Domestic release, once more, accounted for slightly less than one-third of the film's total income.[34]

For the films at the bottom of the list in earnings, video release plays an even greater role in generating money. The 129th ranked film of 1996, the animated feature, *All Dogs Go to Heaven 2,* made $8.6 million in domestic gross and $28.7 million in video gross. The 138th ranked film of 1996, the horror film, *Bordello of Blood,* generated $5.8 million in domestic gross and $14 million from video. The 146th ranked film of 1996, the hard-boiled crime drama, *Heaven's Prisoners,* made $5 million in domestic box office income and $11 million from video. And the Clive Barker production for 1996, *Hellraiser: Bloodline,* nearly doubled its $9.3 million take in the video market.[35]

CONCLUSION

During its hundred-year history, movies have always been tied to business practices. Economic factors, such as where and how films are exhibited, have always been a crucial element in how motion pictures are produced and sold to an audience. Historically, these economic factors included the technological invention of a more profitable way to exhibit movies to a wider audience, as well as the film industry's invention of the star system and the studio system as more lucrative ways to produce and promote movies. Many of these marketing developments that first appeared over eighty years ago remain an important part of contemporary filmmaking. The notion of high concept that evolved in Hollywood during the 1970s fully embraced marketing as the single most important aspect of film production. George Lucas, in his blockbuster *Star Wars,* created an entire Film Environment that established an audience for the film even before the picture was released theatrically, and that also created many levels of merchandising that psychologically reinforced the filmgoing experience. Steven Spielberg, in *Jurassic Park,* demonstrated how the Film Narrative Cycle provides a storytelling history for the making of new movies, as well as providing an artistic point-of-reference for the filmmaker during production. And Clive Barker, in his horror movie, *Nightbreed,* demonstrated how Film Saturation constructs an economic safety net for films that do not enjoy a profitable theatrical release, thus allowing filmmakers additional artistic freedom in the production of their movies. The business of making movies is not a corrupting influence on art. Rather, when business and marketing strategies work cooperatively with the creation of movie content, the result produces a storytelling medium yet unchallenged by its rivals. As Steven Spielberg remarks in an interview with Gene Siskel, "I think motion picture's a unique medium. Film and cameras and everything we have right now is all we need. I really believe that. It's all we need."[36]

NOTES

[1]John Belton, *American Cinema/American Culture* (New York: McGraw-Hill, 1994), 61.
[2]Robert Sklar, *Movie-Made America: A Cultural History of American Movies* (New York: Vintage Books, 1975), 17.
[3]Ibid., 23.
[4]Gerald Mast and Bruce F. Kawin, *A Short History of the Movies,* 5th ed. (New York: Macmillan, 1992), 19–21.
[5]Ira Konigsberg, *The Complete Film Dictionary* (New York: Meridian, 1989), 223.
[6]Kristin Thompson and David Bordwell, *Film History: An Introduction.* (New York: McGraw-Hill, 1994), 37.
[7]Richard Maltby and Ian Craven, *Hollywood Cinema: An Introduction.* (Oxford, UK: Blackwell, 1995), 89.
[8]Mast and Kawin, 95.
[9]Konigsberg, 347–348.
[10]Ibid., 331–332.
[11]Thompson and Bordwell, 215.
[12]Sklar, 67–68.
[13]Ibid., 19.
[14]Belton, 257.
[15]Konigsberg, 410–412.
[16]Ibid.

[17]Belton, 261.

[18]Ibid., 268.

[19]Justin Wyatt, *High Concept: Movies and Marketing in Hollywood* (Austin, TX: University of Texas Press, 1994), 12–13.

[20]Ibid., 13.

[21]Ibid., 21.

[22]Belton, 64.

[23]Michael Conant, *Antitrust in the Motion Picture Industry: Economic and Legal Analysis* (Berkeley, CA: University of California Press, 1960), 100–102.

[24]Bruce Handy, "The Force Is Back," *Time* (February 10, 1997), 72.

[25]George Lucas, "Introduction," *Star Wars: A New Hope* (New York: Del Rey, 1976), i.

[26]Tom Russo, "'Star' Struck," *Premiere* (February, 1997), 86.

[27]Chris Nashawaty, "Shooting Star," *Entertainment Weekly* (February 14, 1997), 6.

[28]Handy, 70.

[29]Don Shay and Jody Duncan, *The Making of Jurassic Park* (New York: Ballantine Books, 1993), 8.

[30]Ibid., 14–15.

[31]Philip Nutman, "Bring on the Monsters! Part One," *Fangoria* (October, 1989), 32.

[32]Ibid., 31.

[33]Stanley Wiater, *Dark Visions: Conversations with the Masters of the Horror Film* (New York: Avon, 1992), 12.

[34]Jess Cagle, "Marquee Marks: 1996 Box Office Report," *Entertainment Weekly* (February 7, 1997), 34.

[35]Ibid., 36.

[36]Roger Ebert and Gene Siskel, *The Future of the Movies* (Kansas City, MO: Andrews and McMeel, 1991), 59.

Appendix A

Microeconomic Foundations

The foundation of any economic analysis of the mass media lies with the basic principles of microeconomic theory. The fundamental problem of economics is the limitation or scarcity of economic resources (land, labor, capital, and entrepreneurship) relative to the limitless demand for goods and services that these resources can produce. This necessitates making choices as to "what" and "how much" of each good and service should be produced, "how" it should be produced, and "for whom" it should be distributed. These economic questions are fundamental to every society; their solution depends on how economic and political power are distributed within society.

In a free enterprise economy such as in the United States, the forces of supply and demand interact in the marketplace to solve these problems. In this market economy, everything has a price—goods and services as well as the factors of production.[1] Everyone receives money for the supply of his/her labor or other factor input and uses this income to demand more of what he/she desires. As a certain product, say A, becomes more popular, its price is bid up and suppliers, seeing the higher price and associated profits, increase their production of this good. Similarly, if less of good B is desired, its price falls and, with less profits, producers now switch to the more lucrative product A.

In this process of consumer-driven production (often referred to as "consumer sovereignty"), the derived demand for factor inputs also changes. More factor inputs will be needed to produce good A and less for good B. If the factor inputs producing A are relatively scarce, their wages will be bid up as part of this process of luring workers and capital away from B to A. Hence, the price mechanism acts as a focal point for translating the different consumer and supplier interests and automatically causes resources to become allocated toward their optimal uses. The selfish desires of the consumers to maximize their utility are counterpoised by the selfish desires of businessmen to maximize their profits. According to Adam Smith, the "invisible hand" of the market balances these opposing forces and guides society towards the greatest wealth.

This ideal notion of the marketplace is closely tied to the wide dispersal of market power associated with the perfectly competitive market structure. When firms become large and command significant market control, the automatic functioning of the market is short-circuited and consumer sovereignty is diminished. Similarly, when the market fails to adequately provide "public goods" or take account of products with harmful byproducts (externalities), then government may have to step in and play a role as well.

DEMAND AND SUPPLY

The wants and desires of consumers are expressed through their effective demand. Demand is often pictured in two-dimensional space as a downward sloping curve relating hypothetical price and output combinations; yet it truly is a functional relationship involving quite a few explanatory variables.

$$Q_d = f \text{ (Price of product, Prices of Substitutes, Complements, Income, Tastes, Population, Time)}$$

with signs: $-\quad +\quad -\quad +\quad +/-\quad +\quad +$

When drawn in two-dimensional space, all other explanatory variables are held constant. The familiar downward slope reflects the fact that as price falls, *ceteris paribus*, this product is relatively cheaper than others thus causing a substitution effect towards it, plus consumers feel wealthier as well and desire to purchase more products of all kinds, including this product (wealth effect). When the other factors originally held constant are permitted to change, the demand curve shifts outward (increase in demand) or inward (decrease in demand) depending on which of the factors changed and its positive or negative relationship to demand.[2] The shape of the demand curve (or portions of it) is known as its elasticity and reflects the relative responsiveness of quantity demanded to changes in prices. Price elasticity depends on the number and closeness of substitute products, the degree of product necessity versus luxury and the proportion of household income the product represents.

If the product is produced under conditions of competition, a supply relationship can also be given.[3]

$$Q_s = f \text{ (Price of product, Prices of Substitutes in production, Technology, Factor Prices,}$$
with signs: $+\quad +\quad +\quad -$

$$\text{# Competitors, Expectations, Institutional factors, Time)}$$
with signs: $+\quad +/-\quad +/-\quad +$

As before, the familiar upward sloping supply curve reflects hypothetical combinations of price and quantity supplied. As price increases, producers make a higher

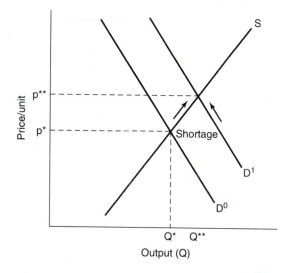

FIGURE A-1 Market Equilibrium

profit per unit and wish to place more product on the market. When one or more of the factors held constant changes, this shifts the supply curve outward (increase in supply) or inward (decrease in supply), depending on which factor changed and its positive or negative relationship to supply. The shape of of the supply curve is known as its elasticity and reflects the relative responsiveness of quantity supplied to changes in prices. Elasticity depends primarily on the closeness of substitutes in production and the amount of time available for producers to respond. When the demand and supply curves for a competitive industry are combined (Figure A-1), an equilibrium market price P^* and quantity Q^* will result. At P^*, the market is just cleared, that is, neither a shortage nor surplus exists. This equilibrium will be stable unless either the demand or supply curves shift due to a change in a factor previously held constant. For example, suppose there is an increase in tastes favoring a certain product; its demand curve shifts to D^1. At the former equilibrium price P^*, there is now a shortage of product $(Q_d > Q_s)$ and pressure will occur for prices to rise until a new equilibrium is established at P^{**} and Q^{**}. Since this new equilibrium entails more output than before, scarce factors of production in use elsewhere automatically transfer (probably at higher prices) to their more valued use in this industry. As Figure A-1 demonstrates, the additional equilibrium quantity produced critically depends on the elasticities of these two curves.

COSTS OF PRODUCTION

To understand the concept of costs, it is first necessary to understand what is meant by the short run as contrasted to the long run. In the short run, plant size is fixed and no entry occurs; hence, the output of a firm is functionally related to the amount of variable input (labor). As labor units increase, the total output at first increases at an increasing rate then eventually increases at a decreasing rate, also known as decreasing marginal product or simply decreasing returns. Since factor inputs are purchased at fixed prices, the average and marginal product relations can easily be translated into corresponding cost curves. Figure A-2 illustrates the familiar average variable cost (AVC), average fixed cost (AFC), average total cost (ATC), and marginal cost (MC) curves.[4] The AVC, ATC, and MC curves are U-shaped to reflect initially increasing returns (decreasing costs) and then decreasing returns (increasing costs) associated with increased output. The MC curve passes through the minimum points of the AVC and ATC curves.

The long-run average cost (LRAC) curve is quite different from its short-run counterpart. In contrast to the short-run situation, there are no fixed inputs in the long run; all inputs are variable including plant size. The firm must now choose not only its profit-maximizing output level but also the most efficient-sized plant to produce it in. It has at its disposal a whole series of hypothetical ATC curves, each associated with a different-sized plant (different possible short-run situations). If one assumes an infinity of different plant sizes (most easily conceptualized in different square footage), there will be one unique minimum cost plant associated with each possible output level in the long run. The long-run average cost curve is pictured in Figure A-3 as an envelope of this infinite number of ATC curves, uniquely connected at the points of tangency. Movements along the LRAC in the region of declining unit costs are called economies of scale while regions of increasing unit

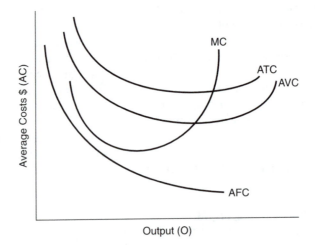

FIGURE A-2 Average Cost Curves

costs are labelled diseconomies of scale; the point of minimum LRAC is known as the minimum efficient scale (M.E.S.).

There are two basic kinds of factors that cause the LRAC curve to decline; they can be grouped in the categories of technical factors and pecuniary (financial) factors. Technical factors refer to the underlying technical process of production. Let's be more specific. As noted above, production can be visualized as a functional relationship with output depending on the combination of labor, land, capital, raw materials, and entrepreneurship—the so-called factors of production. In mathematical form this would be represented as $Q = f(X_1, X_2 \ldots X_N)$ where Q = output and X_i = the factors of production. In the long run, all factors of production are variable.

Assume an initial level (and price) for each factor and a process for combining them to yield a value for Q. If one now hypothesizes a 100 percent increase in all factors of production and permits them to be combined in whatever manner is most efficient, then three possible outcomes can occur: (1) a more than proportional increase in output, (2) an exactly proportional increase in output, or (3) a less than proportional increase in output.

The former case is referred to as increasing returns to scale and suggests a greater productivity for the factor inputs, and given constant factor prices, this translates naturally into lower average costs per unit of output. In the second case, which is known as constant returns to scale, one finds the same productivity of the factor inputs at the initial and doubled level and hence a constant average cost per unit of output. The latter case is known as decreasing returns to scale and demonstrates lower productivity of the factor inputs when they are doubled and hence higher average costs per unit of output.

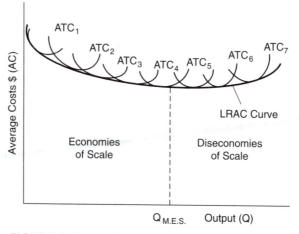

FIGURE A-3   Derivation of the Long-Run Average Cost Curve

These, then, are the technical factors underlying the presence or absence of scale economies. Rising productivity associated with larger scale can be explained by the fact that larger units can be more efficiently organized through greater specialization of tasks and division of labor, more effective use of byproducts, and more effective matching of optimal equipment to the size of the task. When the LRAC curve turns upward into the diseconomy range, this is often attributed to managerial inefficiencies (red tape) associated with running very large enterprises—the requirement of additional layers of bureaucracy, more rules and regulations, and loss of effective control by top management.

Pecuniary efficiencies are financial economies attributed to being large within one's own industry or as a major employer within a local area. Big firms are able to contract for large quantities of raw materials or other intermediate product from various suppliers. Such large orders reduce transaction and transportation costs to the supplier who can pass some of these savings along to the large purchasers. Furthermore, to the extent that these supplies are specialized or tailor-made and oligopsony buying power resides in the hands of a few major purchasers, they may be able to secure other discounts and concessions as well. An excellent example of quantity discounts is found in the purchase of advertising time and space in all the media.

ECONOMIES OF SCOPE AND SYNERGY

Models of industrial organizations focus almost entirely on economies of scale as the traditional source of efficiencies in most industries, yet there are other related factors that may be important sources of cost savings as well for the multiproduct firm. Economies of scope refer to cost savings that arise when a firm produces joint products as part of the normal production process. There may be special cost savings that accrue to a multiproduct firm that are unavailable to firms producing only one of the products but not both. In short, the single firm can supply a bundle of products demanded by the market at a lower total cost (and price) than some combination of two or more single-product or low volume producers. These byproduct savings may further entrench economies of scale and enhance the overall barrier to entry.

Synergy is a form of economies of scope in the sense that the subadditivity of two or more production, marketing, or distribution processes yields more than proportional results (2 + 2 = 5) by creating additional efficiencies. These synergistic efficiencies are usually touted to accompany mergers of firms that combine related or unrelated business patterns in unique ways that increase productivity or save costs. Such special synergistic effects could arise from: achievement of new markets, stronger combined product lines, buying raw materials in large volumes, eliminating duplicate general and administrative functions/ departments, risk reduction in capital markets, acquiring new strategic locations for distribution or warehousing (see Bulinski, p. 11).

MARKET STRUCTURES

Microeconomic theory categorizes industries into four different market structures according to the degree of market power held by the individual firm. The four structures include perfect competition, monopoly, monopolistic competition, and oligopoly. The degree of market power and control is smallest with perfect competition and highest with the pure monopoly case. We shall now examine these economic structures in greater detail.

Perfect Competition

The perfectly competitive market is composed of a large number of identical firms that have such an insignificant share of the market that their presence or absence is scarcely noticed. In this context, the firm is virtually powerless and totally subservient to the forces of the market. The market determines the appropriate price through the intersection of industry supply and demand.

Each firm acts as a "price taker" since it faces a horizontal demand curve, which indicates that it can supply as much product as it wants at the prevailing market price without affecting that price. The horizontal demand curve is said to be perfectly elastic, indicating that all firms produce *identical* products that are perfect substitutes for one another. This also implies that should any firm raise its price, by even

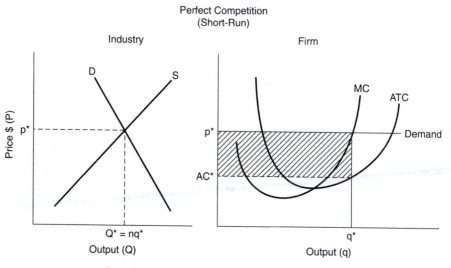

Excess Profits for the firm are cross-hatched in graph

FIGURE A-4   Perfect Competition (Short Run)

the smallest amount, it faces the loss of its entire product supply since it will be abandoned by the *all-knowing* consumer in favor of the identical product from another firm at a lower relative price. Thus, in Figure A-4, the firm takes the industry price P* as a given and responds with the appropriate profit maximizing output level, Q*, where the marginal cost curve intersects the price line. According to the diagram, this profit-maximizing combination yields excess profits for the typical firm in the industry.

As market supply and demand conditions change, the firm experiences shifts in its financial position. However, the theory of perfect competition permits no long-term fortunes to accrue to the individual firm or the industry since entry is assumed to be very easy. In Figure A-5, short-term excess profits are dissipated as new firms enter the industry, increase the industry supply curve to S^1, and drive down the price to P**, where normal profits (zero excess profits) are restored.

Actual entry becomes the disciplinary force that establishes the familiar conditions of long-run equilibrium—a stable state of affairs that often is used as the benchmark to contrast "imperfect" market structures. Let's examine these equilibrium standards in greater detail.

1. *Optimal allocation of society's resources.* Since price is equated to long-run marginal cost at the long-run equilibrium point, the proper amount of product is being produced in this industry. Price represents the valuation to consumers of the marginal unit of output, while marginal cost represents the opportunity cost to society of allocating scarce economic resources to the marginal unit of this

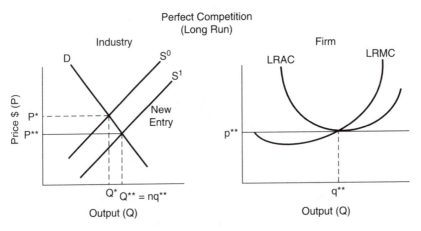

At final long-run equilibrium, P = LRMC = LRAC$_{min}$.

FIGURE A-5 Perfect Competition (Long Run)

product as opposed to some other product. At equilibrium, marginal benefits equal marginal costs.

2. *Optimal plant size.* At the point of long-run equilibrium, the long-run average cost of production is at its minimum. Hence, society is not only producing the socially optimum quantity of product, it is producing it in the socially optimal, minimum-cost plant.

3. *X efficiency and technological progressivity.* Due to the extreme degree of competition between firms, each firm must stand ready to take advantage of every available opportunity to minimize costs and stay on the frontier of technological progress. Firms that are slow to innovate will soon discover they have higher costs and face severe financial repercussions. Ultimately, they cannot survive in this industry. Furthermore, since the consumer is blessed with perfect information, it will be unnecessary to advertise or spend excessive amounts of money on other product differentiation devices.

4. *Normal profits.* Normal profits prevail at the long-run equilibrium position of stability. Normal profits mean that prices just cover the average costs of production in which average costs include payments to the factors of production plus a fair rate of return to entrepreneurs for their time and invested capital. Normal profits, when combined with the aforementioned cost efficiencies, imply that consumers need pay only the *minimum* price necessary to bring forward production. This "reasonable" price will not distort the distribution of income in society but rather will be neutral.

5. *Automatically functioning market.* The market mechanism works automatically and effortlessly, triggered by the selfish desires of producers to maximize their profits and the sovereignty enjoyed by consumers in the valuations they place on different products. As consumer wants, needs, and tastes change and as technology makes the production–distribution process more efficient, the market automatically adjusts to a new long-run equilibrium and transfers scarce resources to their most valued uses.

Besides the fact that the assumptions underlying the perfectly competitive model are unrealistic, other shortcomings also should be mentioned. First, the market mechanism tends to ignore certain goods that are not easily priced in a market economy ("public goods") and fails to account for harmful externalities such as pollution, which are not internalized as private marginal costs by firms.

Second, there may not be enough excess profits in this industry to permit research and development that brings forth the technological progress that benefits the consumers. Such industries may be reliant on their input suppliers or government-sponsored research projects to achieve the desired level of innovation.

Finally, life under perfect competition may be very dull since by definition no variety exists among the standardized products, and there is no incentive created within the system for product differentiation of any kind. Hence, the utopian world of economists may be as dismal as the dismal science of economies itself!

Monopoly

The monopoly firm encompasses the entire market for a specific product; the industry demand curve is its demand curve and all the power of the marketplace is embedded within its corporate headquarters. It is generally assumed that no close substitute for the product exists; hence, the demand curve is relatively inelastic, and the consumer must either deal with the monopolist on its terms or abstain from consumption of the product. Whereas the perfectly competitive firm was pictured as a slave to the market price, the monopolist is the price-maker and supplies product according to its own profit-maximizing dictates. Figuratively speaking, the monopolist "stands at the gateway of commerce and can extract a toll from all who pass."

Looking at Figure A-6, the profit-maximizing output Q^* for the monopolist occurs in the short run where marginal revenue equals marginal cost.[5] The associated optimal price P^* is simply taken from the demand curve. Notice that the marginal revenue curve (MR) lies below the demand curve (price line) because the monopolist must lower price to all customers to sell additional units of quantity; hence, it must in essence rebate money to those who would have been willing to pay a higher price but now need pay only what the product is worth to the last user.[6] Notice the excess profits for the monopolist.

In the long run, we only need substitute the long-run cost curves to demonstrate the persistence of excess profits. In the perfect competition model, freedom of entry

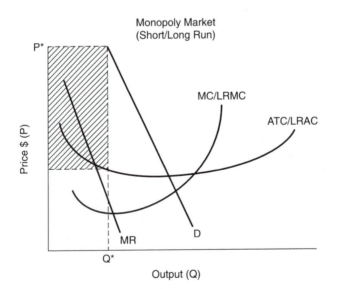

Excess profits for the firm are cross-hatched in graph

FIGURE A-6 Monopoly

dissipated any excess profits in the long run. In monopoly, these excess short-run profits are perpetuated in the long run through various barriers to entry. The barriers to entry may take the form of pervasive economies of scale, control over strategic resources and patents, absolute cost barriers, and various predatory practices designed to discourage entry. In sum, short-run positions of power can be transformed into long-term control if the barriers to entry are sufficiently high.

However, barriers to entry and strategic control are never totally impregnable. Schumpeter talked about a different form of long-term competition that threatened the possessors of monopoly power. He called this competitive force "the gale of creative destruction."

> *The competition from the new commodity, the new technology, the new source of supply, the new type of organization—competition which commands a decisive cost or quality advantage and which strikes not at the margins of the profits and outputs of the existing firms but at their very foundations and their very lives. . . . The competition we now have in mind acts not only when in being but also when it is merely an ever present threat. . . . The businessman feels himself to be in a competitive situation even if he is alone in his field.[7]*

Examining the monopoly market structure according to the same performance standards used in the competitive model, we see that at the long-run equilibrium point, the monopolist:

1. Misallocates society's resources by producing at the output level where price exceeds long-run marginal cost. Hence, consumers value additional product more than the cost to society of producing that marginal product; yet, it is not produced because it would diminish monopoly profits.
2. Produces in a suboptimal-sized plant at a unit cost exceeding the minimum point of the long-run average cost curve, thereby wasting scarce economic resources.
3. May not have the incentive to be cost-efficient or technologically progressive. Whereas the monopolist clearly has the financial resources to invest in research and development and could be vigilant in minimizing its costs, it lacks the compelling pressure to excel in these endeavors.
4. Earns excess profits that have been perpetuated by high barriers to entry. Such excess profits reflect excessive prices greater than the minimum necessary to bring forth production. Depending on the importance of monopoly products relative to consumer disposable income, this may adversely affect the distribution of income in society in favor of monopoly stockholders.
5. Controls the market and determines how it functions and its timing. Power vests in the monopolist, not in the market. Furthermore, the monopolist may obtain such control that there are no external checks and balances on its behavior. In the extreme, it could perform society's planning function according to its own self-interests.

Regulated Monopolies

If the monopoly has continuously declining long-run average costs and the product has an element of necessity associated with it, it may be in the "public interest, convenience and necessity" to regulate this "natural monopoly" by placing maximum limits on its prices and profits. These monopolies/utilities are generally regulated on a "cost-plus" basis that permits them to charge prices (tariffs) and earn revenues only large enough to recover the actual outlay costs plus a "fair" rate of return on invested capital, intended to approximate normal profits.[8]

This pricing scheme is often known as "average cost pricing" since the total revenues allowed just equal the total costs, which includes this "fair" rate of return. In Figure A-7, we see output is determined where the average cost curve intersects the demand curve (price line) and normal profits result. Contrast this regulated price P^* with P^{**} which would be the nonregulated monopoly price (MR = MC) and P^{***}, the perfectly competitive price (P = MC). The regulated price and associated output more closely approach the competitive ideal but can never equal this level since the marginal cost curve lies below the average cost and such a price would entail economic losses.

In more practical terms, the total cost component (TC) just equals the actual outlay expenditures on such items as supplies, labor, interest, depreciation, and so forth (E), plus a fair rate of return (r) multiplied by the depreciated value of the stock of accumulated plant and capital equipment (K_d):

$$TC = E + r(K_d)$$

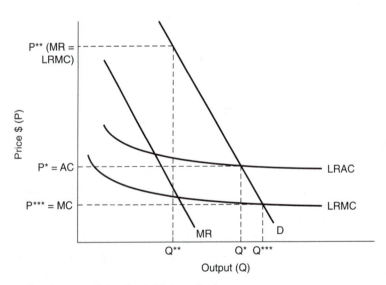

FIGURE A-7 Regulated Monopoly

The permissible total revenues (TR) equals the price per unit multiplied by the number of units sold (Q):

$$TR = PQ$$

Typically, the regulatory commission is only interested in verifying that TR does not exceed TC; thus leaving the regulated monopolist free to design its *rates* on different product lines.

Suppose the firm has five separate product lines/services, then P and Q are broken down into vectors, $[p_1, p_2, p_3, p_4, p_5]$ and $[q_1, q_2, q_3, q_4, q_5]$. So long as $p_1q_1 + p_2q_2 + p_3q_3 + p_4q_4 + p_5q_5$ just equaled TR, this satisfied the regulatory agency. The regulated firm might even further divide its customers in a particular product service into two or more subgroups (i.e., residential versus business); hence, within the first product class above, there may be a $[p_{11}, p_{12}]$ and corresponding $[q_{11}, q_{12}]$.

The flexibility associated with rate design provides for the possibility of internal cross-subsidization,[9] that is, charging uneconomically low prices for one product line or customer group and very high prices for another product line or customer group. Usually, the former has very elastic demand for the product while the latter has an inelastic demand. This type of demand-oriented pricing scheme, often known as price discrimination, is still quite common in many regulated industries. While it may provide social benefits to a class of customers that ordinarily would be denied service, it also can be used in a predatory fashion to fight off potential competition from inter-industry firms.

Finally, there is no incentive for the regulated firm (or defense contractor) to minimize costs since they are automatically recouped by building them into the revenue requirements and passing them along to consumers. Hence, many economists believe that such industries exhibit excessively wasteful managerial and production–distribution inefficiencies.

Consumer Surplus and Deadweight Welfare Loss

Economists often measure consumer welfare by the amount of consumer surplus that accrues from various prices under competitive and noncompetitive market structures. To illustrate this concept, look at Figure A-8—the demand for a firm under monopoloid conditions. Let's assume standard average and marginal cost curves but not worry about whether the curves represent short-run or long-run conditions. The monopoloid firm maximizes profits where MR = MC, produces q^*, and charges a price of P^*. Consumer surplus is the difference between the highest price consumers would be willing and able to pay (what is called their "reservation price") and the actual price charged. At inframarginal output units before q^*, say at $1/3\,q^*$ or $1/2\,q^*$, consumers would be willing and able to pay higher prices than P^*, say P_1^*, but the single price monopoloid producer will only charge its profit maximizing price, P^*. Hence consumers receive an increase in their welfare through dividend, bonus, or

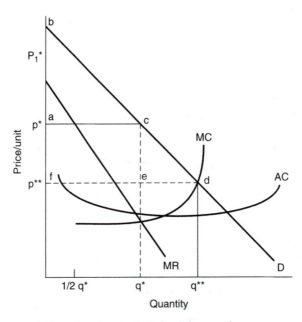

FIGURE A-8 Consumer Surplus and Deadweight Welfare Loss

subsidy, which is the difference between P_1 and P^*. If we look at all the inframarginal units preceding q^* and add them together, we would see that the aggregate consumer surplus is the triangle abc in the above diagram.

Suppose the price and output level of the producer were adjusted closer to the competitive ideal—the output level q^{**}, corresponding to the point where $P = MC$. At this output level, the aggregate consumer surplus is now represented by the triangle bfd—a significant increase in consumer welfare and one of the clear-cut advantages of the competitive market economy.

Notice that under conditions of monopoly, the rectangle acef was part of monopoly profits, also known as "producer surplus," but the triangle cde was neither part of consumer nor producer surplus. It is referred to as the "deadweight welfare loss" triangle associated with the monopoloid firm's decision to restrict output and misallocate society's scarce resources. Only when the industry approaches competition does this deadweight welfare loss change to consumer surplus and benefit consumers.

Price Discrimination

The above analysis assumed that the monoploid firm could only charge a single profit maximizing price, but what if we relax this single price assumption and permit the firm to charge multiple prices for the same quantity to different product classes of consumers—what is referred to as "price discrimination." We can now demonstrate how the price discriminating monopolist can earn higher profits than the single price firm. For price discrimination to work, special conditions must, however, hold: (1) Customers must be separable into different classes based on differing elasticities of demand; (2) there must be a way of identifying and keeping track of the customers in each class; (3) there must be no resale (arbitrage) between customers from one class to another. Given these conditions, it is now possible to charge customers in each class their *highest reservation price* rather than the common price for the last marginal consumer. This tactic then confiscates consumer surplus and changes it into monopoly profits (producer's surplus). Note that the more inelastic customer classes will have higher reservation prices and will be charged the highest prices.

Suppose there are five customer classes, each succeeding class with lower reservation prices. For class 1, the corresponding reservation price is P_1, for C_2 it is P_2, and so on. By charging P_1 to the first class, P_2 to the second, and so on, the monopolist will receive the revenues associated with the rectangle $P_1C_1 + P_2C_2 + P_3C_3 + P_4C_4$ to the point at which $P = MC$. The fifth class will not be included since the price lies below AC, thereby earning a loss for this extra output. Note that the single price monopolist would equate $MR = MC$ and produce at an output level near C_2 and a corresponding price near P_2. It should be fairly obvious that the sum of the producer surplus rectangle for classes 1–4 greatly exceeds that of the single price monopoloid producer. It should also be understood that the producer surplus comes directly from consumer surplus, although pockets of consumer surplus triangles still remain as illustrated above. As the firm carves out more and more distinct customer classes, even these pockets of consumer surpluses will be absorbed.

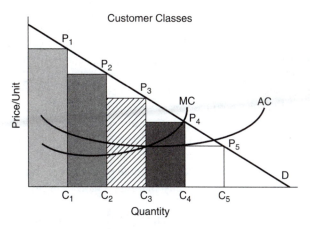

FIGURE A-9 Price Discrimination

One redeeming feature of price discrimination is that it does positively impact on society's allocation of resources by bringing forth additional output and lower prices, and now permits new classes of customers to be included in consumption than would have occurred under the single price case. Firms can also take fuller advantage of scale economies through increased output possibilities.

This same analysis can be applied to the regulatory firm that faces the dilemma of setting optimal prices under conditions of declining costs (see Figure A-7). If the monopolist is permitted to price discriminate by separating out different classes of customers, then it can cross-subsidize production in elastic markets with higher prices in the inelastic ones. The total output will approach competitive levels but this kind of cross-subsidization may be viewed as a predatory tool against competitive firms or as a way to prevent new entry in competitive submarkets.

Monopolistic Competition

This hybrid model of monopolistic competition has elements of both monopoly and competition and for that reason often is pictured as more closely corresponding to real-world industries than the market structures at either end of the continuum.

Like its perfectly competitive counterpart, the monopolistically competitive firm is one of many such firms in the industry and individually accounts for a very small share of the total industry product. Unlike its counterparts, this firm has some control over its economic fortunes, some ability to act independently by virtue of a downward sloping demand curve. The significance of the downward sloping demand curve (as contrasted to the horizontal one of perfect competition) is that small increases in price do not drive away all consumers to the outstretched arms of rivals; the firm retains a loyal following of customers.

The shape of the demand curve is related to the nature of the product. Firms in monopolistic competition produce similar but not identical products (as in perfect competition). To coexist in the industry, the firm must utilize some means of product differentiation to create a market niche—to distinguish itself in the minds of consumers as providing some unique product or attribute. Common techniques available include quality differentials, service and location differentials, and, most prominently, advertising.

As long as consumers believe some difference exists between two firms providing essentially the same product, this is sufficient for the firm to establish a loyal following of customers. The impression should not be created that the monopolistically competitive firm can act with impunity and exploit its position in the same way as the monopolist. Rather, the demand curve for the firm will be relatively elastic (flat) due to the large number of close substitute products within the industry,[10] and this will constrain its behavior to only marginal changes in price and product attributes.

Within its range of discretionary action, the firm believes it is independent and seeks to establish the profit maximizing levels of prices, output, quality, and advertising expenditures, where MR = MC in Figure A-10. Since the monopolistically competitive firm is representative of a large number of similarly situated rivals, all firms tend to react the same way to the same economic stimuli, and thus the individual firm's assumption of independence from its rivals is never achieved. The industry slowly gropes toward a short-run equilibrium with the rival firms having similar prices, product quality levels, and advertising expenditures.

Should excess profits exist at the short-run equilibrium position, these profits will be dissipated in the long run due to the relative ease of new firms in entering the industry—the same assumption used in the perfectly competitive model. The entrance of new firms is visualized in Figure A-10 as reducing the share of the market of existing firms (a leftward movement in their "representative" demand curves)[11] until long-run equilibrium is achieved (where MR = LRMC and P = LRAC), all excess profits are squeezed from the industry, and no further incentive remains for additional firms to enter or existing firms to expand their level of operations.

Since the monopolistic competition model is a hybrid, we therefore discover that its performance standards are not as desirable as those of perfect competition, yet not as obnoxious as monopoly, rather, somewhere in the middle. In this regard, prices are above what would occur in a perfectly competitive industry and a resulting misallocation of society's resources occurs since prices exceed marginal costs. The resulting "shortage" of product is produced in suboptimal-sized plants (as with monopoly). In addition, there may be excessive expenditures on advertising, especially of the persuasive kind, or other nonutility generating means of product differentiation.

While it is true that in the long run the favorable standard of normal profits occurs, this is achieved only partially by falling prices (due to entry and loss of

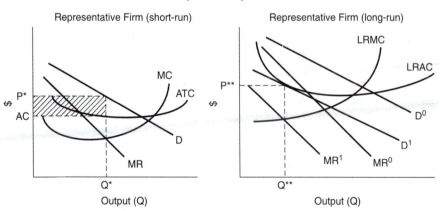

Monopolistic Competition

Excess profits for the representative firm are cross-hatched in diagram

FIGURE A-10 Monopolistic Competition

market share) in conjunction with the rising level of costs associated with product differentiation. As a result of such excessive costs, many economists believe that excess capacity exists and that the industry is populated by too many small-sized firms inefficiently producing and distributing their product.

Oligopoly

As with monopolistic competition, the oligopoly market structure is a hybrid form but generally pictured as lying closer to the monopoly side of the ledger than to the competitive ideal. The salient feature of oligopoly is that there are relatively "few" firms that collectively comprise the entire industry. Within this grouping of relatively large firms, the distribution of market shares may be balanced or else dominated by one or two industry giants. Often, the disparity in firm sizes are related to their history of merger activity. The product may be relatively homogeneous or highly differentiated.

Each firm and the industry as a whole face a relatively inelastic demand curve indicating that there are no close substitute products. Like its monopolistically competitive counterparts, the individual oligopoly firm seeks to differentiate itself by carving out a market niche, obtaining a loyal following of customers, and making its individual product demand more inelastic. This can be achieved through advertising, branding, or the other forms of product differentiation mentioned above; furthermore, the fewness of sellers within the industry and the resulting lack of viable substitutes creates a naturally inelastic demand curve for the product class. It is usually assumed that some barriers to entry exist within the industry, which helps to perpetuate excess profits in the long run. The barriers, whether in the form of economies of scale, absolute cost advantages, or whatever, may not be as formidable as those discovered under monopoly, and hence the oligopoly structure may not be as impregnable.

Because of the fewness of sellers, each oligopolist is so powerful that its pricing, product differentiation, or research activities cannot go unnoticed; such actions *directly* affect the market as a whole and impinge on market shares of rival firms. Since rivals desire to maintain their relative standing, they must react (usually in kind) to any precipitous action of competitors. Because all rival firms face similar industry conditions and economic stimuli, each oligopolist contemplating changes must assess how its rivals will respond to any action it may initiate.

This process is what is referred to as *mutual interdependence,* and, depending on the assumptions a firm makes concerning the rivals' reactions, different theoretical models of oligopoly behavior may result. The range of reaction assumptions and the corresponding behavior of rival firms can cause oligopoly performance to move closer to the results discovered under monopolistic competition or alternatively nearer the monopoly end of the spectrum. Let us discuss a few of the possible scenarios.

First, assume that rivals choose to disregard totally each other's reactions to changes in prices and advertising. As one firm lowers price and initiates an advertising campaign, the other firms protect their market shares through corresponding actions and thus trigger a second and succeeding series of price cuts and advertising expenditures until full-fledged warfare breaks out. This warfare continues until all excess profits are squeezed from the industry through compression of the profit margin from above and below. This nonlearning scenario continues time period after time period with market shares approximately the same as initially existed, and with performance standards similar to those associated with monopolistic competition.

Under a second scenario, assume the rival firms closely monitor each other's reactions but totally mistrust each other's motives, believing their rivals are out to inflict the worst possible economic damage on them. This is operationalized in the following way: Given an initial market price, the representative oligopolist assumes that if it initiates a price increase, its rivals will not follow suit; hence, it will lose a significant share of business because its prices for a similar product are now relatively more expensive. At the same time, if it lowers prices, its rivals will exactly match such price cuts to avoid having market shares siphoned off by this relatively lower priced competitor. Perfectly matched price cuts gain some minor additional sales (less than proportional) for all firms at the expense of inter-industry products. A kinked demand curve, as pictured in Figure A-11, therefore exists for each representative oligopoly firm. It is damned if it raises prices, damned if it lowers prices, and so does neither.

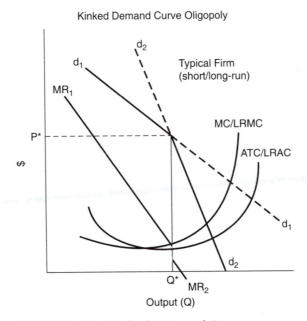

Kinked Demand Curve Oligopoly

FIGURE A-11   Kinked Demand Curve

The kinked demand curve is the combination of two demand curves of differing elasticities; d_1 reflects an *elastic* response associated with unmatched price changes while d_2 reflects an *inelastic* response associated with matched price changes. The heavily shaded d_1d_2 portions of the two demand curves are now joined to become the relevant operational demand curve, with the standard marginal revenue and associated cost curves also shown. Note that the marginal revenue curve is now discontinuous because of the differing slopes of the original demand curves from which it is derived. Profit maximization occurs at the output level where MR = MC. The resulting price P^* is rigid and stable for this industry unless wide variations in costs shift the industry toward a new output level and new equilibrium price.

This scenario of the kinked demand curve formerly was considered the general theory of oligopoly but was found not to correspond to a variety of industry situations; it now seems relegated to new industries and industries in which different companies enter *de nouveau* or via acquisition and are unfamiliar with existing industry practices and untrusting of their new rivals.

A more likely scenario occurs through a modification of the first two scenarios. Under this hybrid approach, firms are assumed to be capable of *learning* from past actions and willing to trust each other to the extent of recognizing the right of mutual existence. At some point, after a few self-defeating price or advertising wars, it becomes clear to all competitors that it is a wiser policy to seek a cooperative posture vis à vis each other than to fight it out in the trenches. If everyone "agrees" to maintain high product prices, low input prices, or limited advertising expenditures, then the industry as a whole can maximize profits, and each firm's share of these higher profits will be "greater" than if it acts independently and engages in a cycle of rivalrous behavior.[12]

If this type of tacit collusion operates smoothly, the result may be a "shared" monopoly indistinguishable from the performance of the single monopolist making all the decisions itself (see Figure A-6). Under this scenario, the spirit of mutual cooperation replaces mistrust and the "live and let live" philosophy accrues financial benefits to all who participate. Therefore, the performance standards of oligopolies may cover the full spectrum from aggressive competition (scenario 1) to collusion (scenario 3), depending on how rivals view and trust each other.

GAME THEORY

Often it is possible to conceive of oliogopolistic consensus in terms of game theory. Game theory models are too numerous to explain here but they generally rely on assessments of expected rival behavior and payoffs associated with each behavior. Generally, matrices of opponents behavior and one's own behavior are constructed to illustrate overall industry actions.

Suppose rivals are considering increasing product profits. If each rival acts independently and selfishly to better its own position, then the end result will be disas-

		Rivals (firms 2 & 3) Behavior	(firms 2 & 3)
		Low P.D.	High P.D.
Firm 1			
Own Behavior	Low P.D.	High Profits for all	Losses (1) Profits (2, 3)
Zero Sum Game	High P.D.	Profits (1) Losses (2, 3)	Low Profits for all

FIGURE A-12   Rivals Payoff Matrix

trous for all firms. On the other hand, if all trust each other, and act appropriately for what is best behavior for the entire industry, then the overall results will be mutually beneficial.

In more specific terms, in the context of a zero sum game at a low level, then rivals 2 and 3 can win away market share and profits increasing to a high PD level. Similarly, if firms 2 and 3 were to institute a low PD policy and firm 1 responded with high PD, then firm 1 would earn greater profits and the rivals would be in a loss position. Because neither trusts each other, each opts for a high product differentiation strategy, thereby reducing profits for all concerned. If all could somehow agree on low expenditures on PD and there was a spirit of cooperation, then everyone would benefit. On the other hand, if there is mistrust and each competitor seeks to undercut its rivals by taking advantage, then the end result is high PD for all and accompanying low profits. The same disastrous results can occur with pricing policies and expenditures on research and development.

One final point should be made with respect to all these theoretical models. Each model by definition is an abstraction of the real world; no real-world industry will exactly fit all the assumptions and theoretical propositions. It is the task of the industrial organization paradigm of Appendix B to take these theoretical constructs and translate them into more meaningful and useful real-world measures.

NOTES

[1]The price of land is rent; the price of capital is interest; the price of labor is wage; and the price of entrepreneurship is normal profits.

[2]Each variable in the demand function given above has a + or − sign above it to indicate its relationship to quantity demanded.

[3]If the product is produced under noncompetitive conditions, the profit-maximizing firm makes a single *supply response* (rather than a curve) to the given demand curve it faces.

[4]$AVC = TVC / Q$; $AFC = TFC / Q$; $ATC = TC / Q = AVC + AFC$; $MC = \Delta TC / \Delta Q$.

[5]Technically speaking, this was true for perfect competition as well since price equaled marginal revenue due to the horizontal demand curve facing each firm.

[6]The difference between what the consumer is willing to pay and what he/she actually pays is known as "consumer surplus."

[7]Joseph Schumpeter, *Capitalism, Socialism and Democracy,* 3rd ed. (New York: Harper and Brothers, 1950), pp. 84–85.

[8]This is a similar method of pricing to that used by the federal government in the acquisition of national defense weapons and materiel.

[9]This cross-subsidization may be demanded by the regulatory agency to meet certain social goals such as universal telephone service, first-class postage delivery, public education, or public affairs programming.

[10]Some economists have criticized the concept of "the industry" as being too nebulous and including what might otherwise be considered inter-industry substitute products.

[11]By "representative" or proportional demand curves, we mean that each of n firms possesses $1/n$ of the total industry demand. If the number of firms increases by m, and total industry demand doesn't change, then each representative firm now has $1/n + m$ (a smaller) share of the total market demand.

[12]The different forms of cooperation and the difficulties of achieving a collusive oligopoly are explained in greater detail in Appendix B.

Appendix B

The Industrial Organization Model

While the four traditional market structures described in Appendix A provide useful insight into categorizing modern U.S. industries, nonetheless, they still are abstractions from the real world and often leave as much unexplained as explained. To illustrate this point, several confusing concepts will be presented.

First, in the oligopoly model, the concept of a "few powerful" firms is typically used to describe this market. Yet how few is few? And what is meant by being powerful? How does one draw the boundary line between a strong and weak oligopoly and between the latter and monopolistic competition? Second, is it realistic to assume that a single plant is magically expandable to whatever size is necessary to achieve economies of scale or rather would the profit-maximizing firm seek such economies at the *firm* level by managing a portfolio of optimal-sized plants, strategically placed at key geographical distribution locations? Finally, how does one grasp (and measure) such slippery concepts as technological change, firm conglomerateness, or even excess profits?

The role of industrial organization is to give substance to these abstract concepts by providing various rules of thumb and practical indicia for their measurement. Furthermore, it arranges these concepts into a particular sequence that provides the means for examining any industry in a systematic fashion.

The order of these concepts is best explained by the familiar schematic of market structure affecting market conduct and in turn affecting market performance.

MARKET STRUCTURE → MARKET CONDUCT → MARKET PERFORMANCE

While some might choose to insert a stronger verb here to indicate causation rather than merely effect, it should be noted that at times the arrows may be reversed through various feedback effects. In any case, we will analyze the components of each of the major boxes in turn.

MARKET STRUCTURE

The structure of an industry refers to all the institutional forces that shape a modern industry. Often, the nature and scope of the market itself is included in such a taxonomy as a means of accounting for the characteristics of the product, the means of production and distribution, and any special governmental rules or regulations that affect this product, the workplace, or its labor force (i.e., minimum wage and safety rules, special tax exemptions, import/export regulations, etc.).

ELASTICITIES

Within this general description should be an indication of the nature of the demand for this product. Under the category of demand are various concepts of elasticity. First is *price elasticity* of demand, which reflects the shape of the demand curve within a relevant range and is defined as the percentage increase in quantity in response to a percentage decrease in product price. This relationship is usually expressed as a fraction:

$$\eta_p = \frac{\% \Delta Q d}{\% \Delta \text{Price}} = \frac{\Delta Q}{Q \text{ base}} \bigg/ \frac{\Delta P}{P \text{ base}}$$

Because of the law of downward sloping demand, this fraction is negative in all but the most extreme cases.[1] By taking the absolute value, one can concentrate on the magnitude of change and ignore the signs. If the fraction is greater than 1, this is a relatively elastic portion of the demand curve since the quantity response is more than proportional to the price change. If the fraction is less than 1, this is an inelastic portion of the demand curve since the quantity response is less than proportional to the price change. If the fraction equals 1, this reflects an equiproportional response and is labelled as unitary elastic.

Firms desire price inelastic demand curves since this gives them the flexibility of raising prices without losing their customers to intra- or inter-industry competitors. While the basic properties of elasticity revolve around the number and closeness of substitute products, the degree of necessity or luxury, and the share of disposable income the product represents,[2] firms spend considerable sums seeking brand awareness, that is, creating actual or perceived product differences in the eyes of the consumer to build a loyal following, especially when prices are raised.

The *cross elasticity* of demand is crucial in determining which products constitute the "relevant product market"[3] for the industry. This finding is preliminary to any determination of market concentration. For any product market, one ideally seeks to include those products that are close substitutes and thus directly compete for the consumer dollar. Cross elasticity of demand asks how responsive are the quantities demanded of one product (say B) to increases in the price of another product (say A).

For close substitutes, there should be a very strong quantity response for B as that product now attracts customers who are not very loyal to A and search out a reasonable (lower priced) alternative. In mathematical terms, the cross elasticity is expressed as:

$$\omega = \frac{\% \Delta Q_B}{\% \Delta P_A} = \frac{\dfrac{\Delta Q}{Q \text{ base}} \text{ (product B)}}{\dfrac{\Delta P}{P \text{ base}} \text{ (product A)}}$$

If this fraction is greater than or equal to .75, this suggests a very strong substitute relationship—a 10 percent increase in the price of A increasing the quantity demanded of B by 7.5 percent. If the fraction is greater than .50 but less than .75, this would be considered a moderate degree of substitutability. Between .25 and .50 would be considered a weak substitute relationship, while below .25 would suggest that there is no substitute relationship—the goods are independent. If the cross elasticity were less than zero, rather than being substitutes, the products are complements, that is, they are used in conjunction with each other and usually in fixed proportions such as with coffee and cream or autos and tires.

The third type of elasticity reflects the *income* dimension and measures the degree to which the product is a superior or inferior good, that is, the relative responsiveness of quantity demanded to changes in income. It is expressed in the following form:

$$\Omega = \frac{\% \Delta Q d}{\% \Delta \text{ Income}} = \frac{\dfrac{\Delta Q}{Q \text{ base}}}{\dfrac{\Delta I}{I \text{ base}}}$$

If the fraction is greater than zero, this indicates a superior good while fractions less than zero indicate inferior goods—goods consumed in smaller amounts as people become wealthier and trade up to better quality merchandise. While income elasticities are often quite large and in some instances exceed 1, there is no simple rule of thumb that can be given for this measure. Firms need to be concerned with income elasticities as they engage in strategic planning over a long-term horizon and guesstimate the varying turns in the business cycle.[4]

Finally, one needs to consider the *strength* of the product demand, that is, whether the demand curve is increasing, decreasing, or stable. This is another way of assessing what stage the industry sits in the product life cycle. Is it growing, stagnant, or on the decline?

It generally is assumed that firms operating in a growing industry can take a more aggressive and independent stance vis à vis each other since, at worst, they simply retain a constant piece of a growing pie of revenues. On the other hand, when the industry demand is stagnant or declining, the firms take greater cognizance and can more closely monitor market shares, and mutual interdependence becomes critical in their interaction with rivals.

MARKET CONCENTRATION

Perhaps the single most important element of market structure is the existing distribution of power among rival firms. As economic theory demonstrates, the greater the degree of market control that is concentrated in a few hands, the greater will be the power of these firms to raise prices above the average costs of production and earn excess profits.

While the microeconomic theories of market structure refer to this size distribution of power in only the most general of terms (*large number, few*), industrial organization requires more precision in conceptualizing these abstractions and thereby separating those firms with significant market clout from those that operate on the fringe of the industry and could exit at any time. In short, it is not sufficient to describe an industry as having 25, 100, or even 1000 firms without some way of describing how market power is distributed among such firms.

One means of adding greater precision here is to visualize the degree of equality/inequality of market shares within an industry by means of a Lorenz diagram. While this technique was first used in examining the inequality of income (and wealth) within a nation's economy, it can be easily transplanted to the industrial context without sacrificing much meaning.

As shown in Figure B-1, the horizontal axis represents the cumulative percentage of firms in the industry[5] while the vertical axis represents the cumulative percentage of market shares as reflected by sales or assets. If there were perfect equality of power, one would witness the 45 degree line (i.e., 10 percent of the firms possess 10 percent of aggregate sales; 20 percent of the firms possess 20 percent, and so on). On the other hand, plotted as a curve is the actual cumulative distribution of market shares. As pictured, the top 10 percent, 20 percent, and so forth of firms now have a disproportionate share of the market. The farther this bowed-out curve departs from the 45 degree line, the greater control of the market is held in a relatively few hands and vice versa.

Using integral calculus and modern computer programs, it would be possible to calculate the area between the Lorenz curve and the 45° line and compare it to the

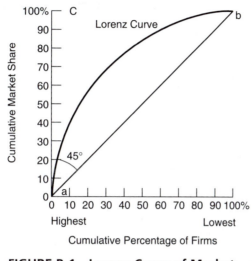

FIGURE B-1 Lorenz Curve of Market Share Distribution

area of the right triangle abc. This procedure is known as calculating a Gini coefficient, which mathematically equals the former area divided by the latter. Gini coefficients have a range from 0 (no deviation) to 1 (total deviation accompanying a pure monopoly). Hence the higher this numerical coefficient, the greater the degree of inequality of market power among the firms. One flaw associated with Lorenz diagrams and Gini coefficients occurs in oligopolies, which have only a small number of firms (say less than ten) with approximately equal market shares. These measures of market power now give a false impression of market competition when, in fact, the industry is very concentrated.

An alternative to Lorenz diagrams and Gini coefficients is the so-called Concentration Ratio (CR). This measures the aggregate market shares (of assets or sales or occasionally "value added") of the largest four or eight or even twenty firms. Since the larger firms have the most influence and wield the greatest market power, the idea is to focus on their control rather than worry about smaller fringe firms. While no common standard has yet emerged to categorize concentration ratios, one that is fairly conservative should suffice for our purposes.

Three categories are established in Table B-1: (1) the first is highly concentrated and corresponds to what theorists would consider a strong or tight-knit oligopoly; (2) the second, a moderate degree of concentration that corresponds to a mild or weak oligopoly; (3) monopolistic competition that indicates a lack of power or, phrased differently, the minimal amount of power necessary to retain a differentiated demand curve, yet not enough to share mutual interdependence with rivals. Finally, we can describe a functional monopoly as whenever one firm achieves at

TABLE B-1   Concentration Ratio Categories

High Concentration	$CR_4 > 50\%$ and/or $CR_8 > 75\%$
Moderate Concentration	$33\% < CR_4 < 50\%$ and/or $50\% < CR_8 < 75\%$
Monopolistic Competition	$CR_4 < 33\%$ and/or $CR_8 < 50\%$

least two-thirds control of the market itself, regardless of the industry concentration ratio.

As noted above in the discussion of cross elasticity of demand, we wish to include the market shares of all companies that compete in the relevant product and geographic markets. This necessitates adjusting concentration ratios to include competition from imports where they play anything above a trivial role in the industry. Furthermore, the geographic market needs to be delineated as well. While the typical default mechanism is to express the geographical market as including the contiguous forty-eight states, in many industries, especially those involving the media, this process may be incorrect and boundaries should more properly be local or regional (e.g., transmission of cable television, delivery of daily newspapers). In fact, the relevant geographic market may change across every stage of production within an industry.

One problem with concentration ratios is that little attention is necessarily paid to medium- or small-sized firms that, under certain circumstances, can play a competitive role. Also, by only looking at the aggregate share of the top four or eight firms, one might overlook significant shifts in power within these groupings over time.

The most consistently used measure of concentration today is the Herfindahl–Hirschman Index (H–H index) because it is sensitive to both differences in the number of firms in an industry and differences in relative market shares as well. It is calculated as the sum of the squared market shares of each competitor in the relevant product and geographic markets:[6]

$$\text{HHI} = \sum_{i=1}^{n} S_i^2$$

Where S_i is the market share of the i th firm in the industry and n equals the number of firms in the industry. The squaring process gives disproportionate weight to the largest firms in the industry, and in this way it reflects the same philosophy as the concentration ratios. While the H–H index requires complete information for every firm in the industry, its calculated value will hardly be affected (because of squaring) if some very small firms with minuscule market shares are purposely or unintentionally omitted.

Another reason for the popularity of the Herfindahl–Hirschman index is that the Department of Justice adopted it as the centerpiece in its new "Merger Guidelines"

TABLE B-2 Categories of Concentration for Herfindahl–Hirschman Indices

High Concentration	H–H > .18
Moderate Concentration	.10 ≤ H–H ≤ .18
Unconcentrated	H–H < .10

of 1982, as revised in 1984 and 1992. Justice categorizes the degrees of concentration as shown in Table B-2.

The Antitrust division of the Justice Department will not object to any proposed merger that creates a post-merger H–H index of < .10 and will only intervene in mergers creating a moderate degree of concentration if the change in the H–H index exceeds .01 and/or other structural factors, especially heightened barriers to entry, are involved. On the other hand, if the post-merger H–H index creates a high degree of concentration, opposition is likely even if the merged firms are only medium in size.

One final measure of concentration is gaining increasing acceptance in the literature. It is known as the *market share instability* technique. It reflects a belief that, over time, tight-knit oligopoly firms will develop an industry consensus on price and possibly other aspects of product quality. Hence stable market shares over time should better represent this aspect of oligopoly control than simply examining concentration ratios or H–H indices.

The instability index is calculated as the sum of absolute value differences in market shares between time period t and t + 1.

$$\sum_{i=1}^{n} \left| S_{t+1}^{i} - S_{t}^{i} \right|$$

The higher this value, the more unstable and hence competitive the industry during the time span; the lower the value, the more stable (and noncompetitive). One problem with such a scale is that once a price consensus occurs, oligopolistic firms may decide to compete in nonprice/product differentiation areas that are more susceptible to wide swings in market shares since, unlike prices, retaliation is very difficult.

BARRIERS TO ENTRY

The market concentration within an industry (however measured) need not be considered in static terms but can undergo changes over time as part of the product life cycle or in response to changes in technology (Schumpeterian "gales of creative destruction"). Conditions of long-run entry determine to a great extent whether and how long an industry will retain its existing market concentration. The greater the difficulty of new firms in entering an industry as significant competitive forces, the higher are the "barriers," and the greater the tendency for current firms to maintain high profit-maximizing prices with accompanying excess profits and misallocation of society's scarce resources.

Structural barriers may take many forms: economies of scale, absolute costs, product differentiation, barriers to exit and government rules, regulations, and favors. Additionally, certain coercive *conduct* practices tied to several elements of market structure may constitute conduct barriers and thereby further frustrate entry. Conduct barriers will be described in connection with other aspects of market behavior.

ECONOMIES OF SCALE

As noted in Appendix A, the concept of economies of scale refers to the shape of the long-run average cost curve (LRAC). The extent of such economies is crucial in determining the existing number of significant competitors in an industry and the prospects for future deconcentration of an industry. Looking at panel (A) in Figure B-2, one sees that efficient-sized firms will produce at or near Q_1^*, the minimum efficient scale, with an average cost of AC_1. Firms producing at approximately one-third of M.E.S. at Q_2 or one-half of M.E.S. at Q_3, will have significantly higher average costs (AC_2, AC_3, respectively). For these firms to coexist, they must be willing to accept compressed profit margins or else compete in a specialty component of the market with very loyal customers who do not mind paying the higher prices needed to cover the higher average costs.

Thus, if the M.E.S. output level is large relative to the total industry output, this industry will have a high likelihood of being an oligopoly and exhibit a propensity for remaining one in the future. Potential entrants will find it difficult to obtain the heavy capital financing needed to establish a cost competitive enterprise and then capture the requisite market share needed to compete on an equal footing with existing firms. In sum, their long-term prospects remain quite dim, and they generally will seek other market opportunities in which the obstacles are not so steep. This is the way that widespread scale economies fortify market concentration and function as a barrier to entry.[7]

If the LRAC appears as in Figure B-2 (B), this would indicate an industry wherein minimum efficient scale is easily achieved from both the financial standpoint as well as capturing a sufficient market share to justify production at M.E.S. Such industries would most closely correspond to the monopolistic competition model and entry would be relatively easy in the long run.

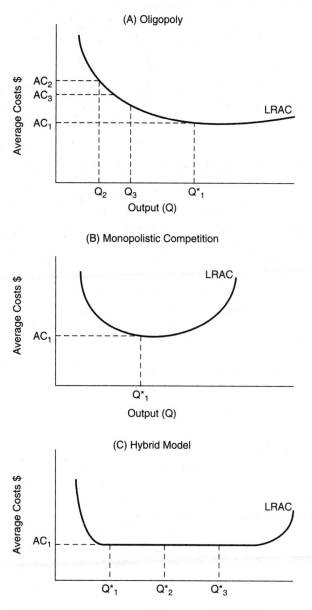

FIGURE B-2   Different Shapes of LRAC Curves

Finally, if the LRAC curve has the shape pictured in Figure B-2 (C), this would indicate that minimum efficient scale is reached at a fairly small level and remains constant over a broad range of output (Q_1^* has the same average costs as Q_2^* and Q_3^*). In such an industry, no advantage accrues to being either a large or small producer; each is equally efficient and entry is relatively easy in the long run. One would then expect a market structure composed of large- and small-sized firms, each able to coexist with one another. Depending on other factors, this cost structure could be consistent with either monopolistic competition or a weak oligopoly situation.

It is also interesting to discuss movements of the long-run average cost curve. Three factors can cause shifts in this curve. The first is a change in process technology, which is usually envisioned as favorably reducing costs through greater efficiency and productivity of the factor inputs, that is, requiring fewer factor inputs to produce the same level of output. This improvement in technology shifts the LRAC curve downward and may also affect its gradient, depending on whether it is labor-saving, capital-saving, or neutral (no change in factor proportions).

A second factor is known as *external diseconomies.* These are diseconomies beyond the scope of an individual firm, diseconomies that occur as the industry itself gets very large and places demand pressure on specialized resources or skilled labor, thereby causing factor prices to rise. These diseconomies raise costs rather than affecting productivity and shift the LRAC curve upward in a balanced or unbalanced fashion.

The third factor reflects the fact that *new firms* may have higher costs of production–distribution than existing firms for some period of time. Reasons for such cost disadvantages are: (1) the extra time needed to learn how to produce–distribute the product efficiently and to learn trade secrets that only come through experience; (2) extra costs may be initially involved in differentiating the product from existing firms, luring away their customers, establishing an identity, and creating a sense of trust with the consumer; (3) extra interest surcharges or underwriting fees may be levied by banks and security dealers to reflect the extra risk associated with new ventures as opposed to older ones; (4) initial royalty payments facing new firms to use existing technologies prior to their discovery of different methods not subject to current patents. These cost disadvantages are collectively referred to as *absolute cost barriers to entry,* and they may reinforce the other structural or conduct barriers.

MEASUREMENT OF LRAC CURVES

While the economic concept of the long-run average cost curve is very rich in theoretical terms, its actual measurement in real-world industries is not so easily accomplished. Often, it can be estimated only through indirect means. To bridge this theory gap, it is first necessary to determine whether output should be measured at the plant level, firm level, or both.

Microeconomic theory discusses scale economies and the derivation of the LRAC curve in terms of an optimal-sized plant—as if a single plant can always be expanded to whatever size is necessary to exhaust all technical cost savings. In real industries, most firms have a portfolio of optimal (and even some suboptimal)-sized plants, and the discussion then changes to wherein multiplant and firm size economies lie.

Several techniques are available for measuring the shape of the LRAC curve. Most have been applied to the single plant or multiplant level rather than to the firm as a whole since economists have generally been interested in separating out *technical* efficiencies involving real resource savings from *pecuniary* efficiencies involving redistribution of income. Such a distinction is not made in this discussion. And while the optimal-sized plant and optimal-sized firm are related, they are certainly not identical concepts.

The first and most accurate technique is called *engineering estimates* and involves obtaining information through interviews and written questionnaires from professional engineers, architects, and plant managers about various costs associated with different-sized plants. Since these people are intimately involved in designing, constructing, and operating new plants within the industry under examination, they will be most knowledgeable about all cost efficiencies at both the single and multiplant levels. In conjunction with data given in specialized trade journals, one can then piece together different data points and construct cost curves for the newest facilities currently in use or on the drawing boards.

This process would presume a wide variation of different plant sizes in the planning, construction, or refurbishing stages throughout the industry. If such proprietary information could somehow be systematically obtained, it would also permit measurement of the gradient (slope) of the LRAC curve—the cost disadvantage faced by firms producing at one-third or one-half the minimum efficient scale.

A second approach is called the *historical cost* technique and involves obtaining original data on plant size and average costs from a wide variety of different firms within an industry. A statistical regression equation would then smooth out these different data points into an average cost curve. The higher the statistical fit, the closer this estimated cost curve would reflect historical cost associations in the industry.

Besides the obvious difficulty in obtaining such confidential data, it is unlikely that the sample will contain plants of the same vintage or capacity utilization. It is possible to make adjustments and allowances and thereby standardize such a data set, but the results will not be as reliable because of variations in accounting practices (such as depreciation allowances) and internal costing discrepancies across firms. Also, this suffers from the fact that the *observed* cost of producing various output levels differs from the *minimum* cost of production. Nevertheless, with all its shortcomings, if the data are available across enough firms and can be appropriately adjusted, this technique can provide a reasonably good estimate of "current practice" cost relationships.

The first two methods primarily involve measurements at the plant or multiplant level and require detailed cost information. The third method looks more broadly at the profitability and survivability of different-sized *firms* in the marketplace and *indirectly* links such performance to the attainment of plant and firm efficiencies of all kinds. This "survival" technique asks the basic question of whether firms can withstand all the pressures of the marketplace and continue operations and thrive in the long run. Such "survivors" must then be efficient firms. The fact that such durability may reflect market position or conglomerate power rather than efficiencies is an obvious shortcoming and explains why this method is referred to as an indirect measure of scale economies. At best, it can only give broad ranges of optimal size; it cannot pinpoint the gradient of the LRAC curve!

To conduct a survivor estimate of minimum efficient scale, one needs data from a large cross-sectional sample of firms in an industry. The analysis needs to encompass a considerable period of time intended to capture the long run. This time period should be a minimum of five years and preferably ten years in length.[8] The data should be broken down (at the firm level) according to sales, number of employees, assets, number and size distribution of plants, profitability before taxes, and similar measures. A series of associations can then be made to relate firm size (assets, number of employees, number of plants) with survivability (profitability, market shares, etc.). These associations can best be illustrated with a series of analytical questions.

1. Have firms of certain sizes exited from the industry or been acquired in merger deals during the time span under examination? These are clearly not the "survivors" and hence these firms are said to be inefficient and have higher average costs. Similarly, what was the minimum size of new entrants to the industry that have remained as viable concerns for a period of time after entry? These new entrants can be expected to reflect the state of the art of minimum efficient scale at the time of their entry.

2. Are firms of certain sizes more profitable (as measured by their percentage rate of return on sales or assets) than other firms? If so, these would be considered the "survivors." Alternatively, is there an optimal range of firm sizes for which profitability is stable (or rising) over time yet above which or below which profitability is unstable or declining?

3. Are firms of certain sizes (as measured by assets, number of employees, etc.) increasing their market shares over time at the expense of smaller or perhaps larger firms?

4. Somewhat easier (but less desirable) would be an analysis that simply measures the mean/median firm size for an industry along with the standard deviation. This could be measured alternatively by the amount of assets, value added, number of plants or employees. Here it would be assumed that firm sizes that constitute "outlying cases" (say, one or two standard deviations) will not be as efficient as those closer to the mean.

Having completed one or more of these survival techniques and thereby sketched out the LRAC curve, one would have greater confidence in assigning it to one of the three market structures presented in Figure B-2. Once again, it should be stressed that these associations only provide a raw, indirect measurement of the scale economy concept and cannot be separated into technical or pecuniary efficiencies; nevertheless, the usefulness of the survival technique becomes immediately apparent in the various media in which questions arise as to the optimal size for a chain organization of newspapers, cable systems, motion picture theaters, or broadcast stations or the minimal efficient level needed to launch a new national newspaper or remain in a competitive situation with another metropolitan daily.

PRODUCT DIFFERENTIATION

Product differentiation refers to the degree to which firms producing similar or identical products can convince consumers that their products differ in at least one important dimension from their rivals'. The differences can reflect actual grades of quality, workmanship, durability, warranties, appearance, packaging, business location, hours of operation, ease of service, or imagined differences induced by advertising.

As noted above, the firm is seeking to create a market niche or brand preference to make its demand curve more inelastic. In cultivating this loyal following of customers, the firm will have more flexibility in pricing behavior without fear of widespread loss of business to slightly lower-priced alternatives. Each method of product differentiation, whether in the form of rock video television ads, fancy packages, or annual style changes requires a financial commitment from the firms. These expenditures often become the most important competitive element between rival firms, especially those operating under conditions of oligopoly. To the extent that the consumer tolerates, sanctions, and rewards those firms engaging in such activities, product differentiation expenditures soon become an integral component (sometimes more critical than price itself) in a firm's demand function and hence its market share.

As these product differentiation costs are continued year after year, they become embedded within the cost structure of all firms wishing to remain viable competitors in the industry; they become almost an indispensible fixed cost that dare not be reduced unless extreme adverse economic conditions prevail. It is at this point that these expenditures become a barrier to entry in the sense that new firms considering entry must be willing to devote the same absolute dollar amount or percentage of revenues to compete on an even basis with existing firms.[9] In terms of our previous discussion on LRAC curves, these expenditures would raise the curve above its previous level.

There is another way that product differentiation may become a barrier to entry. If we conceive of the product market in spatial terms, then new entrants can be thought of as jockeying for advantage by seeking a product niche, that is, an unfilled need in product space. To the extent that existing firms also recognize this and other market niches in anticipation of new entry and occupy the product space themselves, then this would reduce the open portion of the market and increase the difficulties of new entry. Using the same logic from a geographical perspective, if certain geographical markets are perceived to be "open" but are filled by existing rather than new firms, then this reduces the opportunity set for new entrants. The phenomenon of flooding the market with new products and alternative brands is known as "brand proliferation" and can fill the product space and deny opportunities to new firms. When brand profileration occurs within the context of limited retail shelf space, the opportunities for new product entry are even more limited.

Because the nature of product differentiation differs from one industry to another and there are no standard classification schemes for reporting such expenditures, it is not possible to provide a single rule of thumb. We are left at best with such gross measures as the percentage of sales revenues devoted to product differentiation activities or more probably with the percentage of sales revenues devoted to advertising.

BARRIERS TO EXIT

In some industries with large fixed capital costs, firms thinking about entering an industry often pose the question: If things don't work out as originally planned (for whatever reason), how difficult would it be to sell off the assets and escape with some of the upfront invested capital?

To the extent that such plant and equipment is very specialized, tailor-made, subject to rapid technological obsolescence, or physical deterioration, the resale or scrap value of such assets may be worth only a fraction of their original costs.[10] In these circumstances, the costs of exit are so large that they swamp the benefits from entering and deter firms from entering in the first place.

GOVERNMENT CONTROLLED BARRIERS

In many industries, it is necessary to obtain government permission (at the local or federal level) to enter an industry. This may come in the form of a license, a permit to construct a facility, or restrictive rules on dealing with environmental surroundings. While the rationale for government involvement in such matters is usually based on sound principles of protecting the public interest, health, or environment (i.e., licensing physicians or taverns, approving new drugs, issuing electromagnetic frequencies, etc.); nevertheless, it restricts the ability of new firms to enter quickly and provide competitive benefits to consumers.

In another light, the patent system (and to a lesser extent copyrights and trademarks) grants monopoly protection to innovative firms for a long period of time while strict import quotas, tariffs, or other trade restrictions protect U.S. firms against offshore competition. In any case, these government sponsored restrictions may be the stiffest of all barriers to entry because they say: "Thou shall not enter!" or "Thou shall not enter until you have met such and such conditions!" Furthermore, the full force and power of government is available to enforce such sanctions.

Finally, governments may grant special favors to existing firms if these firms provide strategic products (often defense related) or are large employers within a community or region. These favors may take the form of government bailouts (grants, guaranteed loans, favorable interest rates) to prevent bankruptcy, preferential tax rates (special investment tax credits, tax abatements, undervalued property assessments), or simply the provision of services that alleviate firms from spending such funds themselves (retraining facilities, access roads and utility hookups, high or extended unemployment benefits). While such favors formerly were exclusively reserved for old-line firms, in today's business environment most states have undertaken such incentive programs as a means of luring new business and diversifying their local economies. Hence, new firms promising to bring significant employment to a local area can probably capture similar government favors.

VERTICAL INTEGRATION

Each product that reaches consumers has already travelled through several "stages of production." These stages are generally presented in a vertical picture (see Table B-3) to emphasize the progression from the lowest (simplest) level to the final retail stage at which the consumer ultimately becomes involved. As the product progresses forward/downstream toward the retail arena, each stage adds additional value to the final price at which the product is transacted. The amount of "value added" within a stage depends on the product transformation or new services that are rendered as well as the market power of firms in setting prices. In Table B-3, the retail stage makes the greatest contribution (expressed in percentage terms) while the raw material stage makes the smallest.

TABLE B-3   Stages of Production

		% of Value Added
Stage 4	Retailing	40%
Stage 3	Distribution	30%
Stage 2	Manufacturing	20%
Stage 1	Raw Materials	10%

Vertical Integration refers to the situation in which various firms in an industry simultaneously operate at more than one stage of production. While such vertical integration normally occurs for adjacent stages, it need not in order to fulfill the definition. Firms become integrated to achieve greater coordination and efficiencies across the production–distribution process or to avoid having to deal with outside firms that are undependable suppliers–customers, have poor reputations for quality, or are unstable or unreliable in some other dimension. On the other hand, vertical integration is much more costly and perhaps riskier than operating at a single stage; there may be considerable inefficiencies that result from trying to operate additional stages at optimal levels. Often the economies of scale do not coincide between adjacent stages.

Vertical integration can take several different forms, the most stable of which is direct ownership and operation by the firm (either fully or as part of a joint venture). Slightly less control accompanies vertical integration by long-term exclusive agreement; here the firm doesn't actually own, but may be able to partially or fully control through contract provisions. Typical of such arrangements are franchise agreements, which are prevalent in many industries including automobiles, fast foods, and some appliances. While independently owned, these retailers agree to exclusively carry the line of a single distributor and abide by various quality control rules and regulations regarding the preparation and sale of the franchised product.[11]

Looking at Figure B-3, one sees a series of firms, each with a different degree of vertical integration within the "industry as a whole."[12] If appropriate data are available, the best method for measuring vertical integration is by calculating the *average value added* across all firms that participate in one or more stages. The higher this average, the greater the degree of vertical power within the industry. There are some

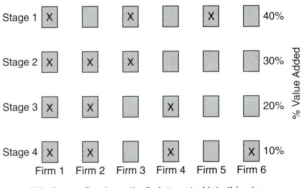

X indicates firm is vertically integrated into this stage

FIGURE B-3   Average Value Added Technique

complications that arise in obtaining value added data by individual firm, but sometimes the information is available by *stage* for the industry as a whole (as shown in Figure B-3) and a gross estimate of average value added can be determined.[13] An even simpler estimate would be merely to calculate the average number of stages operated per firm.[14]

Finally, vertical integration may be conceptualized by comparing any two stages and asking what is the average degree of self sufficiency per firm in the industry.[15] This is a somewhat different concept than the previous measures since it assumes that just because a firm physically produces (distributes or retails) in a particular stage, it may not satisfy the entire product needs of its subsidiary in the adjacent stage—it may have to depend on other outside firms to fill the void.

One final note should be added concerning vertical integration; in its simplest form, it is a neutral concept. However, depending on how it is used, it may reflect the essence of a competitive economy, as firms search for efficiencies across stages of production, or the worst features of monopoly power if it is used to drive non-integrated rivals from the industry. This latter action will be explored more fully below.

CONGLOMERATENESS

Firms may be economically powerful *relatively* within a particular product market and *absolutely* within the economy as a whole. Absolute firm size is known as "deep pockets" and refers to control over assets or sales (often in unrelated product lines) of the parent corporation whose subsidiary is competing in the product line under consideration.

Differences in absolute size among rival firms may either exaggerate or reduce the relative disparity in market shares in the relevant product line. It means something quite different in terms of market clout if the leading firm in an industry is owned by say a top 10 corporation on the *Fortune* list than by one ranked 1000. Conversely, if a new entrant has deep corporate pockets, it may be better able to withstand the normal learning period through corporate cross-subsidization than a similar-sized entrant operating on its own.

There are several techniques for assessing absolute firm size and conglomerateness. The simplest is to seek some sort of ranking such as the *Fortune* 500 or 1000 and identify those firms whose corporate parents occupy such positions. Alternatively, one can calculate the sales or assets of the firm in the product line under investigation and compare them to those of the parent corporation. The *lower* the percentage of sales–assets attributable to the particular product line, the greater the degree of conglomerateness or diversification of the parent corporation and thus the deeper the corporate pockets and "staying power."

There are no standard rules of thumb for assessing the degree of conglomerateness or absolute size differentials. One can only look for wide variations between firms in an industry as possible explanations for unconventional or unusual market behavior.

BUYER CONCENTRATION

It should be recalled that there are two parties to every financial transaction—a seller (supplier) and buyer (demander) of product. In a competitive world of large numbers of buyers and sellers, the market itself retains power and establishes a compromise price somewhere between the high prices desired by suppliers and low prices sought by demanders.

In the previous description of seller concentration, the implication of significant market control was that a small group of oligopolists, collectively encompassing the market, could be expected to provide a supply response to aggregate consumer demand that approximated that of how a monopolist would react if it controlled the industry. Such a transaction price naturally would favor the sellers and disadvantage the buyers.

On the other hand, the behavior of sellers would be constricted if they must deal with a small group of powerful buyers on the other side of the market. To the extent these buyers individually and (more importantly) collectively encompass the major customer class, their purchases become absolutely critical to the sellers; should they act or threaten to act in concert, they may be able to drive prices below the profit-maximizing level of the suppliers.

In short, when bilateral power exists on each side of the market, complex bargaining strategies ensue and whichever side has the strongest bargaining position and/or the deepest pockets generally prevails.[16] Thus, it is crucial to understand (and assess) the nature of such "countervailing power" before attributing too much control to highly concentrated sellers.

Buyer concentration is measured in the same fashion as seller concentration, generally using concentration ratios or Herfindahl–Hirschman indices. To underscore this point, the four-firm buyer concentration ratio would be the aggregate market share *purchased* by the largest four buyers of the relevant product line. This concept of buyer concentration is quite important for media industries in which the product tends to be very specialized with few alternative uses (e.g., newspapers, television and radio programs) or is tailor-made for a particular medium (e.g., made-for-TV or cable movies). Contrast this with the production of steel or aluminum, which has many different end product users.

MARKET CONDUCT

Our second major area of examination refers to the interactions of firms in such dimensions as pricing, product differentiation, and research and development. Since public policy analysis is generally focused on various gradations of oligopoly power (market concentration), we will confine analysis to this area.[17]

Mutual Interdependence

Oligopoly firms are said to have a high degree of mutual interdependence that requires cognizance of each other's moves and countermoves in the areas of interaction. Failure to understand such a web of entanglements can lead to mutually destructive action for all firms. This concept can best be explained through illustration.

Suppose you have a strong oligopoly and, during a period of excess capacity, one of the industry leaders decides to lower its price from the equilibrium agreed-on level. The firm believes that other firms will not match the decrease and hence its price will be relatively lower. By moving down the elastic portion of its demand curve, it could lure away business from its rivals.

However, the rivals do not sit idly by and watch their market shares dwindle; rather they match the price cuts, thereby negating the advantage of the firm initiating the action. Such an industry-wide price cut would now bring only a slight increase in business—not from intra-industry rivals but from inter-industry substitute products that are now relatively more expensive. This type of unrewarding, self-defeating price cut reduces industry revenues and profits and may trigger further price wars.

In another light, suppose instead of risking a price war, the maverick firm now launches a major advertising campaign aimed at luring away customers from rivals and enhancing its brand awareness. To the extent that such a campaign catches everyone by surprise, it may temporarily increase market share of the initiating firm and decrease that of rivals. However, the rivals will soon counter with their own campaign, which can be expected to win back many if not all of its customers.[18] In short, there will largely be a restoration of initial market shares although the initiating firm may get a small permanent increase in its share by dint of its surprise attack.

During the course of this skirmish, the rival firms may up the ante to fully recover their lost business or to teach a lesson to the maverick firm. Soon, a full-fledged advertising war ensues and, when the dusk finally settles, market shares appear to be similar to their original levels, but industry-wide costs have skyrocketed and drained profits.

After enough of these mutually destructive price or advertising wars, the firms come to realize their degree of mutual interdependence and the undeniable fact that rivals instinctively respond in kind to grandstand attempts to steal market shares. The firms come to understand that *cooperation* rather than competition is the key to industry survival. More specifically, if common industry standards for price and other potentially disruptive practices can be established, then the joint industry-wide profits can be maximized and each firm's piece of this large pie of revenues and profits will be greater than if it acts independently, ignores its rivals, and triggers economic warfare.

Achieving Consensus

The means of achieving a "spirit of cooperation" are varied and run the gamut from the closest type of consultation inherent in a formal cartel to a "meeting of minds" associated with tacit coordination. We will now explore these different methods.

First, the rival firms may decide to openly consult with each other on optimal prices, geographical spheres of influence, quality gradations, transportation costs, bid rigging, and other matters. These open discussions could occur at special meetings, trade conventions, country clubs, or through written correspondence or telephone conversations. This formal cartel arrangement is the most stable of all consensus-building arrangements because differences of opinion can be straightened out through interpersonal bargaining. Nevertheless, these agreements are considered to be per se illegal forms of price-fixing under the United States Antitrust Laws.[19] Even with the associated fines, criminal sentences, and triple damage sanctions, some firms continue to pursue such overt cartels.

A second means of achieving industry consensus is through *price leadership.* Usually, the dominant firm in the industry acts as the spokesperson, and other leaders closely monitor the words and actions of this company as it signals to them what new price or other related action needs to be established. The communication can come from newspaper and broadcast interviews or simply from press releases announcing new policies. The remainder of firms soon follow the leadership of the dominant firm, which, by virtue of its position, has the financial clout to reprimand maverick firms that do not follow suit.

Occasionally, smaller firms with solid reputations, respect, or charismatic leaders act as price leaders for the industry. These "barometric" firms feel out weather conditions affecting the industry and signal their response to the economic stimuli. The other firms then follow suit. Notice that neither the dominant nor barometic price leaders are in direct consultation with their rivals; this indirect "signaling" process acts as a loophole for escaping price-fixing charges, yet may be nearly as effective as open consultation.

A third less intrusive approach is known as *common pricing practices.* Here, the firms have been in the industry for many years and have watched each other under varying economic stimuli. They know each other's pricing and product differentiation strategies[20] and can predict with near certainty how each other will react to common industry conditions. There is no need here for open discussions; a "meeting of minds" in a common design and purpose occurs, and the firms grope toward an industry consensus. Sometimes, trade associations can legally circulate information about general industry trends in terms of sales, prices, costs, and other matters that can facilitate this common understanding.

Obstacles to Consensus

If the process of reaching and maintaining an industry consensus were so simple, it would naturally become standard operating procedure for every oligopoly. However, there are obstacles that make such a consensus problematic for certain industries.

One such problem is widespread differences in true product quality. If the product has several different quality gradations, no single standard price will suffice. Firms producing higher quality merchandise will seek higher prices than those selling lower quality product. While it is possible to have fixed price differentials between the grades, this may unduly complicate the tacit agreement or make it very unstable.

A similar problem arises with differences in the cost structures between the firms. These differentials may arise from different market shares and associated scale economies, different plant vintages, x-inefficiency or whatever. The crucial point is that the high unit cost producers will seek higher prices to cover their excessive costs while the efficient firms will discover their profit-maximizing point at a lower price. The greater the range of average costs, the harder to establish and maintain a single optimal price.

Another impediment to forming a spirit of cooperation lies with the number of significant firms in the industry. Since true consensus requires participation of all major firms, the larger this critical mass, the harder it will be to obtain an agreement. As the number of firms increases, the number of interactions rises exponentially, thereby increasing the likelihood of miscommunications or misunderstood signals. Furthermore, the chances increase that one or more firms will deliberately "cheat" on standard prices and destabilize the fragile agreement. While a half dozen firms should pose no major hurdle, once the critical mass exceeds a dozen, industry consensus becomes all but impossible without overt collusion.

Industry members must continually be monitored and cheaters disciplined before economic warfare ensues and the agreement is destabilized. Cheating is most easily detected in the greater the number of market transactions that occur. Firms that enter the market frequently and with relatively small-sized orders expose themselves to discovery more readily than those that enter intermittently and with large and/or custom-made orders. Furthermore, the ability to detect price cheaters will only be as effective as the measures of enforcement and punishment handed out. It is generally the responsibility of the dominant firms to discipline recalcitrant rivals by some temporary predatory conduct. If enforcement or punishment is ineffective, this can further destabilize a spirit of cooperation.

Suppose that all of the aforementioned obstacles regarding achievement and maintenance of a price consensus are somehow overcome, can the tacit cartel truly operate as a shared monopoly? The answer is generally "no." The agreement can never run as smoothly or operate with the precision of a single monopolist making a single set of operating decisions. The competitive instinct cannot be totally suppressed; it usually surfaces in those nonprice areas where retaliation is not so swift or predictable. In concentrated industries that have eliminated price competition, market shares are usually distributed to those who successfully compete in such nonprice areas as product quality, new product development, warranties, and so forth. While these areas of rivalry are costly and can erode industry profits, emergency adjustments or limits can be imposed if things get out of control.

Thus, while no oligopolistic consensus is likely to be complete in all possible dimensions, the smart firms will *cooperate* in the most important revenue-generating areas and *compete* in minor areas that don't significantly jeopardize industry profits. In essence, this cooperation–competition strategy places a floor below which profits cannot fall.

To document a spirit of cooperation requires extensive knowlege of the industry. It is necessary to observe an industry over a period of years as various firms individually respond to different economic stimuli. The *manner* of response is often as crucial as the uniformity of action.

Coercive Conduct

Sometimes, the conduct of powerful firms gets carried to the extreme that it may become injurious to smaller rivals or firms considering entry. At this point, such coercive conduct takes on the character of a *conduct barrier* to entry, with the inherent power to exclude those who wish to engage in commerce in the industry. Each of these coercive practices is tied to specific structural characteristics; each can become the basis for an antitrust violation if "intent" can be proven in a court of law.

Predatory Pricing

The concept behind predatory pricing reflects the idea that powerful firms in an industry wish to teach a lesson or reprimand existing rivals or send a message to firms contemplating entry. In the first instance, this will usually be the response of one or more industry leaders to a smaller maverick firm that perhaps has engaged in a series of secret price discounts or some other disruptive action.

The nature of the message is that this industry will follow certain rules of engagement with respect to pricing, and that orderly conduct is the watchword! Such warnings are usually backed up by the economic clout of the industry leaders who not only match the original price reduction but cut prices below average costs, thus causing the entire industry to suffer economic losses. By possessing "deeper pockets" from this industry and through corporate conglomerateness, the plan is to outlast the smaller resources of the firms being disciplined. Either these smaller rivals leave the industry or else they remain but with a considerably lower profile, having learned "fear of the almighty." In either case, market power is solidified over the longer haul.

Such predatory conduct takes on the nature of a barrier to entry when it is done to scare away prospective firms who are poised on the outskirts of the industry contemplating entry. What firm will want to enter an industry suffering economic losses even though they be artificially contrived? Some economists do not believe that the sacrificing of short-term profits for long-term control is sensible. They argue that the minute excess profits reoccur, a new round of entry will ensue unless additional new barriers are created. While partially true, this criticism neglects the aspect of optimal timing associated with entry; frequently firms that are likely entrants today will seek another window of opportunity elsewhere should this one be temporarily closed. Furthermore, the disciplinary lesson taught to maverick firms, once widely recognized by outsiders, does not go unheeded.

Vertical Supply and Price Squeezes

The second type of coercive action reflects a significant but unbalanced degree of vertical integration in an industry combined with a strong degree of market power. Looking at Figure B-4, one sees the production and distribution stages of an industry. Assume firms A and B are industry leaders in both stages; they are vertically integrated, self-sufficient, and also major suppliers of input to firms C and D with whom they compete at the distribution level. Firms C and D get a small amount of input product from independents E and F as well.

Should A and B wish to reprimand C or D or drive them from the industry, they could slow down, halt, or temporarily disrupt the supply of input to these companies, thereby making them appear to be unreliable distributors to their customers. This is known as a supply squeeze. Alternately, they may have the power to raise the general level of prices of stage 2 (expecting firms E and F to follow) while keeping prices of stage 3 products constant. Price increases of input represent real cost increases to firms C and D and hence compress their profit margins (in stage 3), yet only represent an accounting transfer to firms A and B because of their vertical structure.[21] Should firms A and B simultaneously lower the prices of products in stage 3, this form of predatory pricing would now squeeze profit margins for the nonintegrated firms from above and below.[22]

Similar results occur when the imbalance of vertical integration is now reversed between the stages. Suppose firms E and F now must rely on A and B for access to

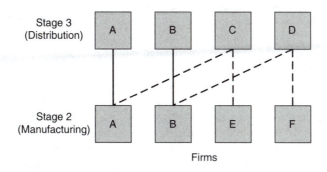

FIGURE B-4   Vertical Squeezes

distribution. Firms A and B may decide to deny distribution rights or only partially handle the products of E and F (an access squeeze) or else lower the distribution prices they will pay to all firms, including their own subsidiaries. Once again, this represents a real price squeeze to firms E and F but accounting sheet transfers for A and B.

Each example demonstrates the flexibility that vertical integration gives large powerful firms in determining which stage should extract the monopoly profits. It also teaches a lesson to the nonintegrated firm or a potential entrant to avoid dependency on these companies. Counterstrategies include seeking additional independent sources of input supply, seeking foreign sources, or else vertically integrating themselves. Should the latter scenario occur, this heightens barriers to entry by necessitating two-stage entry and eventually may lead to enhanced concentration of power across several stages.

Pricing to Deter Entry

The third coercive practice generally occurs in a concentrated industry that only has partial barriers to entry. The industry leaders have to determine a joint profit-maximizing price, bearing in mind that the size of their excess profits may stimulate entry. Should they choose to fully exploit the short-run profit-maximizing price, entry may be quickly enticed by such a profitable industry while price moderation may slow down the entry process. Hence, they face a series of possible prices, each associated with a different level of excess profits and a different speed of entry.

Let us examine two such pricing strategies. In strategy 1, they follow the standard short-run profit maximization strategy and charge P^1 and earn large excess profits for two years, after which significant entry drives down the price and profits to competitive levels. In strategy 2, they charge a moderate price P^2, earn moderate excess profits for four years, after which significant entry drives down prices and profits to competitive levels. Which strategy is best?

One needs to examine the stream of profits arising from each strategy for the five-year time interval to see which has the highest yield. However, since the value of a dollar today is worth more than one coming three or four years down the road, one needs to standardize the disparate values by applying appropriate time discount factors. This technique is known as finding the *present value* of the stream of profits. The discounting factors are the compounded rate of interest for the "out" years.[23] The present value formula is shown in Figure B-5.

Firms following strategy 2 are said to be "limit pricing" or "pricing to deter entry." This effective strategy is not quite so simple as pictured above. There are likely to be a dozen or more possible prices that should be considered, each with a different stream of profits and entry date for new competitors. Furthermore, the estimates of profitability and interest rates may not be the same each year but subject to business cycle trends. Interest rates may be especially unstable since they incorporate an estimate of future inflation. As a result, only general propositions can be

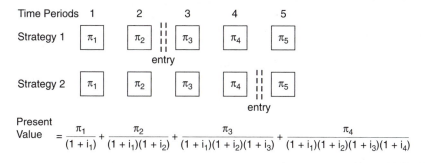

Compare the present value of both streams of profits to see which is higher

FIGURE B-5   Pricing to Deter Entry

stated, such as the lower the expected interest rates, the lower the rate of time discount; hence, the more valuable are the "out years" and the more viable are limit pricing strategies.

As noted above, when the degree of monopoly is insecure because of weak barriers to entry, it often is useful for the firms to consider price and output modifications to slow down the rate of new entry and thereby maintain their industry consensus. Many economists are skeptical about such strategies as limit pricing or predatory pricing because of the sacrifice of short-term profits for some abstract and possibly unattainable future goal or objective. The issue revolves around what the poststrategic situation will look like once prices are restored to their normal levels. For example, will entry reappear at this point and the entire cycle be repeated again? Firms considering entry must also make strategic guesses as to how the incumbent firms will behave over the long haul, once entry has been committed by the new firms. If the incumbent firms act irrational and unpredictable, that may be enough of a message to scare new firms in and of itself. Let's examine a few of the possible scenarios.

Suppose industry demand is stable or slightly increasing and looks favorable for the foreseeable future, and excess profits exist for incumbent firms. New firms contemplating entry must then judge what the post-price and profit situation will be once their new output is added to existing industry production. If their marginal output depresses prices severely, then entry may be infeasible and opportunities elsewhere may be more lucrative. The price depressing impact of their entry depends on how large they must be to achieve comparable economies of scale relative to total industry output, what the cost disadvantages are if they enter at less than MES, elasticity of demand, and, most importantly, whether incumbent firms will reduce their own outputs to accommodate the output of the new firms without depressing prices. If new firms believe that incumbent firms will eventually give ground to avoid spoiling the market, then the threat of short-term price aberrations is not credible and the firm can proceed without hesitation.

On the other hand, if incumbent firms send a consistent and credible warning that they won't allow entry without a fight, this can be a very strong message to deter new entrants. The threat will be most credible if it is carried out in concrete terms, is irreversible, and the message is obvious. Investment in new capacity by incumbent firms is the most clear-cut message since it indicates that the investment opportunity envisioned by new firms is most likely to be diminished by expansion of existing firms, already well versed in industry product. It should be noted that investment to deter entry is more expensive and more permanent than pricing modifications. Thus, pricing to deter entry and investment to deter entry are really two sides of the same coin and can be used in conjunction to send a warning to new firms considering wide scale entry, marginal firms considering expansion, or others waiting in the wings as "potential" entrants.

Another variant on the limit pricing model involves a special case in which the amount of such costs associated with new entry are small or nonexistent. Under such market conditions of "contestability," the behavior of existing firms in seeking to deter entry will be much more limited. As noted above, when assets are subject to physical deterioration, fast technological obsolescence, or other single uses—so-called "sunk" costs—the opportunity for quickly exiting an industry is diminished, thereby reducing the possibility of entering in the first place.

On the other hand, where such costs are nonexistent, it may be possible for a new entrant to quickly enter an industry, reap its profit potential, and then exit before existing firms have reacted through price or investment strategies. According to this theory of contestable markets, this threat of "hit and run" entry by fast moving firms can be a very credible threat of entry that will act as a modifying force on firms and their ability to maintain prices over costs successfully. Hence, the potential/likely entrant doctrine and contestability situation can act as a narcotizing element that freezes the strategic pricing ability of firms in an industry from exerting market power except during special short-run situations.

Of course, the assumption of zero sunk costs is very questionable in most markets, the presence of product differentiation, widespread scale economies, and government grants of privilege create advantages for incumbents and diminish the incentive and financial gain for such hit and run tactics. Furthermore, the expectation that the time lag for firms will be so long to respond to such overnight entry may be mistaken as well. Contestability may thus only work under very special circumstances and cannot be expected to affect conditions of entry in most industries.

Alternative Frameworks

While the industrial organization framework has persisted over time and become the standard for industry studies, it is by no means the only framework for analysis. In recent years, a rival approach championed by management guru, Michael Porter,[24] has gained popularity, especially in business schools. The Porter paradigm is in many ways quite similar to the industrial organization approach, with similar terms and concepts serving as the guiding principles. The one distinguishing factor in the Porter paradigm is the extreme focus on the competitive strategy of the firm. For Porter, the paramount activity for the competitive firm should be to establish a "sustainable competitive advantage."

Porter believes that competition is at the "core of the success or failure of firms," and that competitive strategy is "the search for a favorable competitive position in an industry."[25] While the overall attractiveness of industries for long-term profitability is rooted in their structure, the relative competitive position of firms depends on how they position themselves vis-à-vis their competitors. Hence, Porter understands that the elements of market structure determine the overall parameters for operation; nevertheless, within this constraint, the firm must maneuver itself and jockey for a strong competitive position. Hence, the conduct of firms takes on greater importance in the Porter framework than in the standard Industrial Organization approach and the feedback and interactive effects of conduct are much more important and under the control and will of the firm.

In more specific terms, Porter sees the firm interacting with five basis structural forces, including suppliers, buyers, potential entrants, current rivals, and substitute products.[26] Each of these forces can change over time and redefine the position of the firm and the health of the industry. The firm must consequently be greatly concerned with this nexus of forces. For example, threats of new entry or increased rivalry among incumbent firms can jeopardize current and future market shares. Fears of technological breakthroughs can create new substitute products that jeopardize comfortable positions of power as Joseph Schumpeter once prophesied. The threats may, therefore, arise from within the industry or outside it. Furthermore, the countervailing bargaining strength of suppliers and/or buyers can infringe on the freedom of the firm to act independently. These five forces stand poised like a snake, ready to strike at any moment, and only the firm that understands the seriousness of these competitive threats and creates strategic plans to counteract or control these forces can sustain itself over the long term.

Porter's main emphasis then is on the way in which firms conduct themselves to establish their "sustainable competitive advantage." Basically, there are three main approaches that any firm can follow.[27] First, the firm can become a "cost leader"—ever vigilant to cut costs, eliminate inefficiencies and wastes, and take advantage of all new technological improvements that increase productivity per hour of labor. This overemphasis on cost reduction will help establish this firm's reputation as the purveyor of a high value product—that delivers a specific level of quality at a reasonable price. As long as the quality of the product remains acceptable and within the parameters of industry standards, the firm can market itself as delivering comparable quality at a bargain to consumers.

A second approach is to focus one's energy on the establishment of product differentiation and to become a leader in this dimension. There are naturally many aspects of product differentiation, some as real as true quality differences between brand X and Y and some imaginary, built on the hyperbole of persuasive advertising that appeals to emotions or other personal attributes such as health, beauty, or popularity. The product differentiation leader can cater to myriad interests of consumers by producing many different brands, each slightly different in one dimension (e.g., laundry soap, cigarettes, cereal, and so on). To become a master of the product differentiation game, the firm must naturally invest some of its sales revenues in this dimension. Presumably, the inelasticity of demand it creates through product differentiation will allow it to charge higher prices than its rivals and thus cover the extra costs of such activities.

Can a firm be both a cost and product differentiation leader simultaneously? This is highly unlikely since the former implies cutting costs to the bare bones, while the latter implies a liberalness in spending money, even to extravagance. Thus, these two strategies are pictured by Porter as representing extremes and requiring a *tradeoff*. This is not to imply that some firms might seek a middle ground with trying to attain both cost efficiencies and product differentiation advantages, but Porter warns against the dilemma of being "stuck-in-the middle" when other firms are aggressive in these dimensions; this can be a formula for stagnancy.

The other dynamic strategy that can prove to be quite fruitful is for the firm to invest in research and technology trying to become a technology leader. As we know from the discussion above, technology is the unpredictable force (the Schumpeterian gale) that can destroy the status quo and redefine the industry. Some industries are more technologically oriented than others, but technological change has the ability to improve the *process* of production and distribution and thereby improve the associated productivity; alternatively, it can improve the quality of the product and thus make it more attractive to consumers in fulfilling their utilities or in providing value. In short, to the extent that technology increases productivity or creates value, it is related to the cost control strategic approach, while to the extent that it creates new and truly improved products, it fits in with the differentiation approach. In fact, firms following either of these two approaches probably should continually invest in research and technology to advance their positions. Firms can also try to be pure technology leaders and establish their sustainable competitive position in this manner.

Porter does also add another dimension to the search for strategic purpose and this involves the target audience. Firms must simultaneously make a decision whether to appeal to a broad constituency of consumers or become more specialized and cater to a narrower demographic or psychographic "focus."[28] Porter advances the notion that maintaining a strict focus on one subsection of the consumer class can be successful in the product differentiation, cost consciousness, and/or technology dimensions but that such a narrow strategic position might be vulnerable to the very successful firm in these primary dimensions that creates breakthroughs that appeal widely across the different consumer subsectors.

In summary, the Porter paradigm is important in the conduct area because it suggests a very active management approach to finding a market niche that is sustainable over time and can withstand the onslaught of competitive challenges arising from new technologies, new substitute products, and intra-industry warfare. Most appropriately, Porter cautions industry leaders to be as vigilant in protecting their industry as themselves and to focus on actions that create long-term stability for everyone. Finally, one should recall that changes in conduct can reverberate through the structure of the industry and create favorable or unfavorable feedback effects.

Market Performance

The final component of the Industrial Organization model is known as *market performance* and reflects those final equilibrium conditions discussed in Appendix A in comparing competitive and monopoloid market structures. In a certain sense, these elements of performance represent the final bottom-line analysis and foundation on which public policy reforms must be based.

To the extent that poor performance can be traced to specific conduct problems, targeted action addressing such practices may be all that is necessary. On the other hand, if the performance criteria are uniformly poor, more complex structural surgery aimed at breaking up concentrations of power or lowering barriers to entry may be required. Such structural reforms can be initiated by agencies entrusted with antitrust enforcement, regulatory agencies (where appropriate), or through legislative proposals.

Profitability

The most common manifestation of market power and control would be the appearance of excess profits in the long run. As noted above, this abstract concept must be operationalized before it has practical significance. By excess industry profits, we imply a sustained rate of return (before taxes) on sales or invested capital that exceeds that of similar products or industries operating under similar conditions of production–distribution with comparable investor risks.[29] The long run should last for a minimum of five and preferably ten years.

While obtaining information on capital investment is sometimes difficult in some industries, sales and profit data are generally available for the industry as a whole if not for individual firms. The critical task is then determining the base of comparison, that is, the grouping of similar products. This base should be broad enough so that it approximates economic activity within a major sector of the U.S. economy, yet narrow enough that the product or industry under investigation clearly fits in and makes sense. A few examples might clear up any confusion.

Suppose one were examining the auto industry, a reasonable basis for comparison might be all manufactured products; similarly, if one were examining the broadcasting or cable industries, an appropriate basis might be all media industries or even all leisure time activities but probably not all service industries. Aggregate data

TABLE B-4 Categories of Excess Profits

Less than 25% difference = normal profits

25–50% difference = above normal profits

51–75% difference = excess profits

greater than 75% difference = high excess profits

suitable for making such calculations are published by the Department of Commerce, Bureau of Labor Statistics or Census of Manufacturers.

After calculating the average rate of return and comparing it to the appropriate base, a judgment needs to be made concerning what constitutes "excess." Unfortunately, no common rule of thumb exists; often it is simply a matter of subjective judgment. Clearly if the rate of return for the relevant product is twice as high as the base, this would constitute excess profits. One suggestion would be to establish different categories reflecting a range of possible differences; represented in Table B-4.

There is one caveat to this analysis. While the existence of significant profit differentials almost always indicates market power, its absence may not since x-inefficiencies of various kinds may camouflage the true profits.

Efficiency

Efficiency refers to the optimal use of society's scarce resources and is the cornerstone of microeconomics. Yet, frequently, the presence of efficiency is extremely hard to detect much less measure. Often, the only tool available to industry analysts is to document its absence, that is, to measure inefficiency.

The first notion of efficiency is known as *x-efficiency,* which is defined as the minimization of cost for whatever sized firm is under scrutiny. In simpler terms, this means operating at a point *on* the LRAC curve rather than above it. Regarding the relationship between concentration and x-inefficiency, the line of thinking runs something like this: Very large firms and concentrated industries will have excessive profits, barriers to entry, and yet no competitive pressure or urgency to maintain a vigilance on costs. The cause of such waste may be the red tape associated with large bureaucracies, extra layers of management, make-work rules by unions or excessive salaries, perquisites, fringe benefits, and other costs.

While occasional high versus low cost comparisons can be gleaned by examining firms within an industry or foreign producers, it should be recalled that unit cost differentials may be as much attributable to differences in size (economies of scale) as extravagant expenditures. The best way for documenting such waste is to choose several standard cost items for the industry of record and compare them to some wider general base of similar industries (as was done for profitability). These measures might be average salaries, bonuses and perks of chief executives, or average wages per hour plus fringes for unionized labor. Since no common rule of thumb applies for categorizing such differences, one could follow a scheme similar to that suggested for profitability or simply highlight the differentials without attaching value judgments.

A subset of x-inefficiency refers to excessive amounts of product differentiation, especially advertising. As discussed above, firms in oligopoly industries may substitute product differentiation for price competition. Depending on the nature of the product and the degree of homogeneity, such product differentiation expenditures may reflect real quality differentials, different packaging, or the creation of imagined differences. As before, one wishes to separate out legitimate expenditures from waste.

However, since each industry has different products, different grades of quality, warranties, added services, and so forth, as well as different reporting procedures, it is virtually impossible to make comparisons across industries. The only hope is to compare advertising expenditures, a subset of product differentiation, between a given industry and a comparable base.[30] This comparison can be made with absolute advertising expenditures or the percent of sales devoted to such expenditures. Data on advertising expenditures are published annually in *Advertising Age*. Once again, we are left with no common rule of thumb categorizing the degree of advertising intensity differentials.

A further refinement of this technique would be to break down advertising expenditures by media, with the greater preponderance of advertising in the broadcast media, especially television, being linked to persuasion rather than the provision of information.

Economies of Scale

As noted above, we are interested in whether firms in an industry take full advantage of economies of scale. If such economies were measured by engineering estimates (or possibly through historical data), one could then see how many firms deviate (and by how much) from the minimum efficient scale. However, if economies of scale were measured by indirect survival techniques, then it would be tautological to compare these estimates with the positions of actual firms (since the estimates come from the firm data). In these circumstances, only the broadest generalizations can be reached about the number of inefficient firms and scale requirements for new entrants.

Allocative Efficiency

Allocative efficiency refers to whether the price per unit exceeds the marginal cost. As noted in Appendix A, concentrated industries can be expected to charge higher prices than marginal cost, thereby restricting the amount of output produced and misallocating society's resources. Yet, the marginal cost concept is often difficult to measure or identify for an individual firm (especially multiproduct ones) much less for an entire industry. Such data, if identifiable and separable, are generally considered to be proprietary information and are unavailable for research purposes.

Therefore, only general conclusions can be reached here and only indirectly based on the presence or absence of excess profits. Presumably, industries persistently earning excess profits are restricting output and misallocating scarce resources.

Technological Progress

Of all the abstract economic theoretical concepts, technological change is the most difficult to measure; sometimes, even difficult to describe because of its subtle nature. For our purposes here, we will examine two components of technological change. The first is "process" and refers to the means by which products are produced and distributed. Improvements in process should increase the productivity of the factor inputs and thus reduce cost per unit of output. For manufactured goods, these technological improvements can be measured by increases in productivity output per hour of labor that translates into lower unit costs. While there are often problems in defining productivity of services, many of the content products and hardware of the mass media (e.g., TV programs, videocassettes) should be measurable.

There is one major hitch in such measures of productivity; they assume that the product itself remains unchanged during the time frame under investigation. Yet, the *innovation of new products* and refinements of existing ones are the second major component of technological innovation. Unfortunately, it is more difficult to measure such *qualitative* product changes. Technological product innovation operates like the old adage of Justice William Brennan (associated with pornography), "I can't define it, but I know it when I see it." Oftentimes, such technological change is not apparent until a new generation of product is introduced either by an offshore competitor or by a firm outside the traditional boundaries of the industry. Such technological breakthroughs may revolutionize and redefine the relevant product market.

A very controversial issue has revolved around whether concentrated industries are best suited toward inventing and introducing technological change or if this is the province of more competitive industries. The former advocates would argue that only concentrated industries have the cushion of excess profits to invest in research and development and "lure capital to untried trails." This is a luxury unavailable to competitive industries that must hover closely to normal profits.

Contrariwise, because of this razor's edge of profitability, competitive firms are pressured to take full advantage of all such technological breakthroughs (especially process innovations) that lower operating costs. Such firms must keep up with rivals or face extinction—there is no margin for error. Yet, precisely because of the excess profits, the concentrated industries lack the incentive to engage in such research and development, often preferring to maintain the status quo until capital has been fully depreciated and all investments fully recouped. Holders of market power are often said to lead a "quiet life" free from the anxieties that accompany being on the leading edge of technology. This idea was best expressed in the famous dictum of the *Alcoa* case:

> *Many people believe that possession of unchallenged economic power deadens initiative, discourages thrift and depresses energy; that immunity from competition is a narcotic, and rivalry is a stimulant, to industrial progress; that the spur of constant stress is necessary to counteract an inevitable disposition to let well enough alone. Such people believe that competitors, versed in the craft as no consumer can be, will be quick to detect opportunities for saving and new shifts in production, and be eager to profit by them (U.S. v. Aluminum Co. of America 148 F. 2d 416, 1945).*

Which side of the debate is correct? There are examples and counterexamples illustrating each side. The best evidence suggests that some small degree of market power and large absolute size is necessary to reach the threshold of product innovation, but there are no further advantages to being a giant. On the other hand, the actual invention and diffusion stages may require a more competitive market structure to reach the full potential, i.e., the invention of new products being more conducive to small entrepreneurial settings with a minimum of bureaucratic red tape. Either a qualitative or quantitative assessment of technological progress should be made for each industry, given the limitations of data inherent in such an analysis.

Other Performance Goals

Some industrial organization models often include under the performance category such goals as full employment, income redistribution, price stability, and worker alienation. These are truly *macro* goals rather than micro performance standards and are beyond the influence of the vast majority of all industries. Hence, they will not be considered within the context here.

Occasionally, specific performance goals associated with public policy considerations can be included. They can range from equal opportunity employment practices to the more esoteric "diversity" goals associated with the preservation of a marketplace of ideas under the First Amendment. This latter category is critical to many media industries and has been the focus of considerable research linking various market structures to program or content diversity.

Finally, one general comment is in order concerning the entire structure–conduct–performance model. Rarely are sufficient hard data available to measure every element of each area. Furthermore, some elements of the model may be totally inappropriate or insignificant within a particular industry. Often, researchers focus only on the most important aspects of structure (or conduct) and relate them to key aspects of performance, especially those elements that have public policy implications.

Another fruitful research area is to perform comparative equilibrium analyses, that is, examine one or more aspects of the model at a particular point in time when it was in a stable equilibrium state and trace through the impact of endogenous or exogenous shocks to the system as a new equilibrium is reached.

NOTES

[1]When the demand curve is vertical, the fraction has a value equal to zero. This is referred to as a perfectly inelastic demand. When the demand curve is horizontal, the fraction has a value equal to infinity. This situation is referred to as a perfectly elastic demand. The quantity and price bases in the fraction usually are the midpoints between the initial and final values for the respective variables (i.e., $Q_1 + Q_2 / 2$; $P_1 + P_2 / 2$).

[2]Inelastic products tend to be necessities, with few close substitute products and small ticket items.

[3]The first issue in antitrust proceedings is determining the relevant product and geographic markets in which the attempted monopoly or "substantial lessening of competition" is alleged to have occurred.

[4]Because price of product, prices of substitutes, and income are three of the standard determinants in demand functions, multiple regression analysis permits one to isolate these elasticities by examining the coefficients (partial slopes) of these respective variables at appropriate bases (usually mean values). For more detail, see Barry R. Litman, "Economic Methods of Broadcast Research," in Joseph R. Dominick and James E. Fletcher, eds., *Broadcast Research Methods* (Boston: Allyn and Bacon, 1985), pp. 114–115.

[5]Suppose one discovered ten firms in the industry. Each firm would then represent 10 percent of all firms in the industry. If there were twenty firms, each firm would represent 5 percent of all firms.

[6]For example, suppose there were only five firms in the industry with market shares distributed as follows: 40 percent, 20 percent, 20 percent, 10 percent, and 10 percent. Then the H–H index would be $.40^2 + .20^2 + .20^2 + .1^2 + .1^2 = .26$.

[7]In the extreme situation of a continuously declining LRAC curve (without limit), the result is known as a "natural monopoly" or utility and such industries typically have some form of price–profit regulation that limits their ability to charge excessive prices.

[8]Periods in excess of ten years usually involve too much "noise"—abnormal economic circumstances such as wars, severe recessions, import restrictions, or government wage and price controls that distort normal performance.

[9]In the previous section, it was noted that these product differentiation expenditures may also represent an absolute cost barrier if new firms must exceed the expenditures of current firms to make their presence known and/or lure away their customers if the industry is not growing fast enough to absorb a newcomer at minimum efficient scale.

[10]The time frame for earning enough profits to retire the debt and recoup research and development costs may also be too short to enter such industries profitably.

[11]Not all franchise agreements are exclusive. Some retailers may have multiple competing "franchised" products (e.g., automobiles, bicycles, computers, and so on).

[12]The concept of the industry can no longer be confined to a single stage of production; it must reflect all such stages.

[13]This would be calculated by examining which particular stage each firm occupies and assigning the value added percentage for the stage to each firm and then finding the mean across all firms. For our example, firm 1 = 100 percent; firm 2 = 60 percent; firm 3 = 70 percent; firm 4 = 30 percent; firm 5 = 40 percent; and firm 6 = 10 percent. The simple mean is thus 51.7 percent.

[14]For our example, firm 1 operates 4 stages, firm 2 has 3; firm 3 has 2; firm 4 has 2; and firms 5 and 6 have 1 each. The mean number of stages per firm is thus 2.17.

[15]To calculate this average self-sufficiency, one would proceed as before by first finding this percentage for each individual firm and then taking a simple average for all the firms in the industry. Firms producing in only a single stage obviously have a zero degree of self-sufficiency between the two stages—they are wholly reliant on outside firms.

[16]If there is equal bargaining power, a transaction price may prevail that is similar to the market price accompanying competition on both sides of the market.

[17]Perfect competition never occurs in the real world while pure monopolies are almost always regulated. Functional monopolies need not worry about interactions with rivals and, in monopolistic competition, the firms act independently of each other.

[18]Advertising is just one avenue of product differentiation. The war could just as easily be fought on warranties, packaging, frequency of style changes, or additional services attached to the product.

[19]Section 1 of the Sherman Antitrust Act of 1890 prohibits all forms of price-fixing agreements in interstate commerce. Until recently, the Webb–Pomerene Act of 1914 permitted such price-fixing agreements to operate for offshore exports.

[20]These pricing strategies may be reduced to simple markup or margin pricing over wholesale cost while product differentiation may occur at specific times of the year or represent a fixed percentage of sales revenue. In some industries, "focal," or pricing points, are established for the product so that firms know where to round off the price, such as to the nearest dollar (for men's shirts) or at .9 cents for gasoline.

[21]For A and B, their production subsidiary raises prices to everyone including their captive distribution subsidiary. Corporation profits from distribution now fall but profits from production correspondingly rise. In fact, the total corporate profits may actually increase, depending on the magnitude of the higher revenues now received from C and D.

[22]This double squeeze also affects integrated firms A and B by lowering their profit margin, but presumably they have deeper pockets and greater staying power and can outwait their smaller rivals.

[23]The present value of $1 coming one year from now at a 10 percent rate of interest is .91; two years from now is .82. Expressed somewhat differently, if I were to take 91 cents today and invest it at 10 percent interest, I would have $1 a year from now.

[24]Michael E. Porter, "Competitive Strategy: The Core Concepts," in Michael E. Porter, *Competitive Advantage: Creating and Sustaining Superior Performance* (New York: Free Press, 1985), Chapter 1.

[25]Ibid., p. 11.

[26]Ibid., p. 6.

[27]Ibid., pp. 11–16.
[28]Ibid., p. 15
[29]In pure economic terms, excess profits is intended to represent a rate of return exceeding the opportunity cost of entrepreneurial time and capital elsewhere in the economy.
[30]This assumes that advertising represents about the same percent of product differentiation expenditures for all industries studied.

Appendix C

The Merger Guidelines

Because of the conflicting and disputatious decisions of the Federal courts in major merger cases, interpreting the precedential language is often quite difficult and complex for U.S. businesses. To facilitate the process of understanding the antitrust laws through examination of the key cases, the Department of Justice over the last twenty years has periodically issued merger guidelines to businesses, indicating the areas of concern that would most likely trigger an antitrust investigation and complaint by the Federal authorities. This certainly is no foolproof blueprint for business as to what is legal or not, but, nevertheless, it does provide some information on current thinking as to what the Department of Justice considers to be important and how it expects to allocate its scarce budget resources.

First issued in 1968, then again in 1984, and most recently, in 1992, the *Guidelines*[1] have evolved over time and certainly do reflect the political philosophy of the extant administration in power and its attitude toward big business in general, and antitrust issues in particular. The 1992 Guidelines highlighted below were jointly conceived by the Federal Trade Commission, which has mutual responsibility for enforcing antitrust laws in the United States. Finally, these current guidelines apply only to horizontal-type mergers; vertical and conglomerate mergers are no longer given prominence by the Justice Department, although they still remain part of the antitrust statutes and are influential in the precedential cases that interpret the antitrust laws. A brief examination of these precedential cases follows the presentation of the Guidelines.

The horizontal merger guidelines[2] are all based on the premise that horizontal mergers eliminate direct competition between firms, increase market power, and create a potential for raising prices and restricting output—the classic situation that has been associated with microeconomic theory for the last century. All elements of market structure and conduct are considered that might facilitate this process of gouging the consumer through above cost pricing and misallocating society's scarce resources; they are weighed in the consideration of whether such horizontal mergers are anticompetitive or procompetitive. The standards, while they appear to be straightforward, can nevertheless be subjectively interpreted and given more than proportionate weight. In sum, it is still possible to use these standards to arrive at political decisions as to which mergers will be prosecuted and which will be permitted.

The first step in determining whether horizontal mergers will be condemned is defining the relevant product and geographic markets. Comparing antitrust law to criminal law, if you accuse someone of an antitrust violation, you must produce the "body," that is, you must define what product line will be affected and in what geographical area the crime will occur. There is great flexibility (and considerable subjectivity) in this determination since the Clayton Act,[3] as amended, requires economic harm "in any line of commerce, in any section of the country." The most commonly used measure of assessing relevant markets is that of cross elasticity of demand, i.e., whether two products (or two geographic areas) are close substitute goods for each other such that an increase in price of one good (or in one geographic area), all other things constant, triggers an exodus of business to the unaffected product (or area) whose price has not changed.

We want to include all products in the relevant markets that fit this description of close substitute products and exclude all products that are weak substitutes or unrelated. Once this trial and error process of inclusion/exclusion is completed, then included products and markets can confidently increase prices without fear of leakage of business to other products or other areas.

The trial and error method works as follows: Suppose product lines A, B, and C are provisionally assumed to be close substitute products and D is being considered. Then A, B, and C are geometrically illustrated by intersecting concentric circles while D is outside the relevant market, shown in Figure C-1.

The cross elasticity of D is then assessed vis à vis A, B, C (taken as a group). If D is discovered to have a moderate or high cross elasticity, than a new provisional product market is drawn with D now included, and the process is continued by evaluating the next most likely product line, E. This interactive process continues until all close substitutes are included within the circle and all weak substitutes or unrelated products are placed outside the circle. The included product lines as a group could now profitably increase price without loss of business to any close substitute product.

The same procedure is then followed for the relevant geographic market. Given the prior identification of the relevant product market, the main question is whether the firms producing this product line (e.g., A, B, C, D) operate in provisional geographic markets 1, 2, and 3 as shown in Figure C-2.

The price is hypothetically then increased in these three areas, taken together, and the leakage or loss of business is assessed in area 4. If the leakage/loss is signifi-

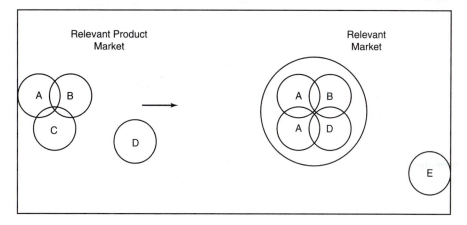

FIGURE C-1

cant, then it is determined that area 4 is a close geographic substitute and should be included in the relevant geographic market. The process then continues with respect to geographic area 5 and so on until no further leakage is expected. Hence, to continue the example, prices could now be profitably raised for relevant products (A, B, C, D) in geographic areas (1, 2, 3, 4). According to the guidelines, one should always choose the "smallest geographic market."

The next step involves figuring out which firms produce the relevant product in the relevant geographic area and determining their market shares. According to the Guidelines, we should include firms currently in production and also those firms

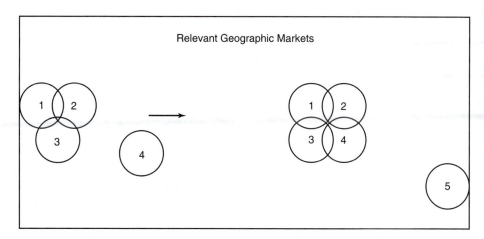

FIGURE C-2

that can *immediately* (within one year) change product lines or geographic localities in response to price increases. Similarly, one is instructed to further include "internal" production (from one captive subsidiary to another), secondary or used production that can be recyclable, and foreign imports. For the latter, one should assess the impact of quotas and tariffs on actual imports, and correspondingly assign market shares by countries rather than individual foreign firms.

Having established market shares, the next step is to determine the market concentration that will result as a result of the proposed merger. The post-merger Herfindahl–Hirschman Index (HHI) is used to measure market concentration. The Guidelines establish four major standards: (1) If the HHI < 1000, then the market is considered monopolistically competitive and the merger is harmless—there is no impact on concentration and no enhanced power to raise prices or restrict output; (2) If the HHI lies between 1000 and 1800, this market is considered moderately concentrated, and the merger can be expected to enhance power over price, especially if the change in the HHI as a direct result of the merger was 100 or more points;[4] changes of less than 100 points are generally considered harmless and will not trigger a challenge by the Department; (3) If the HHI > 1800, this market is considered highly concentrated, and the merger can be expected to enhance power over price, especially if the change in HHI exceeds 50 points; if it exceeds 100 points, the likelihood of Justice Department challenge is even greater; (4) If the post-merger market share of the acquiring firm exceeds 35 percent, then this leading company's control over price is considered to be inherently dangerous, thereby triggering a challenge. The *Guidelines* also suggest that if an industry is subject to technical change, current market shares may not be appropriate and the investigation may need to be expanded beyond the normal one-year time horizon.

The next major step to consider involves conditions of entry. As explained in Appendices A and B, the ease of entry can evaporate or moderate any preexisting market concentration and thereby negate the newly established power over price and resource allocation. Hence, even if an industry has triggered Justice Department concern because of its market concentration, low or nonexistent barriers to entry can countervail this initial negative impression and forestall antitrust intervention. Similarly, if the barriers to entry are high, this will provide corroborating evidence to support intervention where concentration is moderate or high. In short, there would be no dynamic force on the horizon to deconcentrate the industry in the long run, except perhaps new technologies, which we have already accounted for above.

The ease/difficulty of entry is considered over a two-year time horizon. (Note: As explained above, firms that can move quickly into an industry in less than a year are already considered as industry members and shouldn't be double counted as new entrants as well.) Entry must be timely, likely, and sufficient. Timeliness means that entry can occur within two years. Likeliness means that they can achieve sufficient, new market share to justify investment in plant capacity and equipment at the MES level. This will be easier if demand is expanding rather than contracting or the economy is in the positive component of a sustained business cycle that "lifts all boats" in the water. Sufficiency means that firms can overcome any conduct barriers imposed by incumbent firms, and that they can establish a product identity competitive with existing rivals. There are also a number of conduct factors that can facilitate or frustrate collusion by the major companies. Collusion, now known as "coordinated interaction," may be necessary for the industry to jointly maximize profits and create a stable pricing consensus. Where collusion is unlikely or unstable, the merger may not create favorable conditions that injure consumers through higher prices or restricted output. The main factors that facilitate coordinated interaction are:

1. Availability of information about recent market transactions. This helps detect and police whether specific firms or the industry as a whole are following pricing standards. Often trade associations provide the clearinghouse for exchange of information.
2. Evidence of previous express collusion. Did favorable conditions exist before that facilitated collusion? If so, they may reappear again in a different or similar form.
3. Homogeneity of products. The more closely the products are related to each other, especially in terms of their quality, the greater the likelihood that a pricing compromise can be reached that won't disadvantage either the low cost–low quality producer nor the high cost–high quality one. Similarly, the simpler the pricing arrangements, the easier it will be to standardize them. Requirements for different grades of quality may frustrate any potential consensus.
4. Frequency of transactions and their size. The smaller the transactions are and the greater their frequency, the easier it will be to determine whether firms are abiding by or cheating on common price agreements.
5. Characteristics about large buyers. If there is market power on the buying side (monopsony) then this can frustrate the achievement of any pricing agreement since the large firms will demand price discounts or rebates as a normal part of doing business with them.
6. Elimination of a maverick firm through merger. If the acquired firm was a particularly disruptive influence and often cheated on agreed-on prices, then its elimination through merger should restore stability to the industry pricing consensus.

DEFENSES

The Department of Justice Guidelines do not automatically assume anti-competitive impacts from most mergers. In fact, the presumption is quite the contrary—the underlying reason for mergers is to achieve operating or distributional efficiency. Hence, the firm contemplating mergers of a horizontal nature (or under challenge) will always be given an opportunity to defend itself by arguing the achievement of economic efficiencies. These efficiencies can arise from economies of scale, scope, better integration of facilities from a geographic standpoint or lower transportation costs. Generally, suggested managerial or marketing efficiencies will receive lesser credence.

Similarly, the accused acquiring firm can also argue that the acquired firm is a "failing firm" in immediate jeopardy of meeting its financial obligations and on the doorstep of bankruptcy and reorganization. Such firms are presumably inactive competitors, and thus their elimination from the market will not impact the vitality of remaining competition. These firms have no other way of exiting absent acquisition from another firm.

PRECEDENTIAL MERGER CASES

There have been a number of very important merger cases since the passage of Section 7 of the Clayton Act (1914) as amended by the Celler–Kefauver Amendment (1950). While it is not the task here to recite the case history underlying these situations, it is important to understand the basic philosophical tenets that have emerged and undergird the enforcement of the laws by Federal authorities. There are several different kinds of mergers that need to first be delineated before these important judicial precedents can be completely understood.

A horizontal merger involves the joining together of two firms in direct competition with each other (e.g., firms A and B or C and D).

A vertical merger involves the joining together of two or more firms that were either suppliers or customers for each other across different vertical strata (e.g., firms A and C or B and D).

A conglomerate merger involves all other possible combinations and may appear in several different configurations:

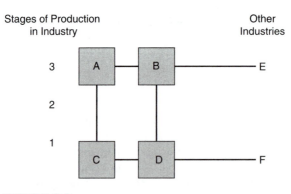

FIGURE C-3

  a. A product extension merger. Here the two firms produce related but not close substitute products. So, if firms B and E produce related products from different industries, their combination would be considered a means of enhancing the product lines of the acquiring firm.

  b. A market extension merger. Here the two firms produce the same product but are located in different geographic regions for which there is no import substitution effect. Hence, they are not true competitors in the same product–geographic space.

  c. A pure conglomerate merger. In this instance there is no relationship between the products at all. Their cross elasticity is zero (e.g., D and F).

The theory of competitive economic injury and line of judicial precedents is much clearer for the horizontal mergers than for the vertical or conglomerate types, and this explains the predisposition of the Department of Justice and Federal Trade Commission to prosecute horizontal mergers when there is no compensating claim of economic efficiency.

For the horizontal merger, absent the achievement of economies of scale, scope, distribution, or transportation, the acquisition of a direct competitor reduces the competitiveness of that firm, enhances market share and power of the acquiring firm, and gives the resulting firm greater control (generally in association with similar sized firms) to raise prices and restrict output. The courts have clearly identified four areas of concern where disturbing economic conditions will trigger anticompetitive harms. These are:

1. Where the direct loss of competition is significant. Here, even the creation of a medium-sized firm can be considered to be a significant loss of competitive vitality.[5]
2. Where there has been a clear trend toward horizontal mergers in the recent past such that the merger in question would continue and enhance and encourage other mergers by similar firms.[6]
3. Where very large firms or industry leaders (threshold of 25 percent) are involved, even a small increase in concentration will not be tolerated. These mergers will be considered presumptively "bad" when condition 4 is coincident.[7]
4. Where industry concentration is already high, further increases in concentration will generally not be permitted.[8]

These instances in isolation, but especially in combination, can prove deadly toward any proposed horizontal merger.

Vertical Mergers

In the vertical arena, there are two major theories of anti-competitive abuse that can exist absent any demonstrable increase in transactional efficiencies.

1. Vertical foreclosure from access. When two firms merge in a vertical fashion, there is the natural tendency for the resulting firm to increase its level of self-sufficiency and decrease its reliance on outsiders. In other words, former suppliers or customers may not have equal access to the newly merged firm as its own subsidiary increases its presence to the detriment of others.[9]

2. Multistage entry. When vertical merger occurs, it may create a situation in which firms become increasingly self-reliant on their own subsidiaries as mentioned in (1). This may constrict the open portion of the market and make it very difficult for unintegrated firms to obtain sufficient product/access to remain viable competitors. *Their response is to seek vertical merger partners themselves to assure stable supply or access.* Alternatively, they may seek business relationships with their competitor–integrated firms, but this dependence on their competitors makes them vulnerable for supply or access squeezes as described in Appendix B.

Under both circumstances, it becomes clear that existing firms as well as new entrants must have a multiple stage vertical operation in order to compete on a level playing field in the industry.[10]

Conglomerate Mergers

In the conglomerate area, where the product or geographic connection is somewhat vague, the impact on competition, prices, and economic resource allocation is considerably less direct. For the product extension and market extension merger cases, the theories of "potential competition" and "deep pockets" are used to illustrate the economic effect, while for pure conglomerate cases only the latter theory is even remotely possible.

The theory of potential competition means that the acquiring firm had a reasonable probability of entering the specific industry from scratch (de nouveau) in hopes of extending its product line into related product or geographic areas. Should it enter without merger, it would provide a major new competitive force that would eventually help *deconcentrate* industry power. By allowing the firm to merge, this potential competitive element is lost since the firm merely replaces an existing market competitor. Even if the firm never actually enters the market de nouveau, its mere presence as a potential competitor may cause current firms to moderate their pricing behavior to forestall or delay entry.[11] While product/market extension mergers involving industry leaders are often prosecuted, if the acquired firm is smaller and considered a minor competitor, there will be greater antitrust tolerance. Such "toehold" mergers enable the acquiring firm to enter by tying in with an already experienced company and then later expanding the merged company to seek a bigger market presence. While toehold mergers are not as desirable as completely new entry from scratch, nonetheless, they are a superior to acquiring an industry leader.[12]

The deep pocket theory suggests that when major diversified companies integrate with smaller companies within a market segment, this can disturb traditional means of interaction among competitors by enhancing the power of firms with well-financed corporate parents. This should act to stabilize industry pricing consensus for fear of predatory actions and cross-subsidization by deep pocket firms.[13]

In summary, the theories and approaches toward prosecuting vertical and conglomerate mergers rely on less direct economic impacts, but nonetheless still are credible in antitrust litigation, especially when brought by private litigants rather than by government officials who seem more comfortable in challenging only horizontal mergers where the economic issues are clearly more direct.

In addition to the antitrust laws involving mergers, there are two other key areas that are available to prevent the loss of competition. These are the proscriptions against price-fixing and monopolization. We will briefly examine these areas in turn, once again focusing on the concepts and theories rather than just following the trail of precedential cases.

PRICE-FIXING

Section 1 of the Sherman Act prohibits "contracts combinations and conspiracies in restraint of trade." This very vague language has consistently been applied to express agreements between horizontal competitors involving prices, territorial rights, secret government bidding, and similar price-related activities. Borrowing from microeconomic theory, the inherent danger of firms getting together to fix prices and related activities leads to a direct loss of competition and interference with the disciplining marketplace forces of supply and demand. By agreeing to common prices, transportation charges, and standardizing other quality aspects of products, the firms act as if they are a single firm rather than distinct rivals. The competitive forces of the market are replaced with a single decision center, and the end result may be similar to monopoly in terms of excessive prices and restriction of output.

For nearly a hundred years, these types of direct, express agreements between competitors have been condemned in antitrust litigation. While initially there was considerable disagreement as to whether such agreements were restraints of trade on the surface, through their conception, and hence illegal per se without any explanation or alternatively, whether the fairness of prices, adverse economic conditions or other explanations would be considered as justification under a "rule of reason" approach.[14]

Eventually, the courts agreed on the former approach by saying that certain contracts such as price-fixing are so obnoxious that further explanation or elaboration is unnecessary. The courts are not in any position to judge the reasonableness of prices nor to regulate prices within an industry. They further elaborated that they cannot accept the age-old cry of ruinous competition nor excuse situations in which only part of the industry is affected. Rather, any tampering with the free play of market forces is considered injurious to competition and is illegal per se. These same strict prohibitions apply to bid rigging, market allocations, or any other areas involving prices.[15]

While these sanctions against express price-fixing appear immutable, there are still several areas that are ambiguous and require a rule of reason approach in each specific case. The most frequent exceptions involve situations in which the price-fixing is only incidental to the main purpose of the agreement or actually perfects competition or enhances efficiency.[16] Similarly, if a trade association merely shares past information rather than acting as a clearinghouse for the operation of a cartel, this now falls within the legal parameters of the Sherman Act.

On the other hand, when there is no express or direct agreement or no actual meeting occurred, the issue revolves around whether a conspiracy actually occurred in the meaning of the law. These indirect agreements generally are not prosecutable under the price-fixing statutes and since they often arise in concentrated industries, they will be further covered under prosecution involving oligopoly power under section 2 of the Sherman Act.

MONOPOLY AND OLIGOPOLY POWER

The original concern of the Sherman Antitrust Law was to attack the large accumulation of market power that had organized under the form of trusts at the turn of the twentieth century and could not be prosecuted under the archaic precedents of English common law. Section 2 of the Act proscribed monopolization through trusts or any other forms of business organization and made it a felony with criminal sanctions and fines to actively engage in monopolizing an industry. The original interpretation of the law suggested that, to be found guilty of monopolization, the firms had to have the requisite monopoly power in the relevant product and geographic markets, but, more importantly, had to evidence a specific intent and purpose to acquire the power and to exclude other firms from their lawful right to engage in commerce. Specific overt acts of aggression against competitors were generally considered necessary to prove this malicious intent and purpose.[17]

In later cases, the courts moved away from a conduct approach toward monopolization and relied more on structural evidence of monopoly power. Specific intent gave way to general intent and the achievement of market power, even if not exercised, was the critical element.[18] As this doctrine of structuralism came to be refined in the *Grinnell* and *U.S. Shoe* cases,[19] the conscious acquisition and maintenance of monopoly power through erection of barriers to entry was all that was required to prove monopolization.

With all these cases, there was always the defense that the monopoly power was acquired innocently through superior foresight, business acumen, or efficiency—it was "thrust upon them"[20] or that monopoly was not properly defined through misapplication of economic reasoning as in the *DuPont* case. Of course, successful prosecutions of monopoly allow the courts great flexibility in restructuring the firms into less powerful independent companies[21] and thereby restoring competition.

The issue of oligopoly is very difficult for litigation under the Sherman Act since monopoly is not achieved by a single firm but only through a combination of firms acting in concert. Owing to mutual interdependence there is a natural tendency for such oligopoly firms to discover means for achieving mutual consensus on price and related matters. Whether the vehicle for the tacit agreement (indirect price-fixing) comes through price or quality leadership, standardized business practices, or merely signaling one's competitors through the print, electronic, or information superhighway, the end result can be a "shared monopoly."

Shared monopolies are very difficult to prosecute under the antitrust statutes unless they border on formal conspiracies. In early case litigation, it was thought that simply proving conscious parallel behavior was sufficient to document the presence of a conspiracy,[22] later refinements left open the door for firms to argue that parallel actions did not emanate from conspiracy, but rather from sound business judgments independently arrived at.[23] In short, if all firms respond identically to the same stimulus, this does not automatically mean conspiracy; it may simply mean they all exercised sound business judgment. Since this doctrine of "independent business judgment" was permitted, the incidence of successful prosecution of oligopoly has severely diminished.

Even if one could successfully prosecute oligopolies, a further complexity involves the kind of structural remedies one would expect to impose on them that would not affect the inherent efficiencies achieved through economies of scale, scope, and the like. Conduct solutions generally are impractical since oligopolists' natural productivity to seek mutual arrangements cannot easily be suppressed nor can every form of such interaction be anticipated and outlawed. With such difficulties in applying the Sherman Act to high concentrations of market power, the antitrust authorities have put more resources into *preventing* the formation of such power bases through strong enforcement of the antimerger statutes.

SHORT-CIRCUITED MERGERS

The Department of Justice does not always have to get involved in blocking newly announced mergers; sometimes the mergers collapse under their own weight and are thereby short-circuited. This can happen with all different kinds and sizes of mergers and in all types of industries. While the threat of antitrust prosecution can play an influential role in terminating a merger prematurely, there are many other factors that individually or collectively can cause the collapse.[24]

In reading the academic literature, the following factors are most often attributed or linked to the success or failure of mergers.[25] First, the concept of "relatedness" between the product lines of the acquiring and acquired firm. Clearly, horizontal mergers are the closest related among the merger types. The acquisition of a direct competitor provides no surprises, uncertainty, or unfamiliarity of product lines and thus should provide the closest fit. Vertical mergers provide access to the materials, inputs, and product markets and involve areas of interaction that may be somewhat new, but clearly are not uncertain or unfamiliar to the acquiring firm. Conglomerate mergers, especially where the product lines are totally different (e.g., pure conglomerates) offer the greatest degree of uncertainty, unfamiliarity, and, of course, risk, and therefore have the highest chance of failure arising from unrelatedness.

The size of the firm or its "critical mass" is another factor often cited as contributing to merger failure. Where there is a significant size mismatch between the acquiring and acquired firm, especially if it is the latter that is disproportionately smaller, the new subsidary may not attract enough attention from corporate headquarters and communication problems and lack of motivation may occur, thereby causing the smaller subsidary to be disenchanted and alienated with the parent corporation. The end result is poor economic performance and eventual divorce if the merger has actually been consummated.

A third very important consideration is the strategic fit between the two merged firms. Most firms claim that there will be new efficiencies in economies of scale, scope, strategic locations, transportation costs, marketing, and so forth that accompany the merger. Similarly, there is also the claim that new managerial efficiencies will spring from joining the two product lines together. Collectively, these managerial and economic efficiencies are supposed to create a new synergy that makes the merged enterprise more profitable in the long run and enhances stockholder value. If these expected efficiencies are not real or are overvalued, then this would put pressure on the newly merged firm to meet its debt requirements if it has borrowed money to finance the merger or on its stock prices, if it has exchanged stock or issued new stock to finance the merger.

The question of "cultural fit" between the management teams of the two affected companies is similar. "The key factors highlighted in the literature are: conflicts in management styles, especially merging conservative firms with entrepreneurial ones, a lack of personal chemistry between the two managements, and a lack of understanding of the other firm's markets, technology or regulatory environments."[26] These cultural differences can be exacerbated by personality conflicts between charismatic leaders of each firm. If such mergers are consummated, their future financial prospects do not look very bright.

A final and very important factor affecting a merger's trajectory toward success is the capital market's reaction to the merger announcement and the impact on stockholder value that ensues. With mergers today, the financing mechanism to acquiring firms is often through exchange of stock—the acquiring firm offering to buy up all or a large percentage of stock of the acquired firm in exchange for stock of the former company. However, if stock prices for the acquiring firm decline as a result of the merger announcement, the total value of the deal may suffer and it may not be completed. Hence, the stock market's reaction can have a disastrous effect unless price protections are initially built into the deal.

Just as important as the market's reactions are the underlying reasons behind this reaction. If the investment community does not see the close strategic and economic fit for the merger, or the cultural fit is wrong, they may distrust the eventual financial returns and express their skepticism by discounting the value of the acquiring firm's stocks. This can act as a bellwether for the affected firms, and often the merger shortly collapses after the stock market indicates its lack of faith or large individual stockholders in the companies question the wisdom of their corporate leaders.

This brief outline of the marketplace factors that can short-circuit a merger is not intended as an argument for a laissez-faire, noninterventionist antitrust policy. Rather, it is simply a reflection of the reality of modern-day antitrust enforcement with its limited budgets and hierachy of priorities. Perhaps the Department of Justice should add these lists of factors to its calculus in making a decision as to whether to intervene and/or prosecute certain mergers. If the merger appears to be doomed because of its inherent inconsistencies, why devote scarce budgetary resources to its prosecution? On the other hand, the threat of prosecution in conjunction with the unstable market forces can add additional concern for the merger partners and cause them to short-circuit the merger without the government ever formally bringing the case.

NOTES

[1] Department of Justice, *1992 Horizontal Merger Guidelines,* April 22, 1992, pp. 1–58.
[2] Ibid. The following section is largely condensed directly from the formal Guidelines.
[3] Clayton Act 38 Stat. 730 (1914), as amended.
[4] The change in HHI can be calculated by substracting the premerger HHI from the postmerger HHI or alternatively by multiplying 2 times the market share of the acquiring firm by the market shared of the acquired firm: (e.g., $2 \times S_1 \times S_2$).
[5] *Brown Shoe Co., Inc. v. United States,* 370 U.S. 294 (1962); *United States v. Von's Grocery Company,* 384 U.S. 270 (1966).
[6] Ibid.
[7] *United States v. Philadelphia National Bank,* 374 U.S. 321; *United States v. Continental Can Co., et al.,* 378 U.S. 441 (1964); *United States v. Aluminum Company of America,* 148 F.2d 416 (2d Cir. 1945).
[8] Ibid.
[9] *Brown Shoe,* op. cit.; *United States v. E. I. DuPont de Nemours & Co.,* 353 U.S.586 (1957).
[10] Ibid.
[11] *Federal Trade Commission v. Proctor & Gamble Co.,* 386 U.S.568 (1967); *United States v. Bendix,* 77 F.T.C., 731 (1970).
[12] *Bendix,* op. cit.; *United States v. Falstaff Brewing Corp.,* 410 U.S. 526 (1973).
[13] *Proctor & Gamble,* op. cit.; *Bendix,* op. cit.
[14] *United States v. Addyston Pipe,* 85 Fed. 271 (1898); *Standard Oil of New Jersey v. United States,* 221 U.S. 1 (1911); *Chicago Board of Trade v. United States,* 246 U.S. 231 (1918); *United States v. Trenton Potteries,* 273 U.S. 392 (1927).
[15] *United States v. Socony-Vacuum Oil,* 310 U.S. 150 (1940).

[16]*Chicago Board of Trade,* op. cit.; *Broadcast Music, Inc. v. Columbia Broadcasting System, Inc.,* 441 U.S. 1 (1979); *NCAA v. University of Oklahoma,* 468 U.S. 85 (1984).

[17]*Standard Oil,* op. cit.; *United States v. United States Steel Corp.,* 251 U.S. 417 (1920).

[18]*United States v. Aluminum Company of America,* 148 F.2d 416 (2d Cir. 1945).

[19]*United States v. Grinnell Corp.,* 384 U.S. 563 (1966); *United States v. United Shoe Machinery Corp.,* 110 F. Supp. 295 (D. Mass 1953).

[20]*Alcoa,* op. cit.

[21]*Standard Oil,* op. cit.; *United States v. Paramount Pictures,* 334 U.S. 131 (1948).

[22]*American Tobacco Company v. United States,* 328 U.S. 781 (1946).

[23]*Theater Enterprises, Inc. v. Paramount Film Distributing,* 346 U.S. 537 (1954).

[24]Patricia Whalen and Barry Litman, "Failed Mergers in the Mass Media: Credible and Incredible Evidence," *Media Management Review.* Lawrence Erlbaum: Mahwah, NJ, 1997, Chapter 7.

[25]This section borrows liberally from Whalen and Litman.

[26]Ibid.

Index

Note: Bold page numbers indicate figures and tables.